HARLAXTON MEDIEVAL STUDIES
VOLUME FOUR
ENGLAND IN THE FIFTEENTH CENTURY

PAUL WATKINS MEDIEVAL STUDIES
General Editor: Shaun Tyas ~ *Consultant Editor:* David Roffe

1. ANDERSON, Alan Orr, *Early Sources of Scottish History AD 500-1286*; a new edition with corrections, in 2 vols. (1990).
2. HARMER, Florence, *Anglo-Saxon Writs*; a new edition comprising the original work together with her later essay 'A Bromfield and a Coventry Writ of King Edward the Confessor' (1989).
3. STENTON, Sir Frank Merry, *The Early History of the Abbey of Abingdon*; reprinted for the first time since 1913 (1989).
4. SPITTAL, Jeffrey and FIELD, John, *A Reader's Guide to the Place-names of the United Kingdom* (1990).
5. HILL, Sir Francis, *Medieval Lincoln*; reprinted with an introductory essay by Dorothy Owen (1990).
6. PARSONS, David (ed.), *Eleanor of Castile 1290-1990, Essays to Commemorate the 700th Anniversary of her Death: 28 November 1290* (1991).
7. COATES, Richard, *The Ancient and Modern Names of the Channel Islands, a Linguistic History* (1991).
8. FOULDS, Trevor (ed.), *The Thurgarton Cartulary* (1994).
9. ORMROD, W. M. (ed.), *England in the Thirteenth Century*, Harlaxton Medieval Studies I (1991).
10. ANDERSON, Alan Orr, *Scottish Annals from English Chroniclers, 500-1286 AD*; a new edition with corrections (1991).
11. LINDLEY, Phillip, *Gothic to Renaissance: Essays on Sculpture in England* (forthcoming, 1994).
12. HICKS, Carola (ed.), *England in the Eleventh Century*, Harlaxton Medieval Studies II (1992).
13. ROGERS, Nicholas (ed.), *England in the Fourteenth Century*, Harlaxton Medieval Studies III (1993).
14. STANNCLIFFE, Clare and CAMBRIDGE, Eric (eds), *St Oswald: Northumbrian King to European Saint. Essays from the Durham Conference* (forthcoming).
15. ORMROD, W. M. and LINDLEY, Phillip (eds), *The Black Death* (forthcoming).
16. ROGERS, Nicholas (ed.), *England in the Fifteenth Century*, Harlaxton Medieval Studies IV (1994).
17. DEMIDOWICZ, George (ed.), *Coventry's First Cathedral. The Cathedral and Priory of St Mary, Coventry. Papers from the 1993 Anniversary Symposium* (1994).
18. GROSS, Anthony, *The Dissolution of the Lancastrian Kingship: Sir John Fortescue and the Crisis of Monarchy in Fifteenth-Century England* (forthcoming).

HARLAXTON MEDIEVAL STUDIES, IV

ENGLAND IN THE FIFTEENTH CENTURY

Proceedings of the 1992
Harlaxton Symposium

Edited by
Nicholas Rogers

PAUL WATKINS

STAMFORD

1994

© The Contributors

Published in 1994 by
Paul Watkins
18, Adelaide Street,
Stamford,
Lincolnshire, PE9 2EN

ISBN
1 871615 67 4

Photoset from the discs and essays of the authors in Garamond
by Paul Watkins (Publishing)

Printed on long-life paper

Printed and bound by Woolnoughs of Irthlingborough

CONTENTS

LIST OF CONTRIBUTORS

Jonathan Alexander	Institute of Fine Arts, University of New York
Rosemary Hayes	Royal Commission on Historical Manuscripts
Michael K. Jones	Winchester College
J. I. Kermode	University of Liverpool
Jane Laughton	University of Cambridge
Philippa Maddern	University of Western Australia
C. W. Marx	St David's University College, Lampeter
Scot McKendrick	The British Library
Nigel Morgan	La Trobe University, Melbourne
Colin Richmond	University of Keele
Nicholas Rogers	Sidney Sussex College, Cambridge
Jenny Stratford	Institute of Historical Research, London
Anne F. Sutton	The Mercers' Company, London
Benjamin Thompson	University of Cambridge
Daniel Williams	University of Leicester

LIST OF ILLUSTRATIONS

15 (McKendrick) *Romuléon*, London, British Library, Royal MS 19 E.v, fol. 196 (photo: by permission of the British Library)

16 (McKendrick) *Romuléon*, Florence, Biblioteca Medicea Laurenziana, MS Med. Pal. 156^2, fol. 294v, colophon naming David Aubert (photo: Biblioteca Medicea Laurenziana)

17 (McKendrick) *Romuléon*, Florence, Biblioteca Medicea Laurenziana, MS Med. Pal. 156^1, fol. 1, Philip the Good visits David Aubert (photo: Biblioteca Medicea Laurenziana)

18 (McKendrick) *Romuléon*, Brussels, Bibliothèque Royale, MS 9055, fol. 25, Gomez Albornoz visits Benvenuto da Imola (photo: copyright Bibliothèque Royale Albert Ier, Bruxelles)

19 (McKendrick) *Romuléon*, Brussels, Bibliothèque Royale, MSS 10173-4, fol. 110, Hasdrubal brings Hannibal to Spain (photo: copyright Bibliothèque Royale Albert Ier, Bruxelles)

20 (McKendrick) *Romuléon*, Florence, Biblioteca Medicea Laurenziana, MS Med. Pal. 156^2, fol. 306v, miniature: the origin of 'Circenses' (photo: Biblioteca Medicea Laurenziana)

21 (McKendrick) *Romuléon*, Florence, Biblioteca Medicea Laurenziana, MS Med. Pal. 156^1, fol. 37, miniature: Romulus and Remus (photo: Biblioteca Medicea Laurenziana)

22 (McKendrick) *Romuléon*, London, British Library, Royal MS 19 E.v, fol. 336v, the Emperor Augustus's vision of the Virgin and Child (photo: by permission of the British Library)

23 (McKendrick) *Romuléon*, Turin, Biblioteca Nazionale Universitaria, MS L.I.4^2, fol. 118, the Emperor Augustus's vision of the Virgin and Child (photo: Biblioteca Nazionale Universitaria)

24 (Rogers) Cambridge, Trinity College, MS B.11.7, fol. 29, St Anne teaching the Virgin to read (reproduced by kind permission of the Master and Fellows of Trinity College, Cambridge)

25 (Rogers) Cambridge, Trinity College, MS B.11.7, fol. 31v, Henry V at Mass (reproduced by kind permission of the Master and Fellows of Trinity College, Cambridge)

26 (Rogers) Cambridge, Trinity College, MS B.11.7, fol. 20, Sir John Cornwall kneeling before the Blessed Virgin and Child (reproduced by kind permission of the Master and Fellows of Trinity College, Cambridge)

27 (Rogers)   Cambridge, Trinity College, MS B.11.7, fol. 21, detail, Princess Elizabeth kneeling before Christ crucified (reproduced by kind permission of the Master and Fellows of Trinity College, Cambridge)

28 (Rogers)   Wenceslaus Hollar, engraving of stained glass formerly in Ampthill Church, Beds., from F. Sandford, *A Genealogical History of the Kings of England* (London, 1677), p. 252 (reproduced by kind permission of the Syndics of Cambridge University Library)

29 (Rogers)   Cambridge, Trinity College, MS B.11.7, fol. 31, procession of relics (reproduced by kind permission of the Master and Fellows of Trinity College, Cambridge)

30 (Rogers)   Cambridge, Trinity College, MS B.11.7, fol. 5, September (reproduced by kind permission of the Master and Fellows of Trinity College, Cambridge)

31 (Rogers)   Cambridge, Trinity College, MS B.11.7, fol. 7, Annunciation (reproduced by kind permission of the Master and Fellows of Trinity College, Cambridge)

32 (Rogers)   Cambridge, Trinity College, MS B.11.7, fol. 38, detail, Christ before Pilate (reproduced by kind permission of the Master and Fellows of Trinity College, Cambridge)

33 (Rogers)   Cambridge, Trinity College, MS B.11.7, fol. 23, detail, St John on Patmos (reproduced by kind permission of the Master and Fellows of Trinity College, Cambridge)

34 (Rogers)   Cambridge, Trinity College, MS B.11.7, fol. 13, the angel appearing to Joseph (reproduced by kind permission of the Master and Fellows of Trinity College, Cambridge)

35 (Rogers)   Cambridge, Trinity College, MS B.11.7, fol. 85v, detail, Job on the dunghill (reproduced by kind permission of the Master and Fellows of Trinity College, Cambridge)

36 (Rogers)   Cambridge, Trinity College, MS B.11.7, fol. 66v, detail, Susanna and the Elders (reproduced by kind permission of the Master and Fellows of Trinity College, Cambridge)

37 (Rogers)   Sotheby's, 19 June 1990, lot 53, Joab's murder of Abner (photo: Sotheby's)

38 (Rogers)   Brussels, Koninklijke Bibliotheek, MS IV.1095, fol. 14v, St Anne teaching the Virgin to read (reproduced by kind permission of the Koninklijke Bibliotheek Albert I)

PREFACE

In February 1466 a party of sea-sick Bohemians, on a diplomatic mission from King George of Poděbrad, disembarked at Sandwich. Leo of Rozmital's visit to England would have remained in the documentary obscurity of most medieval embassies had not two of his retinue compiled accounts of their travels. At points these are garbled and confused, but they noted things which an English observer would have disregarded as familiar. We learn of the musicians who announced the wind direction throughout the night at Sandwich, the etiquette of a royal churching and the subsequent banquet, the English custom of kissing rather than shaking hands, the great numbers of fallow deer in Windsor Park, and the mechanical images of the Adoration of the Magi and the Resurrection at Salisbury Cathedral. From Schaseck and Tetzel's admiring descriptions of the shrine of St Thomas at Canterbury, the beautiful image of the Mother of God at Reading and the sweet music sung by choirs up to sixty strong we get a vivid sense of what was lost at the Reformation.

The contributors to this volume, which is based on the proceedings of the 1992 Harlaxton Symposium, provide a series of passports to fifteenth-century England. Our view is often limited by the fragmentary nature of the evidence, and many conclusions must remain speculative. But these essays, which embody some of the most interesting recent research in their various fields, enable us to become as familiar with the realm visited by the Bohemians as the passage of time will allow. Several of the papers are biographical studies, or at least contain a strong biographical or prosopographical element. Analysis of the motivation of individuals, whether it be their spiritual life, their political approaches, their artistic tastes, or their social and economic ties, enables an appreciation of the richness of an age, and reveals the limits of historical generalization.

I wish to thank all the contributors for their help, which made the task of editing much easier. As before, I am indebted to the support of the Harlaxton Steering Committee, proof-reader Philip Riley, and above all, Shaun Tyas of Paul Watkins Publishing, who has devoted his usual care to the publication of the fourth volume in the series Harlaxton Medieval Studies. I must also thank the various libraries and other organizations, individually acknowledged elsewhere, for granting permission to reproduce material.

Nicholas Rogers
St George's Day 1994

The 'Private Life' of a Late Medieval Bishop: William Alnwick, Bishop of Norwich and Lincoln
ROSEMARY HAYES

It is almost impossible to write a true biography of all but a few medieval men. One may be able to discuss their actions at length but rarely can one look clearly at the person behind those acts. Arguably, this is even harder for the late medieval period than for the high Middle Ages when more assistance is available from chronicles and hagiography. William Alnwick, who was bishop of Norwich from 1426 to 1437 and then of Lincoln until his death in 1449, is no exception. He is unique in the quantity of surviving records of his official acts, and this has led previous historians, perhaps mistakenly, to single him out as having been exceptionally conscientious among his fellow bishops.[1] Nevertheless, he seems to have left no personal letters, no-one wrote a contemporary biography of him, and there are few references to him in the chronicles of the period. There are not even any household accounts such as the wonderful series that enabled Margaret Aston to shed such light on the everyday life of Thomas Arundel, while he was bishop of Ely.[2] Consequently, this attempt to get closer to the man who was Bishop Alnwick is pieced together from a wide variety of hints and sources, and may well be inconclusive.

On a basic level, very little is known of Alnwick's family background and early life. That he came from, or near, Alnwick in Northumberland may safely be assumed from his name and his benefactions. Nothing is known of his parentage, although the papal collector, Piero da Monte, a hostile witness, described him as 'rusticanus homo ... et ex vili genere natus'.[3] His will indicates that he had a brother whose daughter, Agnes, had married a Richard Hayton by whom she had a daughter.[4] Perhaps, therefore, he was related by marriage to the William Hayton who served as Henry VI's secretary during the king's French coronation tour of 1430 to 1432, and lost his post at the same time as

---

1   A. R. Myers, *England in the Late Middle Ages* (London, 1952), p.157; W. W. Capes, *The English Church in the Fourteenth and Fifteenth Centuries* (London, 1900), p. 205; *Visitations of Religious Houses in the Diocese of Lincoln*, ed. by A. Hamilton Thompson, 2 vols, Canterbury and York Society, XXIV, XXXIII (London, 1919-27), I, p. xxx. I am most grateful to Dr M. R. Foster for her helpful comments on earlier versions of this paper.

2   M. E. Aston, *Thomas Arundel. A Study of Church Life in the Reign of Richard II* (Oxford, 1967), pp. 165-261.

3   *Piero da Monte: Ein Gelehrter und Päpstlicher Beamter des 15 Jahrhunderts*, ed. by J. Haller (Rome, 1941), p. 74.

4   Lambeth Palace Library, Register John Stafford (Canterbury), fols 178v-179v, translated (with some omissions) in *Visitations*, I, pp. xxiv-xxx.

Alnwick was deprived of the Privy Seal.[5] Alnwick's will also reveals that he considered Stephen Scrope, archdeacon of Richmond, and chancellor of Cambridge University, to have been an important patron.

If there is little to be learnt about his early life, perhaps in death he left a few clues. His tomb in Lincoln cathedral was destroyed in 1644.[6] Fortunately, a few years earlier, Bishop Sanderson had recorded most of the epitaph engraved on it:

At Bp. Smith's Feet, this Circumspection, on a Brass, round a Marble.
Mortis vi rapide de mundi valle vocatus,
Alnwyc sub Lapide jacet hic Wilhelmus humatus.
Quondam privati Custos fuit ille Sigilli,
Noluit ille pati falsum, dum constitit illi.
Primo Norvici Pastoris fulsit Honore.
Postea multiplici stetit hic non absque Labore.
Multos sudores pro ....
.... Errores sua sicut Cor petivit.
Etheris Aularum proprius sit Participator,
Qui pretiosarum Domuum fuit edificator.
Anno C. Xti. quater, M, quater X, Decade dempto
Uno, Mors isti nocuit Pretio Crucis empto.

At the Feet of [his] Pourtraiture in Brass.
In Cinerem rediet Cinis, et nequit hic remanere.
Mortem non fugiet Homo natus de Muliere.
Ut Flos egreditur Etate virente decorâ,
Et cito conteritur, cum Mortis venerit Hora;
Hic Labor, hicque Dolor, hic Languor, et hic Ululatus;
Omnis transit Honor; Homo nunc, cras incineratus.
Si velis, si nolis, tua non hic Gloria stabit.
Et Patris et Prolis fera Vitam Mors superabit.
Decessit Solomon sapiens, mitis quoque David.
Fortis erat Sampson, tamen illum Mors superavit.
Me Mundus renuit, potior nunc Jure paterno
Quem Virgo genuit Regnum cum Rege superno.[7]

The composer of these rhyming couplets, apart from his propensity to philosophize on the vanity of life, had clearly decided what was significant about Alnwick's life. It is not surprising that he concentrated on his distinguished career as Keeper of the Privy Seal and bishop of Norwich and Lincoln.[8] However, it was perhaps something more than poetical convention

5   J. Otway-Ruthven, *The King's Secretary and the Signet Office in the Fifteenth Century* (Cambridge, 1939), pp. 154, 156, 169.
6   E. Venables and G. G. Perry, *Lincoln Diocesan History* (London, 1897), p. 297.
7   *Desiderata Curiosa*, ed. by F. Peck, 2 vols (London, 1732-35), II, Lib. VIII, p. 15.
8   This career has been examined elsewhere. See R. C. E. Hayes, 'William Alnwick, Bishop of Norwich (1426-1437) and Lincoln (1437-1449)', Bristol University

that suggested he end his first verse with a prayer that he who had been an erector of costly buildings should be a participator in the halls of heaven. It may be helpful, therefore, to start this investigation of the man by looking at some of the buildings he inhabited or had constructed.

The most important building in a diocese was, of course, the cathedral. By Alnwick's time, cathedral administration was much more the concern of the chapter than of the bishop. Nevertheless, the latter was expected to participate there in the great festivals of the church year. Alnwick was frequently in his cathedral cities, and seems to have made a special effort to share in the Easter festivities with his chapters.[9] Significantly, he chose to be enthroned at Lincoln on Maundy Thursday 1437, inserting a note of that fact in the chapter acts, with his own hand (Pl. 1), which read '*Hic scripsit W. Alnewyk episcopus qui fuit installatus Lincoln' die cene domini set occupavit in episcopatu prius quia vacacio duravit per unum annum tantum*'.[10]

But did he adorn his cathedrals with anything more than his presence? At Norwich the answer is a resounding yes. There he was responsible for the almost complete remodelling, not beloved by connoisseurs of the original Norman architecture, of the west front (Pl. 2).[11] During his episcopate, the cathedral's great western entrance was erected. The two figures at the top of the porch probably represent King Henry VI, seated on the left, and, kneeling on the right, the bishop. Even if this is not so, Alnwick's association with the porch is obvious. The spandrels above the doorway contain, on the left, the arms of the see of Norwich, *Azure three mitres labelled or* (Pl. 3), and, on the right, the arms of Bishop Alnwick himself, *Argent a cross moline sable* (Pl. 4). Around both coats of arms are the words '*Orate pro Anima Domini Willelmi Alnwyk.*' Both sets of arms are repeated at the top of the door itself. The doorway was clearly only the start of Alnwick's plans for the west front of his first and, one suspects, more beloved cathedral. After his death, his executors clearly obeyed the instructions of his will to 'cause to be made at my costs a great window of fit sort above the western entrance into the church of Norwich, for the adornment and enlightening of the same church, in stone-work, iron-work, glass, workmanship and every other needful material'.[12]

---

9   Ph.D. (1989).
    His itinerary is traced in ibid., pp. 410-42.
10 Lincolnshire Archives, Dean and Chapter A 2/32, fol. 121v.
11 E. Sansbury, *An Historical Guide to Norwich Cathedral* (Norwich, 1986), pp. 4, 40. The cathedral priory's chronicler (Bartholomew Cotton, a monk of Norwich) recorded that he '*fieri fecit ex sua gratia majus hostium occidentali cum fenestra supereminente in Ecclesia cathedrali Norwicensi*' (*Anglia Sacra*, ed. by H. Wharton, 2 vols (London, 1691), I, p. 417).
12 *Visitations*, I, p. xxvii.

Alnwick was not unusual among fifteenth-century bishops in leaving bequests to the cathedral church of a previous diocese,[13] but this does seem to have been a particularly munificent one; especially when compared with his legacy to Lincoln cathedral: the princely sum of £20![14] His attitude to Lincoln may well have been soured by the continual wrangling between dean and chapter which marred his episcopate there.[15] Nevertheless, he clearly considered he had contributed to the church during his episcopate. On making his will, he left £100 to his successor in case the latter should complain of any dilapidations;

> albeit I received from my predecessor, by the hands of his executors, only in the first place a hundred marks, and at another time a hundred shillings and a pontifical valued at twenty marks and three small cruets for oil and chrism to the value of forty shillings,[16] ... notwithstanding that I found great dilapidation in the buildings of my church and have laid out and spent no small sums of money in their repair and in the construction of new buildings from money procured far beyond the sum for which the rents and revenues of my church of Lincoln, after the victuals and raiment of me and mine had been deducted from the same, could be sufficient, as may clearly appear to anyone who will look into it by my yearly accounts.[17] But if my aforesaid successor will not be able to be so contented, but is bent on encroaching on my goods through right or wrong, I will that my executors, before they in any wise go beyond the sum defined by me above, spend four hundred pounds in defending themselves and my goods.[18]

On what had these great sums been spent? There is no surviving part of Lincoln cathedral that can safely be attributed to him, and no known documentary evidence to support the suggestion that he erected the three wooden spires that have long since disappeared.[19] So what were these

13 J. T. Rosenthal, 'The Fifteenth-Century Episcopate: Careers and Bequests' in *Studies in Church History*, 10. *Sanctity and Secularity. The Church and the World*, ed. by D. Baker (Oxford, 1973), pp. 117-27. He analysed the thirty-nine surviving wills of the eighty bishops in England, 1399-1485. Twenty-one had held more than one see and, of these, ten left bequests to their previous cathedral (p. 126).

14 Lambeth Palace Library, Reg. Stafford (Canterbury), fol. 179. Omitted from *Visitations*, I, p. xxvi.

15 Hayes, 'William Alnwick', pp. 39-58. The best published description of these disputes is in A. Hamilton Thompson, *The English Clergy and Their Organization in the Later Middle Ages* (Oxford, 1947), pp. 90-98.

16 That is a total of £87: not far short, surely, of his own figure?

17 Sadly, they have not survived. Was it this passage of Alnwick's will which inspired the composer of his epitaph (who may well have been one of his executors) to describe him as '*pretiosarum Domuum ... edificator*'?

18 Lambeth Palace Library, Reg. Stafford (Canterbury), fol. 179; *Visitations*, I, p. xxix.

19 T. Allen, *The History of the County of Lincoln, From the Earliest Period to the Present Time* (London, 1834), pp. 149, 157, 159.

'buildings of my church' to which he referred? Munificence to his cathedrals was, in a sense, part of a bishop's public life. Perhaps one can come closer to Alnwick's 'private life' in the buildings on his estates.

Recent study of Lancastrian bishops has demonstrated that, contrary to the assertions of Thomas Gascoigne, most of them were in their dioceses for much of the time.[20] Alnwick was no exception. Given the size of his two dioceses, covering, between them, more than ten of the most populous counties in England,[21] continual residence in any one place would not assist him in overseeing the affairs of his flock. Like his contemporaries, Alnwick led a peripatetic life, staying nowhere for more than a few weeks at a time. He therefore needed comfortable houses conveniently scattered through the diocese.

As bishop of Norwich, Alnwick used six principal residences. Of these, the grandest was the palace in the cathedral city. There are only tantalising hints in his receiver-general's accounts of work done on the palace.[22] However, it is known that Alnwick was responsible for the erection of its principal gateway. This was described as a 'lofty and magnificent stone pile vaulted over' by Francis Blomefield, in whose day (c.1736) Alnwick's arms survived on the shields above the entrance.[23] One can still see evidence of his devotion to the Virgin Mary in the crowned 'M's above the gateway (Pl. 5); and it is perhaps not too fanciful to see, in the rather garishly painted corbels at the base of the gate's internal arch, a portrayal of the boy king, Henry VI, and his confessor-bishop, William Alnwick. The bishop depicted in the central boss of the arch is another possible portrait of Alnwick (Pl. 6).[24] Something of the comfort and grandeur Alnwick expected in this palace is indicated by the sums (in excess of £35) spent in 1428/9 on blue, white and green worsted for bed hangings and other adornments for the bishop's chamber.[25]

[20] *Loci e Libro Veritatum: Passages Selected from Gascoigne's Theological Dictionary illustrating the Condition of Church and State, 1403-58*, ed. by J. E. Thorold Rogers (Oxford, 1881), pp. 36-37. Cf. R. G. Davies, 'The Episcopate in England and Wales, 1375-1443', Manchester University Ph.D. (1974); J. A. Nigota, 'John Kempe, a Political Prelate of the Fifteenth Century', Emory University, U.S.A., Ph.D. (1973), esp. pp. 320-24.

[21] The diocese of Lincoln encompassed the counties of Lincolnshire, Huntingdonshire, Buckinghamshire, Northamptonshire, Leicestershire, Bedfordshire, Oxfordshire and Rutland, with about half of Hertfordshire forming part of the archdeaconry of Huntingdon; that of Norwich comprised the counties of Norfolk and Suffolk with parts of Cambridgeshire.

[22] Norfolk Record Office, EST 15/1/1, m. 6.

[23] F. Blomefield (and C. Parkin), *An Essay Towards a Topographical History of the County of Norfolk*, 2nd edn, 11 vols (London, 1805-10), III, 531.

[24] A. Whittingham, *Norwich Cathedral Bosses and Misericords* (Norwich, 1981), p. 11.

[25] Norfolk Record Office, EST 15/1/1, m. 5.

Despite these embellishments of the palace, Alnwick's favourite residence in the Norwich area seems to have been his manor at Thorpe, situated very pleasantly on the river, a couple of miles from the city centre. The surviving house has been much altered since Alnwick's day, but its basic structure is medieval. In 1428/9, 10s. 10d. was spent on a new great table for this house and nearly £5 on roofing the bake-house and hall.[26] The bishop's two other favoured residences within the diocese were at Hoxne on the Norfolk/Suffolk border, of which nothing survives, and at Thornage in north Norfolk where the house was altered, if not completely rebuilt, late in the century by Bishop Goldwell. Thornage's popularity with the bishops may be explained by the fact that it provided deer for the lord's table in other manors.[27]

His two other major residences were outside the diocese. *En route* to London was his manor at Terling near Chelmsford. Once situated near the church, the original manor house is now to be found over a mile to the south-west, surviving as the frame of a building now known as Ringer's Farm.[28] In London itself, during his frequent visits there on royal and episcopal business, Alnwick used two main residences. Until he relinquished the Privy Seal, episcopal *acta* were usually dated from St James's Hospital, Westminster, of which he was warden, and which was also often used by his colleague, the chancellor, Archbishop Kempe.[29] The bishop of Norwich's own house, which Alnwick used increasingly after 1432, was situated near (if not next to) this hospital at Charing Cross. Nothing is known to remain of either building. The same is true of the inn of the bishops of Lincoln on the site of the 'Old Temple' in Holborn, possibly where Southampton Buildings are now on the corner of Chancery Lane.[30]

Apart from his London house, there were six major bases from which Alnwick chose to oversee the sprawling diocese of Lincoln. The furthest south and west was at Bishop's Wooburn, conveniently *en route* for the Oxfordshire part of his diocese, and not too far from Windsor castle. Nothing survives of this house, although parts of its moat remain. Several of the bishop's other manors served as staging posts on the route from London to Lincoln. Most conveniently situated was the southernmost of these, directly on the Great North Road, at Buckden in Huntingdonshire. The surviving parts of the palace date from the late fifteenth century. However, Alnwick's connection with the place is vividly recalled in the nearby church of St Mary. He may have been responsible for the south porch and other

---

26   Ibid.
27   Ibid., m. 1.
28   Department of the Environment, *Statutory List: Essex: District of Braintree*.
29   Nigota, 'John Kempe', p. 281.
30   C. L. Kingsford, 'Historical Notes on Medieval London Houses', *London Topographical Record*, 11 (1917), 28-81, esp. pp. 59-61, 63.

fifteenth-century work in the church including parts of the nave. Here his arms are still to be seen on the shields held by the rather smug stone angels acting as corbels (Pl. 7), although the work may have been undertaken not by Alnwick himself but by John Depyng or William Alnwick junior, successive prebendaries of Buckden between 1427 and 1461, both of whom were closely connected with the bishop.

Not far north of Buckden, a few miles west of Stamford, was the bishop's manor of Lyddington.[31] Originally a hunting lodge, this was a favourite residence for several bishops; and Alnwick often spent Christmas here. The great hall has disappeared but the chamber block, to its south, survives. On the upper storey there remain rooms that were probably a chapel (now divided in two), the great chamber and the presence chamber. The basic building seems to date from the fourteenth century with late fifteenth-century alterations. However, it seems clear that Alnwick instituted at least some work there. The glass in the windows of the great chamber contains numerous illustrations of his arms and of his motto, 'Delectare in Domino'. It is even possible that the bishop depicted in one of the windows is a portrait of Alnwick himself (Pl. 8). Certainly, his prayer, addressed to a 'digna patrona', accords with Alnwick's devotion to the Blessed Virgin, as does the somewhat strained expression with what is known of his character.

In Lincolnshire itself, only some fallen masonry remains where the bishops had a castle at Sleaford. Nothing at all survives of the palace at Nettleham, situated, like Thorpe, just outside the cathedral city. Alnwick left money to the churches of all these manors, perhaps signifying his relative affection for them by leaving to Lyddington and Buckden ten marks and 100 shillings respectively, and only forty shillings each to Nettleham, Wooburn and Sleaford. It seems fitting that it is at Lyddington and Buckden that he is best remembered today.

The palace at Lincoln itself suffered from the suggestion made in 1726 that it be used as a quarry for renovations to the cathedral.[32] Nevertheless, enough remains to form some idea of Alnwick's alterations to it.[33] In the great west hall he inserted a bow window which was filled with 'Pictures of many of the Kings of *England*, with Verses underneath their Effigies'.[34]

---

[31] C. and P. Woodfield, 'The Palace of the Bishops of Lincoln at Lyddington', *Transactions of the Leicestershire Historical and Archaeological Society*, 57 (1981/2), 1-16.

[32] The architect, James Gibbs, provoked a riot with another suggestion made that year that the spires of Lincoln cathedral, perhaps erected by Alnwick, should be taken down (J. W. F. Hill, *Georgian Lincoln* (Cambridge, 1966), pp. 27, 38-41).

[33] T. Ambrose, 'The Bishop's Palace. Lincoln', *Lincolnshire Museums Information Sheet, Archaeology Series*, 18 (Lincoln, 1980).

[34] *Desiderata Curiosa*, II, Lib. VIII, p. 32. The description continues: 'Particularly, under *William Rufus*, no great Friend to the Clergy, this Spiteful Distich: *Grata*

However, his principal surviving addition was the three-storied gatehouse, still known as the Alnwick tower, where his arms were placed in the base of the newly restored oriel window in the nineteenth century. Next to it, he built a range described thus by the Parliamentary Survey of 1647: 'In the florye over the parlour is a very faire chappell with seates and many other conveniences and very faire painted glass windowes, with a small studye there and allsoe a lobye, a withdrawinge chamber with a closset Pewe lookinge in at the end of the chappell'.[35] This chapel was dedicated to the Virgin Mary, and its windows filled with prayers addressed to her and the Holy Trinity, on the bishop's behalf:

In a window, just going into the Chapel, at the Bishop's Palace there,

Istam Virgo, novellam do tibi, meque, Capellam
Alnwyc; tu pie, Natum fac mihi propritiatum

In every Window of the said Chapel Memorials of the said Bishop, as,

O benedicta satis, Flos et Rosa Virginitatis,
Luminis ad Regnum duc Alnwyc, Virgo, Wilelmum.
O Pater! O Proles! O Consolatio! Flamen!
Quem refovere soles Alnwyc ostende Solamen.
Triplex Persona, sed simplex in Deitate,
Wilelmum Alnwyc dona Celis, precor a te.
O Lux eterna, qua fulget Turma superna,
Post Vite Cursum rapias Alnwyc, tibi sursum.
Principis almifici Genitrix, O digna Patrona,
Alnwyc Pontifici precor assistas Prece prona.
Principis ....Celi Dulcedine plena,
.............................Alnwyc succure Wilelmo[36]

Little of this range remains today; but Buck's view gives us some idea of how it looked in 1726 (Pl. 9).

These buildings then were substantial, if not enough to confirm Alnwick as an *'edificator pretiosarum domuum'*.[37] However, in order to have some idea of his 'private life' it is necessary to know something of the people who inhabited these buildings and accompanied the bishop on his journeys round his estates. Some idea of the size of his Lincoln household is given by the account of the expenses of Richard Assheton, the newly elected abbot of Peterborough, in 1438. This included the prior and another monk riding over

---

Sagitta fuit Willelmum *que permiebat*; | *Dira Morte perit, qui dira frequenter agebat.* Under K. *Henry I: Henrici Regis Discretio summa patrabat,* | *Neglecte Legiis .... dum reparabat.'* Was it mere coincidence, or did Alnwick, in commissioning this glazing, concentrate on those kings who shared their names with himself and his royal patrons?

35 Lincolnshire Archives, BP Surveys 1, p.3.
36 *Desiderata Curiosa*, II, Lib. VIII, pp. 32-33.
37 Ibid., p. 15.

to visit the bishop at Buckden where they distributed tips to the clerks of the bishop's chapel (26s. 8d.); to the bishop's registrar, and his clerks (33s. 4d.); to the bishop's chaplain, marshal, and chamberlain (6s. 8d. each); to his six gentlemen (20s.), twelve valets (20s.), and nine bòys (9s.); the serjeant of his cellar (6s. 8d.); the clerk of the chancellor and the bishop's second clerk (2s. 8d.); the stable boys (40d.); and the kitchen boys (12d.). This makes a total of something between fifty and eighty household members considered worth tipping by the abbot's representatives.[38]

Some of these individuals can be identified. The bishop's registrar was Thomas Colstone, a married notary public, like John Exeter, Alnwick's Norwich registrar. His 'second clerk' may have been John Bugg, another notary, who frequently acted instead of Colstone. His chancellor was John Depyng, prebendary of Buckden, who together with two other lawyers, John Derby, who may have succeeded him as chancellor, and Thomas Balscott, formed the core of the bishop's *jurisperiti*. Alnwick's chaplain may have been Thomas Twyer, rector of Glatton, who often preached during visitations, and who was to be one of his executors. Other members of, or visitors to, the household are indicated by the names of those acting as witnesses to the bishop's acts. This is vividly illustrated by the seventy-seven people recorded as having either assisted at or witnessed Alnwick's proceedings against Lollards in his Norwich diocese between 1428 and 1431.[39]

During Alnwick's Lincoln episcopate, those most often noted as present, both in his court of audience and during his monastic visitations, apart from those noted above, were John Colstone and John Depyng junior, probably relatives of the registrar and chancellor, Thomas Holden, priest, and three notaries, Master John Malyns, Thomas Thorpe and John Walbrond. Others were Master William Alnwick, John Depying's successor as prebendary of Buckden, John Breton, and Gregory Byrkes.[40] Byrkes was a kinsman of William Estfield, the eminent London mercer, who may well have placed him in the bishop's household.[41] Three of the others had been members of Alnwick's Norwich household. His receiver general's accounts record that in the years between 1428 and 1430, the bishop's 'clerks', William Alnwick, John Breton, Thomas Bullock, Thomas Holden and John Fyket, were clothed, fed, schooled and barbered at his expense.[42] Four of these boys

[38] Cambridge University Library, Peterborough Cathedral MS 2, fol. 4. Published in *English Historical Documents, 1327-1485*, ed. by A. R. Myers (London, 1969), pp. 93-95.

[39] *Heresy Trials in the Diocese of Norwich, 1428-31*, ed. by N. P. Tanner, Camden Society, 4th series, 20 (London, 1977).

[40] For further discussion of the household and its members, see Hayes, 'William Alnwick', pp. 104-12.

[41] Lambeth Palace Library, Reg. Stafford (Canterbury), fol. 140v.

[42] Norfolk Record Office, EST 15/1/1-2.

received their board from the collegiate church of St Mary in the Fields in Norwich. The fifth, William Alnwick, received his at the cathedral priory, perhaps an indication that he was a favoured kinsman of the bishop. He may, of course, have been an illegitimate son, but there is absolutely no evidence to support such a supposition and, on the whole, it seems unlikely. He is not mentioned in the bishop's will and his own seems not to have survived. All, except Alnwick, had received collation of rural deaneries in the diocese of Norwich, as had John Malyns; an indication that Alnwick used these benefices, which were without cure, to supplement the income of his favoured protégés. Clearly then, at least some of his favourites followed Bishop Alnwick from Norwich to Lincoln.

Nevertheless, it seems that not all was well in the bishop's household. Giles's *Chronicle* gives the sad report that after Alnwick's death, 'because he had been too strict with his household they openly carried off from his executors 2,000 marks to distribute among themselves'.[43] It has been suggested[44] that '*nimis strictus*' should be translated not as 'too strict' but as 'too mean' or 'tight-fisted', a translation that might be supported by Alnwick's strictures, referred to above, concerning the grasping potential of his successor. However, his bequest of 100 shillings to every gentleman, five marks to every yeoman, forty shillings to every groom and twenty shillings to every page of his household, and his instruction to his executors to keep the household together for six months after his death, although not unusual, does not seem to have been ungenerous.[45]

The household did not exist merely for its own sake. As Gascoigne's complaint that bishops '*nec hospitalitatem tenent*' suggests, they were expected to entertain visitors.[46] The loss of Alnwick's household accounts means that there is little indication of who these visitors were. The accounts of the chapter of Lincoln cathedral record the expenses of several of its members travelling to see and stay with the bishop, to discuss chapter business with him at Sleaford, Lyddington, Buckden and even as far away as Wooburn.[47] Of these, the most congenial visitor was probably the provost, Thomas Ryngstede. Alnwick had known him early in his career, had employed him as receiver general in Norwich and had collated him to a Lincoln canonry.[48] On at least one occasion, probably in October 1448, Alnwick entertained

---

[43] *Incerti Scriptoris Chronicon Angliae Temporibus Ricardi II, Henrici IV, Henrici V, et Henrici VI*, ed. by J. A. Giles (London, 1848), Henry VI section, p. 39.

[44] By Dr M. R. Foster.

[45] *Visitations*, I, p. xxvii.

[46] *Loci e Libro*, p. 43.

[47] Lincolnshire Archives, Dean and Chapter, Bj/2/12, m. 9v.; Bj/2/13, 1443/4 section, fols 59v, 61, 1444/5 section, fols 22v, 23.

[48] A. B. Emden, *A Biographical Dictionary of the University of Cambridge to 1500* (Cambridge, 1963), pp. 499-500; Hayes, 'William Alnwick', pp. 120-22.

Henry VI in his newly adorned palace at Lincoln.[49]

Other visitors have, sadly, gone unrecorded. In his turn, Alnwick spent much of the period between Christmas 1433 and Easter 1434 in and around Bury St Edmunds while the young king, to whom he was confessor, was staying in the abbey there.[50] He also visited Ralph, Lord Cromwell, at both Tattershall and South Wingfield.[51] Cromwell was one of several royal councillors with whom Alnwick had established close ties by serving as feoffee for their lands and executor of their wills. These included Thomas Beaufort, duke of Exeter, the chancellor, Archbishop Kempe, Bishop Thomas Langley, and Lords Walter Hungerford and John Tiptoft.[52] However, despite such highly placed connections, the only man of any standing whom Alnwick appointed as his own executor was Sir William Estfield, who predeceased him. This may account for the theft of his goods by his household which the Giles chronicle blames on the fact that his executors 'sacerdotes senes fuerunt, et non timore digni'.[53]

Friendships, as opposed to political connections, can perhaps be guessed at from some of the personal bequests to Alnwick. He received several silver-gilt goblets: a covered one from Thomas Beaufort, duke of Exeter;[54] one that had belonged to Bishop Langley from the latter's steward, Thomas Holden (perhaps a connection of the clerk of that name in Alnwick's household); and one of his choice from those owned by William Estfield.[55] Thomas Montagu, earl of Salisbury, left him a jewel worth forty marks; and Sir Ralph Rochford, a leading Lincolnshire gentleman, a gold ring with a great sapphire.[56] More personal perhaps was the bequest by his early patron, Stephen Scrope, archdeacon of Richmond, of a piece of gold plate and a

---

[49] B. Wolffe, *Henry VI* (London, 1981), pp. 361-71 (Henry VI's itinerary); Lincolnshire Archives, Dean and Chapter, Bj/2/15 (1448/9), m. 15: payment for bell ringing at king's coming to Lincoln this year. Allen, *History of Lincoln*, p. 116, and J. W. F. Hill, *Medieval Lincoln*, 2nd edn. (Stamford, 1989), p. 272, both state he came in 1445/6 but there is no support for this in Wolffe, *Henry VI*.

[50] Hayes, 'William Alnwick', p. 419; British Library, Add. MS 14848, fol. 128; W. Dugdale, *Monasticon Anglicanum*, ed. by J. Caley, H. Ellis and B. Badinel, 6 vols in 8 (London, 1817-30), III, 113.

[51] Lincolnshire Archives, Register XVIII, fols 85v, 86v, 119.

[52] Hayes, 'William Alnwick', pp. 298-301.

[53] Giles, *Chronicle*, Henry VI section, p. 39.

[54] Perhaps like the contemporary parcel-gilt Lacock cup now on loan to the British Museum.

[55] *Register of Henry Chichele, Archbishop of Canterbury, 1441-1443*, ed. by E. F. Jacob, 4 vols, Canterbury and York Society, 42, 45-47 (London, 1937-47), II, pp. 361, 581; Lambeth Palace Library, Reg. Stafford (Canterbury), fol. 140v.

[56] *Reg. Chichele*, II, p. 363; *The Fifty Earliest English Wills in the Court of Probate, London*, ed. by F. J. Furnival, Early English Texts Society, 78 (London, 1882), part I, p. 120.

covered silver salt bearing Scrope's arms.[57]

Perhaps most interesting are the bequests of two men who had a shared history with Alnwick of loyalty to Henry V and his son. Sir John Wodehouse left him 'a gold tablet of the Trinity which I had from his predecessor' (Bishop Wakering of Norwich).[58] The bequest of Lord Walter Hungerford was even more splendid: 'a silver gilt tablet, standing on a silver mount, of the Assumption of the Blessed Virgin Mary: with two leaves of silver, on the outside of which are two silver images, one of St John the Evangelist and the other of St Matthew: and on the inside two other images, one of St Katherine and the other of St John the Baptist'.[59] It was apt for Wodehouse and Hungerford to bequeath him images of the Trinity and Mary during his tenure of two sees whose cathedrals had those two dedications, Norwich to the Holy Trinity and Lincoln to the Blessed Virgin.

If these bequests show who cared for him, Alnwick's will indicates where his own affections lay.[60] To the prior of Norwich (and not to the excommunicate dean of Lincoln) he left a silver-gilt goblet to the value of £10; to the walls of Alnwick £10, and to that town's parish church, besides £10 for its repair, 'my third missal in value, an antiphoner, a purple suit of vestments of mine of cloth of gold with golden lions interwoven, to wit, a chasuble, dalmatic, tunicle, three albs, three copes of the same suit, and a chalice'; to the Carmelites at Hulne near Alnwick he left forty shillings; and to the Austin canons at Alnwick 100 shillings and 'a pair of little basins of silver with flowers enamelled in their bottom and a spout in the side of one of the said basins for their high altar'.[61] Alnwick also left vestments to each of the churches appropriated to the bishop of Lincoln.[62]

If on death he left no treasure to Lincoln cathedral, in life he would seem to have been generous to its treasury. One of the longest entries in an inventory of 1536 records a processional cross described thus:

[57] *Testamenta Eboracensia*, ed. by J. Raine, Part I, Surtees Society, 4 (Durham, 1836), p. 389.

[58] *Reg. Chichele*, II, p.438. A close analogy to this tablet would appear to be the Middleham jewel, which is a pendant with the image of the Trinity on one side and of the Nativity on the other, now in the Yorkshire Museum.

[59] Lambeth Palace Library, Reg. Stafford (Canterbury), fol. 117Av.

[60] Ibid., fols 178-79; *Visitations*, I, pp. xxiv-xxx.

[61] These were perhaps similar to the surviving pair left by Bishop Foxe to Corpus Christi College, Oxford (C. Oman, *English Church Plate 597-1830* (London, 1957), p. 87).

[62] At least one of them, Thame, received their bequest. The churchwardens' account for 1450/1 records 'Item, to John Waltan for the bryng a peyr of vestmentys of the quest of the Beschope of Lynkole, xijd.' (Oxford Record Office, MS dd. Par. Thame C5, fol. 14v). I am grateful to Mrs Julia Carnwath for this reference.

a great cross, silver and gilt, with images of the crucifix, Mary and John ...; having four evangelists in the four corners weighing one hundred and twenty-eight ounces, of the gift of William Alnewick; and a foot pertaining to the same, silver and gilt, with two scutcheons of arms and a scripture 'Orate pro animabus Thome Bewford', etc.[63] And the said foot hath a base with six images; the coronation, and the salutation of Our Lady, St George, St Hugh, weighing eighty-six ounces, of the gift of the said William; ... and a staff to the said cross, silver and gilt, with two ..., silver and gilt, with this scripture 'Delectare in Domino' weighing eighty-four ounces.

Also in the treasury in 1536 was

a costly cope of blue velvet with costly orphreys of gold, with images set with pearl, and in the morse an image of Our Lady with her Son, and four angels,[64] in the hood the Trinity set with pearl and stone, and in the back a large image of the Assumption garnished with pearl and stone, with many angels of gold set with pearl, ex dono Wilielmi Alnewike episcopi.[65]

Finally, two other treasures connected with the bishop are revealed by the list of New Year's gifts presented by Henry VI in 1437, which included

Item, delivered by your said commaundment to send to my lady of Stafford the moder, on that same day, a tabulet of gold maad with ij levys and with ynne an ymage of the Salutacion of oure Lady garnized with roses maad with rougeclere and with xl perl hangyng by a cheyne weyng vij unc' j qrtrn, the which tabulet some tyme was yove the Kynge by the bysshop of Norwych.

Item, delivered by your said comaundment on that same day to the bysshop of Norwych, being with the Kynge at Estham [sic, for Eltham], j rounde tabulet of gold garnized with xij garnades and xxiiij perl hangyng by a cheyne weyng v unc' j qrtrn, the which tabulet some tyme was yove the Kyng by the abbot of Westmynster.[66]

Bishop Alnwick's presence with the king at this festive time of year, together with the fact that he was the only cleric, apart from Cardinal Beaufort, to receive a gift that year from the king, is perhaps an indication of the level of intimacy between the bishop and Henry VI at this time.

Although none of the treasures known to have been Alnwick's survives, their description perhaps reveals something of his artistic and liturgical tastes.[67] Similarly, his books may give some indication of his intellectual

---

[63] Unfortunately there is no indication of what the 'etc.' stood for.

[64] A similar morse from Warden Abbey (although without angels) is displayed in the British Museum (M & LA 53, 6-7,1).

[65] Monasticon, VI, part III, 1280, 1283.

[66] Excerpta Historica, ed. by S. Bentley (London, 1833), pp. 148-50.

[67] The concentration on the Holy Trinity and the Blessed Virgin Mary, particularly her Assumption, is not, perhaps, surprising. However, it does tie in nicely with the centrality of these two images to the theology of the period. Cf. Professor Morgan's article in this volume.

preferences. He could, of course, have little control over those he inherited. In 1418, Stephen Scrope, archdeacon of Richmond, left him two books outright: the *Sext* and the *Constitutions* of Otto and Ottobon with John Acton's commentary on them. For his life, he was left four books that were then to go to the library of York cathedral. These were Gratian's *Decreta* and Gregory IX's *Decretals*, together with the Archdeacon of Bologna's *Rosarium* and Henry Cardinal of Ostia's *Lectura*, commentaries on the *Sext* and *Decretals* respectively.[68] In other words, Scrope gave a splendid boost to his protégé's ecclesiastical career by giving him all the basic texts and commentaries needed to administer the canon law in England. In 1439, Bishop Langley, another early patron, bequeathed Alnwick his best copy of Pope Gregory the Great's *Moralia*, a book that may have been as helpful to Alnwick's pastoral role as Scrope's bequest was to his legal one.[69] In addition to these text-books he inherited a great portiforium from William Estfield.[70]

These, while useful, were not necessarily his books of choice. However, in 1441 he requested from the king three books that had belonged to Richard Haroweden, the recently retired abbot of Westminster. These were the *Corpus Juris Civilis*, very meat and drink to a civil lawyer like Alnwick; two volumes of Henry Bowyk's *Commentary* on the *Decretals*; and Roger de Waltham's *Compendium Morale*.[71] That he had a real interest in theology is confirmed by his borrowing from Garendon Abbey, also in 1441, a volume of Origen 'upon the first three books of the Pentateuch, Judges, and somewhat upon the first [book of] Kings, and some little upon the Song of Songs, Isaiah, Jeremiah, Ezekiel'.[72] From his will it is apparent that he owned at least three missals and an antiphoner. However, perhaps most suggestive of private piety is the bequest in the will of Henry Bennett of Lincoln, made in 1468, of 'my boke of meditacions that was Alnewykes, Busshop of Lincoln'.[73]

---

[68] *Testamenta Eboracensia*, Part I, pp. 385-89. The *Lectura* may have belonged to Archbishop Scrope, Stephen's uncle, who was left a copy by his uncle, Geoffrey le Scrope, canon of Lincoln in 1382 (*Lincoln Wills Registered in the District Probate Registry at Lincoln*, I, *A.D. 1271 to A.D. 1536*, ed. by C. W. Foster, Lincoln Record Society, 5 (Lincoln, 1914) pp. 11-16).

[69] *Historiae Dunelmensis Scriptores Tres*, ed. by J. Raine, Surtees Society, 9 (Durham, 1839), pp. ccxli-ccxlvii.

[70] Lambeth Palace Library, Reg. Stafford (Canterbury), fols 139-41.

[71] *Proceedings and Ordinances of the Privy Council of England (1386-1542)*, ed. by N. H. Nicolas, 7 vols, Record Commission (London, 1834-37), V, 140-41. A Bowyk (not a very well-known book) was owned by John Newton, treasurer of York, d. 1414 (E. F. Jacob, *The Fifteenth Century*, rev. edn (Oxford, 1969), p. 286).

[72] *Visitations*, I, 112-13.

[73] 'Lincolnshire Wills Proved in the Prerogative Court of Canterbury, 1471-90', ed. by C. W. Foster, *Associated Architectural Societies' Reports and Papers*, 41 (1932/3), 179-218 (p. 179). I am grateful to Dr Dorothy Owen for pointing this reference

His books would seem to indicate that William Alnwick, although despised as a 'rustic man' by Piero da Monte, was no academic nonentity. He was a doctor of civil law and, like many of his contemporaries on the episcopal bench, clearly appreciated the value of a good education. In his dioceses, he promoted graduates, predominantly of his own university of Cambridge; he saw to the schooling of his household clerks during his lifetime; and at his death he left not only £150 to pay thirty secular priests of the university towns to celebrate Mass for his soul, but also much of the residue of his estate to support poor scholars of his dioceses 'for their study in the universities of Oxford and Cambridge ..., or elsewhere as regards those who do not know their grammar', giving preference to those boys who dwelt in his household.[74]

In his lifetime, he assisted Henry VI in founding Eton and King's Colleges, being one of the compilers of the original statutes of the latter, and its designated visitor, as well as being one of the bishops commissioned by Archbishop Stafford to consecrate its chapel and cemetery in 1444.[75] On his own behalf, he was remembered for having built the south part of the Cambridge schools.[76] As a result, it would seem, of initiatives in recent general chapters of Benedictine monks,[77] in 1428 Bishop Alnwick joined with the abbot of Crowland, Bishop Langley of Durham and John Hore of Childerley to found a residence for Benedictines studying canon law and theology at Cambridge 'who have hitherto been compelled to dwell with secular persons in their inns'.[78] This hall was later re-founded, first as Buckingham and then as Magdalene College. Perhaps closest of all to his heart was the chantry he founded in St Michael's church, Alnwick, in 1448,

---

out to me.

[74] *Visitations*, I, pp. xxv, xxvii. Cf. H. Jewell, 'English Bishops as Educational Benefactors in the Later Fifteenth Century', in *The Church, Politics and Patronage in the Fifteenth Century*, ed. by R. B. Dobson (Gloucester, 1984), pp. 146-67.

[75] Hayes, 'William Alnwick', pp. 269-72, 311-13, 322. Although Alnwick was the designated visitor of King's College, Perry was mistaken in his statement that 'A full account of the visitation of King's is to be found in Bishop Alnwick's register' (G. G. Perry, 'Bishop Beckington and King Henry VI', *English Historical Review*, 9 (1894), 261-74 (p. 267)).

[76] F. Godwin and W. Richardson, *De Praesulibus Angliae* (Cambridge, 1743), p. 298n.

[77] At the Northampton chapters of 1423 and 1426, the prior of the Benedictine students at Cambridge urged the necessity of giving such students proper support and the advisability of their having a common hostel (*Documents Illustrating the Activities of the General and Provincial Chapters of the English Black Monks, 1215-1540*, ed. by W.A. Pantin, 3 vols, Camden Society, 45, 47, 54 (1931-37), II, pp. 149, 173).

[78] *Calendar of Patent Rolls, 1422-29* (London, 1901), p. 475.

together with the earl of Northumberland.[79] One of this chantry's two priests was to teach grammar to poor boys, without payment. Perhaps, towards the end of his life, Alnwick envisaged the possibility of other boys of lowly parentage from his home town progressing in their careers, thanks to a sound education.

Education was not, however, the sole, or even the primary, purpose of such foundations. Their main aim was to worship God and to pray for their benefactors. In addition to those establishments with an educational bent already mentioned, Alnwick was intimately concerned with the foundation of Lord Cromwell's college at Tattershall in 1440.[80] Seven years later the two joined with an impressive array of other magnates to found a guild dedicated to St Christopher at Thame, one of the bishop's own churches. This guild was to employ a chantry chaplain and support a hermit who was to maintain the highway and pray for the founders' intentions.[81] Alnwick was in less lofty company when he joined John Doffield, clerk, and ten parishioners of Louth, another of his churches, to form a similar guild there in honour of the Virgin Mary.[82] These pious foundations came noticeably towards the end of his life. In laying the foundations for his own chantry, Alnwick requested 'that for five years ... my executors find at some altar as nigh as may be to the place of my burial an honest priest that shall celebrate for my soul and the soul of Master Stephen le Scrope, sometime archdeacon of Richmond', as well as for the souls of all the faithful departed.[83] He was clearly a man who remembered his debts.

It is difficult to judge the depth of the faith expressed by such foundations. Conventional Alnwick's piety may have been, but his well-known devotion to his episcopal duties, no less than his benefactions, would seem to indicate that it was real and profound, His three visits to Walsingham during his Norwich episcopate may have been inspired by a pilgrim's desire to visit the Marian shrine there.[84] The verses set in his Lincoln chapel windows calling on his head the blessings of the two patrons of his dioceses, the Holy Trinity, as depicted in his seals as bishop of Norwich (Pls 10, 11), and the Blessed Virgin, as depicted in his large seal as bishop of Lincoln (Pl. 12), reflect a devotion that was none the less real for being conventional. Similarly, his motto, '*Delectare in Domino*', 'to delight in

79   *Calendar of Patent Rolls, 1446-52* (London, 1910), pp. 170-71.

80   Hayes, 'William Alnwick', p. 271.

81   The other founders were Archbishop Stafford, Humphrey, duke of Buckingham, William, earl of Suffolk, Lord Sudeley, Sir William Lovell, Drew Barentyn, Richard and Sibyl Quartermain (*Calendar of Patent Rolls, 1446-52*, pp. 180-81).

82   Ibid., p. 81.

83   *Visitations*, I, p. xxvi.

84   14 January 1428, 1 April 1430 (an ordination ceremony) and 20 November 1432 (Norfolk Record Office, REG 5/9, fols 10, 128v, 58v).

the Lord', suggests that the faith that drove him to do his duty could also inspire him.

Is it possible to judge his character? That he could be self-righteous is indicated by the passage in his will concerned with his suspicions about his successor's potential depredations. That he stood on his dignity is illustrated by his actions against the prior of Binham who neglected to ring his church's bells at the bishop's approach.[85] A certain austerity may be inferred from his instructions to nuns, with whom he could find no other fault, to make sure that they pulled their veils down to their eyes.[86] Nevertheless, apart from the strictures of da Monte, who was trying unsuccessfully to procure a Lincoln canonry for a papal nephew, and of the abbots of Bury St Edmunds and St Albans, who clashed with him over their exemptions, judgements on him by contemporaries were generally positive. To the writer of Giles's *Chronicle* he was a 'very discreet and virtuous man', if too strict or stingy; and to the Crowland chronicler 'he was singularly distinguished among his fellow-bishops of England for bearing the highest character and an unblemished name' as well as being 'a man of the most consummate skill in the transaction of business'.[87] It is tempting to suggest that it was more than common form which inspired his cathedral chapter to inform the archbishop of Canterbury, '*lacrimandens*', that, because of his death, the church of Lincoln now lay '*destituta*'.[88]

Certainly, at least one member of the chapter felt his loss. This was John Breton, who had been educated in Alnwick's Norwich household and promoted by him to a Lincoln canonry. As related earlier, Alnwick originally provided for a chantry of only five years' duration. However, in making his own will, in 1465, more than fifteen years after Alnwick's death, Breton instructed his executors to employ a priest to celebrate for twenty years for their two souls. The residue of Breton's estate was to be spent for the benefit of their souls, primarily in the building of bridges and roads. Breton's devotion to Alnwick was further expressed by his request to be buried 'at the side or feet of my most singular lord, William Alnwick'.[89] Their tombs have been lost but they are united armorially. Side by side on

---

85 *Annales Monasterii S. Albani, a Johanne Amundesham, Monacho, ut videtur, Conscripti (A.D. 1421-1440)*, ed. by H. T. Riley, 2 vols, Rolls Series (London, 1870-71), I, 30-32 and ff..

86 *Visitations*, I, 118, 319-20.

87 Giles, *Chronicle*, Henry VI section, p. 39; *Ingulph's Chronicle of the Abbey of Croyland with the Continuations by Peter of Blois and Anonymous Writers*, trans. and ed. by H. T. Riley (London, 1854), pp. 405-06.

88 Lambeth Palace Library, Reg. Stafford (Canterbury), fols 32v-33 (11 December 1449).

89 Lincolnshire Archives, Dean and Chapter, A 2/34, fols 59, 81; A 2/35, fols 96v-98; Dij 50/2/21.

the east end of the tithe barn of the Lincoln vicars choral are fixed the arms of Bishop Alnwick and the rebus, 'bre' on a tun, for Breton (Pl. 13). It may be impossible to approach anywhere near a true understanding of the 'private life' of a late medieval bishop; but perhaps these arms may serve as a reminder that, if the private lives of medieval men remain hidden from our view, it is our sight that is at fault and not the lives themselves.

The Laity, the Alien Priories, and the Redistribution of Ecclesiastical Property
BENJAMIN THOMPSON

On 13 November 1399, Henry IV issued the following order:[1]

To whom it may concern:

> Whereas priories, houses and other religious places staffed by aliens have been laudably founded and built within our realm of England and Wales by our noble progenitors and other leading men and magnates of our realm, in order to perform and support divine offices and burdens of hospitality and alms and other works of piety and devotion;
>
> [yet because of the war with France, Edward III took them into his hands and the priors were expelled and replaced by various secular and other farmers]
>
> with the result that both in their houses and in their goods and possessions they are so greatly destroyed, dilapidated and devastated, that divine worship and regular observance have ceased in them, hospitality and alms and other works of charity, which were accustomed to be surely performed, are withdrawn, and moreover the pious wishes of the founders are repeatedly defrauded and frustrated, to the great displeasure of and offence to Almighty God, so we believe;
>
> we, wishing more liberally to provide, for the honour of God and Holy Church, for the augmentation of divine worship, and the renewal and continuance of the said charitable works and other burdens;
>
> restore to such and such a prior, who is instituted and inducted *or* whose priory is conventual, such a priory with all its possessions etc., rendering the ancient apport during the war;
>
> in order that the prior and his successors will find and sustain monks, secular chaplains, and other English ministers in that priory to the due and accustomed number established at its foundation,
>
> and perform and support other burdens and works of piety anciently incumbent on that priory according to the first foundation.

This writ offers a convenient starting-point for analysing the background to and the climax of the story of the 'alien religious of the power of the king of France' in the early fifteenth century. In it, Henry IV justified his restoration of alien priories in terms of the lay view of their function. My object here is to show not only that this attitude was a major cause of the fate of the priories in the preceding and following years, but also that its consistent application led to different practical results in different

---

[1] *Calendar of Patent Rolls* (London, 1891-) [*CPR*] *1399-1401*, pp. 70-72; *Foedera, Conventiones, Litterae...*, ed. by T. Rymer (The Hague, 1745, marginal references to original edition), VIII, 101-06. My translation.

19

circumstances. First, therefore, we must pay attention to the writ and its context in order to ascertain the attitudes of king and laity, and the story so far.[2]

In the first place, Henry asserted that religious houses owed their foundation to kings and nobles, who had given property to support religious works of piety and charity. This was almost a commonplace in the later Middle Ages: the phrase used in the opening paragraph, '*ad divina officia et ... onera facienda et supportanda*', and particularly that characteristic use of the gerundive, was the standard form of late-medieval foundation charters. Such a link, between the (secular) property with which ecclesiastical institutions were endowed and the (spiritual) objects they existed to realize, lay at the heart of the laity's attitude to ecclesiastical patronage, and perhaps to the whole of the endowed church. The preamble to the Statute of Provisors, drawing on a petition of 1307 but reissued as recently as 1390, explicitly asserted that the church in England owed its existence to the endowments of kings and nobles, for the specific purpose of procuring the salvation of the souls of the founders.[3] The arrangement was, to the lay mentality, contractual and tenurial: founders gave lands, and in return they were rendered spiritual services leading, they trusted, to salvation.[4]

This attitude was applied directly to the condition of the alien priories in 1399: the damage to the possessions of these priories was so great, Henry argued, that spiritual works were diminished, and as a result, the wishes of the founders were frustrated. Other texts putting across this argument made the damage to founders even more explicit: these works had been established for their souls (*pro animabus*, as the charters say), to help them through Purgatory. Therefore not only were their prospects of attaining Paradise put in jeopardy, but also the lineage was disinherited, as if it had been seised of

2   I have looked at two aspects of the history of the alien priories before in 'The Statute of Carlisle, 1307, and the Alien Priories', *Jnl of Ecclesiastical History*, 41 (1990), 543-83; and '*Habendum et Tenendum*: Lay and Ecclesiastical Attitudes to the Property of the Church', in *Religious Belief and Ecclesiastical Careers in Late Medieval England*, ed. by C. Harper-Bill (Woodbridge, 1991), 197-238 (pp. 224-33). Here I offer only light footnoting, since a more comprehensive account will appear in my book. I rely heavily on D. J. A. Matthew, *The Norman Monasteries and their English Possessions* (Oxford, 1962); M. M. Morgan, *The English Lands of the Abbey of Bec* (Oxford, 1946); C. W. New, *History of the Alien Priories in England to the Confiscation of Henry V* (Chicago, 1916).

3   *Statutes of the Realm*, Record Commission, 11 vols in 12 (London, 1810-28), I, 316-17, II, 69-74; *Councils and Synods with Other Documents relating to the English Church, II, 1205-1313*, ed. by F. M. Powicke and C. R. Cheney, 2 vols (Oxford, 1964), II, 1232-33.

4   See my '*Habendum et Tenendum*', passim, especially pp. 212-16; and 'From "Alms" to "Spiritual Services": the Function and Status of Monastic Property in Medieval England', *Monastic Studies*, 2 (1991), 227-61.

the spiritual works as services owed from the land. Equally, the restoration of the priory would lead to the renewal of such spiritual services and (again, by implication here but explicit elsewhere) to continued help for the souls of the founders. Henry, therefore, who had until recently been merely the doyen among chivalrous nobility, was acting on a series of attitudes fundamental to the aristocracy in its dealings with the church.[5]

In so doing Henry assessed the eligibility of alien priories for restoration on the basis of criteria which had become common currency. A prior was either to be restored because his priory was *conventualis*, fully conventual, or because the prior was instituted and inducted (as to an ecclesiastical benefice). The latter was thought to provide some guarantee that the priory was an autonomous institution, rather than merely a grange or an office for the exploitation of lands and churches; the prior was not removable at will by the abbot of the mother-house ('dative') as if he were an obedientiary running a monastic department.[6] The nature of the relationship between the French mother-house and its English priories or cells was therefore crucial in 1399.

This relationship dated back to the establishment of the priories in the eleventh and twelfth centuries, in the wake of the arrival of an aristocracy endowed with honours on both sides of the channel. Here again the motives of the benefactors provide a point of reference, because they had an important influence on the form adopted by each priory. Some Norman barons wished to augment directly the endowment of monasteries in Normandy (themselves established relatively recently) with the newly-acquired English lands. Others proposed to locate new monastic houses in the conquered realm, although they were to be staffed by French monks and affiliated to continental mother-houses and orders. This distinction must have sprung from different attitudes among the conquerors to the lands which they had won. William I's foundation of Battle Abbey as a thanksgiving and penance for the Battle of Hastings publicly marked his conquest and his assumption of the throne.[7] Others followed his lead: William Warenne brought monks of Cluny to Lewes, his Sussex castle and

5 See the references in note 3; also *Councils and Synods*, II, 1239; Thompson, 'Statute of Carlisle', 546-53; and the parliamentary petitions cited below, notes 23-27, 65-68, 75-78; e.g. *Rotuli Parliamentorum*, Record Commission, 6 vols (London, 1783), II, 342.

6 Matthew, *Norman Monasteries*, pp. 28-65; Morgan, *English Lands*, pp. 9-12, 18-25; New, *Alien Priories*, pp. 1-44.

7 The facts about the foundations of these houses can generally be found in the *Victoria County Histories* [*VCH*]; William Dugdale, *Monasticon Anglicanum*, 2nd edn, ed. by J. Caley, H. Ellis, B. Bandinel, 6 vols in 8 (London, 1817-30); T. Tanner, *Notitia Monastica*, 3rd edn (Cambridge, 1787). For Battle, see *VCH Sussex*, II, 52.

the centre of the rape responsible for defending the coast, and Gilbert FitzRichard established monks of that most famous of all Norman monasteries, Bec, in the castle chapel at Clare.[8] Such monasteries, like those at Castle Acre and Thetford in Norfolk and Eye in Suffolk, gave notice that this new aristocracy intended to regard its English lands as of significance in themselves, and not as mere adjuncts to continental possessions.[9] The *caput* of the honour needed its monastery as well as its castle, to ensure both temporal and spiritual domination of the locality.[10]

On the other hand, the Beaumonts gave manors and churches to their family house at Préaux, the Giffards to Longueville, the Tonys to Conches, and the Lovels to Ivry, just as William I and his sons continued the endowment of the houses of St Stephen and Holy Trinity at Caen from English property.[11] These lands were the gifts of families whose large interests in Normandy before 1066 made it unlikely that they would move their centre of gravity to England, as did some of their poorer companions.[12] The French abbots exploited these properties in the following centuries by despatching monks and secular proctors charged with returning the profits to the mother-house; these units of either stable or peripatetic monks and clerks became the alien cells.[13]

[8] Lewes: *VCH Sussex*, II, 64-65; *Early Yorkshire Charters*, ed. by W. Farrer and C. T. Clay, Yorkshire Record Society, 12 vols (1914-65), VIII, 54-55, 59-62. Stoke: Morgan, *English Lands*, p. 11.

[9] Castle Acre: *Early Yorkshire Charters*, VIII, 4; *Monasticon*, V, 49. Thetford: *Monasticon*, V, 148; *VCH Norfolk*, II, 363. Eye: *Monasticon*, III, 404-05; *VCH Suffolk*, II, 72.

[10] See note 6. Matthew, *Norman Monasteries*, pp. 56-58; B. Golding, 'The Coming of the Cluniacs', *Anglo-Norman Studies*, 2 (*Proceedings of the Battle Conference 1980*), (1981), 65-77, esp. p. 68; J. Martindale, 'Monasteries and Castles: the Priories of St-Florent de Saumur in England after 1066', in *England in the Eleventh Century*, ed. by C. Hicks (Stamford, 1992), 135-56: I am most grateful to the author for drawing my attention to this piece.

[11] Préaux: Matthew, *Norman Monasteries*, p. 53; *Calendar of Documents Preserved in France, 918-1206*, ed. by J. H. Round (1899), pp. 111-12. Longueville: *Newington Longeville Charters*, ed. by H. E. Salter, Oxfordshire Record Society (1921), pp. 1-7. Conches: *Monasticon*, VI, 995; *The Complete Peerage*, ed. by V. Gibbs et al., 12 vols in 13 (London, 1910-59), XII (ii), 762-64. Ivry: A. J. Taylor, 'The Alien Priory of Minster Lovell', *Oxoniensia*, 2 (1937), 103-17 (pp. 103-04). Caen: Matthew, *Norman Monasteries*, p. 31, n. 2; *Calendar of Documents Preserved in France*, pp. 143, 149, 150; *Monasticon*, VI, 1072; *Calendar of Charter Rolls*, 6 vols (London, 1903-27), V, 158, 160.

[12] Cf. Matthew, *Norman Monasteries*, pp. 28-30, 44-45. The origins of these families may be found in L. C. Loyd, *The Origins of Some Anglo-Norman Families* (Leeds, 1951); I. J. Sanders, *English Baronies: a Study of their Origin and Descent, 1086-1327* (Oxford, 1960); *Complete Peerage*.

[13] See note 6.

The royal example shows that families could maintain a balance between England and Normandy by both founding new houses in England and adding endowments to Norman ones. The two types were not incompatible. Rather, they represent different aspects of the conquest, which witnessed both the acquisition of England by the aristocracy of Normandy, and the introduction into England of French mores in the ecclesiastical sphere (as in the secular). Moreover, between the two types of alien priory there was in practice a spectrum of different constitutional links between mother- and daughter-houses, and of arrangements for exploiting English property. A specific variant arose when donors gave churches to French abbeys to support two monks at a particular place, as Maud Lovel did at Minster Lovel (Oxfordshire, given to Ivry), and Robert Stafford, a Tony cadet, at Wootton Wawen (Warwickshire, staffed by monks from Conches).[14] One accidental result of the arrangement was the institution and induction of one of the monks to the parish church, which was to have important consequences in 1399. These priories can be regarded either as mini-convents, in that they were intended to secure local spiritual services, or cells, because they supported only a small number of monks and sent some revenues back to France. Nevertheless, the contrast between the principles underpinning cells and those underpinning convents was sharp: the function of one was to provide for the spiritual activities of French religious, whereas the other existed to support monastic life in England of the reformed type which had recently taken hold on the continent.

This contrast was to be exacerbated in the course of time, because of the dislocation between property in England and spiritual activities in France. The circumstances in which the houses had suffered the destruction, dilapidation and devastation referred to in Henry's writ flowed ultimately from the severing of the political connection between England and Normandy in 1204. Even before then, families had divided their English and Norman possessions between different sons, and therefore different lineages. But after 1204 the position of priories in England subject to foreign abbeys was bound to be difficult, especially when the naturally competitive kings of England and France went to war: in 1294, after Philip IV's seizure of Gascony, Edward I set a precedent by seizing property and persons of the 'alien religious of the power of the king of France', ostensibly for the security of the realm.[15] He also assessed their wealth and tapped it by granting custody of the priories back to their priors, who became royal farmers paying

---

[14] See note 11.

[15] The story set out in this paragraph is best told in Matthew, *Norman Monasteries*, and Morgan, *English Lands*. Much of the detail can be followed in the *Calendar of Fine Rolls* (London, 1911-) [*CFR*]. For 1294-5 see also Thompson, 'Statute of Carlisle', pp. 553-55.

an annual farm often amounting to a high proportion of income. The same procedure was followed when war was renewed in 1324, and when Edward III did the same in 1337 the seizure was more than a temporary hiatus in the religious's control of their possession; furthermore, the resumption of alien control in 1360 turned out to be but a breathing space which for most was not even long enough to pay off the arrears of farm still owing from the preceding twenty-three years of war. On the resumption of the war in 1369 the alien possessions were taken by the crown again, and again (in most cases) granted to their priors for annual farms which, in the tight financial climate of the 1370s, as in the ambitious 1340s, were gradually forced upwards.[16] Moreover, in 1378 many of the alien religious were expelled, and those who subsequently left or died were not replaced.[17] The fundamental link between temporal property (in England) and spiritual services (in France), physically but not politically dislocated at foundation, had been sundered by the circumstances of time and place. Such were the demands of the world which, medieval churchmen whined, made their spiritual task on this earth so hard.[18]

The plight of the alien priories in 1399 resulted not only from changed political circumstances, however, but also from changed notions of the operation of spiritual services. In his writ Henry assumed that the monks' spiritual services to donors consisted of specific acts of liturgy and alms. The restorations were intended to support the 'due and accustomed' number of monks established at the priories' foundation, and the 'anciently incumbent' burdens and works of piety which were specified then. Such specification was certainly the practice of founders in the later Middle Ages, as their charters show: they detailed the number and types of Masses and prayers (and collects and antiphons) to be said, which souls were to benefit, and even the daily timetable. Late-medieval ecclesiastical foundations were the creations of the founders who laboriously acquired the land for them and who stamped their own identity on to them at every turn.[19]

---

[16] *CFR* VIII, passim. For explicit statements of the policy of pushing up farms, see *CFR* V, 449, and below at note 27. For an example, see below at notes 50-55.

[17] Matthew, *Norman Monasteries*, pp. 109-11; A. K. McHardy, 'The Alien Priories and the Expulsion of Aliens from England in 1378', in *Church, Society and Politics*, ed. by D. Baker, Studies in Church History, 12 (1975), 133-41.

[18] See, for instance, in this context the complaints of the clergy in 1300-01 against the royal farming of alien priories (*Councils & Synods*, II, 1218 [no 34]); and the petition of the abbot of Cluny trying to persuade Henry V to allow him to enjoy his manors (*Charters and Records among the Archives of the Ancient Abbey of Cluny*, ed. by G. F. Duckett, 2 vols (1888), I, 240). Both these texts show the clergy's acceptance of a strong link between temporal goods and spiritual works.

[19] Thompson, 'From "Alms" to "Spiritual Services"', esp. pp. 250-53. E.g. the statutes of Rushworth College, founded in 1342, *Monasticon*, VI, 1385-87; E. K.

When founders in the eleventh and twelfth centuries made their endowments, however, they usually did so with no specific provision for spiritual services. They did not lay down what the monks were to do; they were buying a package not of their own making – Cluniac liturgy, or Cistercian and Carthusian asceticism, or the pastoral vocation of the canons – which would get them to Heaven through the superior efficacy of whichever way of life and suffrages they chose. The merit of the grant lay first in the very fact of the gift, often seen as a gift of alms to the poor which would earn divine favour, and secondly in the general participation in the spiritual benefits acquired through the monks' activities known as confraternity. The detailed arrangements for securing eternal life for the donor, including what was actually done for them in terms of alms liturgical and charitable, were left to the monks.[20]

The transformation by which high-medieval gifts of alms were replaced by grants for spiritual services in the later period explains Henry's anachronistic assumption about the foundation of the alien priories: the writ asserted that both express spiritual services and particular numbers of monks (which translated into numbers of Masses to the late-medieval mind) had been specified at foundation. It was therefore by these standards that the writ (and other royal documents relating to the alien priories) proposed to measure the priories' performance.[21] Because these criteria were anachronistic and projected current demands back into the past, they raised the possibility that ancient institutions might be found irrelevant to contemporary needs.

This was exacerbated by the loss of the 'locality of lordship' between England and Normandy. If English convents had no specific services incumbent upon them, at least it would have been possible to see what was actually being done; but hardly anyone can have known precisely what liturgy and alms were being performed in the French houses receiving English revenues. Moreover, it is difficult to see who might have cared. Not

---

Bennet, 'Notes on the Original Statutes of the College of St John the Evangelist, Rushworth, co. Norfolk, Founded by Edmund Gonville A.D. 1342', *Norfolk Archaeology*, 10 (1888), 50-64 (pp. 51-52); for those of Stoke-by-Clare, see below, note 47. In general on late-medieval secular colleges see Thompson, '*Habendum et Tenendum*,' pp. 233-36, citing B. J. Thompson, 'The Church and the Aristocracy: Lay and Ecclesiastical Landowning Society in Fourteenth-century Norfolk' (unpublished Ph.D. dissertation, Cambridge, 1990), pp. 157-92.

20 Thompson, 'From "Alms" to "Spiritual Services"', pp. 229-37; 'Free Alms Tenure in the Twelfth Century', *Anglo-Norman Studies*, 16 (1994), forthcoming.

21 e.g. *CFR*, I, 362-64; VIII, 13; *CPR 1330-34*, p. 504; *1338-40*, p. 146; *Calendar of Close Rolls* (London, 1892-) [*CCR*], *1330-33*, pp. 406, 419. See also the petitions cited below, notes 23-27, 65-68, 75-78. See further Thompson, '*Habendum et Tenendum*', pp. 225-26.

only would it have been hard for English families to maintain their connections with Norman mother-houses; but the operation of inheritance in patrilineal families also meant that over the centuries almost all suffered inheritance through heiresses, so that sooner or later the lineage which had established a monastery or added an endowment ceased to exist.[22] The result might be that the lands had been given for the benefit of souls which no longer had representatives on earth, and therefore no-one to support their spiritual services. It was after all primarily heirs who had both the duty to support such suffrages, and the incentive to do so through the benefits which they were offered in donations made, as they commonly, were, 'for the souls of me and my heirs'.

The alien priories therefore looked vulnerable on a number of counts. The farms they owed to fourteenth-century kings had crippled them financially, and therefore depleted the spiritual services they performed. But if these were supposed to have been done in France, few can have felt that they benefited from them, and would certainly not have been in a position to enforce them. In any case, the application of anachronistic assumptions might find the priories wanting in terms of performance. This applied equally to convents in England, as did the problem of the founding family dying out and leaving no representatives to support the house. But at least in England ties of locality might allow such links to be renewed with other families, and allow houses to offer spiritual services which matched more closely the expectations of late-medieval aristocrats.

This is the background to the fate of the alien priories. The debate in the parliament rolls from 1369 onwards reveals the views of lay landowners and the royal response to them; and the individual stories of the alien convents and cells show how what was ordained at the centre was put into practice in the locality.

The importance the laity attached to the performance of divine services may be gauged from its use in support of conflicting solutions to the problem presented by the alien priories. In 1373 one petition sought a remedy for the fact that 'the alien religious of your enmity have great possessions in the realm without sustaining the number of monks and chaplains and other works of charity and charges ordained and established by the founders'.[23] It picked out for especial censure the sending of money – or 'apports' – abroad, especially by those 'which are neither convents nor colleges'. In 1376, on the

[22] K. B. McFarlane, *The Nobility of Later Medieval England* (Oxford, 1973), pp. 143-61, 172-76, 269-78. Detail for Norfolk may be found in Thompson, 'Church and Aristocracy', ch. 2, esp. pp. 43-49; 'Statute of Carlisle', p. 575, n. 162; 'Monasteries and their Patrons at Foundation and Dissolution', forthcoming in *TRHS*, 1994.

[23] *Rotuli Parliamentorum*, II, 320.

other hand, the complaint was directed against farmers whose replacement of alien monks had resulted in the destruction of their churches and possessions, 'to the withdrawal and diminution of divine service, alms and other works of charity which were accustomed to be done for the souls of the founders'. Its proposed solution was nevertheless that English monks should replace the aliens.[24]

Another petition in the Good Parliament returned to blaming the alien religious. The king's progenitors and others, it opened, founded the convents and cells (demonstrating, like the 1373 petition, awareness of this distinction); but the foreign monks sent to govern them conducted a 'notoriously feeble life, suffer their houses to fall down and divine service to be cut off, and waste the goods of their houses'. English monks ought to be presented to the patrons, to restore 'religion, divine service, and other alms and charges pertaining to those houses'.[25] In the first parliament of Richard II, a petition reiterated the damage done by the removal of goods abroad to the use of the enemy, and asked for the expulsion of aliens from the realm; then the money could be used instead both for the war, and for 'founders and patrons to have the possessions in their lordships, to ordain in each place that divine service should be done by a reasonable number of English monks'.[26]

The response to this petition set the agenda for the fate of the alien priories in the next generation. The government agreed that the alien religious ought to be expelled for the duration of the war; and although conventual priors and those holding life benefices were excepted, this was only for the tenure of the then holders, who, when they died or resigned, were to be replaced only by English monks or priests, 'to accomplish divine service'. 'And in order that divine service be sustained in the said alien priories, it is ordained that each bishop in his diocese, at the presentation of their patron-founders, should accept and place in them honest religious from English houses, or good and honest secular chaplains, to live and have reasonable sustenance in the said priories, to perform divine service in them during the war, up to the number currently in the said houses.' The profits over and above these charges were to go to the king to augment his estate and relieve his people. To this end the possessions of the alien priories were to be put out to farm, the spiritualities to clerics, the temporalities to the laymen who tendered the highest price; but both were to give security that they would maintain the divine services and alms due and accustomed and keep the monks and chaplains fed and clothed.[27]

[24] Ibid., II, 342.
[25] Ibid., II, 342-43.
[26] Ibid., III, 22.
[27] Ibid., III, 22-23; Matthew, *Norman Monasteries*, pp. 109-11. Although this ordinance only provides for replacement of monks 'up to the current number', the security which farmers had had to give in individual commissions of farm

These measures did not so much draw the distinction between cells and convents, as put to practical effect the functional criteria which lay behind that distinction. Those revenues which ought to support divine services in England were to be so applied, by the presentation of English monks by patrons. Other revenues (those which went abroad to the enemy, the petition claimed) were to be exploited for the war effort, and the profits maximised by open competition for the farms. The fate of the priories was therefore to be determined by local action, according to the individual circumstances of each cell or convent. In particular, it would be patrons who would secure the continuation of conventual life by presenting monks or chaplains.

This must be set against the background of the lack of any spiritual services specified for twelfth-century foundations and donations. Farmers bound to keep up Masses and alms due and accustomed would often find either that there was no such legal requirement (except in the case of rectory-cells where the performance of services in particular places had been laid down); or that in practice there was no-one who minded what was actually performed. The crucial factor was whether anyone had an interest in reviving or maintaining religious life – which farmers on the whole did not, but patrons might. The reasons why they might therefore need to be carefully examined.

These can be discerned by examining what happened to particular alien convents and cells, using here a sample with East Anglian connections.[28] The group turns up the crucial finding that all the conventual priories survived in some form, apparently as a result of patronal action. The Warenne family had acted long before 1377 to secure the removal of Lewes and its Norfolk daughter, Castle Acre, from royal custody; the latter presented less difficulty because, as the daughter of a priory in England, it was not formally alien. The last two Warenne earls of Surrey secured its exemption from royal seizure in 1296, 1325 and 1337, precisely on the grounds that Castle Acre was staffed entirely by English monks and paid no tax or pension abroad.[29] In 1340 John Warenne was able to do the same for Lewes, this time arguing more tendentiously: the priory was not alien because it was founded by Warenne ancestors, and it only paid five pounds a year to Cluny 'of its alms' rather than as a due.[30] The acceptance of this line of argument shows the

---

specified the number 'anciently ordained', just as the 1399 order spoke of the 'due and accustomed number according to the first foundation'; *CFR*, VIII, 13.

[28] This includes conventual priories, and cells/bailiwicks which included Norfolk property, even if they were run from centres elsewhere in England, a total of twenty.

[29] *CCR 1288-96*, p. 470; *1323-27*, p. 251; *1337-39*, p. 151; *Monasticon*, V, 54 (which ought to read 24 Ed. I, not xxxiiij).

[30] *CPR 1338-40*, p. 505.

force of the lay attitude to ecclesiastical endowment: this house was founded by my ancestors (and everyone knew that they were all buried there, and that it was the family's main ecclesiastical investment), and therefore, whatever its constitutional status in the order of Cluny, it is functionally English. The most important defining factor for the laity was that English souls depended upon it. These restorations were formalized by letters of 'denization', or naturalization, in 1351 for Lewes and in 1373 for its cells, including Castle Acre, which secured houses against any further royal seizure or payment of farm.[31]

The original founding family was not the only one which might take an interest in a foundation. The houses founded in the immediate post-conquest years by the holders of new Anglo-Norman honours were inherited and granted with those honours to other noble families down the generations.[32] Because they tended to be well-endowed and impressive (and from a later perspective, old), they were able to attract the support of these new patrons. By the later fourteenth century, none of the families which founded the East Anglian convents was extant in the male line. But patrons played a role in saving most if not all of them. The 1373 denization of Lewes's cells was granted at the request of the Earl of Arundel, heir to the Warennes as patron of Lewes and Castle Acre, and himself buried at Lewes which he intended to be his family's burial house.[33] Roger Bigod had tried in 1300 to displace Cluny's right of appointing the prior of Thetford with a free election under his patronage; and in 1341 Mary, countess of Norfolk, secured the halving of the farm owed to the crown, so that the priory could keep up the service of God.[34] In 1376 it was said that Thetford only contained English monks, and had bought from Cluny the right to elect its priors, 'with the support of certain laymen who of their devotion bore the costs'.[35] Perhaps this initiative was taken in the previous year by Margaret Marshal on becoming countess of Norfolk and sole heir to the inheritance on the death of her niece.[36] A role was almost certainly played by William Ufford, earl of Suffolk, who had been married to Margaret's deceased niece and was therefore patron of the priory by the courtesy of England:[37] Thetford was used as a vehicle for the

---

31 CPR 1350-54, pp. 47-48; 1370-74, p. 286; Monasticon, V, 15-16.
32 See note 22.
33 See note 31. Complete Peerage, I, 244; Lambeth Palace, Reg. Sudbury, fols 92v, 102; A Collection of Royal Wills, ed. by J. Nichols (London, 1780), p. 120.
34 Calendar of Papal Letters (London, 1893-), I, 594-95; Registrum Roberti Winchelsey, ed. by R. Graham, Canterbury & York Society, 2 vols (1952-56), II, 703-04, 793; CPR 1307-13, p. 140; CCR 1341-43, p. 227.
35 CPR 1374-77, p. 301; Monasticon, V, 153.
36 Complete Peerage, IX, 599-600.
37 Calendar of Inquisitions Post Mortem (London, 1904-), XV, 249; Complete Peerage, XII (i), 433-44; it may not be insignificant that William Ufford's son had married

survival of Eye priory, which was also in Ufford patronage because the honour of Eye was the central focus of the earldom granted to William's father in 1337.[38] In 1379 he procured for the prior of Thetford the custody of Eye priory, and in 1380 a monk of Thetford was presented as prior of Eye.[39] The terms of the texts quoted for Castle Acre and Thetford show that, even before 1377, filling a convent with English monks was a prerequisite to getting it out of royal hands; this seems to be what Ufford was doing for Eye, therefore, perhaps after he had done it for Thetford.

Patrons did not need to be descended from founders at all to take an interest in ancient monasteries. The Uffords and Eye illustrates the case of those who had come into advowsons by grant (after escheat to the crown). Moreover, when Ufford died in 1382 the honour and advowson were granted to Richard II's queen, who made the prior of Eye himself its farmer, and secured the priory's recognition as denizen in 1385. The object, stated the letters patent, was to augment divine obsequies, so much diminished by the ruinous state of the priory, and to pray for the king and queen while alive and for their souls when dead.[40]

Horsham St Faith underwent a similar process: the patron can be seen playing a role before denization in that between 1381 and 1389 he had joint custody of the house with the prior, in which time the priory apparently increased from six to nine monks, and in the latter year a monk of the house was elected prior freely, and given custody.[41] It is not therefore surprising that the denization of 1390 (secured through John of Gaunt) described the priory as 'founded by the ancestors of Robert Ufford, knight'.[42] The Clare houses of St Neot's and Stoke-by-Clare exhibit the same consciousness of patronal foundation and function. St Neot's – 'of the foundation of the earl of Stafford's ancestors and of his patronage' – was naturalized in 1409 'to the end that there may be there a prior and convent of English monks to celebrate divine service for the king and the patron and his ancestors, the

---

Richard Fitzalan's daughter, providing another bond amongst the alien-priory-saving nobility of East Anglia.

[38] *CPR 1334-38*, p. 418; *Complete Peerage*, XII (i), 430.

[39] *CFR*, IX, 129-30; Norfolk Record Office, Norwich Episcopal Registers, VI, fol. 71.

[40] *CFR*, IX, 329-30; *CPR 1381-85*, p. 491; *Monasticon*, III, 308: the link between Thetford and Eye is perhaps strengthened by the echo in these letters of the phrase quoted above for Thetford, in this case 'certain laymen who of their alms intend to bear the costs...'.

[41] *CFR*, IX, 261, X, 304; J. C. Russell, 'The Clerical Population of Medieval England', *Traditio*, 2 (1944), 177-212 (p. 189, n. 'g'); Norwich Episcopal Registers, VI, fols. 136v-137, 139.

[42] *CPR 1388-92*, p. 366: the priory was to be as free as the prior and convent of Thetford.

patrons and founders of the priory'.[43]

In the case of Stoke-by-Clare, the patronal role was even more self-conscious. Denization was granted in 1395 (on the achieving of his majority by the young earl of March, heir to the honour of Clare) in much the same terms as for St Neot's;[44] but little had been done at the earl's death, so that when his son came of age in 1413 further action had to be taken. Edmund Mortimer now made the priory into a secular college, and he justified changing the form of the priory by appeal to the actions of his ancestors: it had originally been founded by an ancestor as a college in the church of St John the Baptist at Clare, but monks of Bec had been introduced by another ancestor, and a third had removed it to Stoke; Richard II had given licence for the house to be denizen, but since the convent of English monks had not materialised, it was now to become a college of a dean and canons to pray for the king [Henry V], Edmund his kinsman, Richard II, and the founders of the college and priory and their heirs [the Clare family].[45] The foundation charter of the college recited the beneficiaries of the divine services to be celebrated there as the souls of Edmund's ancestors, heirs, and himself (showing that we need not always take seriously the prayers kings were offered in petitions for denization and licences).[46] But the actual statutes of the college only mentioned three beneficiaries by name, the founder, the dean and the bishop. The daily requiem mass was to be for Edmund himself and the first dean of the college (whose obits were also to be kept), and all benefactors of the college.[47] In theory this would include those past generations of Clare patrons; but in the later Middle Ages it was important to be named to enjoy significant spiritual benefits.[48] The terms on which Mortimer established the college make it abundantly clear that in both its temporal form and its spiritual function this was an institution directed to the fifteenth century, not the eleventh. It was changed into a college of secular canons, both because monks were no longer held in much respect and because secular priests were equally fitted to perform the suffrages which the later Middle Ages regarded as valuable, Masses for the dead. And it was to the current generation, not those of bygone Clares and Mortimers, that the effect of these Masses was directed. This was a refoundation, an updating;

---

43 *Rotuli Parliamentorum*, IV, 42-43; *Monasticon*, III, 479-80; *CPR 1408-13*, p. 76; *Cal. Papal Letters*, VI, 250.

44 *Monasticon*, VI, 1415-16; *CPR 1391-96*, p. 640; Sanders, *English Baronies*, p. 35; *Complete Peerage*, III, 245-46, 257-58; VIII, 447-51.

45 *CPR 1413-16*, pp. 291-92; *Cal. Papal Letters*, VI, 456; *Monasticon*, VI, 1416-17.

46 *Monasticon*, VI, 1417.

47 *Monasticon*, VI, 1417-23, esp. p. 1421.

48 J. le Goff, *The Birth of Purgatory*, trans. by A. Goldhammer (London, 1984), pp. 267, 274-77.

Mortimer re-used old material for new purposes, going further than the letter of the ordinance of 1377, but perhaps not infringing its spirit.

For the great body of alien cells the story was quite different. Although the convents lost large numbers of monks at the expulsion in 1377, the cells were more vulnerable in the longer run, because mother-houses, in order to hold on to their English properties and (in better times) to extract the revenues, depended upon being able to send monks as proctors. The ordinance of 1377 inaugurated a slow process of attrition to sever the connection between French abbey and English property, which was alleviated only by the action of Henry IV in 1399, permitting monks to return and act as proctors.[49]

The experience of one cell illustrates what happened locally in the years after 1377. Panfield and Well Hall consisted of a manor in Essex and a church in Norfolk belonging to the abbot of St Stephen's, Caen, which were assessed for taxation at over £70 (although in 1295 only £20 was recorded as having been sent abroad to Caen).[50] In 1370 the prior was given custody in return for a farm of forty marks, of which thirty went towards the £350 arrears still outstanding from the 1337-60 period. In 1371 the prior left, and an Essex layman was given the farm for ten pounds more (a total of fifty-five marks), to account for the now redundant maintenance of the monk who had left; but the farmer was to support the other monk. No new prior appeared, and in 1373 Hugh Fastolf was keeper, for sixty marks plus ten pounds to the remaining monk for his sustenance; if the latter died, that figure was to be added to the farm, making a total of seventy-five marks (fifty pounds). It appears therefore that the process of laymen bidding farms upwards pre-dated 1377, and that the procedure then ordained turned this occasional practice into a policy.[51]

Another phase began in 1382, when one of Richard II's knights, John Devereux, was granted licence to acquire the property from St Stephen's on a lease for three lives, as long as he continued to render his farm of forty pounds to the crown during the war. Devereux was succeeded by his daughter in the 1390s, and in the changed circumstances of 1400 custody was formally re-granted to her and her husband, Walter Fitzwalter, still for forty pounds.[52] In line with Henry IV's aims, on this occasion a clause was added

[49] See in general Matthew, *Norman Monasteries*, pp. 111ff., 121; McHardy, 'Expulsion'; and *CFR*, IX ff.

[50] *VCH Essex*, I, 454; *VCH Norfolk*, II, 465; Matthew, *Norman Monasteries*, p. 151; *Taxatio Ecclesiastica Angliae et Walliae auctoritate papae Nicholai IV, circa 1291*, Record Commission (London, 1802), pp. 12b, 17b, 21b, 22, 22b, 29b, 80b, 96, 96b, 112, 112b, 122b, 266; PRO, E 106/3/10, 3/11, 3/19, mm. 2, 9 (on these figures see Thompson, 'Statute of Carlisle', p. 554, nn. 42, 44).

[51] *CFR*, VIII, 38, 135, 232; IX, 22, 90.

[52] *CPR 1381-85*, p. 111; *Complete Peerage*, IV, 298-300; *CPR 1396-99*, pp. 559-60;

that the farmers or lessees must maintain the divine services, alms and other works of piety due from the priory. Henry had allowed one monk to return to Panfield from Caen, who in February 1403 was granted joint custody with a layman for the increased farm of sixty-five marks.[53] Another change followed the death of Joan Fitzwalter in 1409, when William Bourgchier, who inherited some of her property, took the farm with his wife, Anne, countess of Stafford, at the much inflated figure of fifty-five pounds (over eighty-two marks); there is no further trace of monks, nor were there any injunctions about divine services.[54] The next year Bourgchier had to offer an extra pound to outbid another tender for the custody.[55] In 1413 another king's servant, John Woodhouse, received licence from Henry V to buy the priory from St Stephen's, but this process was pre-empted by the act of 1414 which was ultimately to give title to the crown. Instead the temporalities were granted to Woodhouse in fee, and the spiritualities to his clerk.[56] The latter Woodhouse used in 1421 to endow a chantry for himself at the charnel house at Norwich Cathedral, but the temporalities continued in his family until 1461.[57] At that point they came again to the crown by Edward IV's resumption of Lancastrian grants, but, although initially granted to laymen, Panfield came to Christ Church, Canterbury, in 1483 by grant of the archbishop of Canterbury (who bought it), and in 1469 Well Hall was granted by the king to St Stephen's, Westminster, to pray for him and for Elizabeth his queen.[58]

The elements in this story were the common experience of the alien cells: even when there were still monks present, they could be outbid by lay farmers, often local men; and when the religious were gone the farm was put up and the farmers allowed to exploit the property fully. Kings used the farms they received to contribute to the endowments of members of the royal family, in this and other cases two dukes of Gloucester, Thomas and Humphrey, and Queen Joan in between.[59] Moreover, kings allowed those

CFR, XII, 61-2, 105-06. Despite the lease by the abbot to Devereux, Henry IV gave FitzWalter the custody in 1400, creating a (deliberate?) ambiguity as to the source of his right in the priory.

53   CPR 1399-1401, p. 368; CFR, XII, 195.

54   CFR, XIII, 148; Complete Peerage, V, 482; CCR 1405-09, pp. 277-78, 284; 1409-13, pp. 5, 446-47.

55   CFR, XIII, 152, 177.

56   CPR 1413-16, pp. 57, 300-01, 340.

57   CPR 1416-22, pp. 376-77; F. Blomefield, An Essay towards a Topographical History of Norfolk, 11 vols (London, 1805-11, originally published King's Lynn, 1739-75), VIII, 428, 436-37; CFR, XVI, 40-41; CPR 1436-41, p. 385.

58   CPR 1461-67, pp. 64, 108, 151-52; 1467-77, pp. 163-64, 240, 375-76, 568; 1477-83, pp. 334-35.

59   CPR 1377-81, pp. 372, 523, 575; 1408-13, pp. 85-87; 1413-16, pp. 164-67; CCR

they favoured to negotiate with the French abbots for the purchase of properties; William of Wykeham acquired much of the endowment of Winchester and New College from this source.[60] Occasionally the abbots tried to insist upon the maintenance of divine services for the souls of the benefactors of the mother-house, but usually such spiritual activities as there had been simply fade away from the record.[61]

A twist in the story of Well Hall shows why. If anyone could be regarded as 'patron' of the Norfolk part of the cell, it was the Staffords (who had inherited the lordship via the Clares from the original donor, William d'Ecouis); yet there is no evidence that Anne, countess of Stafford *suo jure*, who was farmer of the priory for a time, made any attempt to restore divine services.[62] Indeed it seems probable that she was unaware of her theoretical patronage of the property; it was lost in the history of the grant to St Stephen's by a Domesday tenant-in-chief quite irrelevant to her, and whose spiritual benefits would have concerned her not at all. When we find patrons consciously farming cells, as with the Lovels at Minster Lovell, it may be that they were using them to provide divine services invisible to us; but it is equally possible that they regarded themselves as resuming lands from tenants who could no longer (perforce) continue to fulfil the spiritual functions for which (they imagined) the lands had been given.[63] In either case, suffrages for the original donors went by the board. Occasionally we can see exactly what happened: Elizabeth de Burgh, one of the three heiresses left by the death of Gilbert de Clare at Bannockburn, re-purchased a property

---

60 *1422-29*, pp. 19-21; *CPR 1436-41*, pp. 188-89, 304.

60 New, *Alien Priories*, pp. 87-90 (see the final column); T. F. Kirby, 'Charters of Harmondsworth, Isleworth, Heston, Twickenham and Hampton-on-Thames', *Archaeologia*, 58 (1903), 341-58 (pp. 342-47).

61 e.g. the prior of Longueville leasing English manors in 1411 with proviso for a monk to live at Newton Longville to celebrate for benefactors; *CPR 1408-13*, pp. 307-08.

62 Above, notes 54-55. For the grant of Well Hall and succession to the lordship: *Monasticon*, VI, 1070; *Calendar of Documents Preserved in France*, pp. 155-57, 162; *Calendar of Charter Rolls*, IV, 271-72; *VCH Norfolk*, II, 145-49; Blomefield, *Norfolk*, VIII, 378, 471, IX, 10, 64; *Feudal Aids*, 6 vols (London, 1899-1920), III, 521, 581, VI, 553. Lordship over the manor should have been part of Anne's dower of five-ninths of the Stafford inheritance as widow of two successive earls (McFarlane, *Nobility*, pp. 204-06), to judge from her possession of other Clare fee in the same hundred; *CCR 1402-05*, pp. 218-19; Blomefield, *Norfolk*, IX, 282-83, 452-53.

63 Taylor, 'Minster Lovell'; there is no evidence of a prior at the priory after 1370 (*CFR*, VIII, 82), and the patrons had the farm 1373-1414, and again from 1437, *CFR*, VIII, 255, IX, 29, XIII, 130, XVII, 17, 39; in the latter case, William Lovel was enjoined to keep up divine services and works of piety, which had not been the case before.

within her overlordship at Wereham in Norfolk from its mother-house, and in 1336 used it to found a chantry in the chapel of the cell for Gilbert, herself, and their ancestors and heirs.[64] As at Stoke-by-Clare, and in the case of the chantries of John Woodhouse and Edward IV, it was the current generation which dictated anew both the form of institutions supported by lands granted long ago to the church, and the beneficiaries of the suffrages which were to be performed. Where divine services were to be kept up, it was only within institutions updated or even completely refounded according to contemporary needs.

The parliamentary petitions of the 1380s and 90s support the finding that lay occupation of alien cells was detrimental to the performance of divine services. The alien religious's loss of custody of the priories was blamed for the ending of divine services and alms which had been established by the founders for – and here the assumption was made explicit – the safety of their souls. But some of these petitions emanated from the priors themselves; the commons increasingly lost interest in the maintenance of suffrages, and became insistent instead on the removal of aliens.[65]

Such was their attitude at the beginning of Henry IV's reign, when they responded to Henry's restorations with petitions in 1401 and 1402 insisting that the king take a tougher line against the alien priories. In the years since 1377 local experience had taught the gentry, who were the farmers of alien possessions, that these were fair game for lay exploitation and royal profit, and that they rarely supported divine services requiring preservation. In 1401 they were quite specific: the alien priories ought to be seized into the king's hands as they had been by his royal predecessors, and not restored as they had been on his entry into England (in other words by a jumped-up noble).[66] An exception was made for conventual priors, which a second petition shows to have been more than a recognition of legal necessities: 'the houses which have a full convent, and perform divine services continually and give hospitality, *like the house at Montacute* and others like it', ought to be released from royal custody altogether and have their farms remitted (as in 1399).[67] The citing of a specific example shows that the petitioners had a clear idea of precisely which institutions were valuable, and that this was derived not just from legal categories but also from experience on the ground. Other so-called

[64] Blomefield, *Norfolk*, VII, 508; *CPR 1334-38*, pp. 252-53; 'Some Early Deeds relating to the Priory of St Winwaloe in Wirham and Lands there, Preserved in the Muniment Room at Stow Bardolph', ed. by G. H. Dashwood, *Norfolk Archaeology*, 5 (1859), 297-312 (pp. 301-02, 305-06) (Norfolk Record Office, Hare MSS 4114-4119); British Library Add. MS 6041, fol. 86.
[65] *Rotuli Parliamentorum*, III, 64, 96, 213, 222, 262, 276, 301.
[66] Ibid., III, 457.
[67] Ibid., III, 469.

priories ought not to remain, they argued both then and in the following year, when they made further requests for resumption of the priories restored in 1399.[68] The commons managed to take over from the crown a distinction originally aimed at a legal impediment – that those beneficed for life could not be removed, except for good cause and by episcopal authority – and transform it into one reflecting functional criteria. The petitions of 1402 excepted from the demand for expulsion and resumption not conventual priors, but conventual *priories*. They thereby applied, on the basis of local experience, standards of functional relevance to the institutional forms of the priories.

These pleas had their effect: after this parliament, the sheriffs were ordered to summon all priors and occupiers of alien possessions to come before the king and council to show by what title they held, and to give evidence of whether they were or had been conventual or not.[69] The results of the inquiry must have pleased the commons. Of the thirty-four priories named for restoration in the letters of 1399, which included instituted and inducted 'priors', twenty-one were taken into royal hands again.[70] Moreover, most of these failed to survive thereafter.[71] Of the remaining thirteen, seven are recorded as having proved their conventuality, and the other six, which included St Neot's and Montacute and other obvious candidates for conventual status, do not appear to have been resumed by the king either. Of these thirteen, only two ultimately failed to survive, and they are both the sort of exceptions which help prove a rule: Andover looks the least like a convent (it was a rectory-cell) and was sold to Winchester College by the prior himself in 1414;[72] and Goldcliff was granted to Eton by Edward IV acting self-consciously as its patron in succession to the Clares, with celebrations provided for the souls of the founders, their heirs, and the donors.[73] Similarly, of the twenty-one taken back to the crown in 1403, two

68 Ibid., III, 491, 499.

69 CCR 1402-05, pp. 25-26 (also, 1399-1402, pp. 334-35).

70 *Proceedings and Ordinances of the Privy Council of England*, ed. by N. H. Nicolas, Record Commission, 7 vols (London, 1834-37), I, 190-96; *CFR*, XII, 191-210, 241. Tutbury was taken back to the crown but restored again to the prior in 1404 (*VCH Staffs.*, III, 337).

71 There are three clear exceptions, two of which had originally been conventual: Tickford: *VCH Bucks*, I, 361-63; Tywardreath (denizen 1416): G. Oliver, *Monasticon Diocesis Exoniensis* (Exeter, 1846), pp. 34-41; *CPR 1416-22*, pp. 12-13. Chepstow was not intended to survive, since it was granted to Christ's in 1442: R. Graham, 'Four Alien Priories in Monmouthshire', *Jnl of the Brit. Archaeol. Assoc.*, n.s. 35 (1929), 102-21 (pp. 102-03, 114, 117-18). Three more survived only as cells or chantries: St Michael's Mount, see below; Pembroke, *Monasticon*, IV, 321; *CPR 1436-41*, p. 567; *1461*, p. 120; Cowick, Morgan, *English Lands*, pp. 122, 133-35.

72 *VCH Hants*, II, 221; *CPR 1413-16*, p. 268.

73 *Monasticon*, VI, 1022; *CPR 1461-67*, pp. 93, 106, *1467-77*, pp. 48, 66, *1477-83*, p.

in royal patronage were transformed by kings, Lancaster Priory becoming part of Henry V's Syon and St Michael's Mount a three-chaplain chantry.[74] These show patrons doing what Elizabeth de Burgh and Edmund Mortimer had done, re-using property for their own new foundations.

Amongst the priories restored in 1399, therefore, there was a rough correlation between those thought to be conventual, and those which ultimately survived. The commons succeeded in reining in the crown's attempt to be liberal, and forced it to apply criteria more in keeping with the local and historical realities of the priories' function and performance. To that extent they complemented the local process of sorting out, individually and gradually, which priories would be saved because patrons wanted to continue their existence, which would be re-used for updated ecclesiastical purposes, and which were swallowed up by the crown because there was no-one to defend them.

From this point onward these parallel stories, at the centre and in the locality, gradually came together. Under Henry IV the commons continued to press for the expulsion of French monks and royal resumption of alien property. More significantly, they began to consider the effect of any conclusion to the war on the property which the laity had enjoyed for at least a generation, so that in 1407 and 1410 they asked for permission to negotiate with the French for leases or outright purchases.[75] On Henry V's accession they urged the expulsion of French clergy and their replacement by Englishmen, and royal resumption of 'all alien priories, with their fees, advowsons, land tenements, rents, services, franchises, liberties and all other appurtenances', excepting convents inhabited by English monks, and lands already purchased from mother-houses. Henry responded with a resumption of all property held by aliens or royal letters patent, excepting that of perpetual and conventual priors.[76] The result was tangible; writs were issued summoning everyone with any sort of title to alien religious land to treat for it with the king, and as a result many confirmations were issued, as well as some new grants.[77]

334; Graham, 'Four Alien Priories', pp. 118-19: the priory had been damaged since it was vulnerable to Welsh devastation.

[74] *CPR 1416-22*, p. 35, *1422-29*, pp. 205-06; *Rotuli Parliamentorum*, IV, 243, V, 552; *CPR 1422-29*, p. 205, *1441-46*, pp. 111-12, *1461-67*, pp. 56-57, 177. Thomas Mowbray was also self-consciously acting as patron in granting Monks Kirby to his new Carthusian house at Axholme (*Cal. Papal Letters*, IV, 537; *CPR 1396-99*, p. 77; *1416-16*, p. 355).

[75] *Rotuli Parliamentorum*, III, 617, 644.

[76] *Rotuli Parliamentorum*, IV, 13 (also 5, 6, 11).

[77] *CCR 1413-19*, p. 31; examples of confirmations are *CPR 1413-16*, pp. 91, 161, 164-67, 174, 230; *CFR*, XIV, 37, 45, 58-59.

In the following year the commons finally drew out the logical conclusion of their previous demand, and requested the king to ignore the effect of any ending of the war on title to alien property, by making the status quo permanent. He should take title to himself and his heirs for ever, excepting conventual priories and instituted priors, and saving the estate which anyone had at present, 'to the end that divine services in the aforesaid places be more fully performed by Englishmen than they were by the French'.[78] The royal assent to this petition was in one respect the most important point in the history of the alien priories: it was the moment the decision was taken to remove title to property from churches who had held it for centuries. It was an assertion in principle of the right of the lay power to dispose of property within its jurisdiction, notwithstanding even ecclesiastical claims to perpetual tenure and to immunity from secular claims. To this extent, the precedent for the Dissolution cannot be ignored. The king, in parliament, implicitly asserted an ultimate sovereign jurisdiction.[79]

In practice, however, it made little immediate difference. Indeed there was to be a long, and instructive, coda to the tale before the alien property was finally settled. In the short term, the operation of the statute was contingent on the ending of the war so that, although grants could now be made in fee (such as John Woodhouse's acquisition of Panfield and Well Hall, and the initial grants to the king's foundations at Syon and Sheen), in general the re-examination of title in the previous year stood.[80] The crucial difference became apparent in 1420 when the statute was brought into operation by the Treaty of Troyes. Those with tenure or title to alien property had to come again to the king, this time to make provision for an endless future; only those already holding in fee or in perpetual 'alms' did not need confirmations.[81] Nevertheless, in practice this too did not mark a significant crux, because the life-titles of such as Thomas Erpingham and John, duke of Bedford, who held large portfolios of alien priory land and farms, were left undisturbed (although Queen Joan's dower was briefly resumed).[82] It was to be another generation before a clearer picture emerged, when these titles fell in with the deaths of Erpingham in 1428, Bedford in 1435, and Joan in 1437 – and even then her interests were granted to Humphrey, duke of Gloucester.[83] The first definitive attempt to rationalize

78 *Rotuli Parliamentorum*, IV, 22.
79 Cf. Matthew, *Norman Monasteries*, p. 133. I see the order of 1420 (see note 81) as a direct result of the statute of 1414, not evidence that the king 'ignored' it.
80 See note 56; *CPR 1413-16*, pp. 235, 354; *Monasticon*, VI, 31-33, 542-53; *CPR 1413-16*, pp. 367, 397; Matthew, *Norman Monasteries*, pp. 127-28.
81 *CCR 1419-22*, p. 129.
82 *CPR 1416-22*, pp. 276, 395, 441-42; *1422-29*, pp. 112-14, 169-71; *Privy Council*, II, 305-06; *CFR*, XIV, 366, 373; *CCR 1422-29*, pp. 19-21.
83 See note 59. *CPR 1422-29*, p. 529; *CFR*, XV, 242, 247; XVI, 337, 348; XVII, 17,

title came in 1440, when priories still held by limited titles were granted to a commission headed by Chichele. They were then passed on to Eton as its first endowment.[84]

The Norfolk cells illustrate the distribution of the property at this point, for the Eton foundation charter included all the possessions in the sample which had not already been granted in perpetuity, or the reversions of them. The others were held by the Carthusians at Mount Grace, New College, two chantries, a king's knight, and the Woodhouse feoffees.[85] Most of the property was therefore in the hands of the new foundations of the era, with a small amount in lay hands. Although there was clearly no taboo on lay possession of ecclesiastical land, some of this last category was thereafter deliberately diminished, for instance by the prising of the priory of Wootton Wawen from a royal knight in 1443 to endow King's.[86] Yet more came by accident. William Porter, another Lancastrian squire, had tried to buy four manors from Cluny but had been granted them anyway in fee in 1414; his lack of heirs meant that the manors came back to the church when two of them were sold to Ralph Cromwell for the endowment of Tattershall College, and two fell to the crown to be granted to Westminster Abbey to support prayers for Henry V.[87] By the middle of the century, the alien priory land was almost entirely in the hands of conspicuously late-medieval institutions: chantries, Carthusian monasteries and academic colleges. The property which under one set of circumstances had been granted to French abbeys was now, under a different set of circumstances, re-used. In practice there was no comparison with the Dissolution because there was no wholesale disendowment of the church. But it is no less significant that a wholesale updating of the use of ecclesiastical property occurred, in terms both of the form of the institutions which held it, and the spiritual functions (and indeed beneficiaries) it was to support.

On the latter issue there was yet one more twist. Edward IV's resumption of Lancastrian grants had the effect of re-assessing title to alien priory land, and thereby secured the remaining land still in lay hands to ecclesiastical purposes (not the most immediately obvious attribute of the 'Wars of the Roses'). Eton lost some of its property to King's, and other institutions such as St Stephen's, Westminster, also benefited.[88] By a nice

---

39, 47.

[84] *Foedera*, X, 802-03; *CPR 1436-41*, pp. 454, 471; *CCR 1435-41*, 493-96; *Monasticon*, VI, 1436-37; *Rotuli Parliamentorum*, V, 47-48.

[85] See above, notes 56-58, 64, 84, 86 (also 60); *CPR 1416-22*, p. 395; *CPR 1436-41*, pp. 516, 558; *Newington Longville Charters*, pp. 99-101.

[86] *CPR 1436-41*, p. 170; *1441-46*, p. 269; *CCR 1447-54*, p. 64.

[87] *Cluny Charters and Records*, I, 219-62; II, 1-15; *CPR 1408-13*, p. 369; *1413-16*, pp. 24, 161, 235, 354; *1422-29*, p. 77; *1441-46*, p. 350; *1467-77*, p. 107; *Foedera*, XI, 89.

[88] *CPR 1461-67*, pp. 64, 73*, 74, 108, 151-52, 161*, *1467-76*, pp. 163-64, 240, 375-76,

irony, then, the willingness of the Lancastrians to resume ecclesiastical property and use it for the benefit of their own souls was trumped in the next generation by a similar process as Edward IV took it back and re-granted it for his. The problem with overlooking the spiritual provisions of previous generations was that your own spiritual provisions might in turn be overlooked. It is surely not too far-fetched to suggest that the increasing focus on the current generation to which this evidence bears witness must have provided the background which made thinkable the sweeping away of old institutions at the Dissolution.[89]

The endowments given to French monasteries in the century and a half after the conquest had fulfilled two functions: they had increased the resources of the houses which the Anglo-Norman aristocracy wished particularly to thank for their own good fortune, and they were part of the conquest process itself in introducing reformed monasticism into England by the foundation of daughter-convents. Both these purposes were now irrelevant. Many families had forgotten that their forebears (who were hardly ever their patrilineal ancestors) had given property to foreign houses, so that much of it was left vulnerable to lay exploitation and royal resumption in default of any patronal interest.

Even where there was a patronal interest, this did not guarantee that the old forms would be maintained. The Plantagenets were the family most likely to remember their forebears and to nurture their ancient connections with the continent, which makes their case particularly interesting here. In resisting the sale of his property for more than a limited term, the abbot of Cluny continually emphasized to Richard II and Henry IV that his monks prayed day and night for the king's noble progenitors because of their wonderful gifts in the past, and offered to continue doing so all the more fervently should he allow the abbey to retain control of its lands; and he also implied a threat, that the loss of the lands would endanger the souls of the predecessors (and therefore of the king).[90] In 1420 the abbot of St Stephen's, Caen, tried the same argument to Henry V with the added reminder that this was the Conqueror's own house.[91] But even in the propitious circumstances of the re-conquest of Normandy, Henry preferred not to turn the clock back by restoring the English possessions, but finally to take them to the crown

---

424, 568; *1476-83*, pp. 107*, 334-35; *Calendar of Charter Rolls*, VI, 196-97*. Those asterisked are confirmations of previous dispositions.

[89] I argue this more fully in 'Monasteries and their Patrons at Foundation and Dissolution', (see note 22); and 'The Church and the Laity in the Later Middle Ages', in *Politics, Society and Religion: Essays in Later Medieval History*, ed. by R. Archer (Gloucester, forthcoming 1994).

[90] *Cluny Charters and Records*, I, 177-79, 190-92, 240.

[91] Matthew, *Norman Monasteries*, pp. 172-73.

for redistribution according to what was now considered appropriate – in his case monasteries of observant religious. The prayers of even Norman monks, guarding the tradition of the Conqueror, were not as valuable as those of the Carthusians and Bridgettines. This was not so much a reclamation of what had been lost in 1204, as an entirely new English conquest of Normandy.

Elizabeth de Burgh's resumption of the cell of St Winwaloe at Wereham illustrates the same attitude on an entirely different scale: the property was more useful and relevant supporting a chantry, the most common contemporary form of ecclesiastical institution, than it could be now in its old form. Even where institutions did not have to be dissolved and refounded, updating took place: English monks replaced foreign, and the constitutional ties with French mother-houses which had been in place for three centuries were dissolved. Moreover, we can see the old vague confraternity, on which twelfth-century founders had relied to get them to heaven, being replaced by more specific suffrages for the current generation, a generation whose support was crucial to the monasteries' survival.

The narrower locality of space seen in the shrinking horizons of English vision, even at the point when the borders of England were expanding again into the continent, was complemented by the narrower locality of time in which the spiritual needs of current generations were put before those of ancestors. Through it all, the laity demonstrated that they were in control of the church. Their original endowment with temporal property, and the essential link between that property and the spiritual function of the church, gave them the handle to impose new forms and functions on conservative and outdated institutions. In doing so they re-asserted their membership of the 'church', which they had lost at the very time of the reform their forebears did so much to support, and part of whose story was the establishment of the alien priories.

The Relief of Avranches (1439): An English Feat of Arms at the End of the Hundred Years War
MICHAEL K. JONES

The relief of Avranches, the key to the Norman Cotentin, on 23 December 1439, was the last occasion in the Hundred Years War that an English army decisively defeated the French in a major military engagement. It has fast become a forgotten incident at the end of a losing war. Surprisingly, this important victory receives no mention in any contemporary English chronicle and has quickly been passed over in recent surveys of the conflict. It took place at a time when English fortunes appeared particularly bleak. The defection of Burgundy at the Congress of Arras in 1435 had led to widespread territorial losses, including not only Paris and the Île de France but also parts of Normandy itself. A deepening mood of pessimism worsened when Meaux surrendered to the French during the abortive diplomatic negotiations of 1439. It was a time, Dr Christopher Allmand commented bluntly, when many English 'were losing confidence in their ability to maintain their rule and make their interests pay', adding ominously that some felt that 'they had little chance of countering the force of France should Charles VII choose to use it'.[1] These concerns were to be put to the test late in 1439, when the French king took the decision that so many had been fearing and ordered a full-scale invasion of Normandy. The decisive defeat of his army had important military and political ramifications. It also had a broader, chivalric significance that poses new questions about the way we view this last phase of the war.

Stories of great and heroic deeds were read by commanders and soldiers alike. If a nobleman was enjoined that 'his comyn speche be of armes, of faytes, of chyvalrye and of the valyaunces of good men', his followers would equally understand the sentiments. When Edmund Arblaster departed from Normandy in the 1440s he left to his close friend Thomas Gower, lieutenant at Cherbourg, a manuscript book entitled 'Le chemin de vallance' alongside helmets, crossbows and other military equipment.[2] These tales did not serve as a diversion from war, or an idealization of it. Rather they formed an exemplar, a scale of values, that was as important in practice as in the imagination of the reader. Feats of arms consisted of acts of daring or particular courage, triumphing against superior numbers through a greater resolution and determination than the foe. A *detail* or memorandum drawn

[1]   C. T. Allmand, *Lancastrian Normandy, 1415-1450* (Oxford, 1983), p. 43.
[2]   C. de Pisan, *The Book of Fayttes of Armes and of Chyvalrye*, trans. by W. Caxton, ed. by A. T. P. Byles, EETS, old series, 189 (London, 1932), p. 23; Staffordshire Record Office, D239/ M2842.

up by the Regent Bedford in 1429 gave various criteria for election to the Order of the Garter. In the case of one candidate, Sir William Oldhall, his war record in France was thoroughly reviewed. He had fought at the battles of Cravant (1423) and Verneuil (1424), served continually on the frontier of Maine and Anjou and assisted John Lord Talbot in the relief of Le Mans (1428). It was an impressive pedigree. But particular attention was paid to one specific feat of arms. Whilst riding from one fortress to another Oldhall's company had been ambushed by a much larger French force. Oldhall and his men had managed to turn the tables on their adversaries, and, fighting their way out of trouble, had killed fourteen Frenchmen, captured nine and put the rest to flight.[3]

It would be unwise to overplay this chivalric context. Much of the war consisted of the drudgery of sentry duty and small-scale, inconclusive raiding. Basset's Chronicle, which gave a soldier's eye view of the 1420s, recognized that a failure to keep the watch could be as important as a spectacular engagement.[4] Yet if one's cause were right it was to be demonstrated, for better or for worse, on the battlefield. It was a natural extension of the notion of the duel of honour. The English champion John Astley had challenged the French jouster Pierre de Masse in August 1438, soon after the Valois reoccupation of Paris. Lists were set up in the Rue Saint Anthoine and the combat was presided over by Charles VII himself.[5] Contemporaries saw these duels not only in terms of the valour of the combatants but the martial worth of their 'nation'. When the Portuguese knight Vasques de Savedra arrived in England in November 1440 to 'runne a cours' with Sir Richard Woodville, Woodville's defence was regarded first and foremost as 'to the worchip of Englond'.[6] Again there was no sharp distinction between literary form and chivalric practice. Allegory and romance were part of many feats of arms in the fifteenth century. A series of thirteen allegorical letters of challenge survive for feats of arms held at Eltham in 1401 to honour Blanche, daughter of Henry IV, who presided as Lady of the Tournament. A feat performed by Richard Beauchamp, earl of Warwick, at Guînes in January 1415, in which he adopted disguises for each joust undertaken, was deliberately modelled on a passage found in the knightly romance *Ipomedon*. Joanot Martorell of Valencia stayed at the English court from 1438 to 1439 with the intention of engaging in a duel of honour under Henry VI's auspices; he later drew on his experiences to embellish his prose romance

---

[3] J. S. Roskell, 'Sir William Oldhall, Speaker in the Parliament of 1450-51', *Nottinghamshire Medieval Studies*, 5 (1961), 94.

[4] B. J. H. Rowe, 'A Contemporary Account of the Hundred Years War from 1415-1429', *English Historical Review*, 41 (1926), 504-13.

[5] Viscount Dillon, 'On a MS. Collection of Ordinances of Chivalry of the Fifteenth Century', *Archaeologia*, 57 (1900), 35.

[6] *The Paston Letters, 1422-1509*, ed. by J. Gairdner, 6 vols (London, 1904), II, p. 47.

Tirant lo Blanc.[7] Equally such exhortation was expected from a leader on the field of battle, 'to comfort his people with good cheer and bold words, rehearsing too the falsehood of his enemy's quarrel and the rightness of his own cause'.[8] The invasion attempt of 1439 was especially significant as it was the first time that a substantial French army had entered Normandy. It was a chivalric challenge. The force was led by Charles VII's constable (Richemont) and marshal (Lohéac), and was ready to test English self-belief and their resolve to defend the Duchy.

It is worth considering in more detail the location and timing of the French invasion attempt. The choice of the Norman Cotentin was particularly threatening to the English regime. The security of the region had been deteriorating since 1436. Early in that year a dangerous peasant revolt under Boschier had been put down with some difficulty by the local commander, Lord Scales. He had been able to prevent neither the loss of Granville to a French force under Jean de Bueil, Jean de la Roche and Lohéac nor the arrival of further reinforcements under the Duke of Alençon.[9] In October 1437 the French at Granville launched a particularly destructive *chevauchée*, reaching Tinchebrai, where they raided the market and seized all the produce, and the suburbs of Caen and Avranches. The French garrison at Mont-St-Michel was also showing increasing confidence. The English forces stationed on the nearby fortified rock of Tombelaine were badly worsted in one encounter; in another raid Louis d'Estouteville's men penetrated as far as Torigni. Underlying these worrying episodes was a growing pessimism, reflected in the fears of local officials, that the English were losing control of the region and the whole of lower Normandy might fall.[10]

Mindful of this opportunity Richemont had been working hard to shore up the French bases on the western frontier and to push the Duke of Brittany, Jean V, into a more aggressive stance against the English. Early in 1438 Richemont had seen Jean V at Vannes and pressed on the Duke the need to reoccupy the fortresses of St James de Beuvron and Pontorson. These strategically situated castles had been abandoned at the end of the

---

[7] J. Martorell and M. de Galba, *Tirant lo Blanc*, trans. by D. H. Rosenthal (London, 1984), pp. 78-117; S. Anglo, 'Financial and Heraldic Records of the English Tournament', *Jnl of the Soc. of Archivists*, 2 (1962), 188-89.

[8] The extract is from the English translation of Vegetius's *De Re Militari*, *Knyghthode and Bataile*, ed. by R. Duboske and Z. M. Arend (EETS, 1935). A useful discussion of the work's importance in the late Middle Ages is provided in D. Bornstein, 'Military Manuals in Fifteenth Century England', *Medieval Studies*, 37 (1975), 469-73.

[9] R. Jouet, *Le Resistance à L'Occupation Anglaise en Basse-Normandie (1418-50)* (Caen, 1969), pp. 133-40.

[10] *Chronique du Mont-Saint-Michel, 1343-1468*, ed. by S. Luce, 2 vols (Paris, 1879-83), II (Pièces Diverses), pp. 103-09.

Anglo-Breton war in 1427 and were essential to the launching of a major offensive in the Cotentin. In September 1439 the opportunity arose. Richemont had successfully commanded the army which had reduced the stronghold of Meaux. The momentum needed to be maintained. Diplomatic negotiations with the English had broken down and Burgundy seemed to be pulling out of the war effort. To strengthen the French hand, and to encourage Brittany to enter the war, Charles VII and Richemont now resolved to invade western Normandy.

The timing was excellent. The English had been badly demoralised by their failure to defend Meaux. The early surrender of the fortified part of the town, the *Marché*, by William Chamberlain had led to accusations of treasonable conduct and raised the broader question of whether the English still had the will to resist.[11] For Humphrey duke of Gloucester the news of 'rodes and courses made in your duchie of Normandie', coming so soon after the loss of Meaux, occasioned a furious attack on the policies of his rival, Cardinal Beaufort, and the accusation that the war effort was not being properly supported.[12] There was no English commander or force in the region, and the invasion was linked with a renewed popular uprising in the Cotentin. A later source, Polydore Vergil, provides the only English account of the offensive. Charles VII, after regaining Paris and many other places in the Île de France, 'now was he in full hope easily to recover Normandie, for from thence he had intelligence that the countrey was given somewhat to sedition'. Then he sent Richemont and the Duke of Alençon 'with a mightie armie into Normandie. They with great speed came to Avranches and besieged it forthwith'.[13] Avranches was the key to the Norman Cotentin and if it fell the whole region would be in jeopardy.

The expedition had been well-prepared and struck rapidly. Charles VII had consulted at Angers with the Bretons Francis, count of Montfort, and Pierre de Bretagne. His force, led by Richemont, Lohéac and Alençon, was to be larger than his army at Meaux, with thirty-four captains and a substantial artillery train. It was, according to the chronicler Jean Chartier, 'un grant ost, avec plusieurs bombardes, canons et autres artilleries'.[14] A smaller contingent

11 M. H. Keen, *The Laws of War in the Late Middle Ages* (London, 1965), p. 125.

12 *Letters and Papers Illustrative of the Wars of the English in France during the Reign of Henry VI*, ed. by J. Stevenson, 2 vols in 3, Rolls Series (London, 1861-64), II, ii, p. 446. Gloucester's charges were probably first made in early December 1439: G. L. Harriss, *Cardinal Beaufort* (Oxford, 1988), p. 308.

13 *Three Books of Polydore Vergil's English History*, ed. by H. Ellis, Camden Society, old series, XXIX (1844), pp. 63-64.

14 J. Chartier, *Chronique de Charles VII, Roi de France*, ed. by A. Vallet de Viriville, 3 vols (Paris, 1858), I, p. 251. The strength of the army is discussed in P. Contamine, *Guerre, État et Société: Études sur les Armées des Rois de France, 1337-1494* (Paris, 1972), pp. 271-72.

had also been recruited, under Jean de Bueil. This moved first, in early November 1439, to reduce the English stronghold of Sainte-Suzanne in north-western Maine. Its capture prevented any possibility of reinforcement arriving from the substantial English garrison at Le Mans.[15] The main army gathered at Laval and La Gravelle, before moving north to occupy St James de Beuvron and Pontorson. An advance detachment under Jean de la Roche then crossed into Normandy to seize Gavray, cutting communications between Coutances and Avranches. The main army had reached the suburbs of Avranches at the end of November: the signal for an uprising amidst some of the townspeople.[16] In the next week government broke down in much of the Cotentin. Garrisons were left isolated, without pay or provisions. Soldiers from Regnéville were forced further and further afield to forage for supplies and in one sortie their captain was killed.[17] The moment of crisis had arrived.

When the news of the invasion reached the English captains in eastern Normandy, they kept their nerve and acted with resolve and courage. Edmund Beaufort, earl of Dorset, was the most senior English aristocrat in the Duchy. He was an experienced and highly able leader. In 1436 the heroic efforts of his small army had helped break the Burgundian siege of Calais. Although faced by vastly superior numbers Beaufort had repeatedly attacked the enemy. His daring won him great renown and was celebrated in a number of popular poems. The fullest of these, 'The Siege of Calais', praised his resilience and self-belief, giving him the following defiant words:

> I trust to god to see that day,
> That for al thaire proude aray
> fful low that they shul lowte;[18]

John Lord Talbot had served almost continuously in the war since 1427. It was his presence of mind in December 1435, at the time of a peasant rising in the Pays de Caux, that had saved the English position in eastern Normandy. The preamble of the letters creating Talbot marshal of France in 1436 made specific reference to the diligence with which he maintained the 'discipline de chevalrie'.[19] His outlook is reflected in the contents of the Shrewsbury Book, compiled under his instructions and presented to Margaret of Anjou in 1445. This superbly produced book included chansons de geste and prose romances

[15] Les Chroniques du Roi Charles VII par Gilles le Bouvier dit le Hérault Berry, ed. by H. Courteault, L. Cellier (Paris, 1979), p. 209.

[16] Chronique du Mont-Saint-Michel, I, p. 40. Details on the uprising are drawn from Archives Nationales (henceforth AN), K68/19, fol. 73v.

[17] Paris, Bibliothèque Nationale (henceforth BN), MS Fr. 26067/4063.

[18] V. J. Scattergood, Politics and Poetry in the Fifteenth Century (London, 1971), p. 89.

[19] A. J. Pollard, John Talbot and the War in France, 1427-53 (London, 1983), p. xi.

alongside chronicles and treatises on war, and it is clear that Talbot made no obvious distinction between the two.[20] All the works emphasized one fundamental principle, to be exercised on any occasion of danger or crisis, that of 'prowesse et grant valliance'. His surprise attack on Pontoise in February 1437 was carried out with only a few hundred men. It succeeded because of its sheer daring, and the ruse by which the English gained access to the town became the centre-piece of one of Martial d'Auvergne's poems.[21]

It would be dangerous to see such deeds as merely isolated and, in a strategic sense, unrealistic incidents removed from the broader problems afflicting the English war effort. The confidence of Beaufort and Talbot in launching plundering raids deep into Burgundian territory (in May 1436 and December 1437) inflicted substantial material losses, the sharp and cruel war advocated by Sir John Fastolf in the aftermath of the Congress of Arras. But their principal significance can be seen in chivalric terms, in the humiliation inflicted on the enemy. The poem 'Mockery of the Flemings' ridiculed the 'exploits' of the local levies, who, despite their numbers, were routed by the smaller but better disciplined English force:

> Ye laid upon the Englisshmen so myghtily with your handes,
> Til of you three hundrid lay strecchid on the sandes.
> Ye fled then...
> This was the first wurship... that ye wan.[22]

Talbot's campaign to relieve Le Crotoy in the winter of 1437 so intimidated the enemy that when he approached their *bastille* the garrison fled in panic leaving behind all their artillery and stores. Burgundian chroniclers show a bitter contempt for the feeble resistance offered by their soldiers, Monstrelet describing how the English pursued them, 'shouting after them as they would have done to a ribald mob'.[23] While this discussion does in no sense mitigate the long-term difficulties facing the English position in France, nor the reactions of such 'realists' as Sir John Fastolf, who departed from Normandy for good in 1439, after a long career in the Duchy as soldier and administrator, it warns against an over-emphasis on a purely strategic analysis at the expense of the code of values that dominated the outlook of those who actually fought in the war. The French invasion of the Norman Cotentin in the winter of 1439 posed a stark and immediate question to the English captains in the Duchy, whether they still believed in their cause and had the courage to risk all in its defence.

---

[20] *Ibid.*, p. 123.
[21] Pointed out in A. H. Burne, *The Agincourt War* (London, 1956), p. 283.
[22] Scattergood, *Politics and Poetry*, p. 86.
[23] Burne, *Agincourt War*, pp. 285-86.

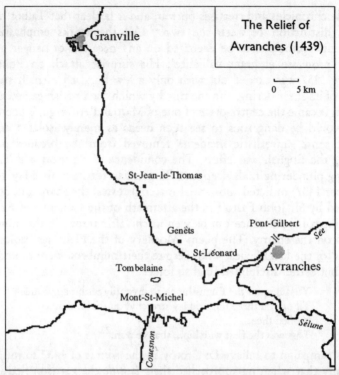

The Relief of
Avranches (1439)

0   5 km

Granville

St-Jean-le-Thomas

Pont-Gilbert

Genêts

St-Léonard

Avranches

Tombelaine

Mont-St-Michel

Sée

Sélune

Couesnon

News of the invasion had reached Edmund Beaufort, earl of Dorset (who was on the eastern frontier) on 30 November 1439. A letter was sent to the inhabitants of Evreux, informing them of the necessity of abandoning the siege of the small castle of Damville and returning immediately to Rouen.[24] Here a council of war was convened consisting of the senior military commanders, Dorset, Talbot, Fauconberg and Scales, and the chancellor Louis of Luxembourg, to consider the measures necessary to meet this terrible new threat. Despite the rebellion of some of the inhabitants of Avranches, the old town was still holding out under the experienced lieutenant John Lampet. Avranches had been fully fortified in the thirteenth century, when walls and towers were constructed joining the twelfth-century castle and *donjon*. At the foot of the ramparts was a substantial moat, fed by water from a large spring in the parish of Saint-Gervais. The English had adapted the defences to the use of heavy artillery, and a number of *bombardes*, along with smaller pieces, were situated along the walls. The garrison of around 180 men was one of the largest in Normandy.[25] Lampet's defiance of

24 BN, Nouvelles Acquisitions Françaises 21289/ 153.
25 Information drawn from BN, Pièces Originales 1374 (Gourdel); MS Fr. 25775/1406; A. Lottin, *Avranches et Ses Environs* (Avranches, 1923).

the French was encouraging but it was clear that a relief force would need to be despatched with all possible haste. It would have to be a scratch field force, recruited from some of the major Norman garrisons and also the pool of soldiers living off the countryside, remnants of former expeditions or lost captaincies, who from 1437 had been drafted into English armies as a matter of policy.

Plans were put into effect with great speed. A war-camp was created south-east of Rouen, between the town of Pont-de-l'Arche and the villages of Pont-Saint-Pierre, Neuville and Franqueville. The open site would have been crowded with makeshift lodgings, stables, leather-workers and carpenters' stalls and forges as the assembling troops were drilled and inspected. Retinues had arrived from Pont-de-l'Arche itself, Gournay, Falaise and Fresnay-sur-Sarthe in Maine. Contingents of soldiers 'vivans sur le pays' were brought in by the experienced captains Richard Harrington and Fulkes Eyton, those from the Andelle valley mustering before Dorset and Talbot on 8 December.[26] Dorset had also been preparing a light artillery train, gathering at Rouen carts of *ribaudequins*. These were mobile field guns with multiple barrels, capable of discharging both stone balls and lead pellets. It was a small but well-prepared mounted force of little over 1,200 men that left Rouen on around 12 December to do battle with a French army five times its size.[27] On 18 December the relief army was described as being in the vicinity of Saint-Lô in the Cotentin, where it paused briefly to gather further reinforcements, supplies and equipment, including cannonballs and lead shot, before undertaking the most hazardous part of its operation.[28]

Avoiding the French at Granville the English were likely to have swung on to the coastal road by the *bastille* of Saint-Jean-le-Thomas, one of a *ceinture*, or belt, of wooden fortifications that had been constructed around the bay of Mont-Saint-Michel. They set up their camp between the *bastilles* of Genêts and Saint-Léonard, overlooking the bay and conveniently close to

---

[26] AN, Collection Dom Lenoir, 26, fol. 347; BN, MS Fr. 26066/3910.

[27] Material on Dorset's artillery is found in BN, Pièces Originales 1202 (Forsted)/6; indication that the force was entirely mounted comes from a muster at Falaise, recording the absence of eight lances and twenty-four others, all mounted, on war service 'on the marches of the Cotentin': BN, Collection Clairambault, 200/87. Field forces drawn from garrisons and soldiers living off the countryside had been used for the relief of Creil (1437) and operations in the Pays de Caux (1438). The strength of both these forces had been around 1,200 men. This form of recruitment is surveyed in A. Curry, 'The First English Standing Army? Military Organization in Lancastrian Normandy, 1420-50', in *Patronage, Pedigree and Power in Later Medieval England*, ed. by C. Ross (Gloucester, 1979), p. 203. I am grateful to Dr Curry for discussing the question of the army's size and composition with me.

[28] BN, MS Fr. 26066/3964.

their garrison at Tombelaine, which they could reach at low tide. The rock of Tombelaine had been transformed into a substantial fortress, with eleven towers, gun emplacements and an observation platform. Its soldiers conducted frequent raids against the enemy, mounted forays that depended on an exact knowledge of the sand spits and fast-moving tides.[29] The river Sée blocked the path of the English army to Avranches and the only crossing point, the bridge at Pont-Gilbert, was in the hands of the French. Richemont had moved a large number of his men north of the city to block the English advance. For three days skirmishing took place along the river, but the French refused to be drawn into battle. In this Richemont was simply following his successful tactics at Meaux, which had forced the English into an eventual retreat, but here he was to be rudely surprised.

Confirmation of the French strategy is found in a passage in Jean de Bueil's *Le Jouvencel*, an allegorical romance that drew heavily on the author's own personal experiences in the latter phase of the Hundred Years War. De Bueil, who was present at the siege, referred to the apparent stalemate in a section on the giving of battle: 'devant Avranches, qui dura par trois jours sans ce que les ungs ne les aultres peussent gaigner ung petit ruisseau qui y estoit'.[30] De Bueil compared the situation with an earlier encounter, at Sillé-le-Guillaume, in 1434. Here the opposing forces of the Duke of Alençon and the Earl of Arundel had faced each other across another small river, the Longuève. Several days of skirmishing ended with the realisation that neither side could attempt an effective crossing without being blocked by the other, and the English retreated. Clearly the French were anticipating a similar withdrawal.

Instead the English resolved on an extraordinarily bold stroke to break the siege and force an engagement. They had located a possible crossing, making use of sand spits, where the estuaries of Sée and Sélune ran into the bay of Mont-Saint-Michel. It was a perilous venture, running the gauntlet of dangerous tides and large stretches of quicksand. Early in the morning of 23 December the English army began to move across the bay at low tide. They were forced to leave their baggage train, with their treasure chest, on the northern bank with the rearguard. Dorset's chaplain chose to remain with it; no doubt offering his prayers for the operation's success from a safe distance. Berry Herald vividly captures the scene: the English advanced slowly across the spits, on foot to lessen the weight, testing the sand with their lances, with the horses being driven behind.[31]

29 Chartier, *Chronique de Charles VII*, p. 251; E. Dupont, 'Tombelaine: une Citadelle anglaise et ses bastilles en France pendant la Guerre de Cent Ans', *Revue de Bretagne*, 42 (1909), 57-79.
30 J. de Bueil, *Le Jouvencel*, ed. by C. Favre, L. Lecestre, 2 vols (Paris, 1887-89), II, p. 227.
31 *Berry Herald*, p. 210. Detail on the baggage train is found in AN, Collection Dom

The terrible risks involved in such a manoeuvre were well-known. The most famous portrayal of them was in the Bayeux Tapestry, which at this time hung in the church of Notre-Dame of Bayeux, where it was listed in a fifteenth century inventory amongst the 'hangings, carpets, curtains and altar frontals kept in the vestry of the aforesaid church', with a detailed description: 'item, a very long and very narrow strip of linen, embroidered with figures and inscriptions representing the conquest of England, which is hung round the nave of the church on the feast of the relics and throughout the octave'.[32] The scene occurs during the 1064 campaign in which William of Normandy agreed to assist the Breton rebels fighting against Count Conan. The monastery of Mont-Saint-Michel is shown in the background, at the point where the river Couesnon runs into the bay. The Norman soldiers had undertaken a crossing of the estuary but suffered near-disaster when part of their army encountered quicksand. The tapestry depicts a rider being thrown and two others pulled to safety.

The English plan depended on complete surprise. Chartier described how at one point their route took them within an arrow-shot of the enemy sentries. But the French did not believe such a crossing was possible. It was a way, the chronicler of Arthur de Richemont remarked ruefully, 'qui jamais n'avoit este trouve'.[33] The English army was almost certainly guided by members of the Tombelaine garrison, whose knowledge of terrain was crucial to the operation's success. Remarkably, they completed their passage without mishap and were able to surprise Richemont's sentries. The southern approaches to Avranches were poorly guarded and they were able to break through to the beleaguered city. Speed was now of the essence: to strike at the French while much of their army was still dispersed along the Sée. Joining forces with the garrison the English stormed out of Avranches, carrying the siege lines after a savage hand-to-hand fight and capturing the main French war camp, with all its guns and provisions. Reforming their battle-line, they then rode north towards the main French position at Pont-Gilbert. They were still heavily outnumbered and decided to risk all in a dramatic engagement. A petition from Edmund Beaufort indicated that they had formed all their men into one single *bataille*, or mounted formation, and charged the enemy.[34] On hearing of the English advance Richemont had

---

[32] Lenoir, 26, fol. 347.

S. Bertrand, 'The History of the Tapestry', in *The Bayeux Tapestry*, ed. by Sir Frank Stenton (London, 1957), p. 76. I am grateful to Dr Richard Eales for discussing this point with me.

[33] Chartier, *Chronique de Charles VII*, p. 252; G. Gruel, *Chronique d'Arthur de Richemont*, ed. by A. le Vavasseur (Paris, 1890), p. 156.

[34] AN, Collection Dom Lenoir, 26, fol. 347. *Berry Herald* (p. 211) and Gruel (p. 156) give the fullest description of the engagement, choosing to emphasize the general panic that overcame the French formations. The later English account (Polydore

hurriedly gathered his troops. The accounts of Berry Herald and Richemont's own biographer reveal that the French had already drawn up their *batailles*, and were in proper military order. But faced with this shock attack a panic set in amongst many of his soldiers, who broke line and fled in terror. Overwhelmed, Richemont was forced to abandon his position and retreat into Brittany with the remnants of his army. Surprise, daring and a remarkable discipline and courage had won the English a memorable victory. A pursuivant, who had joined the relief force in the vicinity of Pont-Gilbert, was moved to record the following:

> auquel lieu de Pont Gilbert ledit poursuyvant arriva le mardi devant le jour de Noel... xxij jour de decembre, et lendemain ensuivent fut levee le siege dudis ennemis qui senfuirent honteusement a leur grant deshonneur et confusion...[35]

The crisis was over and all over Normandy the English rejoiced. Captains of garrisons on the eastern frontier, Gisors and Gournay, were informed of 'la joyeuse recouvrance de la ville d'Avranches', and Dorset's own pursuivant, 'Cadron', carried the news to England.[36] A numerically superior French army had been humiliated. The Bourgeois of Paris recorded bluntly that they had vastly outnumbered the English, 'et firent lever le siege a grant deshonneur'.[37] The victory stabilized the entire Cotentin. Granville was recaptured and fortified by Lord Scales and the French base of La Gravelle in Maine was also seized. Those who had supported the invasion were fully punished. French hopes of involving Brittany in the war effort were dashed. Jean V promised to support the English at Avranches in defensive operations and the port of Saint-Malo, which had provided supplies to Mont-St-Michel and Granville, was placed under the governorship of the pro-English Gilles de Bretagne.[38] Normandy had gained a valuable respite, and the following year saw another great success, the recapture of Harfleur.

The English had performed a notable feat of arms that had important ramifications for all the combatants concerned. Both the accounts of the pursuivant and the Bourgeois of Paris emphasized the dishonour of the French, who had fled from the field of battle after banners had been unfurled. It was a humiliating reverse for Richemont, who may have briefly been in danger of a trial in the court of chivalry. Christine de Pisan's *Fayttes of Arms*,

---

Vergil, pp. 63-64) stresses the ferocity of the relief army's assault: 'they met with many, whom they slew in the encounter'.

[35] BN, MS Fr. 26066/3920.

[36] Archives Départementales de la Seine-Maritime, Fonds Danquin, Carton 11, nos 152, 154.

[37] *Journal d'un Bourgeois de Paris*, ed. by A. Tuetey (Paris, 1881), pp. 350-51.

[38] G. Knowlson, *Jean V, Duc de Bretagne et L'Angleterre* (Rennes, 1964), pp. 167-68. Knowlson saw Charles VII's failure at Avranches as the chief factor that persuaded Jean V to risk plotting with the malcontents in the *Praguerie*.

in listing the duties of the constable, stressed that order and discipline were to be imposed upon his troops, 'that he knowe to governe his own peple and holde in ordre and drede'. He was to be alert to the movements and intentions of his adversary, 'in serchyng alleway their estate... and be he sybtyl pourveyed and wyly to deffende hym fro theym'.[39] Richemont was, as constable, the personal representative of the king, 'that for hym and in his name excercyseth the fayt of his warres'; he now carried the stigma of having retreated in the face of the enemy. At a skirmish at Conty in November 1430 Lewis Robessart had preferred to fight to the death rather than retreat and sustain such a dishonour.[40] Sir John Fastolf's flight from Patay in June 1429 led to accusations of conduct unbecoming a knight. For a time Fastolf may have been stripped of his Garter and the case was still being heard before king and peers in the early 1440s.[41] The chronicler of Arthur de Richemont, only too aware of this chivalric context, is defensive in the extreme: again and again emphasizing the flight of many of the soldiers 'sans ordennance', and how the constable, despite having so few remaining troops ('certifie quatre cens combatans'), wished to make a stand and was only reluctantly persuaded to retreat to Dol.[42] It is not entirely convincing.

There is no doubt that in a chivalric rather than a purely strategic sense the English had re-established an ascendancy. The humiliation of Avranches led to a direct breach between Charles VII and some of his nobility. It was no coincidence that the plotting of the *Praguerie*, which included Alençon and Bourbon, began at the end of December 1439, just after the military debacle.[43] Amongst the English forces a new mood of optimism prevailed. Commanders now believed that if the French could be drawn to battle they could still be decisively defeated, and perhaps even Charles VII himself

[39]   C. de Pisan, *Book of Fayttes of Arms*, pp. 20, 23. Fifteenth-century military treatises accepted that the king himself should flee in the face of a rout, 'car mieulx vault perdre bataille que roy, car pour perdre roy se pert royaume', but a duke or any other commander should never run away, because the king would always avenge or ransom him: BN, MS Fr. 5365, fol. 50v (kindly communicated to me by Mr Peter Lewis).

[40]   D. A. L. Morgan, 'From a Death to a View: Lewis Robessart, Johan Huizinga and the Political Significance of Chivalry' in *Chivalry in the Renaissance*, ed. by S. Anglo (Woodbridge, 1990), pp. 93-98.

[41]   C. A. J. Armstrong, 'Sir John Fastolf and the Law of Arms', in *War, Literature and Politics in the Late Middle Ages*, ed. by C. T. Allmand (Liverpool, 1976), p. 56. Interestingly Armstrong identifies an increasing reaction against the more mercenary forms of chivalry, noting that the statutes of the Order of the Golden Fleece were drafted to encourage personal valour rather than private profit.

[42]   Gruel, *Chronique d'Arthur de Richemont*, pp. 156-57.

[43]   G. Fresne de Beaucourt, *Histoire de Charles VII*, 6 vols (Paris, 1881-91), III, pp. 118-20, adding that a plot to seize Charles VII and execute some of his councillors involved some of the captains returning from Avranches to Angers.

captured. Such aggressive thinking lay behind the Seine and Oise campaign of 1441, which did indeed come very close to capturing the French king.

In an overall analysis, such bold operations ultimately came to nothing. The prime concern of the English government was the financial cost of the war effort, and the reason for their failure to promote or publicize the remarkable military achievement at Avranches can be found in the arguments for the release of the Duke of Orléans and the search for a peace treaty, expressed in the spring and summer of 1440. Here the alternative view was expressed, that victories on the field of battle did nothing to solve the economic problems arising from a continued commitment to the war, a 'grete and grevous cost'.[44] During the truce of 1444-49, whilst Charles VII effected a wholesale reform of his army, the English deliberately ran down their garrison strength and shipped home most of the soldiers living off the countryside, ensuring that when war broke out in 1449 the kind of army that had performed so heroically ten years earlier could no longer be recruited.

Yet the memory of this great triumph, one of the last military successes recorded in the *Boke of Noblesse*, helps us to understand a little better the disgruntled 'war lobby' that existed in the last years of Henry VI's reign. In the view of these old soldiers the war with France was not an irretrievably lost cause, if given proper backing. It was an outlook that commanded enough general sympathy to make the campaign of 1475 as well supported as that of Agincourt sixty years earlier. The letters of ordinary soldiers in Edward IV's army show that honour and renown won through battle against the French remained important objectives, and had in no way died with the loss of Normandy and Gascony.[45]

The very real economic problems afflicting the English in the last phase of the Hundred Years War have quite properly been emphasized in most recent studies, alongside the piecemeal, and often inconclusive, military operations that seemed to offer no chance of resolving the conflict. However, a purely materialistic or pragmatic analysis separates the combatants from the literature that they read and the values that they would have understood. A critical study of John Lord Talbot, one of the principal architects of the feat of arms at Avranches, concludes:

> In the long drawn-out campaigning in the defence of Normandy after 1435 Talbot seems to have constantly subordinated notions of chivalric heroism to overall strategic and tactical requirements. It was a manner of fighting noticeable for eschewing of unnecessary personal risk.[46]

[44] Stevenson, *Wars of the English*, II, ii, pp. 351-60.
[45] C. Richmond, '1485 and All That, or what was going on at the Battle of Bosworth', in *Richard III: Loyalty, Lordship and Law*, ed. by P. W. Hammond (London, 1986), pp. 190, 205-06.
[46] Pollard, *John Talbot*, p. 129.

This view detaches the *gestes* and chronicles of the Shrewsbury Book from the beliefs of the nobleman who commissioned them: Lord Talbot 'did not live up to the ideals of the chansons which he apparently knew'. It is difficult to reconcile such a critique with the astonishing courage shown in the crossing of the bay of Mont-St-Michel on 23 December 1439. In the course of this hazardous venture Dorset and Talbot were prepared to set at risk their entire baggage train, including their own treasure chests, which had to be left on the far side of the estuary: it was later plundered by the fleeing French.[47] Acts of valour were not seen merely as diverting reading material, but a path to true ennoblement. A grant of arms by the herald John Smert to Edmond Mylle was made on 12 August 1450, in the aftermath of the loss of Normandy. Smert recorded how Mylle had

> ...long time followed the career of arms and in this and his other affairs has borne himself so valiantly and honourably as to be fully deserving that he and his posterity shall in all places be honourably admitted...

In the preamble to the grant the herald reiterated the sentiment that gives us a surer understanding of those who fought outside Avranches:

> Equity wills and reason ordains that men of virtue and noble courage shall have the reward of renown for their merits, and that not just in their own persons in this mortal and transitory life, but in such a way that after their day the issue of their bodies shall in all places be held in honour perpetually before others...[48]

In the *Boke of Noblesse* the relief of Avranches was recalled with admiration alongside such well-known earlier triumphs as the victories of Cravant and Verneuil.[49] This important work, originally compiled in the 1450s, extols 'the avauncement and encrece of chevalrie and worship in armes'. It is a point of view that needs to be more firmly integrated into our understanding of the closing stages of the Hundred Years War.

[47] AN, Collection Dom Lenoir, 26, fol. 345.
[48] M. Keen, *Chivalry* (New Haven, 1984), p. 163.
[49] *The Boke of Noblesse*, ed. by J. G. Nichols (Roxburghe Club, 1860), p. 28.

Richard III and his Overmighty Subjects: in Defence of a King
DANIEL WILLIAMS

The short and crisis-ridden period of the Yorkist ascendancy between 1461 and 1485 presents the historian with a series of seemingly intractable problems which have stimulated debate over half a millennium. Convincing interpretations of the actions of the Yorkist kings are hampered by the apparent absence of any tangible theory or statement upon the nature of monarchy during this period. The debate, so it seems, was predicated upon inheritance and not upon political theory, in stark contrast to the situation under the early Tudors. In particular, the reign of Henry VIII witnessed a substantial political and intellectual awareness of the exalted nature of kingship and its central role in the government of both church and state.[1]

This problem can be explained, in part, by the *de facto* nature of the swift process of usurpation between October 1460 and March 1461 which propelled a youth of barely nineteen to supreme office. In the event Edward IV ascended to the throne of England like a young nobleman entering into his inheritance. No new theories of kingship were expounded; none were deemed necessary. It was the restoration of the Plantagenet blood line. The death of Richard duke of York at Wakefield and Henry VI's implication in that act absolved the surviving Yorkists from the terms of the parliamentary settlement of October 1460.[2] To the men of the fifteenth century the spectacular victory at Towton was an obvious divine vindication of the legitimacy of the young king's title. The Yorkist case was set out succinctly by the Crowland Chronicler:

> ... after mature deliberation, the council having come to the conclusion that King Henry, by taking part with the murderers of his father, had used his utmost endeavours to annul the decree of Parliament above-mentioned, the earl [of March] was pronounced to be no longer bound to observe his fealty towards him. Royal honors were now paid him by all the people, with universal acclamation, and he commenced his reign and in the power of his might won and earned the victory and the crown...[3]

---

[1] J. A. Guy, 'Henry VIII and the Praemunire Manoeuvres of 1530-1531', *English Historical Review*, 97 (1982), p. 498; J. A. Guy, *Tudor England* (Oxford, 1988), p. 110; T. F. Mayer, 'Tournai and Tyranny: Imperial Kingship and Critical Humanism', *Historical Journal*, 34 (1991), 257-77.

[2] *Ingulph's Chronicle of the Abbey of Croyland with the continuations...*, ed. & trans. by H. T. Riley (London, 1854), p. 456 (hereafter, *Crowland*).

[3] Ibid.

Once king, all Edward did from time to time was to express good intentions. At the first parliament of his reign he promised his subjects at large 'I shall be unto you youre veray high wisse and lovyng liege lord.'[4] In 1467 he made his famous statement, again before parliament:

> I propose to live upon mine own and not to change my subjects, but in great and urgent causes concerning the Weal of themselves and also the defence of them and this my realm... I shall be to you a good and gracious king and reign as right wisely upon you as ever did any of my progenitors.[5]

This was all very laudable but it certainly does not add up to a theoretical statement of new monarchy; quite the reverse. Sir John Fortescue's works *De Natura Legis Naturae, De Laudibus Legum Angliae*, even the more promising title *The Governance of England*, are all equally disappointing.[6] Their approach is descriptive rather than analytical; their scope legalistic, theocratic and what is worst, by the Yorkist period, distinctly old-fashioned.[7] The Crowland Chronicle's description of Edward IV's plans for monarchy in 1476 does give a more promising statement of intent.[8] But, in the context of this source's uncritical eulogy of the king throughout the second reign, it must be treated with some caution. 1476 is also very late.

Are we looking for theories of monarchy or even statements of future policy that simply do not exist? Was there no difference in contemporary eyes between a king ascending the throne and a nobleman entering his family title and inheritance? This is a superficially attractive theory given support by the rather mundane inheritance argument of Fortescue's *De Natura Legis Naturae*. Perhaps the Yorkist dynasty fell because it broke the first rule of

---

4   *Rotuli Parliamentorum...*, 6 vols (London, 1767-77), V, 487.

5   Ibid., 572.

6   *The Works of Sir J[ohn] F[ortescue]*, ed. by Lord Clermont, 2 vols (London, 1869): *The Governance of England*, ed. by C. Plummer (Oxford, 1885); *De Laudibus Legum Anglie*, ed. by S. B. Chrimes (Cambridge, 1942).

7   Fortescue's legalistic approach, 'that all human laws were either customs or statutes', speaks for itself (*De Laudibus*, p. 37). In the words of S. B. Chrimes, 'His originality lay not in any exceptional constitutional enlightenment nor in liberal sentiments, but in his attempt to array bare constitutional facts in the imposing raiment of political theory' (*English Constitutional Ideals in the Fifteenth Century* (Cambridge, 1936), p. 324). Even this is to make a virtue out of necessity (ibid., pp. 14-15, 322). What glimmers of insight Fortescue has to offer seem to have stopped dead in 1461. In the light of his experiences of that year this is hardly surprising. From then on he devotes his mind to administrative proposals (Chrimes, *English Constitutional Ideals*, pp. 329-32). Despite its post-1471 provenance, *Governance of England* could have been written at least a decade earlier. See also A. Fox and J. A. Guy, *Reassessing the Henrician Age* (Oxford, 1986), pp. 126-28.

8   *Crowland*, p. 474.

dynastic survival – family loyalty? This principle was well enough known. In his will of July 1485, Henry Percy, earl of Northumberland, made generous provision for his second son William, but only on a specifically stated and axiomatic condition:

> to the intent that he shall serve his brother Henry mine heir apparent next to his allegiance and be of loving and lowly disposition towards him and this I charge him upon my blessing as he will answer before God.[9]

The failure of the Yorkist brothers to keep to this first commandment of family survival was the tragic theme of the dynastic history used by the Crowland Chronicler, predicated upon the statement of 1473:

> These three brothers, the king and the two dukes, were possessed of such surpassing talents, that, if they had been able to live without dissensions, such a threefold cord could never have been broken without the utmost difficulty.[10]

The problem with this particular line of thought, however attractive, is that it is a further aspect of Crowland's eulogy of Edward IV that exonerates the king from all blame.[11]

Yet a whole range of surviving evidence and the exalted vision of monarchy under the Tudors reveal that there was a quantum difference between nobility and monarchy.[12] The Wars of the Roses occurred because the essential difference between the two became blurred by the existence of too many claimants of the blood royal and the ready support such 'idols' were able to call upon both within and without the realm. The Yorkists, like the Tudors, were well aware of this situation. Edward himself

> was by no means ignorant of the condition of his people, and how readily they might be betrayed, in case they should find a leader, to enter into rebellious plans, and conceive a thirst for change.[13]

Such 'conditions' made Yorkist England virtually ungovernable as set out in Crowland's second interpretative and analytical theme: the tragedy of King Richard III.

As Professor Lander has recently shown, fifteenth-century kings attempted to counteract these dangerous propensities of their great subjects by emphasizing the theocratic nature of kingship and its high purpose within the state as the focus and embodiment of the nation itself.[14] Thus its divine

---

9 *Testamenta Eboracensia*, ed. by J. Raines, III, *Surtees Society*, 45 (1864), p. 307.
10 *Crowland*, p. 470.
11 Ibid.
12 See for example *The Governance of England*, ed. by S. B. Chrimes (Cambridge, 1936), p. 125; *Crowland*, passim.
13 Ibid.
14 J. R. Lander, *The Limitations of English Monarchy in the Later Middle Ages* (Toronto, 1989).

and superior mission elevated monarchy far above the localized aspirations of even the most magnificent and powerful of the aristocracy in the overall scheme of things.[15]

This could be made manifest in the increasing splendour of court ceremonial and life style and through the munificence of crown patronage of the arts, architecture and religious life.[16] By the late fifteenth century the endowment of educational institutions became the new vogue with the foundations of King's and Queens' Colleges, Cambridge, and Eton College under the walls of the crown's *caput honoris* at Windsor. All this had a calculated purpose to enhance the dignity of the crown. In retrospect it must be recognised for what it was: an innovative policy identifiable in the spirit if not in the concept of New Monarchy.

Such actions, predicated upon political realities and the urgent necessity for a new high ideal of the role of kingship, were limited by the financial constraints within which monarchy was forced to operate. They had to be, therefore, long-term and progressive. This legacy from the Yorkists to the Tudors constituted a faltering link of continuity between the reigns of Edward IV, Richard III and Henry VII, culminating in the exalted magnificence of the court of Henry VIII.

In the middle of this triumphant progression comes the short and tragic reign of Richard III, two years sandwiched between Edward's effective twenty-one years and Henry's effective twenty-three years. Did this fleeting period of crisis contribute to New Monarchy or was it merely an aberration that is best forgotten? In truth Richard's reign is central to the progressive legacy of the growing strength and self-confidence witnessed by English monarchy during this period. For the early Tudors the episode also served as a cautionary example of the perils of faction, conspiracy and bad counsel from which both the crown and the nation had to be rescued and preserved.[17] Richard's fall was seen as an object lesson in the dangers of overmighty subjects whose selfish ambitions rocked the ship of state and made it vulnerable to the malice of its traditional enemies abroad.[18]

All this focuses upon the two themes of the remainder of this paper: Richard III's own 'manifesto' for New Monarchy and the intractable

---

[15] C. Ross, *Edward IV* (London, 1974), p. 257.

[16] Fortescue, *Governance*, p. 125; *Crowland*, pp. 474-75.

[17] *The Complete Works of St. Thomas More*, ed. by R. S. Sylvester et al., II, *History of Richard III* (New Haven, 1963), p. lxv; Mayer, 'Tournai and Tyranny', p. 258: This is also the main theme of Edward Hall's *Chronicle...*, ed. by H. Ellis (London, 1809). Hall was a near contemporary of More.

[18] The extent of foreign intervention in the domestic affairs of England and its consequences have still to be measured and assessed. The most recent study of this neglected subject is R. A. Griffiths and R. S. Thomas, *The Making of the Tudor Dynasty* (Gloucester, 1985).

problem of the singularly awful batch of overmighty subjects with whom he had to contend. Such themes also encompass an equitable and historically valid defence of Richard III which is as necessary today as it was in the time of Sir George Buck. For that king, for centuries the victim of historical tradition, has in recent years become the butt of current historiographical dogma. The tragedy of the interpretation of the reign has taken over from the Tudor tragedy of the reign itself. Both dogmas obscure the truth.

To understand this we must begin with the wisdom of William Stubbs who wrote, a century ago:

> Richard III yet owes the general condemnation with which his life and reign has been visited, to the fact that he left no one behind him whose duty or care it was to attempt his vindication.[19]

The truth lies even deeper than this. It was not only convenient for the Tudor tradition and its fellow travellers to denigrate Richard, but his reign was also seen as a useful example for the new Renaissance modes of historical writing to exemplify their contrasting antique moral themes of good kings and bad kings, a device that dramatized the shameful downfall of the latter, thereby stressing the success and harmony of the former.

The historiographical consequence of all this is that he has suffered from being contrasted with two traditional, though dubious, paragons. The reputation of Henry VII has been buttressed by a series of eulogies that span at least the four hundred years between Bacon and Chrimes.[20] Although modern scholarship has from time to time suggested some glaring holes in the fabric, his reputation is now implicitly preserved by the powerful Tudor History establishment.[21] Over the same period Edward IV's reputation has been more vulnerable. In Stubbs' sane and balanced judgement:

> viewed beside Edward IV he (Richard III) seems to differ rather in fortune rather than in desert.[22]

The recent rehabilitation of Edward by Charles Ross, however, has upset that balance.[23] In the current vogue of the favourable rehabilitation of medieval kings, Richard seems to have lost out. Good King Edward's successes left no evil legacy to his successors.[24] This simply cannot be true. Edward's reign had its successes but these were overshadowed by

---

[19] W. Stubbs, *The Constitutional History of England*, 5th edn (Oxford, 1903), p. 232.
[20] See also M. V. C. Alexander, *The First of the Tudors* (London, 1981), pp. 217, 261.
[21] Sir Francis Bacon, *The History of the Reign of King Henry the Seventh*, ed. by R. Lockyer (London, 1971); S. B. Chrimes, *Henry VII* (London, 1972); *Tudor Rule and Revolution*, ed. by D. J. Guth and J. W. McKenna (Cambridge, 1982); Guy, *Tudor England*.
[22] Stubbs, *Constitutional History*, p. 232.
[23] C. Ross, *Edward IV*, passim.
[24] Ibid., pp. xi, 432.

circumstances and above all by inconsistencies of judgement. Indeed the king's only real consistency is to be found in a predilection to indulge rather than discipline his subjects. Despite Ross's vigorous arguments to the contrary the first part of his reign reveals little policy or judgement, more of a headstrong young man reacting to events beyond his control.[25] By 1470 his subjects were bitterly disillusioned after the great expectations of 1461. In Warkworth's intelligent and objective observation:

> the common people seyde, if they might have another King he should get all again (that is, recover the lost lands in France) and amend all manner of things that were amiss and bring the realm of England to great prosperity and rest. Never the latter, when King Edward IV reigned the people looked for all the fore said prosperities and peace but it came not.[26]

The second period of his reign witnessed greater stability but his indulgences to a select few exacerbated the dangerous predilections of overmighty subjects of the royal blood.[27] The actions of his court and council made more enemies than friends. Edward IV's death in 1483 just before his forty-first birthday was of course unexpected. But, as often happens in such cases, his insurance policies proved to be woefully inadequate. In the words of T. B. Pugh, 'the death of Edward IV .... resulted in a struggle for power which soon exposed the failure of Yorkist rule'.[28]

Most seriously Edward's failures exasperated the greatest of his overmighty subjects, his hitherto loyal surviving brother Richard, duke of Gloucester, a prince motivated not just by the fear and ambition of the Tudor tradition but by a feeling within an experienced and talented mind that he could do better. For the people of England in 1483 the central question was whether Richard had policies which might bring about the peace and prosperity to which they aspired. This is a point set aside by both Tudor and modern orthodoxy.[29] The smoothness of the usurpation and much surviving evidence suggest that contemporaries found a lot to commend in the new king, and aspects of those beliefs lingered on into the next reign.

---

[25] John Warkworth, *A Chronicle of the First Thirteen Years of the Reign of Edward IV*, ed. by J. O. Halliwell, Camden Society (London, 1839), pp. 1-12.

[26] Ibid., p. 12.

[27] M. A. Hicks, *False, Fleeting, Perjur'd Clarence: George, Duke of Clarence 1449-78* (Gloucester, 1980); D. Dunlop, '"The Redresses and Reparacons of Attemptates": Alexander Legh's Instructions from Edward IV, March - April 1475', *Historical Research*, 63 (1990), p. 350.

[28] *Fifteenth-century England 1399-1509*, ed. by S. B. Chrimes *et al.* (Manchester, 1972), p. 112.

[29] C. Ross, *Richard III* (London, 1981), p. 94.

Even his betrayers, the Stanleys, felt some remorse. In the obscure Stanley ballad *Scottish Field* describing the battle of Flodden there is nostalgia, even regret for their slaying of a brave warrior king:

> Richard that rich lord: in his bright armour.
> He held himself no coward: for he was a noble king.
> He fought right royally and vigorously his foeman amongst
> till all his bright armour was all besmirched
> with blood
> then was he done to death with many cruel strokes.[30]

Others more loyal saw him as a king worthy of following and suffering for, even in August 1485. The epitaph of Thomas Howard, duke of Norfolk, who died in 1524, throws some interesting and not unfavourable light upon the legitimacy of Richard's reign and by implication his qualities of leadership and inspiration. There is also some significance in what this long inscription drawn up at the duke's command did not say:

> And after Kinge Edward was ded and King Edward the Fyfte his son; than K. Richard was king ... And the Lord Howard ... was creatt Duke of Norfolk and he creatt Earle of Surrey : And so they bothe served the seid King Richard truly as his Subgettis duringe his lyffe ... And they went with him to Boswrothe Feld, where the seid King Richard was slayne and also the seid Duke of Norfolk And the affirseid Erle hert and takyn upon the Feld and put in the Tower London.[31]

This source also describes the circumstances in which the earl was restored to favour a few years later. In part:

> for the true and faithfull service that the seid King Henry herd of him doon to his other Prince (i.e. Richard III); and also that he (Henry) saw himself, he dide on Boswrothe Feld.[32]

By implication, after his experiences at the battle of Stoke, even Henry VII felt some respect for the loyalty inspired by his predecessor.

Richard, then, had qualities but did he also have policies? Was it merely ambition, or ambition as a means to a more laudable purpose? What were his ideals of good lordship and kingship? The evidence that answers such questions is there to be found in a political programme of sound and productive intentions, predicated upon a constructive exasperation at the deficiencies and errors of his late brother's reign. Evidence of this is to be found in even hostile sources if one looks carefully. Even Edward Hall's *Chronicles*[33] allude to a London memory of Richard's good government well

---

[30] *Bishop Percy's Ballads and Romances*, ed. by J. W. Hales, et al., 4 vols (London, 1867-68), I, p. 213.

[31] F. Blomefield, *An Essay towards a Topographical History of the County of Norfolk*, 11 vols (London, 1805-1810), II, p. 121.

[32] Ibid.

into the next generation. The confrontation between Wolsey and the City of London in 1525 over a proposed benevolence of that year is one example. Faced with the Cardinal's demands a councillor representing the City replied that such extractions were contrary to a statute made in the parliament of Richard III. Wolsey, a sharp and a clever debater, went in for the kill:

> Sir I marvel that you speak of Richard III which was a usurper and a murtherer of his own nephews, then of so evil a man how can the acts be good?[34]

The reply was equally quick and astute, it was also reflective:

> And it may please your Grace although he did evil, yet in his time wer many good acts made not by him only but by consent of the body of the whole realm which is in parliament.[35]

This is certainly revisionist food for thought; Richard III remembered not as a tyrant but as an upholder of the sovereignty of parliament. There is in fact some important corroborating evidence to support such a view. In truth, what we know of the range and nature of this king's concept of good lordship is sufficient to merit the designation of policy even within the traditional limitations of late medieval monarchy.[36] The dynamic behind such a policy was exasperation at the failures of the previous reign, as British Library, Harleian MS 433, 'a remembrance made as well for the hasty levy of the king's revenues', dating from the beginning of the reign clearly shows.[37] As Somerville pointed out, both the criticism of Edward's slack policies within the Duchy of Lancaster and the more positive solutions to the problems created by such slackness that appear in the document come from Richard's own experiences as Steward of the Duchy lands north of the Trent.[38]

The most detailed statements of Richard's ideas for the strengthening of the royal office and the furtherance of good government are to be found, significantly, in speeches, made, or intended to be made, before parliament. They were clearly drafted by the learned Chancellor, John Russell, bishop of Lincoln, but the monarch's own personal commitment cries out over the centuries, at least to those who bother to listen. The first was drafted during the protectorate and was clearly intended for a parliamentary audience.[39] It

---

33 Hall's *Chronicle*, p. 698.

34 Ibid.

35 Ibid.

36 Lander, *The Limitations*, passim.

37 R. Horrox and P. W. Hammond (eds), *British Library Harleian Manuscript 433*, 4 vols (Gloucester, 1979-83), III (1982), 118-29 (hereafter *Harl. 433*).

38 R. Somerville, *History of the Duchy of Lancaster*, 2 vols (London, 1943), I, 270.

39 *Grants ... during the Reign of Edward the Fifth*, ed. by J. G. Nichols, Camden Society (London, 1854) pp. xxxix-xlix.

contains a justification for Gloucester's protectorate but also an explicit indictment of the previous regime:

> remembering what fluctuation and change amongst the nobles has fallen in this realm ... all our own ground is set within a sea all subject to ebb and flow, to winds, blasts and storms.[40]

The nobility can only preserve their own prosperity and wealth by not coveting the assets of their fellow peers. They must apply also the principles of fairness and equity to their judgement of, and conduct towards, the commons under them. The people in turn must obey the commands of the nobility acting as they are upon the authority of parliament,[41] the king's most high and sovereign court. The operative and executive part of the body politic of England is the king and his council. They too have the duty to act justly and in the common interest and not, as in the time of Edward IV, allow

> the crafty and fraudulent dealing of the outward princes with whom he allied. How unjustly they vied for marriages, payments and sureties and other great and noble appointments passed amongst them and to others.[42]

A child king, if he is to win the affection of his people, must render true justice and deliver them from extortionate fiscal innovations. He must not renew the over-generous grants of his predecessors. He must trust to the power and wisdom of his uncle whose protectorate must be endorsed by the authority of parliament.[43] This is not just an affirmation of will and power but a policy document to rectify the manifold deficiencies of the previous reign.

The second source is the rough draft of a speech to be delivered at Richard III's first parliament, scheduled for 11 November 1483 but postponed because of the Buckingham Revolt.[44] The ideas expressed are more philosophical but with clear practical implications, something very close to those of a manifesto. The body politic consists of three estates as principal members under one head. The sovereign lord the king is the head, the lords and the commons are the members. Parliament is the mystical or political body that constitutes the congregation of the whole people.[45]

If the members follow the common good and not their own selfish self-interest, then the commons will not be ruined by enclosures and evictions[46] (one of the first references to this growing social and economic problem to be

---

[40] Ibid., p. xli.
[41] Ibid., pp. xliii-xlv.
[42] Ibid., p. xlvi.
[43] Ibid., pp. xlviii-xlix.
[44] Ibid., pp. l-lxiii.
[45] Ibid., p. lviii.
[46] Ibid., p. lii.

found in the royal records). Nor will there be the unlawful assemblies and violent insurrections which jeopardize the nobility as well as the people. The king too must, by implication, follow such a path. Was not the mortal sickness of Edward IV made worse by his memories

> of dark ways of his crafty and false friends. We must unite to restore the land to its former prosperity.[47]

The full fervour of Richard's pent-up exasperation alluded to here is most clearly expressed in the act endorsing his title to the crown passed at his parliament of January 1484:

> them that such had the rule and governance of this land, delighting in adulation and flattery and led by sensuality and excess, followed the counsel of persons insolent vicious and of inordinate avarice despising good virtuous and prudent persons ... the prosperity of this land daily decreased ... it is likely that this realm is to fall into extreme misery and desolation ... without due provision of convenient remedy be had in this behalf in all godly haste.[48]

Seen through objective and sympathetic eyes all this amounts to a deeply held policy for change, an indictment of the previous regime and a blueprint for a new order of things. To set the prevailing orthodoxy on its head, the 'tyranny' of Edward IV sprang from a failure of counsel, 'of despising the counsel of good, virtuous and prudent persons...'[49] Richard's analysis of the underlying causes of Edward's tyranny bears a striking similarity to Thomas More's indictment of his own in *The History of Richard III*.[50] Was it that Henry VIII's Chancellor attacked the wrong Yorkist king? Certainly a case can be made. At all events More's solutions to this problem of failure of counsel set out in his *Utopia* bear a distinct similarity to the manifesto of Richard III drafted by an earlier learned Chancellor.[51]

As has been shown, the main thrust of Richard's innovations lay in the enforcement of the law in a spirit of equity and impartiality, traditionally the primary and most lauded attribution of medieval kingship, to which the new king was determined to return.[52] Like so many aspects of New Monarchy innovation often meant a return to traditional values. There is a wealth of

---

[47] Ibid., p. lxiii.
[48] *Rotuli Parliamentorum*, VI, 240-42.
[49] Ibid.
[50] *The Complete Works of St. Thomas More*, II (1963), 83-87; XV (1986), 329ff.
[51] *Utopia*, ed. by E. Surtz and J. H. Hexter, *The Complete Works of St. Thomas More*, IV (New Haven, 1965), pp. 124-25, 192-93.
[52] See John Rous, *The Rous Roll* (London, 1859; repr. Gloucester, 1980), no. 63: '...all avarice set aside, ruled his subjects in his realm full commendably, punishing offenders of his laws, especially extortioners and oppressors of his commons'. See also the first clause of his coronation oath in *Registrum Thome Bourgchier*, ed. by F. R. H. Du Boulay, *Canterbury and York Society*, 54 (1957), p. 60.

corroborating evidence of Richard's determination to be an upholder of justice and law to his subjects as set out on the unadulterated version of the *Rous Roll*.[53] But what was the quality of his justice? Was it anything more than a machiavellian exercise in pious hypocrisy? In the last two decades of the fifteenth century the Plumpton family at least would not have subscribed to such a view. Recent scholarship has emphasized the growing importance of the crown's arbitration in serious disputes as a means of keeping peace and order during the later Middle Ages.[54] It was in this spirit that Richard and his administration arbitrated in a major dispute concerning the Plumpton inheritance in Yorkshire.[55] It was to be one of his last acts before the untoward and disastrous events of the Buckingham Revolt and its aftermath distracted the rest of the reign. In the preamble to this judgement of 16 September 1483 the new king set out his motives and due process:

> We, intending rest, peace and quiet amongst our liege people and subjects have taken upon us the business and labour in that behalf and replete with good deliberation have heard and examined the interests and title of the said parties in the premises by the advice of our Lords of our Council and of our judges thereunto called.[56]

In the event such justice was done that the Plumptons abided by the arbitration for a considerable period of years. It was to be overturned in his own selfish interests by Henry VII, described in this context as 'a monarch who under the pretence of a rigid enforcement of the law sought only the means to glorify his avarice'.[57]

As the rebellion of October 1483 revealed so early in the reign, Richard III's task was to defend not only his subjects but the crown itself. He was from the beginning only too well aware of the potential dangers of the king's relationship with the 'overmighty' magnates of the realm. In the considered judgment of his own Chief Justice, the aristocracy were a law unto themselves.[58] By 1483 they constituted a relatively small class, whose individual power and influence was augmented by extensive kinship connections within and beyond their peer group. The dynastic conflicts of the fifteenth century created a propensity to ally in rebellion or conspiracy and to take sides for reasons of self-interest and inter-family rivalry. In addition to the powerful relations of Edward IV's queen Elizabeth

---

53   *The Rous Roll*, no. 63.
54   E. Powell, 'Arbitration and the Law in Medieval England', *Trans. R. Hist. Soc.*, 5th ser., 33 (1983), 49-68. See also *Henry V, The Practice of Kingship*, ed. by G. L. Harriss (Oxford, 1985), pp. 59-60.
55   *Plumpton Correspondence*, ed. by T. Stapleton, Camden Sociey (London, 1839), pp. lxxxix-xcvi.
56   Ibid., p. xc.
57   Ibid., p. xcvi.
58   *Les reportes des cases*, 11 vols in 8 (London, 1678-80), XI, p. 13.

Woodville, the other magnate families, the Staffords, the Bourchiers, the Stanleys, the Nevills, the Percies, the de la Poles and the Tudors were all connected by blood, marriage, or both, to the royal dynasties of Lancaster and York.

Richard III manifestly lacked the Tudor asset of dynastic remoteness.[59] He lived in a world of kinsmen endowed with near-royal dignities and aspirations. Against this he could only maintain the security of the throne and the tranquillity of the realm by offering successful 'good lordship'. This meant arbitrating in their quarrels, supporting their rights and titles to inheritances and dignities, above all using crown patronage to reward their often suspect loyalty. Like his brother Edward, Richard sought to counteract the near-regal dignity of his aristocracy by emphasizing the superior role of monarchy. The splendour and aloofness of a Renaissance prince was predicated upon the honourable service of his nobility to the royal estate. In this respect there was a strong sense of continuity between the policies of the two Yorkist brothers, particularly on the occasions of the investiture of their respective sons as Princes of Wales. The spirit which motivated such glittering ceremonial as that of September 1483 at York is clearly set out in the preambles to documents relating to it. The patent bestowing knighthood upon the Spanish Ambassador relates:

> Since it is the office of princes and kings befitting their rank and magnificence to show munificence and liberality and to adorn with honours those who serve them faithfully or desire to serve them ...[60]

The exalted ideal of the king as an inexhaustible fount of patronage to those nobles who serve him is most vividly expressed in the document of investiture itself.[61]

With such high ideals and expectations and with such a laudable 'manifesto' to prosper the realm and enhance the dignity of kingship why was the failure of King Richard III so swift and tragic? The orthodox and traditional explanation – the moral reaction of his subjects to the murder of the Princes[62] – begs too many questions. Despite the great mystery that surrounded their disappearance it is astonishing how quickly and completely the veil was drawn across their fate.[63] The accusations, lurid details and the culprits were for the most part a product of Tudor historiography or of

[59] M. L. Bush, 'The Tudors and the Royal Race', *History*, 55, no. 183 (1970), 37-48.
[60] *Harl. 433*, I, 1-2.
[61] Ibid., I, 2-3.
[62] Ross, *Richard III*, p. 94 and passim.
[63] P. M. Kendall, *Richard the Third* (London, 1955), pp. 398-406. See also Chrimes, *Henry VII*, p. 93, for the dubious nature of Sir James Tyrell's 'confession' of 1502, '... a confession which was calculated to lay the ghosts of the princes in the Tower for ever... the only real attempt to actually achieve this end, almost twenty years after the event'.

hostile continental rumour.[64] There appears to have been no concerted effort by Henry VII to ascertain their fate.[65] It was a brutal age which consumed many victims. The disappearance of the Princes only assumed a relevance to the fall of Richard III after Bosworth. Then it became a convenient alibi for those magnates who had acquiesced in the usurpation for their own ends and two years later brought down a second liege lord for the same selfish purpose. Indeed the whole episode is most plausibly seen as a casuistic cover story for sordid acts of treachery that brought down an expendable royal dynasty, cobbled up by those hard men who did rather well out of the process. To find a true historical parallel for the fall of Richard III one is forced back to the first half of the twelfth century and the time of King Stephen, another king bought and sold by the forces of treacherous self-interest in the last years of his reign.[66]

The Buckingham Revolt, tenuously linked to a Tudor sub-plot, the connection with which has still to be made, was motivated by a trimmer's instinct for the elusive benefits of the reversionary interest.[67] Had Henry Stafford succeeded in October 1483, what might have been the fate of Henry Tudor? K. B. McFarlane has described the Staffords as a race of trimmers.[68] Their royal lineage elevated their ambitions far beyond that. It was the fall of Buckingham which opened up the prospects of a successful Tudor conspiracy although it was in the interests of the new dynasty and its propagandists to put their particular cart before the horse.

It has been suggested that Richard should have brought these shifty rebels and conspirators to a decisive battle in the autumn of 1483.[69] What prospects were there for such a fight? The two major factions, the Staffords and the Stanleys, were both ancient enemies and devious trimmers; the Courtenays were a forlorn and spent force; Henry of Richmond was a fragile pawn to continental interests. Nor were the Woodvilles a fighting race.[70] In the event, the king was faced with unco-ordinated outbreaks of armed defiance and wet and dispirited Welshmen.[71] The resistance was so contemptible as not to merit the expense of keeping an army together for any length of time.[72]

---

[64] Chrimes, *Henry VII*, p. 33, n. 2. See for example the lurid and detailed account of John Rastell's *The Chronicles...* (1529) (London, 1877), pp. 292-93.

[65] See note 63 above.

[66] See D. Crouch, *The Beaumont Twins* (Cambridge, 1986), pp. 86 ff.

[67] K. B. McFarlane, *The Nobility of Later Medieval England* (Oxford, 1973), p. 212.

[68] Ibid.

[69] R. Horrox, *Richard III* (Cambridge, 1989) p. 324.

[70] There is scant evidence of their personal 'involvement' in the so called Buckingham Revolt (ibid., pp. 138-77).

[71] Ibid.

[72] *Crowland*, p. 495.

How could Richard III, as conventional historical wisdom would have us believe, have over-reacted to this pathetic outburst of faction? Did he really go to the lengths of plantations whereby his southern subjects were subject to the tyranny of the king's northern supporters?[73] Or was it just another example of the Crowland Chronicle's paranoia against the North?[74] Such a policy is supported by little convincing evidence, nor does it make much *a priori* sense. The fact is Richard needed his northern supporters where they were, that is in the North defending the Marches against Scotland. The Huddlestons of Millom, for example, were to acquire in the aftermath of the revolt a receivership, a master forestship, two porterships, three stewardships, four constableships and annuities worth some 170 marks.[75] The purpose of these grants was not to set the family up as prosperous southern gentlemen but to sustain their vital and continuing role in the defence of the West March. Richard III's most famous northern supporter, Sir Richard Radcliffe, was granted lands worth £666 from the earldom of Devon for the same purpose.[76] The king clearly intended others to remain central to the defence of the North, for in 1484 Lord Dacre received £200 from the revenues of the Duchy of Cornwall to support his Lieutenancy of Carlisle.[77] The most plausible interpretation of Harleian 433 and other evidence of this period is that Richard was moving resources north and not warriors south. He was using his windfall in a sensible way.

Indeed, throughout the post-Buckingham reign the king kept his cool. He dealt harshly with the ringleaders but mercifully with the lesser men. His commissions of array and of the peace, along with his other appointments, show that he continued to trust local men throughout his southern counties while using a small number of Northerners to fill obvious gaps, most likely as a temporary measure.[78] In fact Harleian 433 reveals not his inept ruthlessness but a diminishing pool of trustworthy supporters.[79] It is hard to blame the king for this situation. He did all the correct things, he was merciful, generous and trusting, and was repaid in the event by a continuous situation of Tudor-inspired propaganda and subversion with sporadic

[73] A. J. Pollard, 'The Tyranny of Richard III', *Journal of Medieval History*, 3 (1977), 147-65.

[74] *Crowland*, p. 496.

[75] *Harl. 433*, I, 153, 178, 201, 222; *Calendar of Patent Rolls 1476-85* (London, 1901), pp. 363, 369, 372, 379, 448.

[76] *Calendar of Patent Rolls 1476-85*, p. 472; *Harl. 433*, I, 233, II, 152, 160.

[77] *Harl. 433*, II, 136.

[78] Horrox, *Richard III*, p. 198.

[79] Supporting the Tudor 'war of words' set out in Collingbourne's subversive lines recorded in *The Great Chronicle of London*, ed. by A. H. Thomas and I. D. Thornley (London, 1938), pp. 235-36.

outbursts of minor insurrection.[80] Worst still, he was subject to the sullen neutrality of those he thought he could rely upon. It was like a modern run on the pound. All this culminated in the notorious treachery of August 1485. Such treachery, as the Crowland Chronicle tells us, was inherent in the progressive uncertainties and kaleidoscopic realignments of this last stage of the Wars of the Roses.[81] Yet even in such uncertain times, individuals cannot escape blame. Treachery lies in men's hearts; it is a canker that destroys political and social cohesion and stability. No king can be blamed for the moral turpitude and political trimming of his liege men. Some, like the Howards, knew where their loyalty lay, too many others prevaricated or worse. William Herbert, earl of Huntingdon, allowed the invading army an unopposed march across Wales.[82] Henry Percy, earl of Northumberland, came reluctantly to Bosworth and did not fight.[83] William Berkeley, earl of Nottingham, proved no better. In the succinct words of the Berkeley family historian he 'gave money to one side, men to the other and his person to neither'.[84]

The Stanleys were of course the most notorious trimmers of all. On that fatal day, 22 August 1485, Lord Thomas surveyed the scene with a king in either palm before deciding at the eleventh hour which one his brother Sir William Stanley was to crush.[85] This deep treachery is recorded for ever in the chilling words of the will of William Catesby on the eve of his execution a few days later at Leicester:

> My Lord Stanley, Strange and all that blood help and pray for my soul as ye have not my body as I trusted in you.[86]

He need not have worried, for the trimming and treason of that family on that day was still remembered by Charles I's advisers some hundred and fifty years later at the beginning of the English Civil War.[87]

The events of Richard's short reign that had begun with such promise and prospects reflect not tragedy and ineptitude but a collective treachery and a king's active, intelligent and measured response to it. In the event there was

---

[80] See I. Arthurson and N. Kingwell, 'The Proclamation of Henry Tudor as King of England...' Historical Research, 63 (1990), 100-06.

[81] Crowland, pp. 506-07; see also p. 474.

[82] Chrimes, Henry VII, pp. 16-17; R. Horrox, 'Henry Tudor's Letters to England during Richard III's reign', The Ricardian, no. 80 (1983), pp. 155-58.

[83] D. T. Williams, The Battle of Bosworth (Leicester, 1973), p. 17.

[84] J. Smyth, Lives of the Berkeleys, ed. by J. Maclean, 3 vols (Gloucester, 1883-95), II, 117-29.

[85] Williams, Battle of Bosworth, pp. 17-19.

[86] London, Public Record Office, Prob. 11/7 (Register Logg), fol. 15.

[87] J. Seacome, Memoirs; containing a genealogical and historical account of the ancient and honourable house of Stanley from the Conquest to the death of James, late Earl of Derby in the year 1735... (Liverpool, 1741), p. 78.

too much for any mortal man to deal with. If historians have come to accept that the failures of Richard II were due in large part to the treacherous kinsmen and nobles who surrounded him,[88] why cannot the same just and compassionate verdict apply equally to the reign of Richard III? Somewhat surprising in the context of 'the child king', Richard II was the same age on his death in 1400 as Richard III was on his in 1485. They were both barely thirty-two.

[88] H. F. Hutchinson, *The Hollow Crown* (London, 1967), p. 238; C. M. Barron, 'The Tyranny of Richard II', *Bull. of the Inst. of Historical Research*, 41 (1968), 1-18; J. A. F. Thomson, *The Transformation of Medieval England* (London, 1983), pp. 153-54, 164-65.

Medieval Indebtedness: The Regions versus London
J. I. KERMODE

In 1394, a collection of goods was delivered in the York mayor's court by one John Middleton of York to the servant of a dead London merchant, Hugh Rose. The goods comprised 5s. in coin, two cloaks, a mantle, a coverlet and blanket, four bonds, one acquittance and 34 *lbs*. of onion seed. We know nothing of any prior business or other arrangement, but these suggest the possessions of a merchant working away from home, and it may be that Middleton was either the host or partner of Rose.[1] The quantity of onion seed might surprise us, but the bonds and acquittance are of greater interest, drawing us into the complicated world of debt and credit: the financial system which powered medieval trade before the age of banking.

From simply pawning goods for cash,[2] through deferring payment for sales, to drawing up legal documents,[3] credit played a crucial role in medieval life. There is no dispute about that. There is, though, some debate over quite what changing patterns of credit reflected. Did the use of credit rise or fall with the money supply? What was the cause and the effect of the bullion famine of the late fourteenth and early fifteenth centuries? Did it lead to a contraction in credit? The monetarist explanation emphasized the loss of coin and specie draining out of the north through a growing trade imbalance towards the Mediterranean and the Middle East as an important cause of the recession which affected northern Europe in the fifteenth century.[4] To this

---

1   *York Memorandum Book*, II, ed. by M. Sellars, *Surtees Society*, 125 (1915), p. 13.

2   e.g. in January 1515 four appraisers were appointed by the Chester sheriffs to value a quantity of iron of the goods of John Smythe, taken in pawn by Sir William Stanley (Chester City R.O., Sheriffs' Book 5, fol. 157). Valuations of items such as horses, clothing, silver and goldware, household furnishings and so forth were a regular feature of the sheriffs' business. They were often the chattels of a deceased person, presumably being valued to settle debts, while other valuations were of goods pawned *inter vivos* as part of a credit agreement (ibid., fols 38v, 40-41, 72, 157-58, 180v, 182-83). See M. K. McKintosh, 'Money Lending on the Periphery of London, 1300-1600', *Albion*, 20 (1988), p. 565.

3   M. M. Postan, 'Credit in Medieval Trade', and 'Private Financial Instruments in Medieval England', reprinted in idem, *Medieval Trade and Finance* (Cambridge, 1973).

4   J. Day, 'The Great Bullion Famine of the Fifteenth Century', *Past & Present*, 79 (1978), 3-54; idem, 'Crises and Trends in the Late Middle Ages', in his *The Medieval Market Economy* (Oxford, 1987), pp. 185-224; J. H. Munro, 'Monetary Contraction and Industrial Change in the Late-Medieval Low Countries, 1335-1500', in *Coinage in the Low Countries, 880-1500*, ed. by N. J. Mayhew, B.A.R., 54 (Oxford, 1979), pp. 95-137; J. H. Munro, 'Bullion Flows and Monetary Contraction in Late-Medieval England and the Low Countries', in

we must add the long-term effects of the Black Death on consumers, and in England, the decline in the wool trade in particular, which reduced imports of coin and bullion into England and depressed mint output.[5] Wool exports and bullion supply fell together through the late 1390s, reaching a nadir in the first decade of the fifteenth century. But what happened to credit, the money of account supply? Was it inevitably tied to cash supply or to trade?

Much that is claimed for medieval England is only evidence for London and the south-east.[6] For historians of provincial England, the experience of London's economy cannot be assumed to be the national pattern, and indeed London's ultimate dominion at the expense of the provinces should not be anticipated either. The late fourteenth and early fifteenth centuries mark a critical period in the transformation of England's economy. In the course of fifty years, London emerged as the central place in an expanding hierarchy of towns, drawing to itself a number of key functions including that of financial capital. By the end of the fifteenth century, if not earlier, the demands of London's markets stimulated the regional specialization which was so fundamental to England's subsequent economic development.[7]

One of the processes which assisted London's emergence as commercial capital was the growing sophistication of domestic and overseas trade. Recent research by Elizabeth Bennett and Pamela Nightingale has provided insights into the role of credit in London's commerce.[8] Both describe trends in levels of indebtedness which paralleled trends in overseas trade.[9] Moreover, and more importantly, Bennett can identify a high degree of credit manipulation

---

    Precious Metals in the Later Medieval and Early Modern Worlds, ed. by J. F. Richards (North Carolina, 1983), pp. 97-158; P. Spufford, *Money and its Use in Medieval Europe* (Cambridge, 1988), pp. 340-62.

[5]   J. L. Bolton, *The Medieval English Economy 1150-1500* (1980), p. 298; Day, 'Great Bullion Famine', pp. 17-18; T. H. Lloyd, 'Overseas Trade and the English Money Supply in the Fourteenth Century', in *Edwardian Monetary Affairs (1279-1344)*, ed. by N. J. Mayhew, B.A.R., 36 (Oxford, 1977), pp. 96-124; P. Spufford, 'Calais and its mint: part 1', in Mayhew, *Coinage in the Low Countries*, pp. 171-83.

[6]   e.g. the Phelps Brown and Hopkins prices index, derived from south-east evidence, is often quoted as though it relates to the whole country and almost all of John Day's price and wage figures are derived from southern evidence (Day, 'Crises and Trends').

[7]   F. J. Fisher, 'The Development of the London Food Market, 1540-1640', *Economic History Rev.*, 5 (1935), 46-64. Joan Thirsk describes the high degree of regional specialization already visible in the 16th century in *England's Agricultural Regions and Agrarian History 1500-1750* (London, 1987), pp. 11, 23-33.

[8]   E. Z. Bennett, 'Credit in the Urban Economy: London 1338-1460', Yale Ph.D. thesis (1989); P. Nightingale, 'Monetary Contraction and Mercantile Credit in Later Medieval England', *Economic History Rev.*, 2nd ser. 43 (1990), 560-75.

[9]   Bennett, 'London 1338-1460', p. 241; Nightingale, 'Monetary Contraction', pp. 567-69.

which worked within short and medium term market conditions as individuals adjusted terms of credit.[10]

Long distance trade demanded particular commercial arrangements and these were increasingly focused through London as European trade became increasingly channelled through the marts of the Low Countries. What we do not yet know is how closely London's financial practices were replicated elsewhere, if and how quickly the ripples of London interest rates extended into the provinces, nor how differently affected were the rural producer and the wholesale merchant.[11]

This paper suggests that provincial merchants continued to rely on less sophisticated arrangements and that, in Yorkshire at least, credit was not finely tuned to the changing market, but that such sensitivity, if indeed there was any, may have been limited to London.

The sources on which this discussion is based are the Staple Certificates, C241 in the Public Record Office. These were the orders sent out from chancery, in response to action taken against debtors defaulting on agreements enrolled in local courts which possessed the seal of Statute Merchant or Statute Staple. They are a useful class, therefore, wherein local debts were drawn into central government records. With a few exceptions, the certificates record the names of the parties, size of debt, date and place where it was enrolled, the date it was due and the date the certificate was issued. Extents of debts, the surveys of possessions of debtors, have not been consulted, since they were a consequence of the issuing of the certificate and, although interesting for individual cases, offer no more information on geographical distribution or details on amounts and duration.

Nearly 10,500 certificates were examined, courtesy of a grant from the ESRC (No. R000231782). The overwhelming majority were generated by enrolments in London or Westminster staple courts. A surprisingly small number, fewer than 600, were registered in York and Hull or related to Yorkshire merchants, and this massive imbalance towards London was the pattern for most other counties (see tables 1.1 and 1.2).

Our main findings were as follows:
1. 97 per cent of the Yorkshire actions derived from debts enrolled in York and about 3 per cent enrolled in Hull and Hedon.
2. Indebtedness under statute staple fell by nearly 50 per cent between 1360-69 and 1370-79 and by almost as much again by 1380-89. The numbers continued to fall and dwindled to a trickle after 1430-39. Tables 1.1 and 1.2.

10 Bennett, 'London 1338-1460', pp. 155, 157. Cf. Nightingale, 'Monetary Contraction', pp. 566, 571.
11 Elaine Clarke points out the dramatic fall in the number of pleaded debt suits in the vill of Writtle from the 1430s, initiated by a decade of poor harvests: 'Debt Litigation in a Late Medieval English Vill', in *Pathways to Medieval Peasants*, ed. by J. A. Raftis (Toronto, 1981), pp. 247-69 (p. 250).

3.   The range of sums loaned was large, from £2[12] to £1,000; the median was in the bands £10-£50 and the most commonly loaned sum was £15-£40. There was no pattern of increase or decrease over time. Table 2.1.

4.   The duration of credit ranged from 4 days to 8 years, but 75 per cent was for less than 6 months. There was a slight variation in the median from 3 months in the 1360s to 6 months in the 1370s. Thereafter it remained at 6 months. Table 2.2.

5.   The interval before action was taken to recover the debt varied according to no discernible pattern. The median throughout was 2 – 2½ years. Table 2.3.

6.   Unlike Bennett's findings for London, there was no correlation between any of the three elements during the period 1360-1430, even for 1370-79, a decade with a large number of enrolments. Table 3 and figure. From 1430 the numbers were so small that no correlations were attempted.

7.   The distribution of parties was throughout the northern counties but was concentrated in Yorkshire and north Lincolnshire. Fewer than 5 per cent involved parties outside that region.

8.   Gentry, clerics and heads of religious houses regularly appeared, but were always a minority. The majority were townsfolk, merchants, mercers, victuallers and a few craftsmen: goldsmiths and bowyers. The majority of the townsfolk lived in York. Table 4.1.

9.   The majority of creditors were townsfolk and their loans outside the town always exceeded the next largest category, that is loans between townsfolk. Table 4.2.

10. At a national level, the majority of debts pursued under statute staple involved debts enrolled in London and Westminster. The second largest group were enrolled in Devon and Cornwall with a significant number enrolled in Kent and Sussex, Oxfordshire, Norfolk and Suffolk, Northamptonshire, Warwickshire and Bristol. Table 1.1.

Comparing the trends in indebtedness between London and Yorkshire, the following points emerge. There were fewer actions taken against defaulting debtors *c*.1400 in both Yorkshire and London. Bennett identifies the 1430s as the time of greatest decline within the period 1390-1460. Nightingale pinpoints the late 1390s and early 1400s[13] and argues that the amount of unpaid debt generally constituted 20 per cent of all debt and

---

12   Following divisions established by the Statute of Gloucester (1278), the 40s. ceiling for debt-detinue actions in local courts was commonly observed from the early fourteenth century: J. S. Beckerman, 'The Forty-Shilling Jurisdictional Limit in Medieval Personal Actions', *Legal History Studies 1972*, ed. D. Jenkins (Cardiff, 1975), pp. 110-17; S. F. C. Milsom, *Historical Foundations of the Common Law* (London, 2nd edn, 1981), p. 245.

13   Bennett, 'London 1338-1460', p. 183; Nightingale, 'Monetary Contraction', p. 567.

declined as coin became increasingly short during the late 1390s. She argues further that the London grocers reacted by reducing the amount of money loaned.[14] Bennett has concluded that there was a positive correlation between the amount and length of loans and concludes that the larger a debt the shorter the credit allowed. During the 1430s the loans were offered for longer periods and the lapse before litigation began also lengthened.[15]

In Yorkshire the marked drop in the numbers of actions brought to recover unpaid debts occurred in the 1370s, slightly earlier than in London, and there was never a return to earlier levels.[16] In addition there were other similarities between the characteristics of debts enrolled in London and Yorkshire. The most common size of loan was the same, that is £15-£40, and the majority were for periods of up to six months.[17]

However, in certain important respects, the evidence suggests that Yorkshire differed from Bennett's analysis of London. There is no correlation between the amount and length of loans, nor indeed between the amount and/or duration of loans and the time which elapsed before litigation was begun. (See figure 1 for 1370; a similar result was obtained for each decade.) There was no sensitive response to the shortage of bullion or trade recession visible in adjustments to credit arrangements as is claimed for London. It is remarkable, for instance, how the same holy days continued to be chosen as terminal dates for loans throughout the 140 years examined. In order of preference, Easter, Michaelmas, Pentecost, Martinmas, Christmas, the Purification of the Virgin, the Birth of John the Baptist, and the feast of St Peter in Chains were chosen in over 80 per cent of the transactions. It is difficult to ignore the conclusion that many parties agreed on the most easily remembered days, and that that controlled the extent of their finely tuned financial response.[18] The choice of Pentecost, Martinmas and St Peter in Chains could have been of special significance in Yorkshire. There were fairs held in York at those feasts,[19] and the local and regional cycle of fairs very likely determined the duration of loans.

14 Nightingale, 'Monetary Contraction', pp. 566, 569, 571.
15 Bennett, 'London 1338-1460', pp. 155-57.
16 Cf. the pattern in Colchester local courts where actions peaked in the 1380s and 1390s, began to fall in the 1420s, and by the 1490s were at only half their 1390s level (R. H. Britnell, *Growth and Decline in Colchester, 1300-1525* (Cambridge, 1984), p. 207).
17 Periods up to six months were the standard in Havering (McKintosh, 'Periphery of London', p. 562).
18 Bennett, 'London 1338-1460', p. 154, noted the Nativity of St John the Baptist, St Michael Archangel, Easter, Christmas, Pentecost, the Purification, and All Saints' Day as dates on which the majority of London staple debts fell due.
19 P. Tillott, in *Victoria County History of the City of York* (London, 1961), pp. 489-91.

Most debts were for sums between £15-£40 and, as in London (and Colchester),[20] there is no indication that the size of debts fluctuated from one decade to another. There was always a significant number for large sums over £100, which are indicated in table 2.1. Large loans continued to be made even during the worst years of the bullion famine. Furthermore, there were very few 'broken' sums, i.e. for shillings and pence, but most were 'rounded' sums which strongly suggests that these debts were negotiated loans or recognizances, which established financial conditions to enforce some other action such as the transfer of land, or non-harassment.[21] Debts enrolled in Hull usually indicated in the certificate that these were loans. Unfortunately there is little direct evidence of interest charged on loans to compare with Richard Helmholz's calculated mean rate of 16.6 per cent on 12 month loans, and 10 per cent on 6 month loans.[22] Hugh Trevor-Roper estimated that sixteenth-century recognizances represented a figure just under twice that actually borrowed and the borrower had to pay the larger sum if he paid late.[23] It is likely that 'rounded' sums represent the principal and interest combined.

There is no discernible pattern in the length of time creditors waited before initiating litigation. The majority commenced within 6 months, some within days, and some soon after the first of several instalments was late.[24] It is clear that in some instances, heirs and executors, in taking stock, decided to try to recover debts which might have fallen due many years previously and acted against several debtors simultaneously.[25] Lapses of over 10 years were not uncommon and in one instance proceedings were begun 61 years after

20 Bennett, 'London 1338-1460', pp. 152-53. In Colchester the size of debt claims remained unaltered until the end of the 15th century when the number over £2 fell between 1482 and 1525, as the number below £1 increased (Britnell, *Colchester*, p. 208).

21 e.g. in some of the few debts pursued under Statute Staple in the mayor's Portmote court in the city of Chester recognizances were registered in 1546 to enforce a conveyance, unmolested occupancy, and payment of a smaller debt (Chester City R.O. MR 112, fols 5v, 6v, 7v).

22 R. H. Helmholz, 'Usury and the Church Courts', *Speculum*, 61 (1986), pp. 373-74. 16 of 22 loans were at rates of 10% to 35% between 1373 and 1515. These estimates were produced by M. K. McKintosh, 'Periphery of London', p. 563.

23 H. Trevor-Roper, 'The Elizabethan Aristocracy: an Anatomy Anatomized', *Economic History Rev.*, 2nd ser., 3 (1951), 279-98 (p. 284).

24 On 20 January 1387 Brian de Stapleton, knight, began an action against John Fairfax, clerk, to recover a total debt of £100 which had been agreed on 27 June 1386. It was to be paid in 5 equal instalments over two years, commencing on 11 November that year, but when the debtor defaulted on the first payment, Stapleton sought litigation (P.R.O. C241/175/86).

25 See Clarke, 'Debt Litigation in a Late Medieval Vill', pp. 247-79, for a rush to call in debts triggered by a cash-flow crisis.

repayment fell due.[26] Such debts cannot be regarded as more than personal defaults and certainly not as part of anyone's financial strategy.

While many familiar Yorkshire merchants appear in the certificates, it is clear that people from a range of occupations and levels in society had recourse to credit. Clergymen,[27] gentlemen, craftsmen not normally associated with long-distance trade appeared alongside mercers, merchants, victuallers, goldsmiths and bowyers (see table 4). This suggests that there was an economic surplus available from time to time, looking for investment opportunities, and in this way other resources such as annuities, rents, and land were converted into working capital.[28] The archbishop, the dean and chapter of the Minster, St Mary's Abbey and St Leonard's Hospital in York made loans, as did the bishop of Durham, the abbots of Meaux and Jervaulx, and the priors of Haltemprice, Kirkstall and Nostell. The majority of these Statute Staple loans had been agreed before 1404,[29] but from patent roll evidence it is clear that Yorkshire houses continued to pursue debtors through the royal chancery well into the fifteenth century.[30] It is difficult to evaluate cases of debt involving high-status clerics, since it not clear if they were acting for themselves or on behalf of their institutions.[31] The number of

26 On 7 June 1402 Katherine de Nutyll, executrix of Emma de Sutton, began an action to recover a debt of £100 which had been registered in Hull on 15 September 1341 (P.R.O. C241/193/7).

27 See B. A. Holderness, 'The Clergy as Money-lenders in England, 1550-1700', in *Princes and Paupers in the English Church 1500-1800*, ed. by R. O'Day and F. Heal (Leicester, 1981), pp. 195-209, where she cites several examples of medieval clerics lending, p. 208, n. 4.

28 J. I. Kermode, 'Money and Credit in the Fifteenth Century: Some Lessons from Yorkshire', *Business History Rev.*, 65, no. 3 (1991), 475-501.

29 Archbishop, C241/151/139; Minster, C241/158/62, 194/59; St Mary's Abbey, C241/149/67, 173/86, 184/34, 190/197; St Leonard's Hospital, C241/144/19, 173/23; Bishop of Durham, C241/188/102; Haltemprice, C241/155/36, as debtor 157/63; Jervaulx, C241/140/66; Kirkstall, C241/151/48; Meaux, C241/143/97; Nostell, C241/157/179.

30 *Cal. Pat. Rolls, 1413-16*, pp. 80, 83; *1416-22*, p. 93; *1422-29*, p. 367; *1429-36*, pp. 13, 17, 166, 228, 237, 430; *1436-41*, p. 111; *1441-46*, pp. 14, 16, 116, 120, 385; *1446-52*, p. 289.

31 There is evidence in the Close Rolls that clerics did act individually. Up to 1384, the evidence is clear: actions were in pursuit of debts. Thereafter actions were increasingly for the execution of recognizances, the majority of which were for such large sums, £20-1,000 marks, as to suggest they were conditional bonds. In the 1350s-1380s, though, a number of clerks regularly appeared in the Close Rolls as creditors in Yorkshire debts. E.g. *Cal. Close Rolls, 1349-54*, pp. 92, 203, 276, 350, 365, 382, 386, 398, 479, 597, 611; *1354-60*, pp. 60, 68, 107, 183, 204, 211, 223, 226, 304, 306, 328, 330, 332, 394, 399, 400, 409, 419, 492, 499, 503, 514, 516, 518; *1360-64*, pp. 291, 300, 423, 516, 553; *1364-68*, pp. 83, 269, 272, 394; *1369-74*, p. 95; *1374-77*, pp. 212, 544; *1377-81*, pp. 323, 478, 485; *1381-85*, p. 328; *1385-89*, pp.

knights appearing as debtors and as creditors might reflect their dealings in wool, but the sums involved were not generally large, and although their numbers fell as the wool trade contracted, so did all actions.

One characteristic of late medieval trade was the practice of individuals to move in and out of short-term partnerships, often for a single venture. These were not the same as the syndicates which emerged during the 1330s and 40s, but were probably convenient arrangements whereby one or a group of creditors invested capital or stood as financial surety for a business venture. The registering of such partnerships may have been the reason for registering some debts in the staple courts, and it is not at all uncommon to find a loan advanced by two, three or more men either to an individual or, indeed, to a group of debtors.[32] What is less clear is the nature of such groups which included one cleric. These may well have been trustees cited as creditors or debtors.

Few transactions involving debtors or creditors outside Yorkshire and North Lincolnshire were recorded in the Yorkshire enrolled certificates. As table 4.2 shows, the majority of transactions were between York, Beverley, and Hull and outsiders, with York loans accounting for the largest group and debts/loans within the towns accounting for the next largest group.[33] This evidence, taken together with the probability that local fairs were used to set dates on loans, gives a clear indication of the regional pattern of finance. It was a surprise to find that few of the debts/loans involved Londoners, since other evidence suggests they were active as traders in the North.[34] Only eleven Londoners appear in the certificates for debts enrolled in Yorkshire (7

248, 476, 603. The most notable were David Wollore (or possibly Tout's Wooler?), prebendary of Fridaythorpe, in St Peter's York (*Cal. Close Rolls, 1354-60*, p. 304), Richard de Ravenser and Richard Thoresby. Both the latter served as Keeper of the Hanaper, and Thoresby was a canon of Beverley. J. L. Grassi, 'Royal Clerks from the Archdiocese of York in the Fourteenth Century', *Northern History*, 5 (1970), 12-33 (25-26); A. Hamilton Thompson, 'Registers of the Archdeacons of Richmond', *Yorks. Arch. Jnl*, 25 (1919), 257-60; T. F. Tout, *Chapters in the Administrative History of Medieval England*, III (Manchester, 1928), p. 215.

32 e.g. in 1406 Laurence Tutbury, merchant of Hull, owed £34 13s.4d. to three men including a merchant from York and one from Beverley (C241/200/6).

33 Richard Britnell found that between 1398 and 1401 only about 6% of creditors and 6.5% of debtors acting alone originated from outside Colchester (Britnell, *Colchester*, pp. 106-07).

34 J. I. Kermode, 'Merchants, Overseas Trade, and Urban Decline: York, Beverley and Hull c.1380-1500', *Northern History*, 23 (1987), 51-73. This argument is based on the declining trade of northern towns from the 1430s and on a scatter of evidence such as London items for sale in northern shops, home counties' butchers in sanctuary in Beverley, Londoners' ownership of property in northern towns, and their continued appearance in debt actions.

between 1482 and 1502 as creditors to Yorkshire gentry). All were creditors and the majority were drapers.[35] Elizabeth Bennett's analysis of London enrolled debts identified only 23 Yorkshire debtors and 3 Yorkshire creditors (including 10 from York and 1 from Beverley) between 1380 and 1460. Overall she identified 18 from Lincolnshire, 6 from Northumberland and Durham and 4 from Lancashire and Cheshire.[36]

Staple registered debts reflect a different level of business from local court debts, even those of regional centres such as Chester, Colchester and Exeter, where most debts were for less than £1 compared with the London average of £14 for the mayor's court and £70 for the sheriffs' court.[37] It is not always clear in local court rolls whether debts resulted from breaches of contract, actions to recover rents, or straight credit agreements. The Chester and Colchester debts were highly localized, over 90 per cent of actions involving local residents and deriving from rent arrears, breaches of contract, and small loans. Exeter debts covered a wider geographical area and frequently resulted from wholesale trade. Local court evidence then seems to support the distribution of staple indebtedness in table 1.1, suggesting greater activity within rather than between regions. Similarly, though Londoners were the major group enrolling debts under statute staple, it seems that these were confined to its hinterland, with 69 per cent of London certificates involving debtors from London, and from the home counties: Bedfordshire, Berkshire, Buckinghamshire, Essex, Hertfordshire, Kent, Middlesex, Surrey, and Sussex.[38]

Several questions remain unanswered. We still have no way of knowing how closely the numbers of defaulters reflected the total number of debts registered via staple certificates since these only record action taken against defaulting debtors and are the only records which have survived in great numbers. Dr Nightingale's recent estimate of a constant 20 per cent offers a credible ratio,[39] but we need to know how popular enrolling debts in the staple courts was and how widespread other forms of credit arrangements were[40] before we rely too heavily on staple certificates as indicators of provincial indebtedness.

[35]   C241/182/8, 194/38, 254/11, 141, 266/32, 268/30, 270/15, 275/177, 179, 262.
[36]   Bennett, 'London 1338-1460', p. 162.
[37]   Britnell, *Colchester*, pp. 101-06, 208; M. Kowaleski, 'The Commercial Dominance of a Medieval Provincial Oligarchy: Exeter in the Late Fourteenth Century', *Medieval Studies*, 46 (1984), 370-74. Research on Chester is in progress and I am grateful to Dr Jane Laughton for information on the 15th century which confirms my analysis of Pentice Court Rolls covering the period after 1500. Bennett, 'London 1338-1460', p. 150.
[38]   Bennett, 'London 1338-1460', pp. 162-64.
[39]   Nightingale, 'Monetary Contraction', p. 566.
[40]   Hubert Hall was sceptical that research would reveal an overwhelming preference

Whatever the supply of coins within the economy, contracting trade removed both an important agency for credit as well as the necessity to employ credit. Just as the decline in staple certificates follows the decline in mint yields, so it follows a decline in England's exports, and in particular exports of wool. The wool trade was a key generator of credit and importer of bullion. The ripple effect of the contraction in wool exports might have imposed limits on credit further down the commercial process, but that has yet to be examined. Relying on staple certificates to answer that question may be misguided.

On the evidence for Yorkshire, and the small numbers of certificates from known wool-producing counties such as Gloucester, Lincoln, Oxford and Wiltshire, it seems likely that other forms of credit were more common there than staple registered loans. We are probably safe in concluding that Londoners' increasing share of defaulting staple enrolled debts, in addition to their use of city courts,[41] was as much a reflection of the rapid expansion of their business as it was their preference. Alternatively it may have reflected the tighter margins that Londoners worked within, which plunged more of them into defaulting.

Commercial life in the metropolis was moving on to a significantly greater and more sophisticated scale. If there was fine-tuning employed by Londoners, it reflected their closer connections with European financial networks through Italian bankers and their closer proximity to international marts in the Low Countries.[42] Provincial merchants, meanwhile, were left with other financial arrangements adequate for the contracting geographical range of their business and their diminishing share in overseas trade.[43]

From this time on, one could argue that provincial came to mean marginal, not just because London emerged as a true metropolis but because, with the increasing integration of the European economy, the margins

---

for registering under statute staple (*Select Cases Concerning the Law Merchant*, III, Selden Society, 49 (London, 1932), p. xii).

[41] Bennett, 'London 1338-1460', pp. 138-51. See also *Calendar of Select Pleas and Memoranda Rolls. City of London*, ed. by A. H. Thomas, esp. *1323-64* (Cambridge, 1926), and *1413-37* (Cambridge, 1953) for commercial actions in the London courts.

[42] London came to dominate the Company of Merchant Adventurers and successfully excluded provincial merchants from prime sites in the cloth marts, and stopped them electing their own northern governor (*The York Merchant and Merchant Adventurers' Company*, ed. by M. Sellars, *Surtees Society*, 129 (1918), pp. 121-26). For Italian financiers in London see E. B. Fryde, 'Italian Maritime Trade with Medieval England (c.1270-c.1530)', *Recueils de la Société Jean Bodin*, 32 (1974), 322-25. See also P. Spufford, *A Handbook of Medieval Exchange* (London, 1986), p. xxxiii, for London's position vis-à-vis European financial centres.

[43] Kermode, 'Money and Credit', pp. 485-96.

became less important relative to the major continental centres. Provincial merchants had to fight even harder to avoid being left on the periphery of European and even of domestic trade.

Figure 1: The correlation between the amount of debt, duration agreed, and
the time lapsed before action was begun to recover the debt, 1370-79

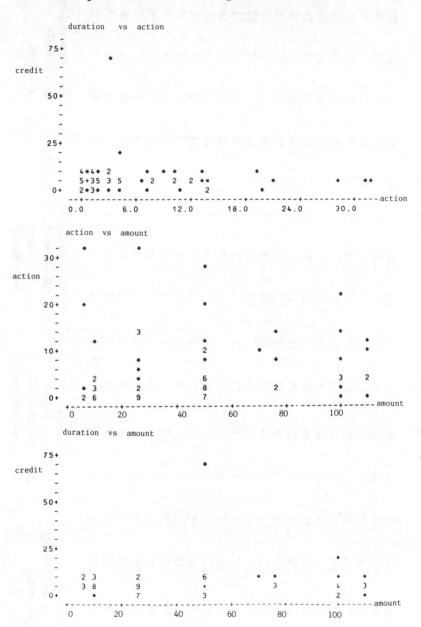

83

Table 1.1 STAPLE CERTIFICATES by 5 years

	total	L	Y	Hu	Br	DC	Hf	Ox	Wa	Sh	Np	Wi	Li	NF	SE	C241/
1360-64	966	339	79	18	52	77	17	31	24	41	8	16	31	116	40	139-44
1365-69	521	161	43	8	14	53	14	15	17	16	14	12	22	64	5	145-49
1370-74	730	386	37	4	38	49	20	10	33	23	14	29	30	71	19	150-55
1375-79	731	313	44	8	50	52	13	13	21	72	17	24	21	71	28	156-62,164
1380-84	667	259	18	3	43	55	16	17	16	10	16	18	14	34	46	163, 165-71
1385-89	737	322	22	6	35	80	8	15	26	10	15	25	13	44	76	172-77
1390-94	624	326	11	4	20	69	11	16	14	10	12	10	18	22	42	178-82
1395-99	600	323	13	5	33	64	6	22	20	4	12	12	5	16	29	183-88
1400-04	545	332	13	3	24	46	4	18	9	4	16	18	5	9	21	189-94
1405-09	409	252	18	4	13	43	3	12	4	6	11	14	4	7	17	194-200
1410-14	281	167	12	1	8	23	2	6	3	4	6	9	3	6	11	201-06
1415-19	240	158	7	0	3	19	2	8	9	3	11	2	0	6	10	207-12
1420-24	204	132	7	1	4	19	0	2	6	4	7	15	2	4	4	213-18
1425-29	192	84	8	0	5	18	0	3	4	0	6	11	0	9	4	219-22
1430-34	175	113	7	3	7	7	0	1	2	1	6	7	5	2	5	223-26
1435-39	190	119	3	1	7	19	0	4	4	1	11	10	3	4	4	227-28
1440-44	165	98	2	1	6	11	0	3	0	0	3	11	2	9	6	229-30
1445-49	112	55	3	0	5	9	0	2	1	1	1	6	0	1	2	231-34
1450-54	192	129	3	3	4	5	0	2	11	0	3	11	2	1	16	235-37
1455-59	89	70	4	0	0	4	0	0	2	0	1	1	0	2	2	238-42
1460-64	330	258	4	1	0	16	0	2	1	0	3	7	0	2	2	243-49

Br – Bristol
DC – Devon and Cornwall
Hf – Herefordshire
Hu – Hull

L – London
Li – Lincolnshire
NF – Norfolk and Suffolk
Np – Northamptonshire

Ox – Oxfordshire
SE – South East (Kent and Sussex)
Sh – Shropshire

Wa – Warwickshire
Wi – Wiltshire
Y – York

84

Table 1.2 STATUTE STAPLE CERTIFICATES C241

Courts in which the debt was first enrolled.
( ) = percentage of the total certificates

	total	London	York		Hull	C241/
1360-69	1,487	500 (33.6)	122	(8)	26 (2)	139-49
1370-79	1,461	699 (48)	81	(5.5)	12 (.8)	150-62,164
1380-89	1,404	581 (41.3)	40	(3)	9 (.6)	163,165-77
1390-99	1,224	649 (53)	24	(2)	9 (.7)	178-88
1400-09	954	484 (51)	31	(3)	7 (.7)	189-200
1410-19	521	325 (63)	19	(3.6)	1 (.1)	201-12
1420-29	492	216 (44)	15	(3)	1 (.2)	213-22
1430-39	365	232 (63.5)	10	(3)	4 (1)	223-28
1440-49	277	153 (55)	5	(2)	1 (.4)	229-34
1450-59	281	199 (71)	7	(2.5)	3 (1)	235-42
1460-69	455		4	(.8)	0	243-52
1470-79	380		10	(2.6)	0	253-60
1480-89	106		2	(2)	0	261-65
1490-99	347		4	(1)	0	266-68

Analysis of Yorkshire Staple Certificates

Table 2.1 AMOUNT of CREDIT

Up to	£5	£10	£25	£50	£75	£100	£100+
1360-69	17	24	31	32	10	10	15
per cent	12	17	22	23	7	7	11
1370-79	8	13	20	22	4	8	5
per cent	10	16	25	28	5	10	6
1380-89	0	7	13	12	1	6	7
per cent	0	15	28	27	2	13	15
1390-99	2	3	6	11	1	3	6
per cent	6	9	19	35	3	9	19
1400-09	3	5	12	10	0	3	5
per cent	8	13	32	26	0	8	13
1410-19	5	0	2	5	3	1	3
per cent	26	0	11	26	16	5	16
1420-29	3	0	1	8	2	2	1
per cent	18	0	6	46	12	12	6
1430-39	1	1	2	2	1	1	1
1440-49	0	2	0	0	2	0	1
1450-59	0	1	0	2	1	0	0
1460-69	0	0	1	1	0	1	0
1470-79	0	1	0	4	2	2	1
1480-89		[blank]					
1490-99	0	0	0	2	0	1	1
1500-05	0	0	0	3	1	0	3

Table 2.2 LENGTH of CREDIT: months

	3	6	9	12	18	24+	total
1360-69	73	33	13	13	4	3	139
per cent	53	24	9	9	3	2	
1370-79	37	24	9	8	1	1	80
per cent	46	30	11	10	1	1	
1380-89	22	12	5	5	0	2	46
per cent	47	27	11	11	0	4	
1390-99	12	15	2	3	1		32
per cent	38	48	5	9			
1400-09	18	8	7	3	1	1	38
per cent	47	21	18	8	3	3	
1410-19	6	6	5	2			19
per cent	31.5	31.5	26	11			
1420-29	6	3	2	6			17
per cent	35	18	12	35			
1430-39	4	1	2	1	1		9
1440-49	0	3	1	0	0	0	5
1450-59	1	1	1	0	3		5
1460-69	1	1	1				3
1470-79	2	2	2	4			10
1480-89	1	1	0	1			2
1490-99	2	2	4				4
1500-05	1	0		1 [1 blank]			7

Table 2.3 ACTION TAKEN within years as percentage

Years	.5	1.5	3	4-5	6-10	10+
1360-69	26	19	14	2	11	28
1370-79	26	21	18	8	10	17
1380-89	33	15	12	18	13	9
1390-99	25	19	31	6	6	13
1400-09	16	15	18	23	13	15
1410-19	50	11	33	0	0	6
1420-29	6	6	24	18	18	28

Table 3 CORRELATIONS

	amount *v* time	amount *v* action	time *v* action
1360-69	0.046	-0.075	0.068
1370-79	0.076	0.070	-0.071
1380-89	0.190	0.060	-0.047
1390-99	-0.209	0.324	-0.233
1400-09	-0.090	0.262	0.009
1410-19	-0.212	0.220	-0.226
1420-29	-0.523	-0.434	0.034
1430-39	0.315	0.612	0.663

Table 4.1 STATUS OF CREDITORS/DEBTORS: Yorkshire

Percentages – those creditors/debtors whose status can be identified, as a percentage of the total number of transactions.

		clergy	knights	townsfolk all	York	Bev.	Hull
1360-69	creditors	13 (9%)	10 (7%)	75 (56%)	60 (43%)	2.5 (2%)	12.5 (9%)
	debtors	1	17 (12%)	18 (13%)	11 (8%)	3 (2%)	4 (3%)
1370-79	creditors	11 (14%)	5 (7%)	41 (51%)	36.5 (46%)	1.5 (2%)	5 (6%)
	debtors	1	9 (11%)	20 (25%)	17 (21%)	2 (3%)	1 (1%)
1380-89	creditors	7 (15%)	6 (13%)	24 (52%)	22 (49%)	1 (2%)	1 (2%)
	debtors	0	19 (41%)	9 (20%)	7 (15%)	0	0
1390-90	creditors	4 (13%)	2 (6%)	17 (53%)	15.5* (48%)	0	1 (3%)
	debtors	2 (6%)	2 (6%)	10 (31%)	7.5 (23%)	2 (6%).	5 (2%)
1400-09	creditors	5 (13%)	2 (6%)	27 (71%)	24 (63%)	0	3 (8%)
	debtors	1 (3%)	2 (6%)	18 (47%)	13 (34%)	1 (2%)	4 (11%)
1410-19	creditors	1 (5%)	1 (5%)	15 (79%)	14 (74%)	0	1 (5%)
	debtors	0	4 (20%)	8 (42%)	6 (32%)	0	2 (11%)

* 0.5 London

Table 4.2 DIRECTION OF DEBT/CREDIT

	YBH creds. to YBH debts	YBH creds.to external debts	Outside creds. to YBH debts
1360-69	24 (17% all)	55 (40% all)	6 (4% all)
1370-79	18 (22% all)	23 (29% all)	2 (3% all)
1380-89	7 (15% all)	17 (38% all)	1 (2% all)
1390-99	6 (16% all)	11 (34% all)	3 (9% all)
1400-09	14 (56% all)	13 (34% all)	2 (5% all)
1410-19	7 (37% all)	8 (42% all)	1 (5% all)

Women in Court:
Some Evidence from Fifteenth-Century Chester
JANE LAUGHTON

As we all know, *cherchez la femme* is now a game which needs must be played by every medieval historian. It is a game which has already been played most successfully by the scholars of a number of English towns, utilizing such evidence as lay subsidy returns, poll tax listings, and probate records.[1] None of these sources is available to the student of late medieval Chester and for this reason the city has long been consigned to the fringes of medieval historiography. This is regrettable since Chester, although never of national importance, did nevertheless serve throughout the Middle Ages as regional capital of the north-western plain and as that area's premier port. It thus exerted considerable influence over a wide hinterland and represented the urban experience for many. It was, quite simply, the largest town for miles around with, in the mid-fifteenth century, a population of perhaps some 3,500.[2] Of these, a majority may well have been female, for it has been suggested that women were numerically predominant in most urban populations.[3] Women were traditionally attracted into towns by the wider employment opportunities on offer there as compared to those available in the countryside. And undoubtedly late medieval Chester, with its bustling markets and fairs, its port and the constant stream of official visitors on palatinate business, did provide a wide range of options to the townswoman. However, as in other medieval towns, women always remained legally, politically and economically subordinate. Indeed, their inferiority in Chester

1   See e.g. P. J. P. Goldberg, 'For Better, for Worse: Marriage and Economic Opportunity for Women in Town and Country', in *Woman is a Worthy Wight: Women in English Society, c.1200-1500*, ed. by P. J. P. Goldberg (Gloucester, 1992), 108-25; P. J. P. Goldberg, *Women, Work and Life Cycle* (Oxford, 1992); M. Kowaleski, 'Women's Work in a Market Town: Exeter in the Late Fourteenth Century', in *Women and Work in Pre-industrial Europe*, ed. by B. A. Hanawalt (Bloomington, 1986), 145-64; C. M. Barron, 'The "Golden Age" of Women in Medieval London', *Reading Medieval Studies*, 15 (1989), 35-58.

2   N. Alldridge, 'The Mechanics of Decline: Migration and Economy in Early Modern Chester', in *English Towns in Decline*, ed. by M. Reed (Leicester, 1986), p. 29, n. 23; C. Phythian-Adams, *Desolation of a City: Coventry and the Urban Crisis of the Late Middle Ages* (Cambridge, 1979), p. 12.

3   M. Kowaleski and J. M. Bennett, 'Crafts, Gilds and Women in the Middle Ages: Fifty Years after Marian K. Dale', *Signs: Journal of Women in Culture and Society*, 14 (1989), p. 484, n. 29; but see P. J. P. Goldberg, 'The Public and the Private: Women in the Pre-plague Economy', in *Thirteenth-Century England III, Proceedings of the Newcastle upon Tyne Conference 1989*, ed. by P. R. Coss and S. D. Lloyd (Woodbridge, 1991), pp. 84-85.

was particularly marked for there they were totally excluded from the franchise and also from membership of all the craft guilds of the city.[4] They were not, however, denied access to the courts and accordingly it is in the court rolls – that uniquely detailed albeit problematical source – that they ultimately become at least partially visible.[5]

In the late medieval period there were two main courts in Chester, the Portmote which was presided over by the mayor and the Pentice which was the court of the two city sheriffs. The mayor exercised the wider jurisdiction, dealing with crown pleas, and with civic ordinances relating to bread, ale and other victuals, as well as those concerning public order and the regulation of trade. All pleas of real estate were heard in his court as too were cases arising from serious breaches of the peace. Petty police cases, initiated by plaint on an inter-personal basis, and pleas of detinue, contract and debt were the preserve of the sheriffs. The boundaries between the two jurisdictions were not clearly drawn, however, or at least appear confusing to us, since a proportion of minor trespasses were also heard in the Portmote. Possibly this was done by referral from the Pentice court. It has been suggested that the two courts were exercising concurrent jurisdiction, with the only difference being the speed with which matters were determined.[6] Certainly the surviving fifteenth-century Portmote rolls indicate a marked mayoral tendency to procrastinate, whereas the sheriffs got through their business with admirable expediency, often seeming to provide instant justice. As their court sat three times each week and that of the mayor only fortnightly, it is their records which are the more voluminous. For this reason they form the basis of this paper. Moreover, since the sheriffs did not deal with breaches of the assize of bread and ale, the in-built bias of some urban court rolls towards the activities of hucksters and regraters is avoided.[7] Such women did indeed appear in the Pentice court but so too did large numbers of other females and it is therefore probable that the sheriffs' records provide a more

4 For women elsewhere see Kowaleski and Bennett, 'Crafts'.
5 See e.g. Z. Razi, 'The Toronto School's Reconstitution of Medieval Peasant Society: a Critical View', *Past and Present*, 85 (1979), 141-57; L. R. Poos and R. M. Smith, '"Legal Windows onto Historical Populations?" Recent Research on Demography and the Manor Court in Medieval England', *Law and History Review*, 2 (1984), 128-52; Z. Razi, 'The Use of Manorial Court Rolls in Demographic Analysis: a Reconsideration', *Law and History Review*, 3 (1985), 191-200.
6 *Selected Rolls of the Chester City Courts*, ed. by A. Hopkins, *Chetham Society*, 2 (1950), pp. xvi-xxiii. For confusion between jurisdictions in other towns see R. H. Hilton, 'Lords, Burgesses and Hucksters', *Past and Present*, 97 (1982), p. 9; and also M. Kowaleski, 'The History of Urban Families in Medieval England', *Journal of Medieval History*, 14 (1988), pp. 50-51.
7 P. J. P. Goldberg, 'Public and Private', p. 85.

representative sample of the female population than elsewhere. Furthermore, the somewhat humdrum business transacted in the Pentice possibly reflects more faithfully the everyday realities of community life than do the more tabloid headlines detailing serious crime and violence.

Women in Chester, of course, never served as court officials, nor as jurors, but came to court solely as litigants, most frequently in the role of defendant. They could appear in person or appoint an attorney to represent them. It was possible for them to act as personal pledge and thus they apparently enjoyed more responsibility than their counterparts in the country, where manorial courts consistently refused to accept female personal pledges, with the exception of a few widowed heads of households.[8] Nevertheless, women remain seriously under-represented in the court rolls of Chester's sheriffs and it is clear that no more than a fraction of the city's female population ever had reason to come to court. An analysis of the surviving rolls for three civic years (1431-32, 1459-60 and 1489-90) reveals that women were involved in only 21 per cent of all cases and that the actual number of women named never exceeded one hundred. These findings are similar to those recorded for rural communities.[9] It should be stressed, incidentally, that since no more than half the original number of Pentice rolls survive for any one year any figures quoted here are totally inadequate for statistical purposes and are used only to give an impression of scale.

The language of the lawcourt showed a tendency to specify women by their relationship with men, frequently describing them either as daughter, wife or widow of X, or as servant, tenant or – on occasion – as concubine of Y.[10] This marked preference to locate a woman firmly within a known household increased as the century drew to a close, perhaps indicative of the decline in her status which has been charted elsewhere.[11] Certainly, the rolls for 1431-32 contain more entries in which a woman is known by Christian name and surname alone than do the later ones studied and it may be that women in Chester did enjoy greater economic freedom in the early decades of the century. Specifying a woman by the familial relationships from which she drew her social and legal identity also served to underline the importance of the household in the medieval economy. Perhaps it also attested to a certain amount of unease on the part of the authorities when confronted with an unattached female.

8   J. M. Bennett, *Women in the Medieval English Countryside: Gender and Household in Brigstock before the Plague* (Oxford, 1987), p. 154.

9   Ibid., pp. 21-22; Z. Razi, *Life, Marriage and Death in a Medieval Parish: Economy, Society and Demography in Halesowen, 1270-1400* (Cambridge, 1980), p. 25.

10   Chester City Record Office SR 84, m.1 (concubine) and SR 281, m.1 (tenant). All other manuscript citations come from the same source: SR (Sheriffs' Rolls).

11   See e.g. P. J. P. Goldberg, 'Female Labour, Service and Marriage in the Late Medieval Urban North', *Northern History*, 22 (1986), pp. 35-37.

References to daughters are in fact seldom found in the Pentice rolls, suggesting that many young girls quickly left their own home in order to become a servant in that of someone else.[12] References to wives are more numerous, in spite of the practice of the common law of England which merged the legal identity of a woman in that of her husband on marriage.[13] This rendered him liable to answer for her debts and misdeeds and, as a result, wives can sometimes disappear from the legal record, failing to be named either as plaintiff or defendant. Thus two male litigants in a case of trespass conceal two women involved in a brawl, while two men named in a case of debt mask the fact that the loan had been contracted between their respective wives.[14]

Conversely, however, in pleas in which a wife is specifically mentioned, if not always by name – for there is often a significant gap where her Christian name should be – it may be legitimate to conclude that she was personally involved in other aspects of the case. Such pleas accordingly allow us to glimpse man and wife operating as an economic unit, with the family home the base of a working partnership. Wives can be seen in a variety of roles – serving in the shop, making purchases, delivering goods, borrowing and lending money. Wives of leading citizens joined their husbands to rent out property, presumably their own; wives of middling craftsmen sold ale which was surplus to household requirements; wives of the poorer artisans helped with wool-carding and linen-weaving. Thus when widows came to court, as many did (litigation being apparently the inevitable accompaniment of bereavement), they were not necessarily inexperienced and faltering *ingénues*, emerging reluctantly from cloistered seclusion into the harsh reality of court scrutiny. Rather were they continuing, albeit on a more intensive scale, activities they had previously shared with their spouse, activities doubtless jointly planned if not always executed side by side.

For wealthy widows, especially if elderly, it could be a matter of business as usual. Cecilia Wotton is a good example. Her husband had served as mayor of Chester in 1433-34, and for many years they jointly used the Pentice court to recover outstanding debts. After his death, in c.1452, and now glorying in the title *Domina*, she continued to play an active role in the commercial life of the community, possibly concentrating on money-lending rather than trading in commodities, and her 'career' continued until her own death in early 1461.[15] Other oligarchic widows pursued similar paths, but

---

12 Ibid., pp. 22-24.
13 Barron, 'Golden Age', pp. 35-37.
14 See e.g. SR 211, m.1; SR 321, m.1v, SR 366, m.1v.
15 SR 219, m.1; SR 224, m.1; SR 250, m.1; SR 302, m.1v; SR 304, m.1; SR 305, m.1v; SR 311, m.1; SR 312, m.1; SR 314, m.1v; SR 315, m.1v; SR 317, m.1v; SR 325, m.1.

some women of all ranks chose to remarry, often finding a new partner among the colleagues of their late husbands. Thus Margaret, a slater's widow, married David Shingler, while Katherine, widow of the butcher Thomas Pekkow, took another butcher as her husband in 1491.[16] These women probably brought with them into the new partnership expertise, experience and equipment pertaining to the trade; just how free their choice was in the matter must remain an open question. Very poor widows had few options of course, but the Pentice rolls have little to say about them.

The common law of England allowed the married woman who wished to trade separately from her husband the status of *femme sole*. This gave her some independence, for she was able to rent a shop in her own name, for example, and consequently became liable for paying this rent. She also became answerable in all cases prosecuted against her, whether they were debt, detinue, covenant or trespass. In London this practice is believed to date back to the early thirteenth century.[17] There is no such early evidence in Chester although a court roll entry of 1486 claimed that the custom of women trading sole in the city dated back to a time 'beyond which contrary memory did not exist'. In fact, the first explicit reference to *sola mercatrix* in the Chester sources comes only in 1459, although there were several cases in the late 1430s and 1440s in which the outcome apparently depended upon whether the woman was or was not sole at the time of the transaction, with defendants vigorously claiming the existence of a husband and corresponding plaintiffs stoutly denying it.[18] During the closing two decades of the century a minimum of fifty-seven *femmes soles* were active in the city, some of whom made regular appearances in the sheriffs' court, implying an energetic role in the commercial life of the community.

In reality their role was severely limited in scope, confined to one solitary art and that the lowly one of huckster. Chester's *femmes soles* were permitted to deal in bread and ale but little else, as one or two explicit references make clear and as an analysis of their debts confirms.[19] Tapsters rather than brewsters, they obtained their supplies of ale from other townspeople, often members of the ruling élite or their widows; occasionally they acted as middlemen, selling on small quantities to more humble female traders. A sizeable proportion of Chester's cellars apparently served as ale-houses. These emerge in the sources as somewhat rowdy establishments, where men got drunk, indulged in fisticuffs and overturned the barrels and other containers. Possibly some of the surviving stone undercrofts along the four main streets were used as tied taverns, with supplies provided by the

16 SR 366, mm.1, 1v; SR 384, m.1.
17 Barron, 'Golden Age', pp. 39-40.
18 SR 240, m.1; SR 249, m.1v; SR 259, m.1v; SR 312, m.1; SR 349, m.3v.
19 SR 352, m.1v; SR 420, m.1; SR 424, m.1.

oligarchic household in residence above. Less grandiose surroundings were perhaps more standard.[20]

As in London, it seems that the majority of Chester's *femmes soles* were married and indeed their husbands were sometimes named with them in the plaint.[21] These men were usually craftsmen or artisans of middling rank – tailors, capmakers, smiths and candlemakers for example. There were also one or two butchers and bakers, whose wives would have had preferential access to bread and tallow, but apparently no men who achieved the rank of councillor. One or two may have served as constable, and the husband of Elena Buccy, a particularly active *femme sole*, was steward of the guild of journeymen tailors in 1485 and again in 1490.[22] Such households would have welcomed the contribution to familial income a wife's efforts could provide, and this contribution may not have been negligible, even though the openings for the *femme sole* in Chester were restricted and indicative rather of constraints than of independence.

Apart from wives and widows there was always a proportion of apparently single women named in the court rolls. Some, especially in the earlier years of the century, can be shown to have been married or widowed, but a substantial number of single females are attested. Among them were former servants who had evidently remained unmarried on leaving service and immigrant women whose names betray their lowly status: Christiana Flanders, for example, and Lisota Walshewoman of Whitefriar Lane.[23] In Chester, occupational by-names, even in the fifteenth century, may be taken as meaningful when applied to the humbler ranks of the population and, significantly, such names were often used by the single women of the city: Emmota Launder, Elena Huxter, Alicia Tynker and Thomasyn Tapster.[24] Unless the victims of assault, these women usually appeared in court as defendants.

Indeed, only a minority of female litigants were named as plaintiffs, appearing, in the three years taken for analysis, in the ratio of 2:3. Wives with their husbands, aldermanic widows and the prioress of the Benedictine convent of St Mary's were the typical plaintiffs, although such women also made regular appearances as defendants. The prioress and her house were poor and were brought to court on one occasion for failing to pay their priest for celebrating Mass and on another owing money for wax candles. The nuns could find no-one willing to act as their pledge and were obliged to use the

20 J. Laughton, 'The Alewives of Fifteenth-Century Chester', paper given at the Conference on Recent Research in Fifteenth-Century History, Oxford, September 1992, forthcoming.
21 Barron, 'Golden Age', p. 40.
22 SR 351, m.6; SR 373, m.1.
23 SR 200, m.1v; SR 248, m.1.
24 SR 226, m.1v; SR 244, m.1; SR 253, m.1v; SR 313, m.1.

convent cart as guaranty.[25] Women often turned to male relatives when they needed a pledge while the unmarried servant girl looked to her master or mistress. It was not unusual for court officials to act in this capacity for the more affluent townswomen but poorer females could find themselves at a loss and the city gaoler would then be pressed to serve on their behalf. Sometimes goods deposited in his safekeeping were accepted as pledges and very occasionally the clerk made the entry *fides quia pauper*.[26] It was perhaps always easier to find a male pledge in cases where the woman was the plaintiff, since decisions in the Pentice court usually went in their favour and the attendant risks were minimized.

Women could themselves act as pledge and did so fairly regularly, although perhaps in decreasing numbers as the century drew to a close; thirteen female pledges were named in 1459-60 but only one in 1489-90. Possibly this may be another indication of women's declining status. Recipients of female pledges were often members of their family or their servants but occasionally they were foreigners, who had perhaps become acquainted with the woman in the hostelry or tavern where she worked.[27] Some female pledges were widowed heads of households but not all; daughters acted for their mothers, female servants for their mistresses, neighbouring *femmes soles* for each other. Women pledges more commonly acted for the defendants than for the plaintiffs.

The majority of plaints in the Pentice court involving women – as indeed the majority of all plaints heard by the city's sheriffs – concerned debt. The sums at issue were not large. In 1431, for instance, the highest debt pursued by a female creditor was the 26s. 8d. claimed by the prioress for rent arrears and the second largest was the 19s. sought by a widow for wine purchased from her husband.[28] In 1459-60 there were two debts in the region of £2, but again these were outstanding debts being chased by oligarchic widows.[29] Thirty years later the highest figure quoted was £3 2s. 8d. owing to a butcher's executrix in repayment of a loan made for the purchase of animals.[30]

Female debtors themselves seldom owed large amounts, the value rarely exceeding £5. The largest recorded in 1431-2 was £4 12s. 6d., in 1459-60 £4 19s. 0d., while thirty years later, apart from the £1 6s. 11d. owed by a gentry widow for buckram, woollen cloth, sarsnet and curtain rings, all purchased by her late husband, no debt exceeded half a mark.[31] Throughout the century

25 SR 318, m.1; SR 321, m.1.
26 See e.g. SR 155, m.1; SR 247, m.1v; SR 318, m.1v.
27 See e.g. SR 249, m.1; SR 259, m.1; SR 277, m.1v.
28 SR 189, m.1; SR 191, m.1.
29 SR 314, m.1v; SR 315, m.1v.
30 SR 368, m.1.
31 SR 186, m.1; SR 319, m.1v; SR 367, m.1.

women rarely seem to have been extended credit above £1 and often their debts were very small, amounting to a few pennies owed for bread, ale, candles, a pair of stockings or a lock for the door. Bread and ale were in fact the commodities most frequently specified in cases involving female debtors and creditors, reinforcing the impression that it was as tapsters or hucksters that the women of Chester enjoyed most economic freedom.

Cases of covenant were pleaded in the Pentice court but were far less common than those involving debt. Only six such cases were heard in 1431-2, five in 1459-60 and three in 1489-90. Four of the plaintiffs were women, but of these just two acted alone, one of them a widow suing a Welshman who had promised to bring sixteen hats to the city but failed to do so.[32] Throughout the century withdrawal of service before the agreed term had expired was the main reason for the appearance of a female defendant in pleas of broken covenant, but occasionally a woman was accused of failing to feed and nurture a child placed in her care. In February 1460, Agnes Hazelhurst's neglect was said to have resulted in the death of a small boy; this she denied, counterclaiming that she was still owed 8s. for her labour. Neither of these pleas was prosecuted any further.[33]

Chester's sheriffs also dealt with cases of detinue. These cases, while more numerous than those of broken contract, were nevertheless relatively infrequent, with women again more likely to appear as defendant.[34] The items at issue were usually of small value – pewter dishes and saucers, brass pots and latten candlesticks for example. The silver horn and belt which had come into the hands of Nicholas Wervyn's widow on his death in c.1432 and which were claimed by a male relative were so out of the ordinary that they merited an extra membrane attached to the court roll.[35] Larger sums were involved when man and wife acted together, either as co-plaintiffs or co-defendants. It seems clear that in Chester, as in Exeter, the woman who had no male partner and who came to court alone would almost inevitably be concerned with goods and debts of the lowest value of all.[36]

Far more numerous than cases of covenant and detinue, and coming second only to debt, were those which came into the category of trespass. This included a variety of offences – assault, larceny, housebreaking and bloodshed – and a casual survey of the court rolls conjures up an image of a very turbulent city. Moreover, in their Pentice court the sheriffs dealt only with petty police cases, involving inter-personal violence; serious felonies and

---

[32] SR 314, m.1.

[33] SR 317, m.1v.

[34] There were ten such cases in 1431-2, four in 1459-60, and seven in 1489-90. Women appeared as plaintiff on nine occasions, as defendant on twelve.

[35] SR 188, mm.1v, 2.

[36] Kowaleski, 'Exeter', p. 149.

most breaches of the peace which led to the raising of the hue and cry were heard by the mayor in Portmote or Crownmote. It is undoubtedly true that court records over-emphasize anti-social behaviour but nevertheless it does seem that squabbles and scuffles, both public and private, were a familiar feature of Chester's daily and nightly life. By medieval standards this was a large town and the crowded conditions within its walls provided plenty of opportunities for dispute. As an important trading centre and port, and lying close to the border with Wales, the city also attracted a sizeable population of outsiders, whose presence almost always provoked disharmony. And of course, there were many items worth stealing in an urban community. Crime therefore flourished and – unlike the countryside – knew no seasons, although the town was possibly more unruly during fairtime, when the population was swelled by itinerant traders, the taverns well-patronized and more merchandise on display. Here was the opportunity for the townsman to take to court the chapman not seen since the previous year and now was the moment when money was urgently needed for rent, for the midsummer fair coincided with the feast of St John the Baptist, one of the city's four quarter days.

Other studies have stressed the low criminality of the medieval woman. In the rural communities of fourteenth-century England male offenders and victims are said to have outnumbered females in the ratio of nine to one, perhaps because women's position and role in society insulated them from most aggressive situations. Should the occasion arise, however, they were found to be quite as capable of aggression as men.[37] The evidence from fifteenth-century Chester supports this view. In this late medieval urban community women were not confined to domestic duties within the house but played an active economic and social role in the town, in tavern, shop and market-place. They came into contact with a wide circle and relationships were not always harmonious.

The Pentice rolls therefore record many instances of hotheaded exchanges, with women frequently named, often – but not always – as victim. Their injuries were rarely serious, although blood could be drawn, and were commonly inflicted by sticks or clubs. Female assailants, and on average one or two such women were brought to court each month, tended to attack other members of their own sex, usually with sticks and stones. It was not unknown, however, for a man to find himself the victim of a female aggressor and one who was quite prepared to act single-handed. An alewife wielding a pewter bowl could prove a formidable assailant, as John Bowyer

---

[37] B. A. Hanawalt, *Crime and Conflict in English Communities 1300-1348* (Cambridge, Mass., 1979), pp. 152-53; A. Finch, 'Women and Violence in the Later Middle Ages: the Evidence of the Officiality of Cerisy', *Continuity and Change*, 7 (1992), 23-45, especially pp. 30-31, 38-39.

discovered in August 1489, subsequently claiming 100s. for the damages she had inflicted to his nose.[38] Only one example of a woman using her traditional weapon, her tongue, has surfaced in the Pentice rolls.[39] Possibly such cases of verbal abuse were heard in the ecclesiastical courts.

Women not infrequently came to court accused of receiving stolen goods, either from a relative or from a runaway servant girl or male apprentice. It was by no means uncommon, however, for them to take a more active role in burglary, personally breaking into a house and carrying away the desired items. Possibly it was easier to do this in a busy town than in the watchful and closed community which was the medieval village. Many urban properties were in multiple occupation, and although it appears that individual tenants were expected to provide a lock and key for their own door, perhaps not everyone took this precaution. Nor did it render the occupant impregnable. At least one female thief merely had a second key made and then let herself in without further difficulty.[40]

Women stole a whole range of items. Sesters of ale were often taken but they were heavy and in these cases husband and wife usually acted together. When acting without an accomplice a woman obviously went for goods which were easy to carry, such as clothing and bedding. Many of the city's upholders doubtless acquired at least a proportion of their wares in this manner. Smaller items such as spoons, dishes and rosaries were also popular with the female thief and occasionally she took raw wool, woollen yarn or linen thread, presumably to work into cloth. Sometimes the Pentice rolls afford a glimpse of the motives behind these crimes. In April 1460, for example, the chaloner who accused a woman of breaking into his house and stealing a tablecloth was said by her to have refused to return a breviary she owned.[41] In the same month Rosa Crumpe had attacked another woman who subsequently claimed 100s. in damages. The reason for this assault would surely have been the 21d. this woman owed Rosa for food and drink.[42] The Pentice court rolls are filled with similar juxtapositions of cases and it seems clear that the inhabitant of late medieval Chester, whether male or female, was unlikely to be attacked without reason by a total stranger.

It is commonly recognized that only a small proportion of medieval lawsuits ever came to judgement; possibly 20 per cent of crown pleas in the court of King's Bench in the fifteenth century reached a verdict and barely 1 per cent of private suits.[43] In the Pentice court, too, the overwhelming

38 SR 376, m.1v.
39 SR 319, m.1.
40 SR 386, m.1.
41 SR 319, m.1.
42 SR 319, m.1v.
43 E. Powell, 'Arbitration and the Law of England in the Late Middle Ages', TRHS, 5th ser., 33 (1983), 49-67.

majority of all cases – not just those involving women – did not proceed for one reason or other; either the plaintiff failed to prosecute, the defendant to appear or else agreement was reached out of court. The vast majority did in fact settle out of court and clearly many cases were only initiated in order to put pressure on defendants so to do.

Punishment imposed by the Pentice court, whether for non-prosecution, non-appearance, reconciliation or jury verdict, almost invariably took the form of an amercement. In 1431-32, when the amounts were regularly entered on the court record, these ranged between 6d. and 3s. for an individual, with 18d. apparently the standard sum. Husband and wife together could be fined 2s. while the usual amercement for the servant girl seems to have been 6d., a heavy enough penalty for someone whose maximum annual wage was perhaps only in the region of twelve shillings.[44] One woman from Whitchurch in Shropshire was fined 3s., indicative perhaps of the marginal – and vulnerable – status of outsiders.[45]

In the socially stratified community which was the English medieval town, women derived their status from their husbands. It was usual, therefore, for the wives of leading citizens to represent all the city's brewsters when charges were brought in the court of the Dee mills against Chester's recalcitrant millers. And in lists of those amerced for breaches of the assize of ale, the wives of middling craftsmen were commonly named separately from more humble female traders. The unattached female found herself gravely disadvantaged in this hierarchy, inevitably ending up at the very bottom of the heap. Lacking family, friends and influence, she it was who would be most likely to be committed to prison, if charged with more serious crime. Lacking goods, chattels and money, she it was who was most in danger of being hanged.

Perhaps this social stratification was mirrored in the urban space. Oligarchic wives and widows would have lived in the major houses found on all the four main streets of Chester, prestige dwellings which were protected from the hurly-burly of everyday life by the screen of shops which fronted the thoroughfare. In these shops the wives of the middling citizens were active – buying, selling, delivering goods. In some of the cellars below, the alewives plied their trade, while in the street in front stood the market stalls of the foreign women, women who had paid an annual fine for the privilege of selling their wares. Also on the streets, perhaps particularly those in the area of the Watergate, roamed the footloose immigrant females, eking out a marginal living as best they could.

---

[44] For wages paid to female servants see e.g. SR 197, m.1v; SR 223, m.1v; SR 247, m.1v.

[45] SR 191, m.1v.

'Best Trusted Friends': Concepts and Practices of Friendship among Fifteenth-Century Norfolk Gentry
PHILIPPA MADDERN

The impetus to write a paper on so diffuse and intractable a subject as friendship arises from recent developments in late-medieval English historiography. Research by Colin Richmond, Nigel Saul and Charles Moreton provides increasingly convincing evidence that vertical social links (patron-client relationships) may have been less prevalent or important in the lives of fifteenth-century English gentry than has been supposed.[1] Some gentry, in their ordinary daily business, may have actively avoided magnates, seeking instead the support of close, reciprocal, functional relationships among their neighbours, kin and marriage connections.[2] Such findings should encourage us to pay closer attention to the horizontal social connections, including friendships, which apparently sustained fifteenth-century gentry society.[3]

The problem has perhaps been complicated by the terms in which past friendships have been discussed. Historians have been quick to accept anthropological classifications of friendship as either instrumental or affective, unbalanced or reciprocal. Though these terms are not mutually exclusive, they tend to construct a comfortable dichotomy between modern and pre-modern friendships. Modern friendships (it is all too easy to infer) are emotional, affective, and spontaneous.[4] Past friendships were patronal and instrumental, often centring on the exchange of purely material assistance.

[1] C. Richmond, *John Hopton: a Fifteenth Century Suffolk Gentleman* (Cambridge, 1981), esp. ch. 4; idem, *The Paston Family in the Fifteenth Century: the First Phase* (Cambridge, 1990); N. Saul, *Scenes from Provincial Life: Knightly Families in Sussex 1280-1400* (Oxford, 1986), esp. ch. II; C. Moreton, *The Townshends and Their World: Gentry, Law, and Land in Norfolk. c.1450-1551*, esp. pp. 23-27; idem 'A social gulf? The Upper and Lesser Gentry of Later Medieval England', *Jnl of Medieval History*, 17 (1991), pp. 255-62.

[2] S. Wright, *The Derbyshire Gentry in the Fifteenth Century*, Derbyshire Record Society, 8 (Walton, 1983), pp. 53-55.

[3] As Christine Carpenter remarks, even the political actions of fifteenth-century gentry cannot well be understood without enquiring 'what, if any, was the meaning of the words that described their foremost preoccupations; words like "family", "lineage", "gentility", "friendship", "allegiance" ... "neighbourhood"...' See her *Locality and Polity: A Study of Warwickshire Landed Society, 1401-1499* (Cambridge, 1992), p. 8.

[4] Modern sociological studies on friendship tend to place it in the realm of affective love; see e.g. S. Duck, *Personal Relationships and Personal Constructs: a Study of Friendship Formation* (London, 1973), and V. Shlapentokh, *Love, Marriage and Friendship in the Soviet Union: Ideals and Practices* (New York, 1984).

Furthermore, reciprocity was not necessary to past friendships; patrons acted as 'friends' to clients from whom they could expect no return but gratitude.[5]

Yet the dichotomy of affective-reciprocal relationships versus instrumental-unequal connections sits uneasily with the evidence of friendship in medieval and renaissance Europe.[6] Could friendship in fifteenth-century England be categorized as either affective or instrumental? Was reciprocity necessarily associated with either end of the affective/instrumental spectrum? These are only two of the problems to be raised about this hitherto largely unexplored relationship. How were friendships made or sustained? Within what social and geographic bounds? What services did instrumental friendship entail? How was fifteenth-century friendship conceptualized? To outline tentative answers to some of these questions, I propose to examine the problem on three levels: first, the high theory of fifteenth-century friendship as it appeared in literary models and classical authorities; secondly the 'low theory' (what late-medieval gentry said about friendship in their proverbs, rhymes and letters); and thirdly, through a case study of the connections of one of the many obscure gentry families of fifteenth-century Norfolk, the actual practice of late-medieval friendship.

Friendship was a relatively common topic in late-medieval English writings. Lydgate wrote a poem entitled 'A Freond at Neode'; and though inclusion in the works of so indiscriminate an author may be poor proof of the general prominence of a topos, other evidence confirms the popularity of his theme.[7] The problems of ideal friendship suffused such widely-read romances as Chaucer's *Troilus and Criseyde*.[8] John Paston II owned a copy of Cicero's *De Amicitia*, which may have been translated by William Worcester.[9] Caxton possibly used this translation when in 1481 he printed an

5 M. E. Mullett, 'Byzantium: A Friendly Society?', *Past and Present*, 118 (1988), esp. pp. 16-18.

6 See e.g. Mullett's reservations, voiced in ibid., pp. 16-18, and G. Fitch Lyttle, 'Friendship and Patronage in Renaissance Europe', in *Patronage, Art and Society in Renaissance Italy*, ed. by F. W. Kent and P. Simons (Canberra, 1987), esp. pp. 48-49 and 53-55.

7 'A Freond at Neode', in *The Minor Poems of John Lydgate*, ed. by H. N. MacCracken and M. Sherwood, part II, Early English Text Soc., original series 192 (London, 1934; repr. 1961), pp. 755-58.

8 Geoffrey Chaucer, *Troilus & Criseyde*, ed. by B. A. Windeatt (London, 1984), of which fifteen manuscript copies and sixteen fragments remain (see pp. 68-76).

9 *Paston Letters and Papers of the Fifteenth Century*, ed. by N. Davis, 2 vols (Oxford, 1971-76), hereinafter referred to as *PL*, I, p. 517; see also A. F. Sutton and L. Visser-Fuchs, 'Richard III's Books: XII. William Worcester's *Boke of Noblesse* and his Collection of Documents on the War in Normandy', *The Ricardian*, 9 (1991), pp. 160-61. (My thanks to Livia Visser-Fuchs both for drawing my attention to this article, and for providing me with a copy.) Paston's ownership of the book of course provides no proof that he read it. The only books in which he expressed

edition of *De Amicitia*, remarking in the preface that the work was 'ful necessary & behoefful vnto euery estate & degree'.[10] Worcester himself felt it appropriate to cite classical doctrines of friendship in moments of acute stress:

> A very frende at nede experience will schewe be deede, as wele as be autorité
> of Aristotle in the *Etiques* that he made of maralité; also by the famous
> Reamayn Tullius in his litell booke *de Amicicia*...

he wrote to an acquaintance in the stormy days of broken alliances following the death of his master.[11]

Classical authors' concepts of friendship are less important in this context than their fifteenth-century audience's interpretation of them. On major points, however, both text and audience evidently agreed. Neither Cicero nor his late-medieval readers acknowledged any disjunction between affective and instrumental friendship. Cicero's Laelius argues both that 'amor' is primarily the wellspring of friendship, and that exchange of good deeds is 'proprium amicitiae'. Similarly, Lydgate characterized edifying examples of classical friendship as combining practical aid with heartfelt affection. Protesilaus and Theseus were 'oone in herte, wille, and dede'. Good deeds for one's friends were thus necessary, but not sufficient, to friendship. Ideally, friendship lasted through any change of fortune; Orestes and Pylades were 'Never to part as seyþe Ovydius, /In frowarde fortune ne in þeire stoundes glade'.[12]

Likewise, friends in late-medieval fiction, rendering one another mutual service, were simultaneously portrayed in lushly sentimental terms. Pandarus and Troilus address each other as 'brother', and may seem, to modern readers, more like lovers than friends. Early in the work, for example, Troilus, struck by what he conceives to be a hopeless and fatal passion, lies weeping on his bed, refusing to confide his troubles to Pandarus. How does Pandarus respond?

> 'Now frend', quod he, 'if euere loue or trouthe
> Hath ben, or is, bitwixen the and me,
> Ne do thow neuere swich a crueltee
> To hiden fro thi frend so gret a care.
> Wostow nauȝt wel that it am I, Pandare?'[13]

---

direct interest concern the more specialized topic of love: Lydgate's *Temple of Glass* (*PL*, I, p. 447) and Ovid's *De Arte Amandi* (*PL*, II, p. 379).

10 *Marcus Tullius Cicero, Of Old Age: Of Friendship* (W. Caxton, 1481), The English Experience: its record in early printed books published in facsimile, no. 861 (Amsterdam, 1977).

11 *PL*, II, p. 203.

12 Lydgate, 'Freond', p. 756; cf. Cicero, *De Amicitia*, Bks VIII and XVIII; *Cicero: De Senectute, De Amicitia, De Divinatione*, ed. by W. A. Falconer (London, 1938), pp. 136-38, 174.

The words 'your true lover' seem to hang in the silence at the line's end.

Constancy and selfless unanimity, quintessential to true friendship, rendered it an intrinsically moral relationship. Lydgate corroborated the classical belief that only good men could be friends; Cicero 'Hyest of vertues frenship doþe preferre'.[14] According to both writers, friendship was so noble that worldly comrades could rarely fulfil its ideal. Lydgate's last verse implicitly contrasts even the purest earthly companionship with that of Christ the Saviour, the matchless exemplar of true friendship:

> O Cryste Ihesu, whos frenship may not fayle,
> For love of man þat suffred passyoun.

Clearly, in Lydgate's mind, Christ's friendship for humankind was perfect in both effect and affect. It was also unequal; the best of human love was but a poor return for, or reflection of, divine charity.[15]

Friendship was also much discussed in less elevated genres. The heading subsumes fifty-one entries in Whiting's collection of proverbs, ranging from the trite ('A true friend is a great help') to the profoundly cynical ('My friend borrowed money and I have lost my friend and my money').[16] Proverbial opinion could reflect classical and literary orthodoxies. Any distinction between instrumental and affective friendship is hard to detect. On the one hand, action on a friend's behalf was clearly seen as obligatory. 'A friend in court is better than penny in purse' ran the proverb. That the services of friendship could be solidly material is shown in William Paston II's succinct advice to Margaret Paston: 'The Abbot of Wymoundham hath sent to me too tymes. Frendship may not hang by the wynde, nor for faire eyne, but causis must be shewid.' His succeeding reference to the widespread belief that he had access to 'your coffers and my brothirs and Maistir Fastolff' indicates the nature of the 'causes' to which he referred. Similarly, William Yelverton's advice to John Paston I in 1450 was to 'Spende sum-what of youre good now, and gette yow lordshep and frendshep þer, *quia ibi pendet tota lex et prophete*'.[17] These practicalities could lead fifteenth-century gentry to calculate, apparently in cold blood, the good or harm accruing from particular services. William Paston II, writing to Margaret in 1469 to urge her

13   Chaucer, *Troilus & Criseyde*, pp. 132, l. 773; 222, l. 1359 (references to brotherhood) and p. 122, ll. 585-88.

14   Lydgate, 'Freond', p. 756, l. 50; cf. *Cicero*, Bks VI-VII, and XVIII, pp. 130-36 and 174. I use the term 'men' advisedly, for reasons which I hope to clarify later.

15   Lydgate, 'Freond', p. 759.

16   *Proverbs, Sentences and Proverbial Phrases From English Writings Mainly Before 1500*, ed. by B. J. Whiting (Cambridge, Mass., 1968), F661, F653 and F666. The latter warning exists also as an advisory verse in British Library Harley MS 116; see *Middle English Lyrics*, ed. by M. S. Luria and R. Hoffman (New York, 1974), no. 123, p. 119.

17   Whiting, *Proverbs*, F633; *PL*, I, p. 170 and II, p. 53.

to grant £20 to the prior of Bromholm, assured her that, considering the prior's capacity to help her son in the future, 'it were a gode frendely dede and no jopardy nor hurt'.[18]

Yet such relationships, seemingly limited to unemotional exchanges of goods and services, also resembled cherished blood connections. Margaret Paston, urging John II to end an estrangement with Robert Clere, wrote 'I wolde þat iche of yow xulde do for othere, and leue as kynnysmen and frendys...'[19] Like kinship, friendship could arouse intense feeling. Roger Taverham's distraught letter to John Paston I employs identically affective language to describe his relationships with both family and friends. Taverham, overcome by the 'wrecchednesse of this worlde', proposed to go to Rome 'in the seruise of God', but wanted Paston to keep a protective eye on his aged father. His request was expressed not as a claim for reciprocal service, but as an appeal for sympathy at parting with both kin and friends:

> And, syr, I suppose I shall neuer see you no more, nor non of myn frendes, whiche is to me the grettest lamentacion that myght come vn-to myn herte... And I haue mervayle ... that I hadde neuer non letter a-geyn [from my father], whiche is to me the grettest lamentacion that euer come to my hert; and nowe, knowing that I shall neuer see hym more, nor you nor non other of myn frendes, mervayle ye not thow sorowe is inprended in myn hert.[20]

Clearly, tepid gratitude was not the only emotion stirred by friendship.

Furthermore, in William Worcester's case, the giving, not receiving, of friendly help roused strong passions. In 1460 he was at odds with the Pastons, with whom he had served the recently-deceased Sir John Fastolf, and to whom he felt he had rendered valuable aid. Writing to another member of Fastolf's household, he complained that rumour ran that 'I straunched me from serteine persones [the Pastons] to moche'. The reverse, he wrote indignantly, was true; when the Pastons took control of Fastolf's *post mortem* affairs, 'I was not put in truste a-mong the seid attourneys there to yeue on peny for my maister sowle, but I paid it of myn owne purse be-foore; nother in trust ne favour to geve an almesse gowne but that I praid for it as a straunger schulde doo.' His bitter outrage at exclusion from the instrumental transactions of friendship was vented in two letters:

> It is not vniversali knowen that I was one of the cheeffe that kepte bothe my Maister Paston and myn oncle in my maister favour and truste, and if I wolde haue labored the contrary, by my sowle (that is the grettest othe that I may swere of my-silff) they had neuer be nygh my maister in that case they stonde now. And if they woll labour to damage or hendre me, all the worlde woll mys-reporte of hem and litel truste hem, nowther they schal not haue wurschip nor profight bi it. I wolde be to them as lowyng and as wele

---

18 *PL*, I, p. 170.
19 *PL*, I, p. 380.
20 *PL*, II, pp. 320-21.

willyng as I gan, so I fynde cause, and other I wolnot be to my fadre, and he weere a-liffe[21]

Among the many remarkable elements in these passages, we may note that for Worcester 'trust' was essential to both friendship and kinship; that the proper conduct of friendship determined public honour and reputation; that friendship and sonship apparently belonged to the same high order of emotional relationships; and that giving help – even in such mundane matters as distributing alms-gowns – had profoundly affective connotations.

This type of friendship can hardly be characterized by a distinction between kin and associates or between instrumental and affective relationships. Instead, a cluster of metaphors delineated the main elements of friendship. Kinship and friendship were easily paired in fifteenth-century minds; Sir John Fastolf reportedly called John Paston I 'the hartyest kynysman and frynd þat he knowyt'.[22] 'Trust' inevitably accompanied friendship. Worcester's emphasis on trust recalls the classical understanding of friendship as comprising constant unanimity of purpose, and may suggest that the common epistolary greeting 'Right trusty friend' was not invariably formulaic.[23] Trust, too, was both expedient and affective. Even the trust (or deceit) involved in mundane business affairs could be represented in terms of almost Chaucerian romance. An account of the devious land transactions between William Burgeys and Reginald Rous alleged that when William 'knewe how he was deseyuyd he was ner deed for sorewe'.[24] Finally, friendship was conceptually connected with a homely sense of close neighbourhood. Proverbial fifteenth-century wisdom was to 'let your neighbour feel your friendship', and to 'love your neighbour' whatever might betide.[25] Margaret Paston, advising John II on his relations with Robert Clere, thought their estrangement was 'a-geynste cortesey, so nyhe newborys as   e be'.[26] Though doubting the suitability of one of her son's college friends, she was convinced that Walter should 'make neuer the lesse of hym, by-cause he is his contré-man and neghboure'.[27] Taverham's distress at leaving his friends evidently stemmed partly from the fact that he was going amongst complete strangers. Worcester thought that only a 'straunger' should have to beg for the gift of an alms-gown. Thus, as in modern usage, 'estrangement' implied emotional, not merely geographical, distance; 'strangeness' was friendship's opposite pole.[28] Taking help from friends in

21 PL, II, pp. 203-05; cf. his letter to John Berney, II, p. 539.
22 PL, I, pp. 154; see also pp. 342 and 380, and II, pp. 296, 313 and 572.
23 For further references to trust and friendship/love, see e.g. PL, II, pp. 270 and 609; for 'trusty' as an address, see e.g. PL, II, pp. 3, 34, 158-59, 184 and 274.
24 PL, II, p. 519.
25 Whiting, Proverbs, N80, N86 and N84.
26 PL, I, p. 380.
27 PL, I, p. 370.

preference to strangers was evidently a duty. In 1461 John Paston II, having cadged five pounds from his father's servant, thought to forestall paternal displeasure by pointing out that he must otherwise have 'boruyd it of a strange man, sum of my felawys'.[29] His 'felawys' cannot have been literally unknown to him; but they were evidently not Norfolk men, neighbours or kinsmen and were hence disqualified in John's mind as acceptable creditors. It was to neighbours, kin, and friends that one could turn in times of need, and for whom one could appropriately feel a deep sense of loyalty, affection and trust.

Services rendered between friends were of varying reciprocity. Such vague promises as 'he hath and may doo for you' presumably encompassed many forms of assistance: lending money, news-gathering, passing on messages, seeking out possible marriage connections, supporting law-suits.[30] Godparenthood could bind together friends, servants, kin, and neighbours. Greater gentlefolk stood godparents to children of their lesser neighbours and dependants, and the relationship could also be reversed. Edmund Norman of Filby was godfather to a child of his much more prestigious neighbour, Robert Clere of Stokesby.[31] Since in canon law a child's godparents became spiritual kin, subject to the same marriage restrictions as blood-relations, the practice of using neighbours and friends as godparents must have reinforced perceived connections between friendship and kinship.[32]

Other spiritual services were rendered impartially for friends and kin. Fifteenth-century Norfolk testators regularly bequeathed money for prayers for the souls of 'parentum et benefactorum', a phrase translated, in Simeon Fyncham's draft will, as 'auncestres and frendes'.[33] Prayers could also sustain living friends. A note in a book of hours belonging to the Fyncham family describes an exhaustive regimen of masses and alms which, the writer advised, would deliver any 'frende' from whatever 'nede or tribulacion or

---

28 Cf. Ralph Lord Cromwell's advice to his 'right trusty' friends, John Paston I and Sir John Radcliffe, to 'forbere' the 'greet straungenesse' between them (PL, II, p. 110; cf p. 203).

29 PL, I, p. 391.

30 PL, I, p. 170.

31 See his testament, British Library Add. MS 34888, fol. 10. Either his godson, or his godson's cousin (Edmund Clere of Ormesby) is described in the testament as 'magistro meo'. Similarly, the Celys sought godparents for their children among servants and friends (A. Hanham, The Celys and Their World: an English Merchant Family of the Fifteenth Century (Cambridge, 1985), pp. 9-10).

32 See J. Bossy, 'Blood and Baptism: Kinship, Community and Christianity in Western Europe from the Fourteenth to the Seventeenth Centuries', in Sanctity and Secularity; the Church and the World, ed. by D. Baker, Studies in Church History, 10 (Oxford, 1973) pp. 132-34.

33 Norfolk and Norwich Record Office (hereafter N & NRO) Hare 5982; not unusually, the bequest depended on the default of other legacies.

syknes that they be inn'.[34] Presumably the material services of friends could be requited by the purchase, on their behalf, of spiritual benefits.

Nor were services rendered only between mortals. Lydgate believed Christ to be one's truest friend; fifteenth-century Norfolk gentry agreed that saints would befriend those who properly rewarded them. William Yelverton, eminently practical, wrote to John Paston I urging him to continued generosity towards the shrine at Walsingham, not only for the sake of their own friendship (and the possibly valuable gratitude of the prior), but also for the celestial relationships at stake:

> for trewly if I be drawe to any worchep or wellfare, and discharge of myn enmyes daunger, I ascryve it vnto Our Lady; preyng yow þerfore þat ye woln ben as frendly to Oure Ladyes hous as I wote well ye haue alwey ben ... *and dought yow not Our Lady shall quyte it yow* ...[35]

Yet within the varied set of actions which sustained good relationships, a series of services, essentially involving trust, were invariably cited as the marks of greatest friendship. Elizabeth Rothenhale, writing to William Paston I around 1426, appealed to his long-standing association with her family: 'I beseche yow for þe grete trost þat my lord hadde in yow, *makyng yow on of his feffeez and also on of his attornés, as for on of his best trosted frendes*'.[36] A group of letters from the 1460s, concerned to establish the identity of those whom Sir John Fastolf would have wished to carry out his will, harped on the same theme. The abbot of Langley considered John Paston and Thomas Howes the most suitable executors, because they were

> þe persones a-boue all other þat þe seyd Sere John Fastolf put in hys most sengulere loue and trust and wold they shuld haue þe kepyng and dysposecion of hys goodes as wele in hys lyue as after hys deseas to dyspose for þe well of hys soule ...[37]

Geoffrey Boleyn, wishing to secure first refusal of Fastolf's manor of Guton, wrote to John Paston I, because 'as I vnderstande, ye be that person that my seid maister ... most trosted to have rewle and dyreccion of his lyfelode and goodes'.[38] This was no mere rhetoric. A surviving writ of Fastolf, dated 1 May 1458, gives the whole supervision of his Yorkshire lands to 'praedilecti consanguinei mei Johnis Paston armigeri plenarie confidens ipsum'.[39] Here,

---

34 Victoria & Albert Museum, MS Reid 44, fol. 134. The book was certainly owned by the Fynchams in the early 16th century, and possibly in the 15th century. The note appears to me to be in a late-15th or early-16th century hand. My thanks to Professor Colin Richmond, who kindly passed on this reference to me.

35 *PL*, II, p. 198, emphasis mine.

36 *PL*, II, p. 3, emphasis mine.

37 *PL*, II, p. 541; cf. Ralph Lampet's declaration of 1463 (II, pp. 542-43); William Barker's and Margaret Worcester's declaration of c. 1485 (*PL*, II, p. 606).

38 *PL*, II, pp. 224-25.

39 N & NRO Phillips 612/2.

the affective terms of kinship and trust were matter-of-factly applied to the trustee of property.

According to fifteenth-century Norfolk gentry, then, the truest examples of trusty friends were those to whom one handed over control of land – either as feoffees, attorneys to deliver seisin, executors or supervisors. This is not surprising; the role of feoffee or executor was vitally fiduciary. Once lands had been granted in an enfeoffment to use, common law could do little to recover them for their original holder, even should the feoffee fail to fulfil the conditions of the grant.[40] Testators' powers over executors were even more tenuous; executors were beyond the reach of the grave, and often depended for their success on the goodwill of feoffees, who must be asked to re-enfeoff the lands of the deceased to the heir.[41] The very livelihood of one's dependants and successors hung on the trustworthiness of feoffees and executors. Where whole estates were at stake, loyalty was hard to ensure simply by means of reward. The only safeguard was to choose as agents people whose friendship rested not on a cold exchange of services, but on bonds of trust and affection strong enough to outweigh cupidity and outlast death itself.

Admittedly not all feoffees, in all circumstances, can be construed as the feoffor's close personal friends. Yet, as Saul notes, 'if friendship is to be found anywhere, it is to be found surely in the choice of a man's feoffees'.[42] Even witnesses to land transactions, who could speak to the intentions of a grant, could become vital links in the network of trust. In Cambridge in 1422, an otherwise obscure witness to a quitclaim was killed, apparently in a dispute concerning the eventual ownership of the property.[43] Consequently, examining these kinds of associates of any individual may show the range of people among whom he found his 'best trusted friends'. This is exactly the process which the well-kept records of Simeon Fyncham, gentleman/esquire of Fincham, Norfolk, enable us to undertake.[44]

Simeon Fyncham is an obscure person. To my knowledge, he never filled any county office, such as sheriff, escheator, or justice of the peace; and he apparently never fell foul of the law.[45] He was comfortably well-off; his

[40] Though Chancery, an equity court, could rule in favour of the original owner; cf. M. Avery, 'The History of the Equitable Jurisdiction of Chancery before 1460', *Bull. of the Inst. of Historical Research*, 42 (1969), pp. 135-37.

[41] Cf. Wright, *Derbyshire Gentry*, pp. 53-54.

[42] Saul, *Scenes from Provincial Life*, p. 62.

[43] See P. Maddern, *Violence and Social Order: East Anglia 1422-1442* (Oxford, 1992), pp. 145-54.

[44] Both additions occur in his documents; see N & NRO Hare 1739 (esquire) and Hare 5879 (for his handsome armorial seal). In his draft will he calls himself 'gentilman' (Hare 5982).

[45] His only known court appearances were as plaintiff, thrice in King's Bench and

terrier, drawn up in the summer of 1427, lists well over 400 acres of arable landholdings in Fincham alone.[46] The handsome church tower of St Martin's Fincham, rebuilt in the mid-fifteenth century with the Fyncham arms proudly emblazoned in the stonework, still stands witness to his prosperous piety.[47] Though he left no letters or memoranda, literally dozens of his business documents remain in the Norfolk and Norwich Record Office. A search through these records from 1409 (the first date at which Simeon is known to have been adult) to the arbitrarily-chosen end date of 1442 yields a list of 149 people whom he enfeoffed, who enfeoffed him, who were his co-feoffees, who witnessed his deeds, whose deeds were witnessed by him, or who were co-witnesses with him to other people's transactions.

This list of potential friends is suspiciously long. However, twenty-five of them occur only as Simeon's co-witnesses or co-feoffees in other people's transactions. This may indicate no more than a slight acquaintance through a third party. Fifty-nine more people left evidence of only one contact between themselves and Fyncham. Some of these may have been closer associates than the figures suggest; the fact that we have only Fyncham's records, and not their own, necessarily limits our view of their joint transactions. Yet caution dictates that we exclude both these groups of people from a consideration of Fyncham's friendships. This leaves sixty-five individuals, of whom four were members of his immediate kin – his father, his brother Thomas, his wife Elizabeth and his eldest son John.

Of the remaining sixty-one, fourteen men from eleven families are distinguishable as Fyncham's most frequent associates. All interacted with him at least ten times over the period studied (see Table 1 below). Their relationships were enduring. Richard Undyrwode constantly acted as witness for Fyncham for thirteen years. John Shuldham esquire, of Marham, died in 1425/6 after only nine years' frequent association with his neighbour, but his son Thomas promptly took his place. Some contacts seem one-sided and uniform (John Allone and Richard Undyrwode, for instance, were almost exclusively engaged in witnessing, or witnessing with, Simeon Fyncham, rather than using him as a witness, or acting as his feoffees); but men such as the Geytons, the Shuldhams, and Nicholas Thurston performed a range of services for him. Can this silent group, identifiable only in statistics extracted from curt business papers, be classed as Simeon Fyncham's friends?

I think they can. Even these mute witnesses displayed, in the patterns of their dealings, some of the qualities which characterized friendship for their

---

once in Common Pleas in the period 1439-1442 (Public Record Office, KB 27 714 m 29d, 714 m 80d, 724 m 74r, and CP 40 726 m 202d).

[46] N & NRO Hare 1685.

[47] My thanks to Professor Andrew Martindale, who kindly insisted on taking me to visit the church.

more articulate contemporaries. Since we know them only through their participation in the mundane business of estate management, they naturally appear as Fyncham's 'benefactors', rendering him day-to-day services which he faithfully returned. Nicholas Thurston, Thomas Trussbut and Thomas Shuldham were among the feoffees of Simeon's own lands, while John Allone, John and Nicholas Miller, Thomas Lovell, Thomas Fuller and Nicholas Geyton witnessed these important transactions.[48] Simeon Fyncham was a feoffee of the Trussbut lands in 1425, apparently inheriting this trust from his father, whom Laurence Trussbut had enfeoffed by Henry IV's time.[49] Simeon took his duties seriously, appearing as plaintiff in King's Bench in 1439 in writs of trespass and maintenance in defence of Trussbut lands.[50] In 1425 he was also a trustee, with Thomas Trussbut, for income for Margaret, daughter of John Shuldham, a professed nun.[51] He acted as Thomas Styward's attorney to give seisin of the Talbot family lands in Fincham to Nicholas Thurston and others in 1433.[52] Presumably such services comprised the 'deeds' essential to the maintenance of good friendship. They also produced the safely moderate profits which trusty friends might expect. In 1427, John son of Nicholas Atte Newhalle of Fincham enfeoffed Simeon Fyncham and two others in various lands and tenements in Fincham and Stradsete. He died, apparently childless, in 1437, whereupon Simeon duly enfeoffed his mother Margaret as his heir. Margaret and her husband later sold the land back to John Fyncham, who must thus have benefited from his father's involvement in the affair.[53]

Friendship and neighbourliness, as we have seen, were closely linked in fifteenth-century minds. Simeon Fyncham's practice matched this theory exactly. Ten of his fourteen most frequent contacts were Fincham men.[54]

[48] See N & NRO Hare 956, 959, 1663, 1697 and 751 (first court of the feoffees). The other feoffees seem to have been William Tendryng, probably Simeon's brother-in-law (see Table 2), Hugh Cook, Thomas Ryngstede and William Goderede (presumably the justice, brother-in-law to Thomas Shuldham).

[49] N & NRO Hare 2414 and 3932; for John Fyncham as feoffee of Laurence Trussbut, see Hare 2692.

[50] Public Record Office KB 27 714 mm 29d and 80d. Depasturing was alleged against Geoffrey Kervyle of Watlington, and the plaintiffs in that case also alleged that Thomas Lovell of Barton Bendish had practised maintenance in Kervyle's defence. The Trussbuts held land in Watlington. Since Kervyle alleged in defence that Thomas Trussbut had granted the land to another man who then enfeoffed him, and since the plaintiffs comprised Thomas Trussbut and two of his feoffees (Fyncham and William Grey), this was probably a dispute over Trussbut's ownership of the land.

[51]   N & NRO Hare 2309.

[52] N & NRO Hare 952.

[53] N & NRO Hare 940, 941 and 944. Margaret had evidently been widowed, and married again.

The Shuldhams and Thomas Lovell came from the neighbouring parishes of Marham and Barton Bendish respectively, both within five kilometres of Fincham. Only Thomas Styward of Swaffham lived as much as fourteen kilometres away. Simeon Fyncham's bonds of ordinary association thus reflect perfectly the ties of neighbourhood friendship evoked by fifteenth-century writings on the subject.

Such extreme neighbourliness may raise the question of whether these men were chosen friends, or whether Fyncham simply used, indiscriminately, those whose lands bordered his own.[55] Closer examination suggests that his most frequent associates were not forced on him by geographical accident. Though all were near neighbours, not all neighbours were frequent associates. Crimplesham, Bexwell and Oxborough, the homes of Thomas Derham, John Bekeswell and Sir Thomas Tuddenham respectively, all lay within the fifteen-kilometre limit of Simeon's radius of association, yet he apparently engaged in no more than two transactions with Derham and Bekeswell, and four with Tuddenham. This is significant, since all were well qualified to be useful friends. Bekeswell was a busy minor office-holder, Derham a diligent lawyer and justice of the peace, and Tuddenham one of the most powerful figures of fifteenth-century East Anglian society.[56] Yet Fyncham appears only twice as a member of a group of feoffees which included Tuddenham, and twice as witness to transactions involving Tuddenham, as if he did not seek, or was not invited to receive, the trust of so great a man.[57] Even within his own village, Fyncham evidently selected his friends. His terrier of 1427 gives the names of men who held lands bordering his own.[58] Since his holdings were in tiny parcels – some only half an acre in extent – he was extremely well-supplied with neighbours. Comparatively few of these appear frequently in his own documents. John Allone, Thomas Fuller, the Miller family, and Richard Undyrwode were literally neighbours as well as friends; but William Algor, the Rykkys family, Andrew Scarlet, Geoffrey Stonham, and William Monfort all held several parcels of land bordering on Fyncham's but seldom appeared in his business transactions. Perhaps final proof is impossible; but the evidence inclines one to believe that Simeon Fyncham made a conscious choice of his friends.

54 See Table 1. I include John Geyton as a member of the family who held Littlewell Hall in Fincham.

55 My thanks to Jennifer Kermode and Sarah Rees-Jones for forcing me to prove this point.

56 For Bekeswell and Derham, see Maddern, *Violence and Social Order*, pp. 138-39 and 249.

57 Fyncham appears as co-feoffee with Tuddenham in N & NRO Hare 2309 and 5029, and as witness, Hare 894a and 953. The latter records an enfeoffment of Talbot family lands.

58 N & NRO Hare 1685.

The Pastons and their associates envisaged friendship in terms of kinship. For Simeon Fyncham too, friends could be kin, and friendship similar to kinship. The Trussbuts were relations by marriage: Simeon's paternal aunt Alice had married Laurence Trussbut, Thomas's father.[59] Simeon apparently decided to reinforce the bond with one of spiritual kinship, asking Laurence Trussbut to stand godfather to one of his sons (see family tree, Table 2).[60] Similarly, Nicholas Fyncham's name suggests that he was godson to Nicholas Geyton or Nicholas Thurston. The former may be the more likely, since his will of 1476 appoints Nicholas Fyncham to the highly responsible position of executor, a post more usually reserved for members of the nuclear family.[61] Simeon Fyncham in turn apparently stood godparent to at least one of his Fincham neighbours.[62] Friendships might pass from father to son, like patrilineal blood. Simeon's father John was a feoffee of the Trussbut lands, and Laurence Trussbut was supervisor of John's will.[63] Descendants of the Trussbuts and other friends trusted Simeon's son John to fulfil the vital duties of a trusted executor or supervisor of their wills. John Fyncham junior acted in one or other of these capacities for Thomas Talbot, John Geyton, Thomas Trussbut, Thomas Shuldham, Katherine widow of William Goderede, and Thomas Sharnbourne.[64] No doubt he gained these confidential appointments partly through his reputation as a 'lerned man in the lawe', as Sharnbourne's will described him. Yet his profession cannot entirely explain his popularity. Of all gentry testators known to me from fifteenth-century Norfolk, only these six used John Fyncham's services. It can hardly be coincidence that five of them were long-standing associates of the Fynchams.[65]

Simeon Fyncham's associates seem like friends. The services they carried out, the kin-like continuity of their connections, the ties of spiritual kinship they formed, the restricted geographical area within which they lived, all recall the image of friendship evoked in the letters and literature of the period – that ideal of restricted but harmonious neighbourhoods whose

---

[59] N & NRO Hare 1594.
[60] The name Laurence is so rare among fifteenth-century Norfolk gentry (only 4 other instances occur) that the coincidence almost certainly denotes godparenthood.
[61] N & NRO Hare 933.
[62] Simeon Rykkys, who witnessed for his godfather (N & NRO Hare 959). Simeon, like Laurence, was an extremely rare name in fifteenth-century Norfolk.
[63] N & NRO Hare 2692 and 5980.
[64] N & NRO Wills Gelour 211-12, Gelour 143, Aleyn 163-64, Betyns 137, and Brosyard 328-30; and Public Record office, PCC Wills, 16 Stockton.
[65] Sharnbourne is the exception. Katherine Goderede was sister to Thomas Shuldham – see her will (N & NRO Brosyard 328-30). I do not count Simeon Fyncham's own will, of which John was an executor.

families relied on old-established, trusty relationships to further their mutual interests and secure a decent prosperity. We cannot prove that Simeon Fyncham felt as strongly about his associates as did Roger Taverham or William Worcester; but there is no reason to suppose he did not. The Fyncham family's fortunes may have been based, as Colin Richmond suggests, on John Fyncham's success in the law. But his legal career in turn was perhaps sustained by the close structure of neighbourly friendship so carefully and patiently fostered by Simeon Fyncham before him.

Some wider observations arise from this study. Firstly, Simeon Fyncham's case supports the argument that patronal connections between great magnates and lesser county personalities may not have been pre-eminent in the social relationships of late-medieval provincial England. Fyncham, like John Hopton, the Townshend family, and the Derbyshire gentry, seemed more intent on maintaining a network of supporting friendships among his immediate neighbours, many of whom were clearly not of gentry status. Secondly, though instrumentality was of prime importance in fifteenth-century friendships, to assume a polarity between instrumental and affective friendships seems unwarranted. The Pastons and their circle felt very strongly about the friends with whom they exchanged services. Thirdly, this kind of friendship may have been typical of late-medieval societies well beyond Norfolk. The Pastons and the Fynchams, discoursing about, and relying on, their neighbours, friends and kin, uncannily resemble fifteenth-century Florentines, comfortably enmeshed in the networks of *parenti, amici* and *vicini*.[66] All these conclusions should be sufficiently intriguing and satisfying; but to a conscientious historian of gender, one puzzle remains. Why, in this analysis of so fundamentally human a relationship, have women appeared so seldom, and so peripherally?

To remark that studies of medieval friendship should do more to illuminate the role of women is hardly original; other modern commentators voice similar misgivings.[67] Yet I suspect that the cause of our bias lies deeper than simple failure to look hard enough for evidence of women's friendships or women in friendship. Each of the three levels of fifteenth-century friendship examined here was constructed as archetypally male, thus tacitly placing any notion of female friendship so firmly beyond the bounds of discussion as to confound even twentieth-century commentators. On the

---

[66] See the fine evocations of Florentine friendship and neighbourhood in F. W. Kent, *Household and Lineage in Renaissance Florence* (Princeton, 1977), pp. 172-73; D. V. and F. W. Kent, *Neighbours and Neighbourhood in Renaissance Florence: the District of the Red Lion in the Fifteenth Century*, Villa i Tatti, 6 (New York, 1982); *Bartolommeo Cederni and his Friends: Letters to an Obscure Florentine*, ed. by G. Corti and F. W. Kent, Quaderni di *Rinascimento*, 10 (Florence, 1991), pp. 3-47.

[67] e.g. Fitch Lyttle, 'Friendship and Patronage', p. 52; Mullet, 'Byzantium: A Friendly Society?', p. 19.

level of high theory, Cicero speaks only of male friendship. Why? Because his presuppositions on the gendered nature of civic virtue (implicit in the ethics of friendship) systematically exclude women from the discourse. That this prejudice appears only obliquely, in Laelius's rebuttal of the claim that self-interest is the origin of friendship, merely adds to its power to silence debate.[68] Similarly, Lydgate's exemplary pairs of friends were all male, described only in archetypally masculine terms – 'Hole, vndeparted of *courage and manhede*'.[69] Friendships in courtly tales are likewise typically masculine. Much of the tension in *Troilus and Criseyde* derives from Pandarus's ambivalent position: uncle and natural supporter to Criseyde, yet Troilus's faithful friend, whose interests he must prefer above those of his niece. As Criseyde sadly remarks:

> Allas, what sholden straunge to me doon,
> Whan he that for my beste frende I wende
> Ret me to loue, and sholde it me defende?[70]

In common usage trust was essential to friendship. It was also a quality proverbially absent in women – 'Who trusts woman is deceived', the saying ran.[71] Perhaps not surprisingly, women rarely acted in the roles reserved for 'best trusted friends'. They were seldom feoffees except in marriage settlements, never witnesses or attorneys. In the Paston letters, women were rarely named as friends. In only two letters, from the duchesses of Norfolk and Suffolk to John Paston III, did women describe themselves as a 'frende'.[72]

The one relationship within which women could be perceived as friends was that of wife to husband. The prior of Norwich, for instance, clearly ascribed to Agnes Paston the qualities of a true friend when he wrote that she

> was in singuler trust with her husbonde and one of his executours, and wele
> knowen in this cuntré ... and knewe hire husbondes mynde and last will as
> wele as ony lyvyng creature.[73]

---

68   Laelius argues that if friendship were based on expediency, then 'mulierculae', who are weak ('sely wymmen', in the Caxton translation), would more often seek friendship than men – which is implicitly ridiculous. See *De Amicitia*, Books XIII-XIV, pp. 156-62.

69   Lydgate, *Minor Poems*, p. 756 (my emphasis). Cf. also Chaucer, *Troilus & Criseyde*, p. 148, ll. 1079-81; the passage lists Troilus's knightly and masculine virtues, one of which is that he is the 'frendlieste wight'.

70   Chaucer, *Troilus & Criseyde*, p. 172, ll, 411-13.

71   Whiting, *Proverbs*, W 505; cf. also W 526 ('Women are oft unstable'), W 532 ('Women can deceive men') and W 534 ('Women can keep no counsel').

72   *PL*, II, pp. 476 and 442.

73   *PL*, II, pp. 609-10.

Certainly many Norfolk gentlemen (including Simeon Fyncham) entrusted to their wives the vital task of executing their wills.[74] Marriages, it seems, produced friendships; though the reverse might not be true. Neither Simeon Fyncham, nor his sons and daughters, nor his elder grandson, married within his friendship circle (the Geytons, Talbots, Shuldhams and Trussbuts). Beatrice Thoresby, wife of Simeon's eldest son, came from Lynn, less than sixteen kilometres from Fyncham; but her family never appeared in Fyncham documents before the marriage agreement of November 1445.[75] Only afterwards did her male relatives become feoffees, associates, and (we must presume) friends, of her husband and son.[76]

This is not to deny that fifteenth-century women carried out the duties and services of friendship among themselves and their male kin. The Pastons sought the company of, and took advice, loans, help, recipes and medicines from, such notable East Anglian women as Lady Morley, Elizabeth Calthorpe, Elizabeth Clere and Sybil Boys.[77] But these wholesome connections were rarely spoken of as friendships. Furthermore, where they were explicitly described in fiction, female friendships could be heavily castigated. In the Chester play of the Flood, Noah's wife's 'gossips' tempt her to drink, and hence to disobedience against God and her husband.[78]

Friendships in the fifteenth century, both in theory and practice, involved a range of connections, material and spiritual, between tightly-knit groups of neighbours who might be chosen without regard to their social standing. The ties of neighbourhood and friendship could be so close, and so warmly cherished, as to recall true kinship. Marriage was apparently seen to originate and maintain lasting friendships. Friendship satisfied both instrumental and deeply affective needs for fifteenth-century gentry. Yet it was also an institution unbendingly defined by male preoccupations and ideals.

---

[74] See e.g. N & NRO Wills, Brosyard 142; cf. Surflete 16-17 and 144-45, Brosyard 234 and 304-05, A. Caston 197, Aleyn 181-82 and Wylbey 40 (wills of Clement Herward, John Aslak, William Bozoun, John Bacon of Baconsthorp, Brian Boys of Rollesby, John Funteyn of Salle, and Christopher Straunge) for some of the many other examples.

[75] N & NRO Hare 2017 (indenture of marriage agreement).

[76] e.g. in 1454 (N & NRO Hare 959) and 1480 (N & NRO Petre Estate Bundle 26).

[77] See e.g. PL, I, 14, 30, 37, 50-51, 171-73, 221-22, 233, 257, 275, 352, 371, 664-65; also n. 16 above.

[78] The Chester Mystery Cycle, vol. I, ed. by R. M. Lumiansky and D. Mills, Early English Text Society, Supp. Ser., 3 (London, 1974), pp. 52-53.

TABLE 1:
MOST FREQUENT CONTACTS OF SIMEON FYNCHAM

Name:	Feoffee	Feoffor	Witness of S.F.	Witnessed by S.F.	Co-feoffee/feoffor	Co-witness	Other	Dates	Total
John Allone, Fincham		2	9			13		1409-41	24
Thomas Fuller, Fincham			8			3		1420-28	11
John Geyton, cleric, Walpole	3	4	3	4				1427-41	14
Nicholas Geyton, Littlewell Hall, Fincham	3	4	10	4		7		1427-42	28
Thomas Lovell, Barton Bendish	1		10	2	1		1	1420-39	15
John Miller, Fincham			13			6		1430-42	19
Nicholas Miller, Fincham		3	12	1	1	8		1416-39	25
John Shuldham, Marham	1	1	8	1	1	2		1416-25	14
Thomas Shuldham, Narborough/Marham	1			3	5	4		1425-41	13
Thomas Styward, Swaffham			5	3	1		1	1410-33	10
Thomas Talbot, Talbot's Hall, Fincham		1	4	6		1	1	1431-41	13
Nicholas Thurston, vicar, St Martin's Fincham, 1424-55	2	5	5	5	4	4		1416-42	25
Thomas Trussbut, Fincham	1	2	5		1	2		1425-39	11
Richard Undyrwode, Fincham			12	2		4		1429-42	18

TABLE 2:

THE FYNCHAM FAMILY IN THE FIFTEENTH CENTURY

```
John Fyncham = Katherine                    Alice = Laurence Trussbut
d. c.1416                                            d. 1425

Simeon = Elizabeth, da. of     Thomas      Christian      Margery
c.1388-1458   John Tendryng    fl. 1419    nun, Crabhouse  fl. 1415
              of Suffolk                    fl. 1415

John = Beatrice, da. of        Alice = John Bachecroft
c.1416-1496   Henry Thoresby
              of Lynn

John I = 1. Alice Bedyngfield   Thomas    Nicholas   Laurence      William   Eleanor
b. c.1452    d. 1474            fl. 1452  cleric,    fl. 1452,     fl. 1452  fl. 1447
fl. 1496  2. Jane Tey (Essex)             d.1503     will d. 1480

                                          John II     = Elizabeth, da. of Thomas
                                          of Outwell    Derham of Crimplesham
                                          fl. 1496      fl. 1499

John
fl. temp. Henry VIII
```

Note: This table was compiled primarily from information in N & NRO Hare MSS. I have added data from the pedigree in W. Blyth, *Historical Notices and Records of the Village and Parish of Fincham, in the County of Norfolk* (King's Lynn, 1863), pp.110-11, only where I could check the author's sources.

Caxton was a Mercer: his Social Milieu and Friends
ANNE F. SUTTON

In his prologue to his first book printed in English, the *Histories of Troy*
(c.1473), William Caxton described himself as 'mercer of the cyte of
London'.[1] This was the legal description of himself that he had been entitled
to since his admission to the Mercers' Company and the freedom of the City
of London in the 1440s. He was even more precise, about ten years later, in
his dedication of his translation of *Caton* (1484) to the City of London:

> William Caxton cytezeyn and conjurye of the same and of the fraternyte and
> felauship of the mercerye ...

He acknowledged he owed to the City of London his service, goodwill and
duty 'as to my moder, of whom I have receyved my noureture and lyvynge',
and his prayers.[2]

At no time in his many prologues and epilogues did Caxton ever
mention his roles as merchant adventurer, governor of the Merchant
Adventurers for nearly a decade, or as participant in many diplomatic
embassies. Despite his long description of his progress as translator of the
Histories of Troy, his frequent but vague chattiness about his acquisition and
choice of texts and their value to his customers, and his fairly frequent
references to places he visited abroad, he was remarkably reticent about his
considerable personal achievements before he was a printer, a fact which in
itself may tell us a little about his own view of his achievements and his
social milieu. Fourteen books were respectfully dedicated to or published for
eleven royal personages and aristocrats,[3] but only twice did he mention
names of high-ranking men he had met while acting as governor or
ambassador: both were interpolations into translations and neither name was
likely to impress his English readers.

---

[1]   N. F. Blake, *Caxton's Own Prose* (London, 1973), p. 97. This paper has benefited
      from the interest and encouragement of the Mercers' Company.

[2]   Blake, *Caxton's Own Prose*, p. 63. On Caxton's translation see *A Manual of
      Writings in Middle English*, gen. ed. A. E. Hartung, III (New Haven, 1972), pp.
      787-88, 938.

[3]   Edward IV (2) – he is mentioned in the dedication of the *Jason* and the
      Polychronicon was published under his 'protection'; Edward, Prince of Wales (1);
      Margaret of York (1); George, Duke of Clarence (1); Richard III (1); Earl of
      Arundel (1); Lady Margaret Beaufort (1); Henry VII (1); Earl of Oxford (1); and
      Arthur, Prince of Wales (1); (the other dedicatees are the City of London and the
      unknown lady of the *Book of the Knight of the Tour Landry*). In the prologue to his
      first book (of 3) commissioned by Rivers it is likely he over-stepped the mark in
      his *camaraderie*, and his next effort was very humble.

The first was an addition to the text of the *Mirror of the World* (1481) which expressed scepticism of the stories about the visitations of demons to anyone who spent a night in St Patrick's Purgatory. Not only had an unnamed canon of Waterford told Caxton he had suffered no hardship but

> in lyke wyse tolde to me a worshipful knyght of Bruggis named Sir John de Banste that he had ben therin in lyke wyse and see none other thyng but as afore sayd.

Sir John de Baenst came from an extremely aristocratic Flemish family and was the owner and commissioner of at least two fine manuscripts, one by Colard Mansion; apart from the contacts of diplomacy, the two men may have met because of their mutual interest in books.[4]

The second interpolation was made in his translation of the *Golden Legend*, a long task finished on 20 November 1484: the pious story of 'Sir John Capons' about King David composing the psalm *Miserere* while buried in the earth and eaten by worms was just the kind of vivid anecdote Caxton liked. Joan Copons was a Catalan nobleman, a past governor of Majorca and a rebel against the king of Aragon. In the rebel cause he was a frequent ambassador in the 1460s to Louis XI and to Isabel, Duchess of Burgundy, and by about 1467 he had achieved the position of a *chambellan* to the Duke of Burgundy's 'grand council'. It must have been about 1467-69 that he and Caxton were travelling companions between Ghent and Brussels and they may have been as well pleased with each other's company as de Baenst and Caxton appear to have been: Copons was cultured, astute, 'malicious, without shame, and very eloquent'.[5]

As these anecdotes were interpolations which only the assiduous reader would find, Caxton can have had no particular motive in mentioning these men's names, except to give authority to his stories – and perhaps it was just because he could remember their names, as he could not that of the canon of Waterford. To his English readers they would have meant nothing; but they show the historian the wide and cultivated acquaintance Caxton enjoyed before he returned to England. A similarly wide and cultivated circle of

4   Blake, *Caxton's Own Prose*, p. 117. Neither N. F. Blake, *Caxton and his World* (London, 1969), p. 128, nor G. Painter, *William Caxton* (London, 1976), p. 110, pursue de Baenst. There is some doubt about the generations of two Sir Johns. See *Vlaamse Kunst op Perkament*, catalogue of the exhibition at the Gruuthuse Museum, Bruges, 1981, no. 117, pp. 274-77; J. van Rompaey, *Het grafelijk baljuwsambt* (Brussels, 1967), pp. 217-18.

5   Blake, *Caxton's Own Prose*, p. 92. Neither Blake, *World*, pp. 37, 128, nor Painter, *Caxton*, p. 110, pursue Copons. I am indebted to Livia Visser-Fuchs for the following references: *Diccionari Biografic* (Barcelona, 1966, in progress), I, s.v. Copons, Joan de; J. Calmette, *Louis XI, Jean II et la Révolution Catalane* (Toulouse, 1903), pp. 172-202, esp. pp. 200-01, n. 6; R. Vaughan, *Charles the Bold* (London, 1973), p. 195.

English acquaintances might be constructed for him from the names of those who served with him on embassies, but he himself never mentions them: John Morton, master of the rolls, Sir Thomas Montgomery, knight of the body, William Hatcliffe, Edward IV's secretary, Sir John Scott and William Roos, the marshal and victualler of Calais, and the London goldsmith, Christopher Eliot, all of whom were engaged in important negotiations along with Caxton in 1474.[6] Perhaps they did not tell good stories; they certainly did not commission him to print books; and perhaps they took no further interest in a man who had left the world of diplomacy to print books in Westminster.

Graham Pollard once said that Caxton 'liked to think of himself as a successful merchant and that his chief claim to commercial fame was that he had introduced a brand new line in the small-wares trade'.[7] This paper explores this point of view that Caxton was content to think of himself as a mercer of the City of London. It seeks to place Caxton in the social milieu he knew to be his own, by examining a few episodes in his career and the lives of several of the men who are known to have worked with him: Robert Cosyn, John Sheffield and William Overey, and in particular the two whom he actually named as his 'friends', William Daubeney and William Pratte. It will also glance at his London competitors in the field of printing.

The members of the Mercers' Company of London included some of the richest, most influential men of the City and, by the time Caxton was a printer, they were used to considering their company's name *fixed* at the head of any list of the companies of London.[8] Their retail speciality was in the luxury cloths of silk and linen, in worsted and fustian (a cotton and linen mix produced in Italy and especially in the Ulm area of Germany), and in small luxury piece-goods which might include anything made of silk, dress accessories, or such items as books. They congregated particularly in the central and most prosperous wards and parishes of the city along Cheapside east of St Mary le Bow, near the church of St Thomas of Acre, and north to the Guildhall in the parishes of St Laurence Jewry, St Mary Aldermanbury and St Michael Bassishaw. Their headquarters were in the buildings of St Thomas of Acre. On Cheapside and the lanes leading off it you were in

[6] W. J. B. Crotch, *The Prologues and Epilogues of William Caxton*, E.E.T.S. O.S. 176 (1928), pp. cxl-cxlii.

[7] H. G. Pollard, *The English Market for Printed Books*, Sandars Lectures 1959, typescript in British Library, p. 12.

[8] Precedence was in fact fixed by custom by the end of the fifteenth century, but the Grocers, in second place, could still fiercely contest this, for example in 1477 when Caxton's friend, William Pratte, was one of the arbitrators (*The Acts of Court of the Mercers' Company 1453-1527*, ed. by L. Lyell and F. Watney (Cambridge, 1936), pp. 101-02).

particular danger of being hauled into a mercer's shop and beguiled by fair words:

> Ainz est crieys plus q'esperver:
> Qant voit la gent q'est desconue,
> Lors trait et tire, huche et hue,
> Si dist: 'Venetz avant entrer!
> Des litz, courchiefs, penne ostricer,
> Cendals, satins, draps d'outre mer;
> Venetz, je vous dourray le vieue,
> Car si vous vuilletz achater,
> Ne vous estuet plus loigns aler;
> Vecy le meilleur de la rue!'

> [...he shrieks more than a hawk. When he sees people he does not know, he pushes and pulls, calls and cries out, saying: 'Step up and come in! Beds, kerchiefs, ostrich feathers, silks, satins and cloths from overseas: Come in, I will show them to you, and if you want to buy you need go no further. Here are the best in the street!']9

The mercers' patter that Caxton learnt as an apprentice proved equally useful to him as a printer for his 'puffs'.

Leading mercers were usually also members of the Merchant Adventurers' Company which dominated the import and export trade to the Low Countries: a mercer-merchant adventurer exported English cloth and brought back the mercery items he retailed or sold wholesale (as well as anything else on which he hoped to make a profit). They did not trade in wool, which was the monopoly of the Merchants of the Staple of Calais, with whom the Adventurers were frequently and increasingly engaged in bitter conflict; all English wool was exported via Calais, except for shipments made under special royal licence. An individual merchant of London who had the Mercers as his parent company might find it convenient to become a member of both the Adventurers and the Calais Staple.10

After an apprenticeship, for which the boy's parents paid a premium, and which varied according to the status of the master and the length of

---

9 *The Works of John Gower*, ed. by G. C. Macaulay, I, *The French Works* (Oxford, 1899), *Miroir de l'Homme*, lines 25273-96, esp. 25285-96 (part of Gower's indictment of fraud); translation here based on W. Wilson, 'A Translation of John Gower's *Miroir de l'Homme*' (unpublished Ph.D. thesis, University of Miami, 1970), II, pp. 623-24.

10 E. M. Carus-Wilson, 'The Origins and Early Development of the Merchant Adventurers' Organization in London as Shown in their own Medieval Records', in her *Medieval Merchant Adventurers. Collected Studies* (London, 1954), pp. 143-182, esp. pp. 143-45. See also J. M. Imray, '"Les bones gentes de la mercerye de Londres": a study of the membership of the medieval Mercers' Company', in *Studies in London History, presented to P. E. Jones*, ed. by A. E. Hollaender and W. Kellaway (London, 1969), pp. 155-78.

service anticipated – anything between seven to ten years – the young man was admitted to the Mercers on payment of a fee; he expected to be admitted to the livery after a few years more, again paying a fee. Membership of the Merchant Adventurers was similarly secured by arrangement with the master, if he was a member, and again for a fee. The last years of apprenticeship of the mercer-merchant adventurer involved going abroad and trying out the skills which he had learnt in his master's house and shop – the ability to recognize and price linens and silks, to make the right purchases and sales, and to speak Dutch and French – at the great seasonal fairs of Ghent, Bergen op Zoom and Antwerp. The older apprentices and newly admitted mercers often acted as factors for their masters. Some of them continued in this role all their lives, having no capital to start out on their own; others were side-tracked into more congenial official jobs; some decided to base themselves mainly abroad; others came home and employed factors in their turn; others played both roles until civic office or old age kept them at home. Caxton's associates and friends fall into several of these categories.

Among the earliest references to Caxton are the three entries of May 1455 in Journal 5 of the Corporation of London published, but not translated or analysed in any detail, by N. F. Blake in 1967.[11] The entries are brief notes of examinations of three mercers, including Caxton, concerning the rights and wrongs of several debts and commercial transactions between Caxton, Robert Cosyn, John Neve, John Shelley and John Harowe, all mercers. The details are not full enough for us to unravel the situation precisely; such debts do not necessarily imply rancour between the parties, they were part of normal commercial life. These men were not dealing in simple cash sales but in the frequent exchange of goods and credit in London and the Low Countries, one bargain paying off another, in whole or in part, turning a credit into a debit or vice versa. But the fact that all of them appeared before the mayor and aldermen does mean at least that some of the debits and credits had become so complicated that arbitration was required over the case involving John Harowe, and prosecution had become necessary over John Neve's failure to settle his debts.

The entries show Caxton in the role of creditor in three more or less separate instances. First for £290 from Robert Cosyn which he expected to be repaid in the form of regular shipments to him in the Low Countries of English woollen cloth *de factura de la vyse* (of the assize) at £19 or less the

11 N. F. Blake, 'Two New Caxton Documents', *Notes and Queries* (March 1967), 86–87. Blake's Latin text is substantially correct, but has minor errors of transcription and some more serious omissions (see n. 16 below); the original has several oddities as it only represents the scrawled and highly abbreviated notes taken by the clerk during the court's session and is not in any sense a full minute; it is also not clear whether it is the court of aldermen or the mayor's court that is in session.

pack and of English pewter vessels at 100s. or less the hundred. So far Cosyn had paid John Shelley for £72 worth of cloth as part of this scheme. It seems likely that this was all part of a business arrangement between Caxton and Cosyn whereby Cosyn acted as the other man's agent in England and laid out his capital in the goods he wanted to sell in the Low Countries – this suggestion may well be supported by a gift of his goods and chattels by Caxton to Cosyn and John Rede, the clerk of the papers in one of the sheriffs' courts, in December 1453, less than two years before.[12] English woollen cloth was the main export of the Merchant Adventurers and English pewter was another solidly reliable export.

Caxton was also the creditor of John Neve, mercer, for £200 worth of linen cloth – one of the main mercery cloths – owing after bargains made between himself, John Neve, and others in Ghent. Ghent was one of the great seasonal fair towns of the territories of the duke of Burgundy much frequented by merchant adventurers. Caxton claimed another £80 from Neve of which £36 had been repaid by yet another business transaction also carried out in Ghent.

Thirdly Caxton described himself as owed many sums by John Harowe, another mercer and an ex-apprentice of Robert Large like himself, but an older man by at least ten years and possibly not one he knew well.[13] The sums involved must have been sizeable because Caxton was bound in 1000 marks to abide by arbitration in the matter; again Robert Cosyn had acted as

[12]   *CCR 1447-54*, p. 476. A gift of goods and chattels was a standard commercial surety (*Calendar of Plea and Memoranda Rolls of the City of London 1437-57*, ed. by P. E. Jones (Cambridge, 1954), pp. xxii-vi; hereafter *CPMR*). John Rede is identified in a chancery suit in which he and Cosyn appeared (PRO, C1/16/488); he was clerk of the papers by 28 Sept. 1452, CLRO, Recognizance Roll 20, m.4; and he was presumably still in office when he was chosen to settle his debts by Thomas Burgogne, undersheriff 1430s-71, in his will of 1471 (PRO, PROB 11/6, fols 4v-5v). The advantages for Caxton in having an associate in one of the sheriffs' courts is obvious. The identification of Rede by R. R. Griffith, 'The Early Years of William Caxton', in *An American Contribution to the Quincentenary Celebration*, ed. by S. O. Thompson (New York, 1976), pp. 20-54, esp. pp. 32-33, is unconvincing.

[13]   All unreferenced biographical details on mercers come from the Mercers' Company (hereafter MC) Biographical Index Cards compiled by J.M. Imray and others. Harowe was apprenticed 1422-3 to Robert Large and on the livery 1439-40; he had an apprentice, Richard Caxston, in 1443-4; 1449, 1450 and 1455 MP; 1450 a warden of the Mercers; 1455-6 he and William Pratte fined over a public quarrel; 1460 he led a London contingent for the Duke of York to the battle of Wakefield and was killed (C. M. Barron, 'London and the Crown 1451-61', in *The Crown and Local Communities in England and France in the Fifteenth Century*, ed. by J. R. L. Highfield and R. Jeffs (Gloucester, 1981), pp. 88-109, esp. p. 98 and n. 77).

Caxton's agent and stood to lose heavily if Harowe did not pay, a loss from which Caxton promised to protect Cosyn by personally prosecuting Harowe if necessary.

The conclusion of none of these matters is known, but it is clear from the few notes of the bonds taken down by the clerk that John Neve was the one being prosecuted, that he had been delaying the case against him, and that the others were witnesses and creditors involved in a complicated series of business arrangements.[14] He had to be bailed by two mercers, William Redeknap and John Shelley, both bound in £300 to have him in court on the following day,[15] and he himself had to swear that he would not attempt to delay the process of the court. When the case was not concluded the following day further recognizances were entered into to ensure that all the parties turned up the next day: Neve was bound in £100 to come and answer the charges against him, while Robert Cosyn, John Shelley (and John Neve again) were bound in £40 simply to appear.[16]

These cases show Caxton had become an extremely successful entrepreneur, mercer and merchant adventurer by 1455, doing business with many other mercers and dealing in large sums of money. The most important detail, however, is that he had as his agent or factor Robert Cosyn, a man about ten years younger than himself.[17] An investigation of Cosyn's career

---

[14] Neve issued from apprenticeship 1448; on the livery 1458-9; he had a row with John Shelley 1461-2, and was fined for uncourteous language; his career continued as a catalogue of fines in the Mercers' Wardens' accounts, 1456-7, 1459-60, 1463-4, and *Acts of Court*, p. 59. In a chancery suit of 1475 he claimed money was owed him by Caxton who was then in Flanders, a John Salford, mercer, having failed to settle the debt completely on Caxton's behalf (E. G. Duff, 'Early Chancery Proceedings Concerning Members of the Book Trade', *The Library*, 2nd ser., 8 (1907), 408-20, esp. p. 412). He also acted as an agent in trade with Italy (M. E. Mallett, 'Anglo-Florentine Commercial Relations 1465-91', *Economic History Rev.*, 15 (1962), p. 253, and PRO, C1/31/80). No will has been found for Neve, but the Thomas Neve who was admitted to the Mercers as his apprentice in 1464 may have been a son; it is perhaps of interest that he took as apprentice a William Squire (1459-60) and that the Squires were relatives of Alice Pratte, née Bothe (see below).

[15] *CPMR 1437-57*, p. 147.

[16] Blake did not transcribe the notes about the recognizances and apparently did not realize they were connected with the preceding entries (Corporation of London Records Office, Journal 5, fols 240v, 241 (the following folios up to 246v have been checked and the case is not referred to again)). Painter's account of the episode is similarly incomplete (*Caxton*, pp. 20-22), and he does not pursue Cosyn.

[17] MC, Wardens' Accounts: apprenticed 1444-5; admitted 1451-2; fined 1455-6 and 1456-7; otherwise not in Accounts and in *Acts of Court* only once for the riding to meet the king from France in September 1475 (p. 75). Valuing mercery in

shows him to have been an extremely competent administrator and that Caxton could hardly have chosen better. His career has a striking similarity to the first career of Caxton: they were both valued for their organizational abilities by their fellow merchants as well as by royal officials; both achieved responsible positions soon after Edward IV came to power. Caxton became governor of the Merchant Adventurers abroad, chosen by his fellows, and Cosyn was appointed collector of the king's customs in Sandwich, one of the major ports on the south coast, as well as controller of the customs in the port of London; his career as an official of the royal customs continued till the mid-1470s and he was clearly both important and trusted.[18]

Just as important was his appointment as clerk of the king's great wardrobe in the City of London, and five years later his promotion to its keepership; this was the department that purveyed woollen cloth, mercery and many other goods to the royal household. He held this post until October 1476, a term which overlapped with Caxton's tenure of the governorship and which ended almost exactly when Caxton took up residence in Westminster. As keeper of the great wardrobe Cosyn could favour, if he chose, particular merchants of London with the king's custom for luxuries and necessities, as well as particular artisans among the tailors, skinners or silkwomen of the city – unfortunately the accounts for his keepership do not survive.[19] He could commission his contacts in the Low Countries to bring to London goods the king might require or like, whether arras, silks or even, perhaps, books; a commission might equally go direct from the king himself to the governor of the Merchant Adventurers in Bruges. The known personal association between Edward IV's clerk and keeper of the great wardrobe and one of the leading merchant-diplomats in the Low Countries in the 1460s-70s may have been of great benefit not only to the king in good service and the acquisition of the trappings of a magnificent court, but also to Caxton and Cosyn in terms of financial profit as merchants and personal status and respect among their fellows.

No personal details are known about Cosyn: he died intestate in 1486. He certainly had some connections with Westminster, where he was a brother of the fraternity of the Assumption of Our Lady in the 1470s, so he could have been a neighbour of the printer; one other thing they had in common was their failure to hold office in the Mercers' Company.[20]

London 1454, *CPMR 1437-57*, p. 141.

[18] *CFR 1461-71*, nos. 5, 6, 7, 131, 263; *CPR 1461-68*, pp. 17, 20, 530; *CPR 1468-77*, p. 340; *CFR 1471-85*, nos. 108, 115. He was also employed organizing the repair of ships, and the taking of ships and men for the French expedition of 1475 (*CPR 1468-77*, pp. 356, 495).

[19] *CPR 1461-68*, pp. 50, 184, 437; PRO, E404/74/2, no. 31. For the work of the great wardrobe generally at this time and for references to Cosyn see A. F. Sutton and P. W. Hammond, *The Coronation of Richard III* (Gloucester, 1983), pp. 47-73.

Details about the Merchant Adventurers are sparse.[21] There is little hope of compiling a complete list of their governors before or after Caxton, or of establishing even his precise term of office. The office went back to the Adventurers' earliest days: in 1296 the Duke of Brabant's first charter granting them extensive trading privileges in his territories, and in particular in his town of Antwerp, included the right to hold their own assemblies; and in the 1315 expansion of this charter he specifically referred to their *capitaneum seu consulem*, the usual title for the leader of any caravan of merchants touring the fairs of Europe elected by themselves. The captain was to punish all trespasses, oversee all contracts, sales and purchases of goods, and manage all the company's affairs, ducal jurisdiction over matters of life and limb only excepted.[22] By Caxton's time the Merchant Adventurers had achieved very similar privileges from the other leading towns of the territories all then under the rule of the Valois dukes of Burgundy.[23]

The governor had to maintain these privileges and renew them as necessary, while maintaining peace and justice between English, Flemings, Brabanters, Hollanders and Zeelanders. Caxton himself was only involved in getting one new charter, in 1469 from Bergen op Zoom, the background details not apparently being known.[24] The governor had an onerous post, part diplomatic, part judicial, made difficult not only by disobedient adventurers but by the war-mongering and bullion-hungry policies of the king of England and duke of Burgundy which so frequently ignored the necessities of trade;[25] he had a salary (by 1421, at least), and expenses were

20 *Materials for a History of the Reign of Henry VII*, ed. by W. Campbell, 2 vols, Rolls Series (London, 1873, 1877), II, 54-55. Westminster Abbey Muniments, Book of the Fraternity of the Assumption of Our Lady, 1474-7, fol. 18.

21 Minutes of their day-to-day activities in London survive for only 1453-1527 among the Mercers' minutes in a heavily edited 16th-century copy; see Carus-Wilson, 'Origins', passim, and A. F. Sutton and P. W. Hammond, 'The Problems of Dating ... the Acts of Court of the Mercers' Company ...', *Jnl of the Soc. of Archivists*, 6 (1978), 87-91, for their often misleading and inaccurate character. Many privileges and charters survive in copies, however, and many of their transactions are recorded in central and local government records on both sides of the channel. Also see J. M. Imray, 'The Merchant Adventurers and Their Records', *Jnl of the Soc. of Archivists*, 2 (1964), 457-67.

22 MC, Book of Privileges of the Merchant Adventurers (1296-c.1490s; made end 15th century), fols 1-12v, esp. fols 2v, 12; J. de Sturler, *Les Relations Politiques et les Échanges Commerciaux entre le Duché de Brabant et l'Angleterre au Moyen Âge* (Paris, 1936), pp. 212-17.

23 MC, Book of Privileges, passim.

24 MC, Book of Privileges, fols 66-72. T. Sj. Jansma, 'De privileges voor de Engelsche natie te Bergen-op-Zoom, 1469-1555', *Bijdragen Mededelingen van het Historisch Genootschap*, 5 (1929), 41-106.

25 J. H. A. Munro, *Wool, Cloth and Gold. The Struggle for Bullion in*

met out of the fines collected;[26] he had lieutenants or deputies, required especially during the seasonal fairs of Ghent, Bergen op Zoom and Antwerp, and a number of advisers or assistants chosen from among his fellows. He was elected each year, but a successful man prepared to stay abroad and with the necessary fluency in languages was frequently re-elected.[27] In Caxton's time William Overey, a stockfishmonger, held the post for several years in the late 1450s and Caxton appears to have been in the post continuously from 1462 to early 1471; and one of his successors, John Pickering, mercer, liked the job so well that he sought re-election off and on from 1471 to his death in 1498. Increasingly in the fifteenth century the post was held by a mercer, a fact reflecting the numerical superiority of mercers among the adventurers.[28]

William Overey's career throws some light on Caxton's subsequent role as governor and illustrates the problems of the office. Overey was the governor who had to sort out the international incident of 1457 precipitated by John Sheffield, the mercer, whose main claim to fame is that he was the one who later told Caxton the story of the eggs which were called *eyren* in a hamlet somewhere along the Thames estuary. It is interesting in the light of the 1457 incident that Caxton says Sheffield grew 'angry' during the confusion with the 'goode wyf' over the 'eyren'.[29] Sheffield was a young man newly admitted to the Mercers' Company in 1457, and one perhaps too used to having his own way since his father's death ten years before.[30] His youth, inexperience and hot temper may have been the cause of his argument with the meter of Antwerp, Martin van der Hove, over a bale of madder which split during the weighing. Sheffield became abusive and provoked Martin to come out with the age-old insult for Englishmen – that they were born with tails like devils, the mark of Cain, the result of a curse laid on them by St

---

Anglo-Burgundian Trade, 1340-1478 (Brussels and Toronto, 1972), pp. 155-85.

26   H. T. Smit, *Bronnen tot de geschiedenis van den handel met Engeland, Schotland en Ierland, 1150-1485*, 2 vols, Rijksgeschiedkundige Publicatien, vols 65, 66 (The Hague, 1928), I, no. 983; M. Sellers, *The York Mercers and Merchant Adventurers 1356-1917*, Surtees Society, 129 (1917), pp. xxxvi, 75-79.

27   Election was 'martly' i.e. made in relation to the four seasonal fairs, but little is known of 15th-century practice (see W. E. Lingelbach, *The Merchants Adventurers of England, their Laws and Ordinances with other Documents* (Philadelphia, 1902), e.g. pp. 5-9, and Carus-Wilson, 'Origins', pp. 158-59).

28   Carus-Wilson, 'Origins', esp. pp. 163-64.

29   Prologue to the *Eneydos* (1490), Blake, *Caxton's Own Prose*, pp. 79-80. Neither Blake, *World*, p. 157 n.48, nor Painter, *Caxton*, pp. 26, 176, pursue Sheffield.

30   His father Edmund was a London vintner, originally from Burton-on-Clay on the banks of the River Trent in Nottinghamshire, who left six children to the care of Leticia, his widow, on his death in 1445-46. She apprenticed John, the eldest boy, with Robert Harom, mercer (PRO, PROB 11/3, fols 239-40; *CPMR 1437-57*, pp. 92, 185; MC, Wardens' Accounts 1456-7). Nothing has been found about John's later life.

Augustine. The authorities of Antwerp decided to take a militant anti-English stand over the quarrel, and the English, led by Overey as governor, packed their goods and left for Bruges, declaring they would not sell any more in Antwerp. In fact both sides had been spoiling for a show-down for some time and each had a catalogue of complaints against the other. Reconciliation, however, was not long in following: the English trade was an extremely lucrative one for Antwerp, and for the English the port was their main access to the German markets for their cloth and where the mercers among them bought German fustian.[31]

They went to arbitration, with the lord of Bergen op Zoom[32] as 'above and upreste arbiter', bearing their books of complaints. William Overey, Robert Worseley, and James Fane[33] were appointed arbitrators or proctors for the English on 26 January 1458, while the town of Antwerp was represented by Francis van der Delft, a lawyer, John van der Meren, steward of the county of Berg, and John Block; there were heavy penalties for those who failed to abide by the resulting arbitration. The final agreement was dated 8 April 1458; innumerable clauses reiterated the privileges of the English and the future recourses for any disputants, and the specific dispute between Sheffield and van der Hove was settled. The latter had declared that his words were 'never said in dispite of the ... king of Englond ne of the said nacion but he spake them of importunyte and hotnesse of blode'; he was to ask forgiveness of the English and both he and Sheffield were to go on a pilgrimage to St Nicholas of Bari in Apulia. It would be pleasant to think of them going off to Italy together, but all it meant was a stiff fine, the stiffest of all 'pilgrimage' fines.[34]

The insult that Englishmen had tails was one that merchant adventurers abroad had to live with. Caxton may well have been in Antwerp at the time

[31] J. H. Munro, 'Bruges and the Abortive Staple in English cloth', *Revue Belge de Philologie et d'Histoire*, 44 (1966), 1137-59, esp. pp. 1143-44.

[32] John of Glymes, nicknamed *metten lippen*, 'with the lips', (1417-94), lord of Bergen op Zoom from 1427 and a man of considerable standing.

[33] Worseley was a mercer; Fane's parent company has not been identified.

[34] The main source for this account and the quotations is the contemporary English translation of the final agreement drawn up at Mechelen on 8 April 1458 by the notary before witnesses. This is entered as 'the pryvelage in English purchased in William Overays tyme beyng gouvernor' in MC, Book of Privileges, fols 51v-66, esp. fols 65, 59-59v, 62v for the quotations. The English translation makes the identity of Sheffield certain; there is also no indication in the Book that any dissatisfaction was felt over this agreement despite the slur of bribery later cast on Overey. Compare M.-R. Thielemans, *Bourgogne et Angleterre. Relations Politiques et Économiques entre les Pays-Bas Bourguignons et l'Angleterre, 1435-67* (Brussels, 1966), pp. 277-80. For the *anglais coué* see P. Rickard, *Britain in Medieval French Literature 1100-1500* (Cambridge, 1956), pp. 165-66. Thanks are due to Livia Visser-Fuchs for additional details about the 'tails' and the pilgrimage-fine.

of this fracas. The curse was variously ascribed to SS. Augustine or Thomas Becket, and the inhabitants of Rochester (and nearby Strood) or Canterbury or Dorchester were variously accused of being the original recipients of the curse. In his translation of the *Mirrour of the World* (1481), Caxton decided to suppress his original's text concerning the insult but in his translation of the *Golden Legend* (1484) he volunteered the information that there was a tradition that St Augustine had put the curse on the inhabitants of Strood in Kent, although he assured his readers that there was now no sign of any such deformity – a remark that is probably the best evidence available that he was born in Strood.[35] This was a private joke for a favoured few, among whom were his friend, William Pratte from Canterbury, and Pratte's most successful apprentice, William Tenacres from Rochester.

The second episode of Overey's career touches Caxton's even more closely: the series of events that led to Caxton's election as governor in succession to Overey. From 1461 Edward IV was the new king of England and the Merchant Adventurers needed a new confirmation of their privileges,[36] a technicality over which they envisaged no problem, apart from expense, as they were part of the London mercantile elite which had thrown in its lot, finances and even some of its blood, behind the Yorkists from June 1460 – at least one mercer and merchant adventurer, John Harowe, had died at Wakefield for York. In the event, an extraordinary document was issued on 16 April 1462 which confirmed many privileges and detailed the governor's rights and duties under the king, but appointed William Overey to the post and entirely failed to mention the right of free election. There is no surviving background information by which to decide whether this was the result of a major clerical misunderstanding or the result of deliberate planning by Overey, but he cannot have acted alone.[37]

It seems likely that there was an internal battle for power going on within the Merchant Adventurers and that Overey, the stockfishmonger, was the leader of a clique trying to circumvent the increasing dominance of the mercers who by force of their numerical superiority could, and indeed did from 1462, monopolize the office of governor.[38] Overey had secured election

---

35 W. Caxton, *The Golden Legend*, ed. by F. S. Ellis, 3 vols (London, 1892), II, p. 499. Blake (*World*, pp. 20-21) knows the Antwerp incident but does not connect it to John Sheffield. And see L. M. Matheson, 'Printer and Scribe: Caxton, the *Polychronicon*, and the *Brut*', *Speculum*, 60 (1985), 593-614, esp. pp. 608-09.

36 Regularly re-issued from 1408 (Carus-Wilson, 'Origins', p. 153).

37 Overey's anxiety to have a royal appointment may have derived in part from past difficulties over defining his authority to officials in the Low Countries; see text of the 1458 agreement with Antwerp, and Bruges Town Archives, Civiele Sententien, 1453-60, fol. 214-214v, kindly checked for me by Livia Visser-Fuchs. See also Thielemans, *Bourgogne et Angleterre*, p. 279 n.653.

38 These were not uncommon (Carus-Wilson, 'Origins', pp. 157-73, and Imray, 'The

as governor several times in the late 1450s,[39] he had had a success with the agreement with Antwerp in 1458, and been appointed to several embassies over trade between England and the Low Countries and over Staple affairs in these years;[40] nevertheless, in 1460 he was actually imprisoned in Bruges on the orders of John Pickering, a mercer and the governor for that year.[41] The imprisonment of such an important past governor by the man in office suggests that power-brokering was going on, and was at its height about 1458-62. It was the Mercers in London who swung into furious action after Edward IV's April 1462 charter: on 28 May a letter under the privy seal from the king at Leicester confirmed the free election of the governor and the holding of their assemblies; on 2 June letters from Antwerp declared that Overey had received bribes from the town and had consequently allowed certain English privileges to be passed over; and on 24 June he was discharged from the governorship. William Caxton, mercer, was elected in his place.[42]

The suggestion that Overey was the loser of a bitter internal battle for power, within the Merchant Adventurers, with the Mercers and William Caxton – whose role in the battle is unknown – as the victors, is borne out by Overey's continuing successful career. He had not incurred official or royal censure, only that of his fellow adventurers, and the astonishing Antwerp accusation of bribery seems to have been more the result of ruthless politicking than truth.[43] He was on diplomatic missions over trade in 1462-3,

Merchant Adventurers and Their Records', p. 462).

[39] Probably governor in 1456 (Smit, *Bronnen*, I, pt. 2, no. 1463); and certainly in 1457 when he obtained from the Earl of Warwick an inspeximus of an old charter to the Adventurers, 15 September 1457 (MC, Book of Privileges, fols 48v-50v); and in 1458 and 1459 (Thielemans, *Bourgogne et Angleterre*, p. 278 n.649).

[40] Thielemans, *Bourgogne et Angleterre*, pp. 278 n.649, 369-75. See also Munro, *Wool, Cloth and Gold*, pp. 151-54.

[41] Bruges Town Archives, Civiele Sententien, 1453-60, fol. 335v (partly destroyed); Overey's sureties included Robert Worsley, mercer, and James Fane of the 1458 Antwerp negotiations, and William Overton, another mercer; thanks are due to Livia Visser-Fuchs for looking at this record. See also Thielemans, *Bourgogne et Angleterre*, p. 278 n.649.

[42] R. Hakluyt, *The Principal Navigations...of the English Nation*, 12 vols (Glasgow, 1903), II, 147-59, is the source for the text of the 16 April 1462 charter which was not entered, for obvious reasons, into the Book of Privileges, as Edward IV's privy seal of 28 May most definitely was, fols 35-37 (Eng. and Lat.); G. Schanz, *Englische Handelspolitik gegen Ende des Mittelalters*, 2 vols (Leipzig, 1881), II, 578, items 34 and 35; Carus-Wilson, 'Origins', pp. 153-4; Thielemans, *Bourgogne et Angleterre*, p. 278 n. 649.

[43] Compare Thielemans' criticism of Overey for being over zealous for the honour of the English which, besides being contradicted by the Antwerp accusation, was in fact his job (*Bourgogne et Angleterre*, p. 278 n. 649). Painter attempts unconvincingly to explain the Overey episodes by reference to the

he was appointed to commissions inquiring into piracy until 1468, and in 1470-1 was organising warships for Edward IV.[44]

The key to his ignominious defeat as governor of the Merchant Adventurers lies in his trade. He came originally from Sheston, Leicestershire,[45] and in London became a stockfishmonger by company. This implied a specialization in dried and fresh fish, and in ship-owning; he dealt in corn, cloth for the Prussian and Danish markets (in the 1450s), horses, steel, potash, whale and cod-liver oil, pitch, tar, and fish;[46] from the 1460s he was part owner of the *New Elyn*, the ship that bore Margaret of York to her marriage to the Duke of Burgundy (one of his partners being Sir John Fogge, a leading officer of Edward IV's household), the *James* of Southwold, and probably other ships.[47] Such a man was an ideal officer for Edward IV in matters of shipping,[48] but as a stockfishmonger he fitted uneasily into a Merchant Adventurers' company increasingly dominated by mercers whose particular expertise lay in the more prestigious imports of silk, linen, fustian and small luxury goods.

The difference between Overey's stockfishmonger world and that of a mercer like Caxton is further revealed in his will of 1473 (he died in 1480). Appropriately enough he lived in the parish of St Magnus at the head of London Bridge and left bequests to both the poor householders of his craft in

York/Lancaster rivalry (*Caxton*, pp. 25-28). The effects of this political rivalry on merchants and London is best described by Barron, 'London and the Crown, 1451-61', 88-109, and J. L. Bolton, 'The City and the Crown, 1456-61', *The London Journal*, 12 (1986), 11-24.

[44] Thielemans, *Bourgogne et Angleterre*, pp. 389 and n.126, 398-99; *CPR 1461-67*, pp. 101-02, 202; *CPR 1466-77*, pp. 100, 217.

[45] He maintained contacts with his home county; a sister was living in Leicester in 1473 and he owned cottages and gardens there; his brother, Thomas, was dead by 1473; perhaps Robert Overey, draper of Leicester, was a relative, *CPR 1446-52*, p. 199, and see his will, below. He had no connections with the Overeys of Southampton as asserted by Painter, *Caxton*, p. 28 (see C. Platt, *Medieval Southampton* (London, 1973), p. 254, for biographies for his namesakes). There must be some doubt over the identity of the man in a few of the *CPR* entries. I am grateful to Lis Lewis for discussing the Southampton Overeys with me.

[46] *CPR 1446-52*, pp. 51, 160; Thielemans, *Bourgogne et Angleterre*, p. 220; Smit, *Bronnen*, I, no. 1620 (6 and 7).

[47] The *New Helen*: C. L. Scofield, *The Life and Reign of King Edward IV*, 2 vols (London, 1923), I, 456-57; Smit, *Bronnen*, I, no. 1611; PRO, C1/32/340. The *James* he bought with Edward Newman, a fellow stockfishmonger and one of his executors, *CCR 1461-68*, no. 405. Edward Stone, his ship-master, received a bequest in his will. See also PRO, C1/36/54 for Overey's ownership of property in Southwold.

[48] This may explain the copious references to 'mariners' in the notorious charter of 16 April 1462.

the nearby streets where they congregated, and money for three 'recreations' for his craft's young men in Old Fish Street, Bridge Street and Thames Street. Unsurprisingly the Merchant Adventurers get no mention, but the fraternity of St Thomas Becket in his parish church received 10 marks (St Thomas was the patron saint of the Adventurers). He had a close, pious relationship with the Hospital of St Thomas the Apostle in Southwark, where he was buried, and leased land from it in Deptford, probably for his ships. He also maintained a 'bierhous' in St Katherine's by the Tower, leased to a 'docheman', no doubt an entrepreneurial interest gained during his long association with the Low Countries. He was prosperous and had many good connections, not least with his partner in the *New Elyn*, Sir John Fogge of Ashford, Kent, and by 1468 he was able to marry his daughter and heiress, Margaret, to Ralph Bawde, esquire, a member of the gentry of Essex.[49] His widow survived him till 1488 and then joined him in St Thomas's.[50]

In 1462 Caxton, as the new *mercer* governor of the Merchant Adventurers, must have considered himself to be a very different man from William Overey, but although he benefited during his term from being a mercer and from the return of strong government in England endorsed by merchants like himself, he had as many political headaches as his predecessor. He had to lead the exodus of the English merchant adventurers from Bruges to Utrecht when Philip of Burgundy yet again banned the import of English cloth into his territories in October 1464 – they only returned in 1467-8. The quarrel between England and the Hansa reached a crisis in 1468, and of all the League's towns only Cologne continued to trade with England. Charles of Burgundy and Cologne acted as arbitrators and Caxton served as an ambassador over both the Hansa quarrel and the cloth ban. Neither issue had been solved by the time of Edward IV's departure into exile in the autumn of 1470.[51]

In 1471 Caxton did not stand for re-election as governor; Edward IV was back on the English throne in May, and in July Caxton departed to learn printing in Cologne. Although he took part in some diplomatic missions in the 1470s and participated in the work of arranging ships for Edward's expedition to France in 1475, he did not again serve as governor of the Merchant Adventurers. He had given them long service in what was an

---

[49] PRO, PROB 11/6, fols 292v-293v, 28 August 1473, proved 14 June 1480; *CCR 1468-76*, no. 187.

[50] She left her estate to Thomas Fulbourne, her grandson by a previous marriage of the daughter, Margaret (PRO, PROB 11/8, fols 170v-171v, 5 January 1488).

[51] W. J. B. Crotch, 'Caxton on the Continent', *The Library*, 4th ser., 7, (1926-7), 387-401, with revision from W. Stein, 'Die Merchant Adventurer in Utrecht (1464-67)', *Hansische Geschichtsblatter*, 27 (1899), 179-89, and Munro, *Wool, Cloth and Gold*, pp. 155-76; T. H. Lloyd, *England and the German Hansa* (Cambridge, 1992), pp. 196-208.

arduous, and largely thankless, job.[52] The good side was the personal fortune he had accumulated, his commercial expertise and his acquaintance with almost everyone worth knowing in trade and diplomacy between Calais and Utrecht, London and Cologne.

After printing a few books in French and English in Bruges he settled in the sanctuary of Westminster Abbey. The king's palace, the government departments, law courts, the great abbey, parliament, and the town's annual fair were among Westminster's many attractions for the printer; and some of his friends, such as Cosyn and Daubeney, may have lived there.[53] Above all, he had easy access to London's markets and trading networks while enjoying sanctuary protection from its laws and prejudices: its aversion to the employment of aliens who made up his press's work-force; the possible jealousy of its book traders, the company of Stationers;[54] and perhaps most important of all the interference of his own powerful company, the Mercers, with its right of search and understandable desire to have such a well-connected and experienced man as himself serve as a warden and an ever-available adviser.[55]

Caxton's own writings expressed pride in his freedom of both the Mercers and the City of London, but there was another side: while translating the *Book of the Knight of the Tower* (1484) he found that his French text had *merciers* in the role of the traders and tricksters who were whipped from the Temple by Christ; he made no changes and in his text too it was mercers who were the object of godly indignation. Whether this was the result of Caxton's sense of humour, his moral sense or just idleness, some

[52] Crotch, *Prologues*, pp. xciv-xcvi, cxl-clvii; S. Corsten, 'Caxton in Cologne', *Jnl of the Printing Historical Soc.*, 11 (1976-7), 1-18.

[53] G. Rosser, *Medieval Westminster 1250-1540* (Oxford, 1989), pp. 209-14.

[54] The Stationers included all the book artisan trades by this date (see G. Pollard, 'The Company of Stationers before 1557', *The Library*, 4th ser., 18 (1937), 1-38, esp. pp. 2-15). Recent research has found little evidence of hostility in London towards the new trade (C. P. Christianson, *A Directory of London Stationers and Book Artisans 1300-1500*, Bibliographical Society of America (New York, 1990), p. 43) but it certainly occurred elsewhere (see R. Hirsch, *Printing, Selling and Reading, 1450-1550* (Wiesbaden, 1967), pp. 27-29).

[55] There is no evidence that he did not advise and attend meetings of both the Mercers and Merchant Adventurers, but he never held office in the former company. He did audit the accounts of the parish of St Margaret's, Westminster, so he was not entirely set on avoiding public responsibility; indeed Caxton's friends and acquaintances in this parish might be a rewarding study – see Rosser, chs. 8, 9 and passim, and the present author's study of the clerk of the parish accounts, John Kendale, public notary, in 'John Kendale: a Search for Richard III's Secretary', in *Richard III, Crown and People*, ed. by J. Petre (London, 1985), pp. 224-38, esp. pp. 228-30.

mercers of London would certainly not have been pleased![56] In the same way his dedication of *Caton* (1484) to the City of London voiced several criticisms: city businessmen no longer thought of the common good as they had in his young days, but only of their personal profit; the city was less rich than it had been; and it lacked the proud dynasties of merchants he had observed abroad. He hoped piously that his book might help improve the younger generation.[57] His clever mixture of flattery and criticism shows how well he knew his fellow citizens' weaknesses and how skilled he was in advertising a book, and it is also a feather in the wind to show how it came about that he declined to live in the City of London.

As a shrewd businessman Caxton had to assess his competitors with presses in England; and they were soon there, if they did not actually beat him to it. Did he choose Westminster because there were printers already in the City of London? Lettou was there certainly by 1480, and by June 1483 he had been joined by several others. At least one unknown printer was established in Oxford by 1478; and Theodoric Rood of Cologne was there by 1481, printing Latin texts, several by English authors, and trespassing into Caxton's territory of English texts with Mirk's *Festial* in 1486 (already printed by Caxton in 1483), apparently his last book before his bankruptcy. In St. Albans a schoolmaster produced a few books in English and Latin 1479-86.[58] Neither of the two provincial printers proved dangerous competitors for Caxton, and perhaps he never saw them as rivals at all; indeed, it has been suggested that they may all have collaborated with or have been employed by Caxton.[59]

The London printers were more numerous and potentially more of a threat.[60] John Lettou was established in the city by 1480, his first known productions being two Latin books paid for by William Wylcocks, a draper and leading merchant adventurer, in 1480-1.[61] It was probably Wylcocks who

56   *The Book of the Knight of the Tower*, ed. by M. Y. Offord, E.E.T.S. S.S. 2 (1971), p. 60, and *Le Livre du Chevalier de la Tour Landry*, ed. by A. de Montaiglon (Paris, 1854), pp. 81-82.

57   *Caxton's Own Prose*, pp. 63-66.

58   N. F. Blake, 'Wynkyn de Worde: the Early Years', *Gutenberg Jahrbuch* (1971), 62-138, esp. p. 65, and his 'The Spread of Printing in English during the Fifteenth Century', *Gutenberg Jahrbuch* (1987), 26-36.

59   It is difficult to see them as 'naturally very much under [Caxton's] influence' (Blake, 'The Spread', pp. 33-34), but he may be only referring to de Worde and Pynson.

60   The main studies on the London printers are *The Revelations to the Monk of Evesham ... edited from the copy ... printed by William de Machlinia about 1482*, ed. by E. Arber (London, n.d.), introd.; H. R. Plomer, *Wynkyn de Worde and his Contemporaries* (London, 1925), pp. 157-62; Pollard, 'The Stationers before 1557', passim.

61   *The Revelation*, pp. 3-4. Arber several times miscalls William 'Wilcock' Thomas.

had encouraged Lettou to set up business in London and he may have acted for him as one of the London citizens required to stand surety for an alien being admitted to the freedom of the City, in Lettou's case possibly as a stationer, possibly as a draper. This status would have been essential to Lettou's position in the City and the support of someone such as Wylcocks would have been invaluable.[62] Wylcocks is another example of a leading merchant adventurer who like Caxton, and the later Roger Thorney,[63] speculated in the early English book trade; the two mercers among them knew the small-wares trade and all three could import the necessary paper – the single most expensive investment of a printing venture – as merchant adventurers and avoid another middle-man.[64] Wylcocks was a prominent royal supplier by the mid-1480s and controller of the subsidies in the port of London.[65] The enterprise of Wylcocks and others like him constituted the really dangerous competition for Caxton – if they started to commission books in English on a regular basis – but he had been used to mercantile competition all his adult life. The rivalry with Wylcocks in particular may have been a friendly one: they were both merchant adventurers and the younger man's enterprise may have been a product of admiration for his elder's venture; both were presumably lovers of books; Caxton had spent

[62] Plomer, *Wynkyn de Worde*, p. 157, suggests Wylcocks brought Lettou to London. Pollard, 'Stationers', pp. 18-22, sets out the importance of the freedom. Also see Christianson, *Directory*, p. 26 and n. 12.

[63] Thorney was apprentice and relative of John Pickering, mercer, Caxton's successor as governor of the Merchant Adventurers in the Low Countries; he requested de Worde to print Higden's *Polychronicon* and a translation of *De proprietatibus rerum*, in 1495, the latter containing laudatory references to Caxton, Thorney and Tate, a third mercer and merchant adventurer who set up the first paper-mill in England, presumably with an eye on the requirements of the printing industry (G. Bone, 'Extant Manuscripts Printed from by Wynkyn de Worde with Notes on their Owner Roger Thorney', *The Library*, 4th ser., 12 (1932), passim, and Blake, 'Worde's Early Years', p. 67).

[64] Hirsch, ch.1, esp. pp. 39-40. The cost of paper must have been a crucial factor in the failure of early printers; merchant adventurers had advantages that only an Italian merchant could have equalled in England. It is probably significant that it was a mercer and merchant adventurer who tried to establish the first paper-mill in England.

[65] Biography in Sutton and Hammond, *The Coronation of Richard III*, p. 414: appears to have been a common councilman for Langbourne ward by 1478, a ward in which several printers were living in 1483 (see below), and a warden of the drapers in 1486; in 1483 living in Candlewick Street ward with an alien wife, *theotonica*, Joanna, PRO, E179/242/25, m. 10d (this corrects the Bishopsgate ward given in error in *The Coronation* above). For further evidence of his involvement in the book trade see the dispute betweem him and a bookseller (Duff, 'Early Chancery Proceedings', pp. 410, 416-17).

much of his life in the Low Countries, and one suspects married there, and Wylcocks certainly had a foreign wife, Joanna.

To return to John Lettou. The little that is known of his books seems to show that he (and his partner and successor) aimed predominantly at readers of Latin and Law-French.[66] In June 1483 he was described as a householder and 'bokeprynter' in the ward of Dowgate – a comparatively poor ward of the city with a river frontage and inhabited by a large proportion of aliens – close to the two churches of All Hallows in the ward according to the colophon of the edition of Littleton's *Tenures* printed in 1482-3.[67] He lived with his wife, Elizabeth, an alien like himself, and he and his partner, William Ravenswalde, together had a staff of four alien servants, Peter Martynson, George van Hawyn, Gerard van Dentour (van Deventer?) and Joste de Fuller.[68] William Ravenswalde can be identified as William de Malines or Machlinia, Lettou's successor.[69] Lettou is presumed to have died shortly after 1483, his business passing to Machlinia who then moved it to 'Fleet Bridge', where Fleet Street crossed the River Fleet in the ward of Farringdon Without, an ambiguous address which was inside the city's boundary but possibly in one of the several liberties near the bridge, such as the Fleet Prison. He then moved to 'Holborn', an address even more difficult to identify. If he was not a freeman of the City, as it is suggested here Lettou was, he might have found it wise to move outside its boundaries.[70] On the other hand it may be that he was simply moving nearer the main customers for his Year Books, the lawyers.

The other three printers listed in the aliens' poll tax return of 1483 have no identifiable surviving books attached to their names and have therefore

[66] *The Revelation*, pp. 3-7; Plomer, *Wynkyn de Worde*, pp. 159-60; Pollard, 'The Stationers before 1557', pp. 21-22.

[67] Pollard, 'Stationers', pp. 21-22, first identified these churches, using the colophon alone.

[68] PRO, E179/242/25, m. 8d (Dowgate) clearly shows Lettou and William as joint employers, with Lettou as the householder. For a commentary on these records see S. L. Thrupp, 'Aliens in and around London in the Fifteenth Century', in *Studies in London History, presented to P. E. Jones*, ed. by A. E. Hollaender and W. Kellaway (London, 1969), pp. 251-72, esp. pp. 265-66 where she points out the printers. This information is not used in *A Short Title Catalogue of Books Printed in England, Scotland and Ireland ... 1475-1640*, III, Indexes, by K. F. Pantzer and P. R. Rider (London, 1991).

[69] Ravenswalde is not known in the neighbourhood of Mechelen but a long-lost monument to Philip Keerman, died 1507, in the church of Our Lady, bore the name 'Ravensfelt'; however, it is not clear from the surviving description of this whether this refers to a place or family. I am indebted for this information to Mr H. M. F. J. Installe, Town Archivist of Mechelen.

[70] Pollard, 'The Stationers before 1557', p. 22; Plomer, *Wynkyn de Worde*, pp. 111-12.

received no attention as printers from historians of the book trade. Each could have deprived Caxton of the commissions on which any press had to rely. If he did not know them automatically, his old friend, William Pratte, one of the sheriffs' deputies collecting the tax, could have informed him.[71] All lived in Langbourne ward, another ward with a sizable alien population. John Hawkes 'bokeprynter' was a householder,[72] but had no alien servants or wife listed with him and may have worked for someone else – possibly the much better known figure, Henry Frankenberg 'bokeprynter' and householder, listed with five alien servants: Stephen Ree, Herman Groce, Dedericus Derikson, Adrian Derikson, and Katerina who is given no surname. Last, listed next to Frankenberg, and presumably living virtually next door, was Bernardus, 'bokeprynter' and householder, with no alien servants or wife.[73]

Of these characters, all *carefully* recorded as book printers in the poll tax return, nothing is known of John Hawkes. Henry Frankenberg's first appearance as an importer of books into England is dated 30 December 1477.[74] He and his partner Bernardo van Stando – undoubtedly the lone 'Bernardus' of the tax return and probably the Bernard of Utrecht who imported large quantities of books in 1480-81 – leased a property called St Mark's Alley in St Clement's Lane, Langbourne ward, on 10 May 1482, at £3 13s. 4d. the year. The acquisition indicates their commercial standing; either or both of them may have taken the precaution of securing admission to the freedom of the City, presumably in the Stationers' Company, as it has been suggested Lettou did. Both have long been known as substantial booksellers and importers, but not as printers themselves.[75] Frankenberg was paying

71 PRO, E179/242/25, m. 1d.
72 Ibid, m. 9d: 'bokeprynter' is inserted above the line.
73 Ibid, m. 10: again 'bokeprynter' has been inserted above the line in both cases, suggesting that the fact was interesting; the recording of trades is erratic, being better for some wards than others.
74 E. Armstrong, 'English Purchases of Printed Books from the Continent 1465-1526', *EHR*, 94 (1979), 268-91, esp. p. 277.
75 The original sources used by commentators are the lease from the Darell estate, PRO, Ancient Deed C1058 (now C146/1058, and badly damaged by gall), and the few surviving customs' rolls of which 1480-1 has now been edited by H. S. Cobb, *The Overseas Trade of London, Exchequer Customs Accounts 1480-1*, London Record Society, 27 (1990). The commentators are E. G. Duff, *A Century of the English Book Trade* (London, 1905), passim; Plomer, *Wynkyn de Worde*, p. 2; his 'The Importation of Books into England in the Fifteenth and Sixteenth Centuries', *The Library*, 4th ser., 4 (1923-4), pp. 146-50; his 'Importation of Low Countries and French Books into England, 1480, 1502-3', *The Library*, 4th ser., 9 (1928-9), pp. 164-68; Pollard, 'The Stationers before 1557', passim; N. J. Kerling, 'Caxton and the Trade in Printed Books', *The Book Collector*, 4 (1955), pp. 190-99; and Armstrong, 'English Purchases', esp. pp. 273, 277.

Machlinia to print a *Speculum Christiani* about 1486 at Holborn[76] so his own press may have been short-lived.

Between them these men represent the main categories of Caxton's competitors: the early presses set up in the City and nearby, and other merchant entrepreneurs like himself, both native and alien, who financed printing projects or who imported foreign books on a large scale. After the 1484 act of parliament exempted aliens in the book trade from the restrictions placed on other aliens, the competition may have increased.

Whether Caxton ever received investments from fellow London merchants in his own projects, or had silent partners, is not known. The translation and printing of the *Mirror of the World* for the alderman and goldsmith, Hugh Brice, partly so that Brice could present a copy to Lord Hastings, his superior at the royal mint, is the only known commission by a London citizen for which Caxton was paid. As has been said, his fellow mercers and merchant adventurers and fellow diplomatists at all levels of church and court are not named in his prologues and epilogues.

William Daubeney and William Pratte are the only two associates and friends whom Caxton himself mentions. Daubeney was referred to with affection as 'a good and synguler frende of myne'.[77] He had requested a translation of *Charles the Great* which was finished on 18 June 1485 in the reign of Richard III and printed on 1 December of the same year, by which time Henry VII was on the throne; Daubeney did not receive a formal dedication and there is no reason to think he paid for the edition in any way.[78] Caxton only describes him as 'one of the tresorers' of Edward IV's jewels, but this allows us to identify him precisely although the details are meagre and he had several namesakes.[79] His family background is obscure; there is no evidence to connect him with the Daubeneys of the West Country and Bedfordshire, nor with the Daubeneys of Norfolk.[80]

---

[76] Duff, *A Century*, p. 47.

[77] See n. 81. Daubeney would have had to be a citizen and therefore a member of a company in order to operate in all his posts; it is possible he was a draper: see his relationship with the Kydds.

[78] As a compilation of several Charlemagne romances and histories it fitted in with Caxton's past publications on two other of the Nine Worthies, Godfrey of Boulogne and Arthur; it also had the recommendation of being quite short, only 96 folios in Caxton's edition (*The English Charlemagne Romances*, III, *The Lyfe of the Noble and Crysten Prynce Charles the Grete, translated by William Caxton 1485*, ed. by S. J. H. Herrtage, E.E.T.S. E.S. 37 (1881), passim).

[79] e.g. the stationer and notary flourishing 1450s-70s (Christianson, *Directory*, p. 99).

[80] His origins are unlikely to be solved as no will of his survives. Giles Daubeney who rose high in Henry VII's service was the West Country family's most famous member at this time. See Herrtage, *Charles the Grete*, pp. vii-xii, for

Daubeney was not a mercer, but like Robert Cosyn he had a useful and respected career in the customs and other royal and civic offices.[81] From November 1480 to the accession of Henry VII he was searcher in the port of London, that is he scrutinized and checked on merchants and their goods going in or out of the port, ensuring that they were honestly valued and that the correct customs dues were paid to the king. From May 1483 he also collected the wool customs in the port.[82] Neither job was popular with merchants, and in both scrupulous honesty and a talent for diplomacy may have helped; it is clear he secured the respect of Caxton and others. Daubeney was sought after as an arbitrator and adviser,[83] for example on two occasions by the Kydd family. Jane Kydd was a single girl living in the precinct of the nunnery of the Minoresses like so many other lone women; she had been promised marriage by the young and rather wild heir of the extremely wealthy draper, Sir Thomas Cook, and naturally his friends and relatives considered her beneath him. When Daubeney spoke up for her he was apparently roundly abused. On another occasion he witnessed the release of William Kydd, presumably Jane's brother, from his apprenticeship to a draper.[84]

From before 1480 he was also a clerk of Edward IV's jewels, and then of Richard III's, a post near the king's person; duties included delivering a covered salt of gold to Richard Gardiner, alderman of London, as a pledge for a loan to Richard III, and making sure a gold livery collar went off to Ireland for the Earl of Desmond.[85] It was probably in this household capacity that he

---

several unsupported assumptions; also Griffith, 'The Early Years of William Caxton', pp. 33, 52. I am grateful to Dr Paul Rutledge of the Norfolk Record Office for checking the Norfolk family; see F. Blomefield and C. Parkin, *An Essay towards a Topographical History of Norfolk* ..., 11 vols (London, 1805-10), IX, p. 437.

[81] The John Daubeney who was an apprentice of William Shore and admitted to the Mercers in 1483 may have been a relative; Shore certainly knew Caxton well but the details of their relationship are vague and it was probably just that of two merchants who had an extensive life abroad (see A. F. Sutton, 'William Shore, a Merchant of London and Derby', *Derbyshire Archaeol. Jnl*, 106 (1986), esp. pp. 128, 133).

[82] *CPR 1476-85*, pp. 223, 375; *CFR 1471-85*, no. 725; *Customs Account 1480-1*, pp. xix-xx and nn. 58 and 66. It was popularly thought that these officials were harsh (*The Crowland Chronicle Continuations, 1459-86*, ed. by N. Pronay and J. Cox (London, 1986), pp. 138-39).

[83] He may be the 'gentleman' receiving gifts of goods and chattels, 1480 and 1482, another indication of trust (*CCR 1476-85*, nos. 621, 966).

[84] His relationship to the Kydds has not been discovered nor anything else about them. BL, Add. MS 48031A, fol. 179* for Jane's petition to Edward IV, to be published in *A Political Memoranda Book of the Fifteenth Century*, ed. by M. Kekewich and others; PRO, C1/64/1108.

had been on 8 August 1482 one of the many witnesses of John Edward's confession that his calumnies against Earl Rivers and the Marquess of Dorset in Calais had been false.[86] Daubeney's value to Richard III was increased by his appointment in April 1484 as one of the commissioners in the office of the admiralty alongside Sir John Wood, the treasurer of England, and Sir Robert Brackenbury.[87]

His other posts were in Southwark as an official of the City of London, acting as the City's bailiff from 25 March 1482 to 25 March 1487 in the tiny area of the Guildable Manor at the foot of London Bridge: administering justice, returning writs and having a small prison under his control; the profits were probably small after he had paid the City its £10 and the wages of his deputies. Richard III's offer of the borough of Southwark to the City at Epiphany 1484 must have interested Daubeney, even if he had little personally to do with the offer.[88]

Bosworth changed Daubeney's fortunes dramatically, but it seems at first only slowly. Caxton was not deterred from mentioning his name in *Charles the Great* at the end of 1485, but he spoke only of his friend's service in the office of Edward IV's Jewels. Daubeney did not secure this office from Henry VII (if he tried) and in April 1486 he made a gift of his goods, chattels, merchandise and debts to Lord Maltravers, Sir Thomas Bourchier, Sir Edmund Shaa and two other London goldsmiths, a method, presumably, of making sure that he had retained nothing of the royal jewels in his possession.[89] He managed to keep his Southwark posts only till March 1487. It seems he had been too closely involved in government under Richard III to survive in office, and he must have had to rely on trade for his new living.

The next reference to Daubeney is at the height of the Perkin Warbeck affair in December 1494 when, as 'late of London gentleman', he was arrested for high treason, along with others he had known in his years of office, such

85   *Materials for a History of the Reign of Henry VII*, I, p. 214 (this document of 12 Dec. 1485 appears to be the only source for Daubeney's knighthood; either the new king's officials got it wrong or he had acquired the title at the very end of Richard's reign). *British Library Harleian Manuscript 433*, ed. by R. Horrox and P. Hammond, 4 vols (London and Upminster, 1979-83), III, 111.

86   J. Gairdner, *History of ... Richard III*, 2nd edn (Cambridge, 1898), p. 339.

87   *CPR 1477-85*, pp. 391-92.

88   D. H. Johnson, *The City of London and Southwark* (London, 1969), pp. 43-60, 408; A. F. Sutton, 'Richard III, the City of London and Southwark', in *Richard III, Crown and People*, pp. 289-95. His loss of all offices does suggest that some close association with Richard III had made him *persona non grata*.

89   *CCR 1485-1500*, no. 91. No pardon is recorded for him in the printed calendars in 1485, as we might have expected. He may have had great difficulty in clearing his accounts with the new regime, given the circumstances of Richard's demise and the extensive loans raised on the security of the royal plate and jewels by Richard.

as Sir Thomas Thwaites, the book collector. The fact that he had bought himself a general pardon in the previous July may indicate he was already nervous about his position. Unlike Thwaites he was executed in January 1495.[90] On 28 December 1496 his widow, Joan, living in Westminster, also acquired a pardon.[91]

The last, and most important, of Caxton's known friends to be discussed is William Pratte. Caxton finished his translation of Jacques Le Grand's *Livre de Bonnes Meurs*, known in English as the *Book of Good Manners* (the 'Book of Morality' would be a more precise modern rendering), on 8 June 1486. Just over a month later his mercer friend, William Pratte, who had inspired his work, was writing his will, and some days later he was dead.[92] The grief and shock of the death of Pratte, who was probably almost exactly the same age as the printer and known to him since he was an apprentice, may have caused Caxton to delay printing the book until the following year (completed 11 May 1487). By that time he had composed a short prologue which honoured the memory of his friend; it contained no publisher's hyperbole and was prompted solely by affection.[93]

> And to thende that every man shold have knowleche of good maners, an honest man and a specyal frende of myn, a mercer of London named Wylliam Praat, which late departed out of this lyf on whos soule God have mercy, not longe tofore his deth delyverd to me in Frensche a lytel book named the Book of Good Maners, whiche book is of auctoryte for as moche

90 Herrtage, *Charles the Grete*, p. xii; Gairdner, *History of ... Richard III*, pp. 286-87, 339; *CPR 1485-94*, p. 471.

91 *CPR 1494-1509*, p. 84; J. Stow, *Survey of London*, ed. by C. L. Kingsford, 2 vols (Oxford, 1908), I, 179, buries the widow of 'Sir' William Daubeney in the Austin Friars and this may be Caxton's friend and his wife.

92 He died between 11 July and 4 August 1486. The thematic coincidence beween the *Royal Book* and the *Book of Good Manners* and the fact that it was translated at the request of a 'synguler frende of myn, a mercer of London', 'a worshipful marchaunt and mercer of London', in 1484, has led to the suggestion that this mercer was also Pratte: see Blake, *World*, pp. 87, 96-97; Blake, *Caxton's Own Prose*, pp. 135, 136, 171; and Painter, *Caxton*, p. 155; followed by Lindstrom, 'The English Versions' (n. 94 below), p. 247. A similar thematic coincidence has led to Pratte's association with the 'frend and gossib' referred to by Caxton in his epilogue to Boethius (1478) (Blake, *World*, pp. 87-88). As Caxton does not name these men speculation over their identity is pointless, however tempting: 'worshipful' may imply an alderman, and 'gossib' a relative in God, assuming Caxton's use of these words meant anything. Neither Blake, *World*, pp. 24, 54, 87, 96-97, nor Painter, *Caxton*, pp. 18, 92, 155-56, 187, pursue Pratte as a personality.

93 A. F. Sutton and L. Visser-Fuchs, 'Richard III's Books: XI. Ramon Lull's *Order of Chivalry* Translated by William Caxton', *The Ricardian*, 9 (1991), 110-29, for an analysis of Caxton's real 'patrons', esp. p. 115.

as there is nothyng sayd therin but for the moost parte it is aledged by scrypture of the Byble or ellis by sayeng of holy sayntes, doctours, philosophres and poetes, and desyred me instantly to translate it into Englyssh, our maternal tonge, to thende that it myght be ... used ... to thencreace of vertuous lyvyng. Thenne I, at the request and desyre of hym whyche was my synguler frende and of olde knowlege, have put myself in devoyr ...

Everything Caxton says about the book and his friend is precisely true. The *Book of Good Manners* is indeed a book of authority: it is composed of many short exempla and texts offering advice on how to live virtuously, with none of the raucous stories of wrong-doing aimed to titillate the audience they were supposed to correct; each story has its source precisely given. It is divided into five books, three on the three estates of church, lords and commons, with the first on Pride and how to overcome it, and the last on the brevity of life and how to prepare for death and the Last Judgement.[94] How did Caxton react to the news of the death of his friend of fifty years, so soon after he had translated this?

At first glance it is a book for a cleric, especially a priest who needed a source book for sermons, not a mercer dealing in luxury cloths or a merchant adventurer fighting for profits in the export trade. An investigation of William Pratte's life shows, however, that the *Book of Good Manners* was the man.[95]

Pratte came from Canterbury; his father was buried in St Margaret's there. Like Caxton he was given a good start in life by prosperous parents able to afford the high premium demanded by a wealthy London mercer; his enrolment was recorded by the Mercers' Company in the same year as Caxton's, 1437-8. His master, John Abbot, was a past warden of the company, sheriff and MP, and owned property in London and Northamptonshire, his home county.[96] He lived in his house in Catte Street

94   There is no modern edition, but there is an incomplete Caxton in the BL, IB 55125 (the prologue is one of the missing sections). B. Lindstrom, 'Some Remarks on Two English Translations of Jacques Legrand's *Livre de Bonnes Meurs*', *Eng. Stud.*, 58 (1977), 304-11; idem, 'The English Versions of Jacques Legrand's *Livre de Bonnes Meurs*', *The Library*, 6th ser., 1 (1979), 247-54.

95   Another book that he may have owned is the equally suitable Diurnal of Syon inscribed 'Liber Willelmi Pratt', Cambridge, Magdalene College MS F.4.12 (M. R. James, *A Descriptive Catalogue of the Manuscripts in the College Library of Magdalene College, Cambridge* (Cambridge, 1909), pp. 22-23).

96   Warden 1415-16, 1422-23, 1428-29 and 1432-33; sheriff before 1428-29; MP 1431. See *CPMR 1413-37*, p. 96, for evidence that he dealt in linen and goods from Cologne c. 1419. Will made 27 Feb. 1444, proved 5 Mar. 1444, PRO, PROB 11/3, fols 272-73. His obit, supported by London properties and entrusted to the Mercers' Company, caused problems in 1476, and Pratte was one of those asked to advise (*Acts of Court*, pp. 93, 108).

(now Gresham St) in the parish of St Laurence Jewry, a stone's throw away from where Caxton lived in the household of a much wealthier mercer, Robert Large, at the north end of the street of Old Jewry in the parish of St Olave. Given the close communities of Mercer apprentices, parish, ward and nearby streets, Caxton's 'olde knowlege' of his friend must have begun in the 1430s.

Both of them lost their masters during their terms: in April 1441 Large bequeathed his enterprising young man 20 marks;[97] and in February 1444 Abbot left Pratte £20 – another bequest of 20s. from Abbot went to Alice Bothe who was to become Pratte's wife.[98]

Thereafter Caxton's career took on the life-style of a merchant adventurer with his base abroad until 1476, undoubtedly with frequent if not regular visits to England, but mostly relying on factors to represent his interests at home. In contrast Pratte, after the obligatory and essential period abroad learning the trade of the Low Countries at first hand, seems to have adopted the more conventional practice of managing his business from London and sending his older apprentices and factors abroad. Perhaps an early inclination to marry Alice Bothe while he was still an apprentice may have decided Pratte's career pattern for him. As a consequence he figures regularly in the Mercers' records in a way Caxton does not. He collected his share of rebukes from his superiors: an exchange of lies and uncourteous language with John Harowe, already mentioned as a predecessor of Caxton among Large's apprentices, landed them both with stiff fines in 1455-56.[99]

By at least 1461 Pratte was thought of by his peers as a mercer and merchant adventurer to be called upon to advise over bills to parliament and embassies to the duke of Burgundy, and to help prepare reports to Edward IV and his council. In 1468, for example, William Redeknap, John Pickering and William Caxton were chosen to go with the king's ambassadors to Flanders to discuss the enlargement of English cloth with the duke of Burgundy's advisers. Pratte and Henry Bumpstede, a past deputy-governor of the Adventurers, were among those set to devise points and articles to be

---

97   W. Blades, *The Biography and Typography of William Caxton* (London, 1877), pp. 151-55.

98   PRO, PROB 11/3, fol. 272v. She is described by Abbot as his servant, not inappropriate for a girl from Derbyshire (see details from her will below), perhaps indentured to him and his wife.

99   Wardens' Accounts 1455-6; for other fines see the same in 1452-3, and 1455-6 (again). He was in the livery from 1452-3. In 1468 he was involved in a furious row with the argumentative Shelley brothers over the recovery of goods sent to France; John Shelley broke Pratte's head with his dagger; one of those chosen to adjudicate was Henry Bumpstede (for whom see below and n. 107), *Acts of Court*, pp. 60-61. This quarrel did not prevent Pratte acting as a feoffee for John Shelley (*CIPM HVII*, I, no. 204).

discussed at the convention and check over the archives of the Merchant Adventurers in London to be certain of their privileges.[100] In other words, Pratte was among those preparing a brief for William Caxton's advocacy.

In the later 1470s and '80s, while Caxton devoted himself to his new career of printing, Pratte was regularly involved in the Adventurers' affairs. Perhaps Caxton offered a word or two of advice to his old friend in October 1477 when Pratte was among several adventurers discussing the problems of English coinage circulating in the territories of the duke of Burgundy with Edward IV's council and the duke's ambassadors at Westminster. From time to time between 1479 and 1480 Pratte was also involved in the protracted negotiations with the king over the money he claimed adventurers had 'embezzled' from the customs duties: the petitions, the legal threats, the merchants' over-enthusiastic 'labouring' of supporters, the suits to the Queen, to her son, the Marquess of Dorset, and her brother, Lord Rivers, and the practical and friendly advice offered by Lord Hastings, the king's Lord Chamberlain, to the Adventurers, make for some of the best reading in the Acts of Court, and must have entertained Caxton if he was regaled with the details. It may have also have convinced him he was well out of it. The Merchant Adventurers finally saved themselves 1000 marks with the help of the Queen.[101]

Although by now in his sixties Pratte was a warden of the mercers for a second time in 1480-81, he rode to meet Edward V on his entry to London in 1483, he was a common councilman for Cripplegate Within, and he acted as a deputy of the sheriffs overseeing the collection of the aliens' subsidy in June 1483.[102]

---

[100] *Acts of Court*, pp. 50, 61-62. Pratte's capacity to prepare reports was called upon again in 1480 over the preparation of a 'book' for the king's council setting out the Mercers' grievances against Hansa merchants who imported mercery into England, and their proposals for reform (ibid., pp. 136-37). He was regularly called upon for similar services by his neighbours and fellow mercers: 1466, executor to John Norlong, mercer, PRO, PROB 11/5, fols 96v-98; 1466, witness to testament of Beatrice Frost, daughter of a mercer of his parish, Guildhall Library, MS 9171/6, fol. 103v; 1479, left 20s. for his prayers by John Sutton, mercer, PRO, PROB 11/6, fol. 285; feoffee of Robert Norbery for property in Kent, PRO, C1/28/199.

[101] *Acts of Court*, pp. 100-01, 115-18, 121-22, 125-26, 127-29, 136-38. He was one of those who went through the formalities of being pardoned their subsidy offences in 1480 and taking an oath before the chancellor (*CPR 1476-85*, p. 243).

[102] He was warden for the first time in 1470 (*Acts of Court*, pp. 138, 147). CLRO, Journal 9, fol. 55v; PRO, E179/242/25, m. 1d. The last entry about Pratte in the *Acts of Court*, pp. 171-72, shows him acting in 1485 in the case of John Salford, the past apprentice of William Shore who also figured in a suit against Caxton by John Neve in 1475 (see n. 14 above).

We have an image of a successful merchant, trusted by his fellows; rich, but certainly not 'seriously' rich as there is no hint of the possibility of aldermanic status; a man with a capacity to prepare reports, useful on committees, knowledgeable on the finer points of trade and capable of finding a precedent in the company's archives; not perhaps endowed with the verbal and diplomatic skills of a Caxton, but a man whose career turns out to be remarkably similar in its solid ability and achievement to that of Robert Cosyn, William Daubeney, or Caxton in his pre-printing days.

When Pratte died he had property in Canterbury, Faversham and Boughton under Blean, Kent, to leave to his wife, for her life, and then to their children: Richard, a mercer, and expected to marry a girl called Gieff Hemp, whose name perhaps indicates she came from the Low Countries; and Alice, wife of Richard Bulle, mercer and merchant adventurer. If they both died without heirs he stipulated that all the property was to be sold and the proceeds devoted to dowering poor maidens and to other charitable works.[103] Both children did in fact die childless a few years later, before their mother, Alice. To Alice fell the duty of arranging a two-year chantry for her husband, herself and her dead children. Perhaps of some consolation on her deathbed in 1491 were the relatives to whom she made many small bequests: the Squire family, and the Bothes of Derbyshire, one of whom had been apprentice to her husband.[104]

The most conspicuous religious bequest in William's will was the gift of 'my table with crucifix' to serve at the altar of St Katherine in his parish church of St Mary Aldermanbury as long as it lasted,[105] but it is Pratte's deposition of his bodily remains that shows most clearly why he in particular gave Caxton the Book of Good Manners. The book devoted a chapter (bk.5, ch.6) to proving how 'none oughte to be curyous of hys sepulture' and how a man's burial was to be according to his estate; the impressive sources cited included the second book of the Vitae Patrum, which was to be Caxton's last translation. Pratte had taken the advice to heart: he asked to be buried in 'cristen sepulture in such place as it shall please God to purvey and ordeyne for me' and his funeral was to

---

[103] PRO, PROB 11/7, fol. 192-192v. Property in Hertford went to Alice immediately with the same reversion to charity. Richard Bulle: admittance date unknown, but on livery and riding to meet king in 1475 (Acts of Court, pp. 89-91); importing linen from Zeeland 1478 (Smit, Bronnen, I, no. 1857); both Bulle and Pratte leased shops in the Crown on Cheapside from the Mercers (D. Keene and V. Harding, Historical Gazetteer of London before the Great Fire, I, Cheapside (Cambridge, 1987), 104/33e, p. 402); no surviving will.

[104] PRO, PROB 11/8, fol. 321-321v: 24 November 1490; proved 9 April 1491.

[105] Both Prattes' wills concentrated on parish charity: poor householders and the dowry of poor girls.

> be done in the most lowliest and devoute wise ... withoute any pompe or
> vayne glorye of the world and no monythis mynde opynly to be kept for me
> ... neyther cloth of gold nor cloth of silk laide upon my body ... but oonely
> as much blak wolen cloth as shall suffice to make two gounes, and a crosse of
> white lynnen cloth to be made theron.

The cloth was to be later made up into two gowns for the neediest
parishioners of his parish; six torches and four tapers were to burn round his
body and four poor men 'if they can be found' were to carry his body. It was
usual for men of the deceased's livery company to carry the body to burial
but Pratte would have none of it: if liverymen of the Mercers were chosen by
the wardens they were only to walk at the side of the body. He knew that
the intercession of the virtuous poor would be the most effective assistance
for his soul in Purgatory.[106]

Pratte's austere funeral and requiem Mass in the parish church of St
Mary Aldermanbury, behind Guildhall, in the second half of July 1486,
would have brought together the dead man's parish, his relatives, his fellow
guild members and the local elite of the common council of the city. Caxton
would have expected to find the customary turn-out of fellow liverymen of
the Mercers, the wardens, the clerk and the beadle, and to recognize many
acquaintances. Among them must have been a prosperous fellow parishioner
of Pratte, Henry Bumpstede, a past deputy-governor of the Merchant
Adventurers in 1461, and a warden of London Bridge 1476-84; he had acted as
a witness of Pratte's will. Bumpstede was of an armigerous Norfolk family in
which he took some pride; like Alice Pratte he was to outlive his children (as
well as Alice and possibly Caxton too), his will being a sad catalogue of
bequests to his nephews, daughter-in-law and friends from his plate cupboard
and the linen in his mercery shop.[107]

Another old friend of the Prattes who must have been well known to
Caxton among the funeral crowd was Alice Claver, a widow, who for thirty
years had run her own highly successful silkwoman's business in the adjacent
parish of St Laurence Jewry, providing silk decorations for Edward IV's
books and mantle-laces and tassels for the coronation robes of Richard III and
his Queen. Like William Pratte she deplored 'pompe' and 'pryde' at burials
and preferred to win heaven by the means of active charity, bringing up
almschildren, and making bequests towards the poor of her parish and
dowries for young girls. To Alice Pratte, whom she predeceased, she was a

---

[106] I am indebted to Clive Burgess for discussing this point.
[107] GL, MS 9171/8, fol. 27-27v: 1 November 1491; proved 21 February 1492; *CCR
1461-68*, pp. 154, 365; *Calendar of Letter Books of the City of London*, L, ed. by R.
R. Sharpe (London, 1912), pp. 144, 215; PRO, C1/66/353. It seems he may have
specialized in linen. Other mercer relatives of Bumpstede, who can also be found
in documents including Pratte, were the Kempes and Burtons.

'gossip', that is a relative in God – they probably had god-children in common. As both Richard Claver, her mercer husband, and Alice Pratte, née Bothe, had come originally from Derbyshire the friendship between the two women may have gone back to their own apprenticeship-days like that between Caxton and the Prattes.[108]

Another parishioner of St Laurence Jewry who should have turned up for Pratte's funeral was Thomas Fabian. He was from Essex and had achieved a wealth and standing among the Mercers and Merchant Adventurers, as well as the Merchant Staplers and the City, comparable to that of Pratte; he was a warden of the Mercers in 1484 and an auditor of the city's accounts in 1486. His personal association with both Pratte and Bumpstede went back to at least 1471, quite apart from their fellowship of trade.[109]

Equally conspicuous was one of Pratte's executors, a past apprentice of his, William Tenacres. Like Pratte and Caxton he came from Kent, Rochester in his case (with relatives in Strood); when he died in 1494, only in his forties, he had inherited lands in Canterbury, Herne Hill and elsewhere in Kent. To the parish church of Herne Hill he bequeathed his 'new massebook prynted of the use of Sarum with all the new festys'; one of his apprentices was John Colyns, that enterprising mercer who dealt in books and, unlike his older and wiser predecessors in the trade, died in poverty.[110] How well Tenacres knew Caxton, many years his senior, is debatable, but he could have met him many times in the Pratte household after 1476.

Last but not least was the widow, Alice Pratte (née Bothe), whom Caxton had known for fifty years. Until April 1491 the hospitality of her house remained available to the printer, and then she too died, not long before his own death.

Caxton's friends were men like himself – they were not Lord Rivers or the Earl of Oxford. They were men who knew a lot of important people,

[108] A. F. Sutton, 'Alice Claver', in *Richard III, Crown and People*, 397-402, of which an expanded version is in *Medieval London Widows 1300-1500*, ed. by C. M. Barron and A. F. Sutton (London, 1994), 129-42.

[109] *Letter Book L*, pp. 99, 235; PRO, C1/66/353; *CPR 1476-85*, pp. 243-44. His will: PRO, PROB 11/8, fols 66-68.

[110] Admitted to the Mercers 1473. He was also Alice Pratte's executor. Tenacres seems to have inherited a lot of his lands; his will of 1494 is full of religious directives, although not as 'plain' as Pratte's, PRO, PROB 11/10, fols 119v-121. For his relatives in Strood and Trottiscliffe, see *CPR 1446-52*, pp. 350, 361; *CPR 1485-94*, p. 447; *CCR 1485-1500*, no. 1138. For Colyns, see C. Meale, 'Wynkyn de Worde's Setting Copy for *Ipomydon*', in *Stud. in Bibliography*, 35 (1982), 156-71, and her 'The Compiler at Work: John Colyns and BL, MS Harley 2252', in *Manuscripts and Readers in Fifteenth-Century England*, ed. by D. Pearsall (Cambridge, 1983), pp. 82-103.

who served the crown and the city; they were prosperous, but not 'seriously' rich; they were 'citizens' of London, or they styled themselves 'gentlemen'; perhaps they aspired to be 'esquires', but they were not hopeful of knighthood; they were never courtiers or aristocrats. It was their burials that William Caxton, citizen and mercer of the City of London, was bound by affection and duty to attend.

The Romuléon *and the Manuscripts of Edward IV*
SCOT McKENDRICK

Six years ago Janet Backhouse sought to define the relative status and personal contribution of Edward IV and Henry VII as collectors of illuminated manuscripts and founding fathers of the present British Library.[1] In order to do this she re-examined several of the large volumes of vernacular non-liturgical texts produced in the Burgundian Netherlands that have frequently been associated with Edward IV and went further than any previous critic since the time of the publication of the catalogue of Royal Manuscripts in 1921 towards defining which manuscripts could confidently be said to have been made for Edward and when his collection came into being.

This paper seeks to address some of the same issues in relation to Edward IV and his manuscripts, but in a different way. As in a previous article on Royal MS 17 F.ii, Edward's manuscript of the *Faits des Romains*,[2] I wish to begin by concentrating on one of the relevant Royal manuscripts, first looking at it in detail and then comparing it with other manuscripts of the same text. On this occasion the manuscript for consideration is Royal MS 19 E.v. I would then like to consider this manuscript in the context of others associated with Edward IV. By these two routes I hope to make further moves towards a clearer picture of the character of Edward's collection and collecting and of how and when the core of his collection was formed.

Royal MS 19 E.v is a very large volume of 418 parchment folios, each measuring 470 x 340 mm. Each folio presents a generous *mise-en-page* of two relatively tall, narrow columns of 40 lines ruled in purple ink with wide central and outer margins. The text is written in a formal bastard secretary which, as Warner and Gilson observe,[3] is close to the script of manuscripts produced by David Aubert between 1458 and 1479/80.[4] In addition to the

1   J. Backhouse, 'Founders of the Royal Library: Edward IV and Henry VII as Collectors of Illuminated Manuscripts', in *England in the Fifteenth Century: Proceedings of the 1986 Harlaxton Symposium*, ed. by D. Williams (Woodbridge, 1987), pp. 23-41. I am particularly grateful to Angela Dillon Bussi and Patricia Stirnemann for their kind help during the preparation of this paper.

2   S. McKendrick, '*La Grande Histoire Cesar* and the Manuscripts of Edward IV', *English Manuscript Stud., 1100-1700*, 2 (1990), 109-38.

3   Sir G.F. Warner and J.P. Gilson, *Catalogue of Western Manuscripts in the Old Royal and King's Collections in the British Museum*, 4 vols (London, 1921), II, p. 348.

4   To the list of Aubert's signed and dated manuscripts in P. Cockshaw, 'David Aubert', in *Biographie Nationale de Belgique*, Suppl. 9 (1971-72), cols. 11-12 should be added Brussels, Bibliothèque Royale (hereafter Bibl. Roy.), MSS 9079 and IV.106, both dated 1461, and MS 9055, dated 1468 (F. Masai and M. Wittek,

minor decoration of illuminated paragraph marks and initials 19 E.v includes eleven illuminated miniatures, nine of which extend across both columns of text and take up at least one third of the text-block area.[5] Most of these miniatures are in a style of Netherlandish painting attributed by Durrieu and Winkler to the Master of the White Inscriptions (Pls 15, 22).[6] The last is inscribed '1480',[7] a date which corresponds with that suggested by the costume of the figures depicted and by the accompanying floral borders.

Two folios on which the miniatures are accompanied by full, four-sided illuminated borders include as an integral part of this border decoration heraldry which establishes the first owner of 19 E.v as Edward IV (Pls. 14, 15).[8] Most significant here are a centrally placed escutcheon bearing the English royal arms and surmounted by a crowned helm with mantling in Edward's colours of red and blue, two flanking escutcheons also bearing the royal arms, but with labels of three and five points relating them to Edward's two sons, the ill-fated 'Princes in the Tower', and finally the Yorkist badge of the white *rose en soleil* on a ground quartered in Edward's colours.

On the first of these two folios (fol. 32) begins the main text contained in 19 E.v, 'le livre intitulé RoCSuléon contenant les fais des Romains'. Openly derived from the works of several classical and Christian authors,[9] this

---

Manuscrits datés conservés en Belgique, IV, *1461-1480* (Brussels, 1982), nos. 394, 398, 467), Florence, Biblioteca Medicea Laurenziana (hereafter Laur.), MS Med. Pal. 156, dated 1464 (A. Collignon, 'Le Romuléon de Charles le Téméraire', *Bull. mensuel de la Soc. d'archéol. lorraine et du Musée historique lorrain*, 2e sér., 13 (1913), p. 162), Vatican Library, MS Pal. lat. 1995, dated 1467 (*Biblioteca Palatina*, Heiliggeistkirche, Heidelberg, exhibition catalogue, ed. by E. Mittler, 2 vols (Heidelberg, 1986), I, p. 314, II, pp. 210, 211 (2 plates)), and Malibu, J. Paul Getty Museum, MSS 30 and 31, dated 1474/5 (P. Cockshaw, 'Some Remarks on the Character and Content of the Library of Margaret of York', in *Margaret of York, Simon Marmion and 'The Visions of Tondal'*, ed. by T. Kren (Malibu, 1992), pp. 58-59).

5   An eleventh miniature on fol. 233, depicting the meeting of Scipio Africanus and Hannibal, is overlooked in Warner and Gilson, II, p. 349.

6   P. Durrieu, *La miniature flamande au temps de la cour de Bourgogne (1415-1530)*, (Paris/Brussels, 1921), p. 61, pl. 65, and F. Winkler, *Die flämische Buchmalerei des XV. and XVI. Jahrhunderts* (Leipzig, 1925), pp. 137, 179. See also G. Dogaer, *Flemish Miniature Painting in the 15th and 16th Centuries* (Amsterdam, 1987), p. 125. Only the opening miniature on fol. 32 and that on fol. 125 are not in this style.

7   London, British Library, Royal MS 19 E.v., fol. 367v. Hereafter Royal MSS are cited by their shelf marks only, e.g. 19 E.v.

8   19 E.v., fols. 32, 196.

9   'souverainement Titus Livius, Saint Augustin de la Cite de Dieu, Valere le Grant, Saluste, Suetonius, Helius Spartinius, Helius Lampridius, Julius Capitolinus, Lucius Florus, Justinius, Lucius, Orose, Vegece, Eutropius' (19 E.v., fol. 32v).

learned but unoriginal text tells in ten Books the story of Rome and the Romans from the time of Romulus and Remus to that of Constantine the Great. Included are accounts of the early kings of Rome, the fall of Rome to the Gauls, the wars with Carthage and Macedonia, the career of Julius Caesar and the lives of subsequent Emperors. Livy's history of Rome is the most important source, providing most of the material and structure for the *Romuléon*'s account of the early and Republican periods. Suetonius's *Lives* are equally closely followed in the account of the Emperors Augustus to Domitian.

Unlike the *Faits des Romains*[10] this text is not an original French compilation from classical sources, but a close translation of a Latin text which survives independently in several manuscripts mostly of Italian origin.[11] According to its preface this Latin work was first compiled at the request of Gomez Albornoz (d. 1377), governor of the city of Bologna.[12] Recent studies have rejected an early attribution to Roberto della Porta and favour instead Benvenuto da Imola as the person most likely to have compiled the text at Florence between 1361 and 1364.[13] The French translator identified in 19 E.v at the end of Book 8 is Jean Miélot,[14] a prolific writer, compiler and translator resident at Lille between 1453 and 1472 who worked in the service of Philip the Good, Duke of Burgundy, from around 1448 to the duke's death in 1467.[15] 1463 is given in 19 E.v as the date of Miélot's translation.

The only other contents of 19 E.v are a prefatory table of chapter headings used in the *Romuléon* and a concluding alphabetical subject and personal name index to the same work. Of these two aids to the reader the

[10]   On the *Faits* and its sources see *Li Fet des Romains*, ed. by L.-F. Flutre and K. Sneyders de Vogel (Paris/Groningen, 1938), II.

[11]   Of the twenty-four manuscripts listed in C. Schaefer, 'Die "Romuleon" Handschrift (78 D 10) des Berliner Kupferstichkabinetts', *Jahrbuch der Berliner Museen*, 23 (1981), p. 126, and a further six in P.O. Kristeller, *Iter Italicum* (London/Leiden, 1963-), III, pp. 161, 475; IV, pp. 550, 574, 605, 612, only two were produced outside Italy, viz. Amiens, Bibliothèque Municipale, MS 480, dated Lyons 1466, and Cologny-Geneva, Bibliotheca Bodmeriana, cod. 143, produced in France in *c*. 1461-65 (Schaefer, 'Die "Romuleon" Handschrift', p. 126, nos. 17, 24, and E. Pellegrin, *Manuscrits latins de la Bodmeriana*, Bibliotheca Bodmeriana, Catalogues, 5 (Geneva, 1982), pp. 349-53).

[12]   On Gomez see *Dizionario Biografico degli Italiani*, II (Rome, 1960), pp. 53-54.

[13]   See Schaefer, 'Die "Romuleon" Handschrift', pp. 127-28 and *Dizionario*, VIII (Rome, 1966), pp. 691-94.

[14]   'Et fut ledit traittie translatte de latin en cler franchois par sire Jehan Mielot chanoine de Lille en Flandres l'an de grace mil quatrecens soixante et troiz en la fourme et stille plus au long declare' (19 E.v., fol. 336).

[15]   See P. Perdrizet, 'Jean Miélot, l'un des traducteurs de Philippe le Bon', *Rev. d'histoire littéraire de la France*, 14 (1907), pp. 472-82.

second is as rare a feature of such fifteenth-century manuscripts of French texts as the first is common.[16] Yet since 19 E.v remained unfoliated until modern times and no folio references were ever added to the prefatory table of chapter headings, the book and chapter references given in the alphabetical index are invaluable to anyone wishing to find specific information in a text of over 400 folios in length.[17]

Besides 19 E.v only five complete manuscripts of the French *Romuléon* survive (see Appendix 1).[18] No further manuscripts are identifiable in contemporary or early documents and no printed edition appears ever to have been made.[19] Of the five complete manuscripts all are very similar products of the professional book producers of the South Netherlands, their texts written in the characteristic *lettre bâtarde bourguignonne* and their decoration executed in the recognizable styles of Netherlandish illuminators. The manuscript now in Florence and Brussels 9055 both contain colophons naming the scribe David Aubert, the first dated 1464 (Pl. 16) and the second 1468.[20] The Florence manuscript is, moreover, one of several manuscripts

---

[16] The *tabula alphabetica* accompanying the Douai version of Vincent de Beauvais' *Speculum Historiale*, for example, is found in only the earliest manuscripts of Jean de Vignay's translation (C. A. Chavannes-Mazel, 'The *Miroir Historial* of Jean le Bon. The Leiden Manuscript and its Related Copies', unpublished Ph.D. thesis, Rijksuniversiteit, Leiden (1988), pp. 10-11, 22). In general see R. H. and M. A. Rouse, 'La naissance des index', in *Histoire de l'édition française I: Le livre conquérant du moyen âge au XVII siècle*, ed. by H.-J. Martin and R. Chartier (Paris, 1983), pp. 77-85.

[17] Because, however, many chapters remain unnumbered, such use is rendered slow and cumbersome.

[18] A sixth incomplete manuscript is Niort, Bibliothèque Municipale, Rés. G 2 F (formerly MS 25) (see *Catalogue général des manuscrits des Bibliothèques publiques de France. Départements*, XXXI (Paris, 1898), pp. 622-23). Two miniatures detached from this manuscript are now at the Musée de Cluny (Inv. Cl. 886, 22607; see A. Boinet, 'Choix de miniatures détachées conservées au Musée de Cluny, à Paris', *Bull. de la Soc. française de reproductions de manuscrits à peintures*, 6 (1922), p. 6) and fourteen were sold at Christie's, London, 21 June 1989, lots 6-11. For two further detached miniatures see J. M. Heinlen, *Mediaeval and Renaissance Miniature Painting* (London, 1989), no. 6 and E.R. Lubin, *European Illuminated Manuscripts* (New York, 1985), no. 29. *Pace* Schaefer, 'Die "Romuleon" Handschrift', p. 142, n. 63 this manuscript does not contain the 1466 translation of the *Romuléon* by Sebastian Mamerot. It is, however, French in origin and therefore closer in this respect to the only three surviving manuscripts of Mamerot's translation discussed by Schaefer.

[19] The only documented manuscript which I cannot now identify is the 'Chronique Romaine depuis la fondation de Rome jusqu' à Constantin' listed in E. van Even, 'Notice sur la bibliothèque de Charles de Croy, duc d'Aerschot (1614)', *Bull. du bibliophile belge*, 9 (1952), p. 22, no. 92.

[20] See note 4 above.

produced by Aubert that contain illustrations attributed to Loyset Liédet who, like Aubert, was then probably active at Bruges (Pls. 17, 20, 21).[21] The manuscript at Besançon can be identified by its *secundo folio* with the manuscript recorded in the 1467 inventory of the library at Bruges of Philip the Good[22] and thereby with a volume bought by the duke's personal reader from Colard Mansion of Bruges on 9 May 1467.[23] All five manuscripts were in fact owned by prominent members of the Burgundian ducal court in the South Netherlands. The Florence manuscript almost certainly also belonged to Philip;[24] Brussels 9055 (Pl. 18) definitely belonged to his illegitimate son Anthony of Burgundy,[25] the other Brussels manuscript (Pl. 19) to Jean de Wavrin,[26] and the Turin manuscript (Pl. 23) to Louis of Gruuthuse.[27]

What more, then, do these other manuscripts of the *Romuléon* tell us of 19 E.v? In the first instance, by collating four passages from each of them[28] it has been possible to draw up a provisional textual stemma and thereby clarify

21 *La miniature flamande. Le mécenat de Philippe le Bon*, Bibl. Roy. exhibition catalogue compiled by L.M.J. Delaissé (Brussels, 1959), p. 126, no. 148. *Pace* Delaissé, Laur., Med. Pal. 156 is dated 1464 (see note 4 above).

22 *Catalogue général des manuscrits des Bibliothèques publiques de France. Départements*, XXXII (Paris, 1897), pp. 535-36.

23 *Pace* J. van Praet, *Notice sur Colard Mansion, libraire et imprimeur de la ville de Bruges en Flandre dans le quinzième siècle* (Paris, 1829), p. 70, and A. Pinchart, *Archives des arts, sciences et lettres* (Ghent, 1860-1881), II, p. 189, the account of Guillaume Poupet for 1450 (Lille, Archives départementales du Nord, B 2004 (formerly F 146)) does not include a payment to Mansion for a manuscript of the *Romuléon*. The only record of such a payment, ordered, on 9 May 1467, is Brussels, Archives Générales du Royaume, CC 25191, fol. 19v, as printed in Pinchart, *Archives*, p. 190. Some explanation of this confusion is given in G. Doutrepont, *La littérature française à la cour des ducs de Bourgogne*, Bibliothèque du XVe siècle, 8 (Paris, 1909), p. 141, n.4. Although Mansion is described in the 1467 payment as 'escripvain', it is not stated that Mansion was the scribe of the text, even in part. It is, therefore, far from certain that Mansion's script can be seen in Besançon, Bibliothèque Municipale (hereafter Besançon), MS 850. For similar uncertainties see *Le cinquième centenaire de l'imprimerie dans les anciens Pays-Bas*, Bibl. Roy. exhibition catalogue (Brussels, 1973), pp. 212, 216.

24 See P. Durrieu, 'Le Romuléon de la Laurentienne', *Comptes-rendus de l'Acad. des inscriptions et belles-lettres* (1910), pp. 442-47.

25 F. Lyna, *Les principaux manuscrits à peintures de la Bibliothèque Royale de Belgique*, III, ed. by C. Pantens (Brussels, 1989), p. 268.

26 A. Naber, 'Les manuscrits d'un bibliophile bourguignon du XVe siècle, Jean de Wavrin', *Rev. du Nord*, 72 (1990), pp. 27, 30, 36-37.

27 As in most of his surviving manuscripts, Gruuthuse's arms on fol. 1 have been erased and painted over with the French royal arms (see *Lodewijk van Gruuthuse, Mecenas en Europees Diplomaat, ca. 1427-1492*, ed. by M. P. J. Martens (Bruges, 1992), pp. 116-17).

28 The passages collated are I.1-2, II.42, IV.1, VI.51.

the descent of the text of Edward's manuscript (see Appendix 2). According to these collations the manuscript in Florence (F) is the best surviving manuscript. It is therefore placed closest to α, the translator's copy of his finished text. The two Brussels manuscripts (Br$_1$, Br$_2$) descend closely from F, but share common differences from it. This relationship is expressed by the intermediary β. Similarly Besançon 850 (B) and 19 E.v (L) are closely related to the Brussels manuscripts, but share common differences from them which are further removed from F. This relationship is expressed by the intermediary Γ. The Turin manuscript (T) is closer to B than to any other manuscript and may have been copied from it. x aims to explain the substantial expansions and additions which 19 E.v alone was found to contain in one of the passages collated.[29]

A re-examination of F, the best manuscript, sheds light on several features of 19 E.v. Most importantly it resolves some apparent problems with the dating and authorship of the *Romuléon*. In the first case the date 1465 which appears at the end of the table for Book 10 in Br$_2$[30] and is apparently at odds with the date 1462 given at the end of Books 8 and 9 in F[31] and Br$_1$ and Book 9 in Br$_2$[32] can be explained by the observation that in F these same tables, each concluding with 'Explicit 1465', are not part of the original structure of F, but written on separate gatherings which have been inserted between the end of one Book and the beginning of the next one.[33] Where these tables could not be neatly inserted between the Books as first written, the original text has been crossed out or erased and the same text written out again at the place left for it in the new structure. In addition the passage in Br$_1$ at the end of the table of chapter rubrics which caused Perdrizet and other critics to suggest that Miélot was the author of these rubrics alone[34] can be explained as merely reflecting this later stage in the production of F when in 1465 Miélot compiled the tables of rubrics for each Book. The rubrics within the text had already been transcribed in F by 1464. F's unique

---

29 II.42.
30 'Explicit l'an iiii^{c}lxv' (Bibl. Roy., MSS 10173-4, fol. 388v).
31 'Cy fine le huitiesme livre ... et fut translate de latin en francois par Jo. Mielot chanoine de Lille en Flandres l'an de grace mil cccclx et deux en la fourme et stile cy dessus declairez au long' and 'Cy fine le noeufieme livre ... translate de latin en francois l'an de grace mil cccclxij' (Bibl. Roy., MS 9055, fols 209v, 252).
32 Masai and Wittek, *Manuscrits datés*, IV, p. 43, no. 467.
33 The inserted leaves are vol. 1, fols 33-36, 80-85, 137-42, 178-81, 231-36, 281-87 and vol. 2, fols 62-67, 125-33, 211-14, 253-57.
34 Perdrizet, 'Jean Miélot', p. 479 and Doutrepont, *Littérature française*, p. 143, n.1. Both authors appear to have been unaware of Laur., MS Med. Pal. 156. The relevant passage is '... et furent faictes et compilees lesdittes rubrices par Io. Mielot chanoine de Lille en Flandres l'an de grace mil cccc soixante et cincq en ladicte ville de Lille' (Bibl. Roy., MS 9055, fol. 23v).

inclusion of the translator's preface, in which Miélot claims to have followed the style of Premierfait's popular translation of Boccaccio's *De casibus*,[35] also explains why in almost all the manuscripts, including 19 E.v, the explicit to Book 8 ends with the statement that the translation was made 'en la fourme et stile cy dessus declairez bien au long'.[36] Since all the other manuscripts lack any such statement on the style of the translation, this explicit on its own appeared an odd false back reference.[37]

Further textual features of 19 E.v are explicable in the context of my provisional stemma. The date 1463, for example, which is given at the end of Book 8 in Edward's manuscript and is at variance with the date 1462 given at the same point by two of the better manuscripts, F and Br$_1$,[38] appears to be the result of a copyist's error of adding one Roman numeral, producing iij instead of ij.[39] Since the other manuscripts to include the date 1463 are B, the manuscript closest to L and T, a close descendant of B,[40] it is likely that Γ was the first to commit this error.

The origins of the alphabetical table and its position in 19 E.v also become clearer in the context of the stemma and of the likely origins of F. Before the insertion of the chapter tables F included only one main aid for readers, namely the alphabetical index, which was placed at the beginning of the volume. In this placement and indeed in its very inclusion F appears to

---

[35] 'Cy commence ung livre intitule Romuleon ... naguaires l'an de grace mil cccc soixante par le commandement et ordonnance de ... Phelippe par la grace de dieu duc de Bourgoingne ... a este translate de latin en cler francois par Io. Mielot chanoine de Lille en Flandres en ensuivant le stille de la translation du livre de Jehan Bocace de Certaldo parlent des cas des nobles maleureux hommes et femmes que fist jadis le tres renomme orateur maistre Laurens de Premierfait secretaire de ... Jehan filz de roy de France, duc de Berry ...' (Laur., MS Med. Pal. 156^1, fol. 1-1v).

[36] Besançon, MS 850, fol. 244; Bibl. Roy., MS 9055, fol. 278v; Laur., MS Med. Pal. 156^2, fol. 209v; 19 E.v, fol. 366; Turin, Biblioteca Nazionale Universitaria (hereafter Turin), MS L.I.4^2, fol. 117v. The explicit in Bibl. Roy., MS 10173-4, fol. 385v is incomplete, ending '... et fut translate de latin en franchois par Io.'.

[37] See note 14 above.

[38] 'l'an de grace mil cccclx et deux' (Laur., MS Med. Pal. 156^2, fol. 209v) and 'l'an de grace mil cccclxij' (Bibl. Roy., MS 9055, fol. 278v; Masai and Wittek, *Manuscrits datés*, IV, pl. 794b). At the end of Book 9 Bibl. Roy., MS 9055, fol. 301 has 'l'an de grace mil soixante et deux' (ibid., pl. 794c), Laur., MS Med. Pal. 156^2, fol. 252 'l'an de grace mil cccclxij', and Bibl. Roy., MSS 10173-4, fol. 385v, 'l'an lxij'.

[39] A similar error seems to be the explanation for the date 1463, not 1468, appearing in Paris, Bibliothèque Nationale (hereafter B.N.), MSS fr. 20311 and 22547, two manuscripts of Vasco da Lucena's translation of Curtius's *Historia Alexandri Magni*.

[40] 'l'an de grace quatre cens soixante trois' (Besançon, MS 850, fol. 244) and 'l'an de grace mil quatre cens soixante et trois' (Turin, MS L.I.4^2, fol. 117v).

have followed the Latin manuscript from which Miélot's translation was made, presumably through the intermediary α.[41] (A very likely candidate, as that Latin manuscript, Brussels 9816, does indeed include such a prefatory index.)[42] Whereas both Brussels manuscripts of the French text dispensed with this index altogether and retained the chapter tables, B, and thereby T, dispensed with the chapter tables and retained the alphabetical table, but now at the end of the volume. L's close textual relations with B and T go together with L's similar placement of the alphabetical table at the end.

Like B and T, L also omits the other subsidiary texts in F, namely the note on the names of the peoples of Flanders and elsewhere, repeated in Br₁, and the alphabetical glossary 'Ampliations ou declarations sur le livre nomme Romuleon', also found in a modified form in Br₂. The almost complete omission of the 'Ampliations' from the manuscripts descending from F is particularly striking given that in F this text of 36 folios in length was thought worthy of no less than three of the fourteen illustrations, all three of which had to be specially worked out in line with the eccentric explanations in the 'Ampliations' of the practices and mythology of the ancient world (Pl. 20).[43] All these moves away from F can, however, be seen as moves towards the production of volumes more standardized in their format and recognizably similar to manuscripts of other similar texts.[44] Motivation for such changes probably lay in the interaction of the interests of book producers and book owners, since in this area at least familiarity probably bred not contempt, but attraction and a satisfactory commercial exchange.

According to the preface in F, Miélot's translation was begun at the instigation of Philip the Good in 1460.[45] B and F were in the Burgundian

[41] Of the manuscripts of the Latin text listed by Schaefer and Kristeller (see note 11 above) virtually all that include this table have it placed before the *Romuléon*. The most notable exception is Laur., Santa Croce MS 21 sin. 10, the earliest surviving manuscript of the *Romuléon*, in which the table is stated to be an addition of the Florentine scribe Tedaldo della Casa. Given that this is also the earliest example of the table, this addition may also be the work of Tedaldo, the editor and compiler of aids to the reader.

[42] Only the concluding part of the table remains in Bibl. Roy., MS 9816, fols 1-2. In 1467 and 1487, when recorded in the Burgundian ducal library (J. Barrois, *Bibliothèque prototypographique, ou librairies des fils du roi Jean, Charles V, Jean de Berri, Philippe de Bourgogne, et les siens* (Paris, 1830), no. 1070/2000) the volume included a complete table. By 1487 it was 'tout dessire' and subsequently seems to have lost its first gathering.

[43] These miniatures illustrate the origin of the 'Circenses' (fol. 306v), the ten Sibyls (fol. 324v) and the story of Menenius Agrippa (fol. 322). For the second see G. Biagi, *Reproduzioni di manuscritti miniati. Cinquanta tavole in fototipia da codici della R. Biblioteca Medicea Laurenziana* (Florence, 1914), pl. xxxii.

[44] Cf. *La miniature flamande*, pp. 183-84.

[45] See note 35 above.

ducal library by 1467,[46] as was Brussels 9816, a manuscript of the Latin *Romuléon* of North Italian origin, which, as has already been suggested, was very probably the manuscript from which Miélot, then in the Duke's service, made his translation.[47] Like F, Br₁ was produced by Aubert, this time in 1468.[48] Br₂ was begun for Jean de Wavrin probably in the late 1460s and certainly before his death, in c. 1472-75.[49] These manuscripts seem therefore to go closely together as direct offshoots of the very interests that gave rise to Miélot's text and as continuing manifestations of interest at the Burgundian court in the classical world, which manifested itself through intermediary

[46] The *secundo folio* of Besançon, MS 850 agrees with Barrois no. 877. The provenance, text and overall appearance of Laur., MS Med. Pal. 156 suggested to Durrieu ('Le Romuléon', pp. 442-47) an identity with Barrois no. 1606, 'Ung livre en parchemin: Romuleum, non lye et historie, et parfait d'escripture', one of several unfinished volumes completed for Charles the Bold (see *Charles le Téméraire, 1433-1477*, Bibl. Roy. exhibition catalogue compiled by P. Cockshaw, C. Lemaire et al. (Brussels, 1977), pp. 4-5). The transcription of the text of Laur., MS Med. Pal. 156 was certainly complete by 1467. Yet it could not have been bound before either Miélot's tables of 1465 were inserted (see note 33 above) or the miniatures were added. Since these miniatures are in the same style as in the manuscripts completed for Charles the Bold (see *Charles le Téméraire*, p. 5) Laur., MS Med. Pal. 156 could very well not have been completed until 1468-70. Some explanation of this delay in completing Laur., MS Med. Pal. 156 may rest in Besançon, MS 850. This manuscript could, for example, have been acquired in 1467 as some sort of easy substitute for Laur., MS Med. Pal. 156. Thereafter its existence may have rendered inessential any particular thought about completing Laur., MS Med. Pal. 156. Only when Charles had decided what to do with all the unfinished volumes he had inherited would it have been illuminated and bound.

[47] Bibl. Roy., MS 9816 – Barrois no. 1070/2000. See *La librarie de Philippe le Bon*, Bibl. Roy. exhibition catalogue compiled by G. Dogaer and M. Debae (Brussels, 1967), no. 173. An earlier ownership mark 'Iacobi rubei de vischis hic liber est' suggests that Miélot's translation did not depend on the Latin manuscript recorded in 1438 in the library of Isabella of Portugal's brother, Duarte (*pace* C.C. Willard, 'Isabella of Portugal, Patroness of Humanism?', in *Miscellanea di studi e ricerche sul Quattrocento francese a cura di F. Simone* (Turin, 1966), p. 538).

[48] Masai and Wittek, *Manuscrits datés*, IV, no. 467.

[49] The miniatures in Bibl. Roy., MSS 10173-4 were attributed by Delaissé to the Master of the Champion des Dames (*La miniature flamande*, p. 83 no. 78). Whereas, however, the style of all the border illumination and at least part of four miniatures (fols 110, 237, 354, 389) is consistent with this attribution, several features of the other miniatures are not. Prominent is the attempted representation of such features of ancient Roman life as togas, tunics (see ibid., pl. 33) and stirrupless cavalry, none of which occur in any other South Netherlandish manuscript dating from before the last decade of the fifteenth century. Given also the perceptible difference of technique used in these miniatures, it seems likely that Bibl. Roy., MS 10173-4 was unfinished at Wavrin's death and was completed only much later.

157

compilations and translations of early Italian humanist works, rather than direct translations of classical texts or translations of Latin humanist versions of Greek originals.[50] They also reflect an interest in Roman history which oddly was not expressed in the making of new manuscripts of the very good and previously popular translation by Bersuire of Livy's history of Rome, but in the generation and copying of such other works as Mansel's *Histoires romaines*.[51] At the same time in France, although new copies of Bersuire's translation were made,[52] a further, independent translation of the *Romuléon* was made for Louis of Laval by Sebastian Mamerot in 1466[53] and one fine illustrated manuscript of the Latin *Romuléon* executed for the younger brother of Louis XI, Charles of France, in c.1461-1465.[54]

By 1480, when 19 E.v was being completed, the *Romuléon* was not an obvious text to choose, the very modest interest that it had aroused being that of two decades before. If, however, one had at that time been searching among the professional book producers of the South Netherlands for texts concerned with Roman history, the choice would still not have been very

[50] See J. Monfrin, 'Etapes et formes de l'influence de lettres italiennes en France au début de la Renaissance', *Atti del quinto congresso internazionale di bibliofili* (Venice, 1967), pp. 38-39 and D. Gallet-Guerne, *Vasque de Lucène et la Cyropédie à la cour de Bourgogne*, Travaux d'humanisme et renaissance, 140 (Geneva, 1974), p. xiv n. 20.

[51] On Bersuire's translation and its manuscripts see C. Samaran and J. Monfrin, 'Pierre Bersuire, prieur de Saint-Eloi de Paris (?1290-1362)', in *Histoire littéraire de la France*, 39 (Paris, 1962), pp. 100-56. New Haven, Yale University Art Gallery, Ac. 1954.17.1 (W. Cahn and J. Marrow, 'Medieval and Renaissance Manuscripts at Yale: A Selection', *Yale University Gazette*, 52 (1978), pp. 245-46 no. 69) and B.N., MS fr. 34, made for Louis of Gruuthuse (J. van Praet, *Recherches sur Louis de Bruges, seigneur de la Gruthuyse, suivies de la notice des manuscrits qui lui ont appartenu* (Paris, 1831), p. 224), are the only South Netherlandish manuscripts of Bersuire's text that I know of. Mansel's *Histoires romaines*, on the other hand, which depends heavily on Bersuire's translation, was copied several times as part of the *Fleur des Histoires* (Samaran and Monfrin, 'Pierre Bersuire', p. 151). For an exceptional manuscript of an Italian translation of Livy's first Decade with South Netherlandish illustrations see C. Limentani Virdis, *Codici miniati fiamminghi e olandesi nelle biblioteche dell'Italia nord-orientale* (Vicenza, 1981), pp. 49-51, no. 9, figs. 22-28, pl. iv.

[52] e.g. B.N., MSS fr. 273-74 (A. Paulin Paris, *Les manuscrits françois de la Bibliothèque du Roi* (Paris, 1836-1848), II, pp. 292-93), 20071-72 (N. Reynaud, *Jean Fouquet, Les dossiers du Département des peintures du Louvre*, 22 (Paris, 1981), pp. 75-77). See also A. Boinet, 'Les principaux manuscrits à peintures de la Bibliothèque de la Chambre des Députés, Paris', *Bull. de la Soc. française de reproductions de manuscrits à peintures*, 6 (1922), pp. 47-56, and J. Meurgey, *Les principaux manuscrits à peintures du Musée Condé à Chantilly* (Paris, 1930), pp. 118-20.

[53] See Schaefer, 'Die "Romuleon" Handschrift', pp. 127-30.

[54] Pellegrin, *Manuscrits latins*, pp. 349-53, pl. 19.

great, particularly as Bersuire's translation of Livy still appears to have been generally unavailable, at least in new manuscripts.[55] The *Faits des Romains*, although reviving in popularity in the 1470s and indeed chosen by Edward, only concerned itself with the career of Julius Caesar,[56] as did the 1474 French translation of Caesar's *Commentarii*.[57] The then still popular translation of Valerius Maximus, although also acquired by Edward, merely complements such a text as the *Romuléon* or Livy.[58] The fact that Gruuthuse owned T may therefore have had little bearing on the selection of the *Romuléon* for Edward. The single hastily added arms of Gruuthuse in T certainly suggest that Gruuthuse's manuscript was not a special commission.[59]

Comparison of the texts of both Aubert manuscripts (Br$_1$ and F) with that of L also shows that, although written in a hand very similar to that of Aubert's Ghent manuscripts dating from the late 1470s, Edward's manuscript is not by Aubert himself.[60] The contribution of the scribe in 19 E.v is very different from those in F and Br$_1$, and includes errors particularly uncharacteristic of Aubert.[61] Removal of such a connection with Ghent[62] allows the possibility of 19 E.v moving back in line with the other *Romuléon* manuscripts, all of which appear to have been produced in Bruges, except

[55] Edward himself did possess by 1480 a manuscript entitled 'Titus Livius' (Sir N. H. Nicolas, *Privy Purse Expenses of Elizabeth of York. Wardrobe Accounts of Edward IV* (London, 1830), pp. 125, 152). This manuscript could, however, have been an earlier volume, such as Royal MS 15 D.vi. Given that Philip the Good's copy of Mansel's *Histoires romaines* was recorded as the 'livre de Titus Livius' (C. Dehaisnes, *Inventaire sommaire des archives départementales antérieures à 1790, Nord. Archives civiles, série B*, IV (Lille, 1881), p. 209, no. 2037), Edward's manuscript could also have been of this text either in separate form or, as was much more common, as vol. II of the long version of his *Fleur des Histoires*.

[56] See McKendrick, '*La Grande Histoire*', pp. 113-14.

[57] R. Bossuat, 'Traductions françaises des "Commentaires" de César à la fin du XVe siècle', *Bibliothèque d'Humanisme et Renaissance*, 3 (1943), pp. 255-354.

[58] For Edward's copy see Warner and Gilson, II, p. 315. The popularity of this translation is evident from the very many surviving South Netherlandish illuminated manuscripts and incunabula (*Le cinquième centenaire*, pp. 185, 188).

[59] This is in fact the only mark of Gruuthuse's ownership in T.

[60] I have compared 19 E.v closely with 16 G.iii, dated by Aubert 1479 (see Warner and Gilson, II, pp. 207-28). The closest hand to that of 19 E.v I have noted is that responsible for Kraków, Biblioteka Czartoryskich, MS 2919, dated 1478 (see M. Jarosławiecka-Gąsiorowska, 'Les principaux manuscrits à peintures du Musée Czartoryski', *Bull. de la Soc. française de reproductions de manuscrits à peintures*, 18 (Paris, 1934), pp. 105-09, pl. xxiii).

[61] e.g. 'Spartinius', 'Justinius' and 'Lucius' for 'Spartianus', 'Justin' and 'Lucan' (see note 9 above).

[62] Manuscripts dated by Aubert between 1475 and 1479 were all copied at Ghent. See *La miniature flamande*, pp. 150-57.

perhaps Br$_2$ which may have its origins at Lille, Miélot's own place of residence.[63]

In terms of its illustrations, 19 E.v is different from all the other manuscripts of Miélot's *Romuléon*. Such individuality, however, both in style and campaign of illustrations is a feature common to all the other manuscripts. None is illustrated in the same artistic style, none has the same campaign of illustration or is even illustrated at the same points in the text beyond the beginning of each Book. Even the two Aubert manuscripts contain very different campaigns executed in different styles (Pls 17, 18, 20, 21).[64]

The particular distinctness of the illustrations of Royal MS 19 E.v is found not in their placement (all except one are placed at the beginning of each Book), but in their artistic style and presentation of their subjects. Its presentation involves the distillation of images to the minimum number of figures needed and narration of only a very small part of the story. In this respect L differs widely from F in which many of the illustrations include multiple scenes of significant actions in generously developed settings. Comparison of their respective opening miniatures to Book 1 shows how little of the story of Romulus and Remus 19 E.v attempts to depict (Pls 19, 21). A similar stark contrast can be drawn with the illustration of Augustus's vision of the Virgin for the beginning of Book 9 in Gruuthuse's manuscript (Pls 22, 23). Such treatment of the subjects in Edward's manuscript is partly explained by the miniaturist's apparent total dependence on the one-line instructions which are still to be found at the foot of six folios of 19 E.v[65] and is a reflection of the shortcomings of the practices of those in charge of producing this book.

By now, I hope, it is clear that despite progressive standardization in its presentation Miélot's text achieved a very limited success and by the time of the production of 19 E.v in 1480 needed to be actively sought. The similarities of 19 E.v to the few other surviving manuscripts of the *Romuléon* are explicable in terms of such standardization and their common origins.

---

[63] An origin at Lille is proposed in ibid., p. 83, no. 78 on the basis of the style of the miniatures. The place of transcription could of course have been different.

[64] F has 14 large, full-colour miniatures without border decoration, all in the style of Loyset Liédet. One of these heads Miélot's prologue, ten each of the ten books and the remaining three the concluding 'Ampliations'. Br$_2$, on the other hand, contains 81 grisaille and semi-grisaille miniatures in at least three different styles, ten of which are two-column miniatures with full borders which head each of the books and the rest one-column illustrations scattered through the rest of the text of the *Romuléon*.

[65] In addition to the directions noted on fols 62, 125 by Warner and Gilson, II, p. 349, there are clear traces of directions at the foot of fols 32, 196, 233, 238. All except those on fol. 32 are by one hand.

Distinctive features, on the other hand, such as the substantial additions found in part of its text explained in the stemma by x, appear to reflect a conscious revival of a Burgundian text. Such a revival may have been motivated primarily by the *Romuléon*'s provision of a concise vernacular account of the history of ancient Rome.

Among the Royal manuscripts in the British Library there are no fewer than 21 large illuminated volumes from the South Netherlands which show by their heraldry that they were owned by Edward IV.[66] Several more such volumes in the Old Royal Library were produced during his reign, but it is far from certain which, if any, were owned by Edward.[67] Of the volumes known with certainty to have belonged to Edward, five are dated 1479.[68] The payment to the foreign merchant Philip Maisertuell for books bought for the king in foreign parts is also dated 1479 and the only substantial record of books under Edward occurs in the Great Wardrobe Accounts of 1480.[69] This evidence alone has already suggested to others the likelihood of Edward having engaged in a very short period of intense book purchasing similar to that of his sister Margaret of York only a few years earlier.[70] The further evidence of the heraldic and miniature painting of Edward's surviving manuscripts, although opening up the possibility of Edward having acquired the core of his library in one principal very large purchase,[71] seems to me to reinforce such a suggestion.

The opening folio of 19 E.v provides an excellent starting point for consideration of the heraldic decoration of Edward's manuscripts (Pl. 14). Both the elements of the heraldry and their disposition immediately form close links with several other relevant manuscripts. The opening pages of five Royal manuscripts all show almost exactly the same disposition.[72] Eight volumes contain the same elements of the central shield charged with the

---

[66] S. McKendrick, 'Lodewijk van Gruuthuse en de librije van Edward IV', in *Lodewijk van Gruuthuse*, p. 159, n. 89.

[67] See Backhouse, 'Founders', pp. 39-40. Further relevant manuscripts include Malibu, J. Paul Getty Museum, Ludwig MS XIII.7 (A. van Euw and J. M. Plotzek, *Die Handschriften der Sammlung Ludwig* (Cologne, 1979-85), III, pp. 257-66) and London, British Library, Cotton MS Nero E.iii.

[68] 17 F.ii, 18 D.ix, 18 D.x, 18 E.iii and 18 E.iv. See Warner and Gilson, II, pp. 261-62, 313-15.

[69] McKendrick, 'Lodewijk', p. 153.

[70] Backhouse, 'Founders', pp. 25, 27, and *Margaret of York*, ed. by Kren, p. 18.

[71] As far as I know, this possibility has until now been suggested only in J. J. G. Alexander, 'Painting and Manuscript Illumination for Royal Patrons in the Later Middle Ages', in *English Court Culture in the Later Middle Ages*, ed. by V. J. Scattergood and J. W. Sherborne (London, 1983), p. 153. The £240 to be paid to 'Maisertuell' would certainly have bought many of Edward's books.

[72] 14 E.i, vol. 1, fol. 3; 14 E.vi, fol. 10; 17 F.iii, vol. 1, fol. 1; 18 E.iii, fol. 24; 19 E.i, fol. 1.

royal arms, surrounded by the Garter, and surmounted by a crowned helm with red and blue mantling and lion crest.[73] Eight include very similar angels with standards bearing the royal arms.[74] Eighteen include the Yorkist badges either halved or quartered with Edward's colours.[75] Two include very similar birds, which, as in 19 E.v, flank the central royal arms, like supporters or personal devices, such as the bombards of Louis of Gruuthuse.[76] Another common link between five manuscripts is the substitution of the crown with the lion for a high crown.[77] All these elements are so similar not only in outline, but often in fine detail of execution, that they appear to have been produced not merely from models supplied to the illuminators, but by the same hands and at a very similar date.[78] When other hands attempt to reproduce these models their intrusion is very obvious.[79]

All these elements appear almost without exception to have formed a planned part of the border decoration of Edward's manuscripts, and on several occasions basic features such as the direction faced by the royal leopards are not faithfully reproduced.[80] It is therefore not the case, as with Matthias Corvinus's manuscripts,[81] for example, that the heraldic painting in Edward's manuscripts was executed in the owner's own country. The same hands were not English ones working after the receipt of the manuscripts in England, but Netherlandish ones working before, probably shortly before,

---

[73] Add to the manuscripts cited in note 72 above 14 E.iv, fols 10, 71. 18 E.ii, fol. 7 and London, Sir John Soane's Museum (hereafter Soane), MS 1, fols 11, 150 differ slightly in including a lion passant guardant surmounted by a fleur de lys. 18 E.ii, fol. 7 also adds lion supporters as in 15 E.iv. See also 16 F.ii, 20 C.ix and Add. MSS 35322, 35323.

[74] 14 E.i, vol. 1, fol. 1; 14 E.iv, fols 10, 71; 14 E.vi, fol. 10; 17 F.iii, vol. 1, fol. 1; 18 D.ix, fol. 275; 18 E.iii, fol. 24; 18 E.iv, fol. 19; 19 E.i, fol. 1.

[75] 14 E.i (2 vols), 14 E.ii, 14 E.iv, 14 E.v, 14 E.vi, 15 D.i, 15 E.i, 16 G.ix, 17 F.ii, 17 F.iii (2 vols), 18 D.ix, 18 D.x, 18 E.iii, 18 E.iv, 18 E.vi, 19 E.i.

[76] For birds flanking the royal arms see 14 E.iv, fols 10, 71 and 15 D.i, fol. 18. The very similar birds found in the marginal decoration of 14 E.ii, 14 E.iv and 14 E.v recur in a few contemporary manuscripts not associated with Edward (see Les manuscrits enluminés des comtes et ducs de Savoie, ed. by A. Paravicini Bagliani (Turin, 1989), col. pl. xxxii, and G. de Domenico, 'Contributo alla conoscenza di Loyset Lyedet: il manoscritto n. 233 della Casanatense ed il Reg. Vat. 736 della Vaticana' in Accademie e Biblioteche d'Italia, 27 (1959), fig. 5 (opp. p. 169).

[77] 14 E.ii, fol. 1; 15 D.i, fol. 18; 17 F.ii, fol. 9; 18 E.vi, fol. 8; 19 E.i, fol. 1.

[78] Compare, for example, the script of the Garter motto and the royal leopards.

[79] e.g. 14 E.vi, fols 110, 215, 288; 17 F.iii, vol. 2, fol. 120; 18 E.iv, fols 71, 109, 163, 229.

[80] e.g. 19 E.v, fol. 32. For similar features see Backhouse, 'Founders', p. 27.

[81] See Cs. Csapodi, The Corvinian Library: History and Stock, Studia Humanitatis, Publications of the Centre for Renaissance Research, 1 (Budapest, 1973), pp. 49-51.

the manuscripts were despatched to England (either singly over a couple of years or *en bloc*). In this respect the heraldry painting is to be clearly distinguished from the binding and furbishing of the books recorded in the 1480 Great Wardrobe Account.[82]

Another important link between 19 E.v and several of the other Royal manuscripts is the style of nine out of its eleven illustrations which Durrieu and Winkler attributed to the Master of the White Inscriptions (Pls. 15, 22).[83] Discernible in more than the four manuscripts noted by Winkler, for example in 14 E. ii and 17 F. iii, this style is distinguished by a palette in which orange, green and grey or black often predominate, and a drawing style which often stresses the ugliness and awkwardness of the male figures, but can also render very elegant, if undistinguished, female figures. Also characteristic are gloomy interiors of grey stone walls, often very bare and sometimes given undue attention within scenes with only a handful of figures. Among the inscriptions that gave rise to Durrieu's name variants on the motto 'tousdis joyeulx', which occur four times in three manuscripts, may be some form of signature.[84] Although not in my opinion the work of one hand,[85] this style has a coherence and distinctness which set it apart from all other contemporary work. It is not a style that I have encountered in any manuscripts other than those owned by Edward.

When this style appears in Edward's manuscripts it is mainly the principal one in each manuscript. Its appearance, however, in 14 E. iv, vol. III of Wavrin's *Chronique d'Angleterre*, is a relatively small contribution and appears by its likely later date to be part of a campaign to finish off the illustration of this volume.[86] In the same manuscript another finishing hand is in the other main style found in Edward's manuscripts, Winkler's so-called Master of Edward IV.[87] In 14 E.i, Edward's manuscript of the *Miroir*

---

82 For an analysis of this work see Backhouse, 'Founders', pp. 28-29.

83 See note 6 above.

84 14 E.v, fols 313v ('Ainsi va le monde tousdis joyeulx'), 391 ('Josne et joyeulx'); 18 E.iii, fol. 24 ('Je suis bien tousdis joieulx'); 18 E.vi, fol. 8 ('Joye sans fin'). See Durrieu, *La miniature flamande*, p. 61. None of these inscriptions relate to the subject of the miniatures, except that in 14 E.v, fol. 313v, a darkly sardonic commentary on a particularly vicious depiction of the murder of Herod. The only other example of such an inscription known to me is the 'Tous iours ioieuls' painted in the marginal decoration of a Book of Hours from Flanders dated 1480 (see A. Matĕjček, 'Manuscrits français et flamandes dans la bibliothèque du monastère de Nová Říše', *Památky Archeologické*, 34 (1924-25), p. 40, pl. xvi).

85 Compare, for example, the principal horseman in 19 E.v, fols 98v, 160v with the simplified version in 14 E.iv, fol. 98v.

86 14 E.iv, fols 81, 98v, 114, 121, 169v, 299. Traces of directions to the miniaturists in a hand very similar to that responsible for most of those in 19 E.v are to be found only in this part of 14 E.iv (see fols 81, 169v, 299).

87 14 E.iv, fol. 293v. On this Master see Winkler, *Die flämische Buchmalerei*, p. 137.

Historial, only the opening large miniature is in the style of the Master of the White Inscriptions,[88] whereas all the one-column miniatures are in the style of the Master of Edward IV.

Named after his contribution to 18 D.ix and 18 D.x, the second of which is dated 1479, the Master of Edward IV has been identified in an ever-increasing number of manuscripts, most of which are datable to the 1480s or 1490s.[89] Without entering into that particularly thorny problem I wish to note that this style is to be found among the large miniatures of two further manuscripts of Edward IV.[90] Although dated 1470, 15 D.i was not at that date intended for Edward IV; only after the erasure of the name of the person for whom it was originally destined was his name entered as 'tres victorieux',[91] a title particularly inappropriate in 1470 and one only again used in Edward's manuscripts in 17 F.ii, the text of which is dated 1479.[92] The illumination of the large miniatures was indeed probably executed at the same time as all those in its two companion volumes.[93] The Soane manuscript, also not originally intended for Edward, is probably to be identified with the Josephus mentioned in the 1480 Great Wardrobe Accounts.[94]

Why then did Edward IV form the core of his library over such a short time and at such a date? The long-proffered explanation of Edward's collecting Netherlandish manuscripts in terms of his stay with Louis of Gruuthuse during the winter of 1470-71[95] seems much less persuasive if it is accepted that the collecting took place mostly in 1479-80. Yet, as is evident from the heraldry of Soane MS 1 and Royal 17 F.ii,[96] Gruuthuse was in some way linked with Edward's manuscript acquisitions.

What I would suggest now is that these acquisitions need to be considered within the broader context of other acquisitions made by Edward IV. Edward's manuscripts do constitute an important development in the collecting of manuscripts in England and as such require some explanation; yet any such explanation should not, I think, be sought solely on the evidence of surviving manuscripts. As is frequently the case, too much or,

[88] 14 E.i, vol. 1, fol. 3 (Backhouse, 'Founders', pl. 3).
[89] See Dogaer, *Flemish Manuscript Painting*, p. 117.
[90] 15 D.i and Soane MS 1. 15 E.iii, dated 1482, also has two miniatures (fols 200, 269) and 17 F.ii, dated 1479, all its small miniatures, in this style.
[91] Warner and Gilson, II, p. 170.
[92] See McKendrick, '*La Grande Histoire*', pp. 110, 116-20.
[93] 18 D.ix and 18 D.x.
[94] Backhouse, 'Founders', p. 28.
[95] For the origins and history of this explanation see McKendrick, 'Lodewijk', p. 158 n. 86.
[96] See McKendrick, '*La Grande Histoire*', pp. 124-27.

worse still, exclusive concentration on surviving works and, dare I say it, on manuscripts fails satisfactorily to explain the origins of those very works.

As I have shown elsewhere,[97] Edward was acquiring tapestries from the Low Countries principally in 1478-80. These works were both more costly to acquire than his manuscripts and more clearly visible manifestations of Burgundian magnificence. Their acquisition, however, demands no explanation in terms of temporary exile in the Low Countries, but can be adequately explained in terms of both the prevailing commercial, political and cultural cross-Channel links and Edward's much greater ease of circumstances and financial resources.[98] Similarly Edward's manuscripts from the Low Countries can be seen as a further reflection of a coherent, if relatively short-lived, indulgence of an interest in Burgundian culture and its luxuries,[99] and Gruuthuse's role that not of an initiator, but an enabler and guide.[100]

As was seen in the first part of this paper and is consistent with his other acquisitions, Edward's manuscripts do not comprise straightforward copies of standard Burgundian texts haphazardly or passively acquired. In particular, history, including that of ancient Rome, appears to have been both an overwhelming preference and active choice. Fifteen of the twenty-one surviving volumes with Edward's arms contain historical texts[101] and a few more provide a mine of historical pleasures and lessons.[102] Thus, although in their outward form Edward's manuscripts clearly reflect an aspiration to emulate the splendour of the Burgundian court and to possess a courtly library which was in harmony with and complemented luxurious furnishings,[103] their contents, the texts chosen and sometimes specially revised, suggest to me a well-focused concern for substance.[104] Determining

---

[97] S. McKendrick, 'Edward IV: An English Royal Collector of Netherlandish Tapestry', *Burlington Magazine*, 127 (1987), pp. 521-24.

[98] See ibid., p. 523.

[99] See C. Ross, *Edward IV* (London, 1974), p. 270.

[100] McKendrick, 'Lodewijk', pp. 153-54.

[101] 14 E.i (2 vols), 14 E.iv, 15 D.i, 15 E.i, 15 E.iv, 16 G.ix, 17 F.ii, 18 D.ix, 18 D.x, 18 E.iii, 18 E.iv, 18 E.vi, 19 E.v and Soane MS 1.

[102] 14 E.v, 14 E.ii, 17 F.iii (2 vols). Although such preferences were not unusual (see M.G.A. Vale, *War and Chivalry: Warfare and Aristocratic Culture in England, France and Burgundy at the End of the Middle Ages* (Athens, Georgia, 1981), pp. 14-22), such an imbalance of preferences was. Louis of Gruuthuse's library, for example, embraced a much more diverse selection of texts (see *Lodewijk van Gruuthuse*, pp. 119-22, esp. 121-22).

[103] Backhouse, 'Founders', p. 38.

[104] Most previous critics seem either to assume a wholesale assimilation, passive or active, of Burgundian fashions or to fail to consider the possibility of an active selection from a court culture which embraced greater diversity and was less monolithic than most such critics allow. They also fail to consider the possibility

the motives behind that concern is, I think, important for a full understanding of Edward and his court, and should perhaps be the focus of future work in this area.

---

of any development on Edward's part of a more selective and individual response. Unfortunately, therefore, the image of Edward buying Burgundian books by the pound has continued to retain its power of naïve seduction. See, for example, C. Meale, 'Patrons, Buyers and Owners: Book Production and Social Status', in *Book Production and Publishing in Britain, 1375-1475*, ed. by J. Griffiths and D. Pearsall (Cambridge, 1989), p. 205.

APPENDIX 1
MANUSCRIPTS OF THE ROMULÉON

Besançon, Bibliothèque Municipale, MS 850 (B)

Parchment. Fols 287. 460 x 320 mm (284 x 192 mm). 2 cols. 48 lines. Formal bastard secretary. Original foliation written in red ink in outer margin (fols 1-287) and illuminated Book numbers at centre of upper margin. Rubricated chapter headings. Illuminated paragraph marks, initials and borders. 1 2-column and 9 1-column miniatures. 15th cent. binding of blue velvet over wooden boards, with 5 leather-covered bosses on each cover.

fols. 1-274	*Romuléon* Books 1-10
fols. 274v-287	Alphabetical index

Brussels, Bibliothèque Royale, MS 9055 (Br$_1$)

Parchment. Fols 322. 445 x 333 mm (285 x 210 mm). 2 cols. 36 lines in purple ink. Pricking. Horizontal catchwords. Formal bastard secretary (colophon naming David Aubert and dated 1468, fol. 322). Book numbers in red ink at centre of upper margin. Rubricated chapter headings. Illuminated line-fillers, paragraph marks, initials and borders. 10 2-column and 71 1-column miniatures in grisaille and semi-grisaille.

fols 1-23v	Table of chapter headings
fols 25-51v	*Romuléon* Book 1
fol. 51v	Note on the peoples of Flanders, etc.
fols 51-322	*Romuléon* Books 2-10

Brussels, Bibliothèque Royale, MSS 10173-4 (Br$_2$)

Parchment. Fols 433. 340 x 240 mm (210 x 165 mm). 2 cols. 34 lines in purple ink. Formal bastard secretary. Original foliation written in black ink in outer margin (old fols 1-323, 334-443) and Book numbers at centre of upper margin. Rubricated chapter headings. Illuminated initials and borders. 1 2-column and 9 1-column miniatures. Binding of gold-tooled marbled brown calf.

fols 1-416v	*Romuléon* Books 1-10, each Book preceded by a table of chapter headings
fols 418-433v	'Ampliacions ou declaracions'

Florence, Biblioteca Medicea Laurenziana, MSS Med. Pal. 156$_1$, 156$_2$ (F)

Parchment. Fols 287, 332. 410 x 280 mm. 1 col. 29 lines (except vol. 2, fols. 297-332, 28 lines). Horizontal catchwords. Formal bastard secretary (colophon naming David Aubert and dated 1464, vol. 2, fol. 294v). Rubricated chapter headings. Illuminated line-fillers, paragraph marks and initials. 14 large miniatures.

Vol. 1.	fols 1-1v	Preface of translator
	fols 1v-2	Summaries of each Book
	fols 2v-31	Alphabetical index
	fols 33-36	Table of chapter headings for Book 1
	fol. 36v	Note on the peoples of Flanders, etc.
	fols 37-287 ⎱	*Romuléon* Books 2-10, each Book
Vol. 2.	fols 2-294v ⎰	preceded by a table of chapter headings
	fols 297-332v	'Ampliations ou declarations'

London, British Library, Royal MS 19 E.v (L)

Parchment. Fols 418+ii. 470 x 340 mm (290 x 185 mm). 2 cols. 39 lines in purple ink, with 2 in upper margin. Pricking. Horizontal catchwords. Formal bastard secretary. Rubricated chapter headings. Illuminated paragraph marks, initials and borders. 9 2-column and 2 1-column miniatures. Half red morocco B.L. binding (1985).

fols 1-31v	Table of chapter headings
fols 32-396v	*Romuléon* Books 1-10
fols 397-418v	Alphabetical index

Turin, Biblioteca Nazionale Universitaria, MSS L.I.4$_1$, L.I.4$_2$ (T)

Parchment. Fols 251, 204. 440 x 350 mm [462 x 355 mm before fire of 1904]. 2 cols. Formal bastard secretary. Original foliation written in red ink in outer margin (vol. 1, fols 1-251; vol. 2, fols 1-180) and Book numbers at centre of upper margin. Rubricated chapter headings. Illuminated line-fillers, paragraph marks, initials and borders. 10 (originally 11) 2-column and 66 1-column miniatures. [Bound as one volume in green velvet before the fire of 1904].

Vol. 1	fols 1-251 ⎱	*Romuléon* Books 1-10
Vol. 2	fols 1-180 ⎰	
	fols 181-204	Alphabetical index

THE *ROMULÉON* AND THE MANUSCRIPTS OF EDWARD IV

APPENDIX 2
STEMMA OF MANUSCRIPTS OF THE *ROMULÉON*

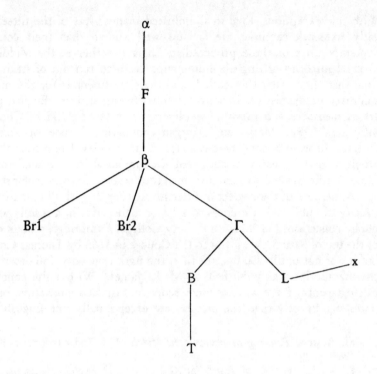

The Artist of Trinity B.11.7 and his Patrons
NICHOLAS ROGERS

With few exceptions, English illuminated manuscripts of the fifteenth and early sixteenth centuries are far less well known than their continental contemporaries or those produced in England earlier in the Middle Ages. General histories of English illumination seem to run out of steam by the time that they reach this period, and their treatment is for the most part summary or dismissive. Rickert presents fifteenth-century English pictorial art as mediocre and passive, 'wholly at the receiving end of Continental influences'.[1] For Marks and Morgan the period is one of accelerating decline.[2] In several cases there is a clear desire to view late medieval English art in natural terms as an autumnal waning, an attitude related to that of those Gothic Revivalists who disdained the decadent Perpendicular style.[3]

A measure of the neglect of fifteenth-century English illumination is the paucity of published references to a major manuscript in a readily accessible public collection. MS B.11.7 at Trinity College, Cambridge, a book of hours of the use of Sarum, was given to the College in 1662 by Thomas Copinger,[4] but it was not until 1900 that the first, and until now only, full description of the manuscript was published by M. R. James.[5] Within the context of a catalogue entry there was not much scope for critical appreciation, but James notes significantly that 'the pictures are exceptionally fine English work'.[6]

---

1   M. Rickert, *Painting in Britain: The Middle Ages*, 2nd edn (Harmondsworth, 1965), p. 198.

2   R. Marks and N. Morgan, *The Golden Age of English Manuscript Painting 1200-1500* (London, 1981), pp. 30-32.

3   This 'natural' approach is apparent in the chapter headings of J. Harvey, *Gothic England: A Survey of National Culture 1300-1500*, 2nd edn (London, 1948): 'Indian Summer' and 'Pregnant Winter'. The most influential 20th-century interpretation of the late Middle Ages as a time of cultural decay is J. Huizinga, *Herfsttij der Middeleeuwen* (Haarlem, 1919).

4   Inscription on fol. 1. Thomas Copinger, rector of Buxhall, Suffolk (c.1600-1674), was the grandson of Henry Copinger of Buxhall (J. Venn and J. A. Venn, *Alumni Cantabrigienses...*, Part I, *From the earliest times to 1751*, 4 vols (Cambridge, 1922-27), I, 396).

5   M. R. James, *The Western Manuscripts in the Library of Trinity College, Cambridge*, 4 vols (Cambridge, 1900-04), I, 342-46 (no. 246). Trinity B.11.7 will be included in Kathleen Scott's long-awaited *Late Gothic Manuscripts c.1385-1490*, A Survey of Manuscripts Illuminated in the British Isles, 6. Also forthcoming is Michael Orr's 'Illustration as Preface and Postscript in the Hours of the Virgin of Trinity College MS. B.11.7'. For a brief description of the contents and iconography see Appendix I.

6   James, *Trinity College*, I, 343.

THE ARTIST OF TRINITY B.11.7 AND HIS PATRONS

Trinity B.11.7 was included in the Burlington Fine Arts Club exhibition of 1908[7] and in Eric Millar's pioneering *English Illuminated Manuscripts of the XIVth and XVth Centuries* of 1928.[8] Millar's comments are more restrained than that of James; for him the book is 'a typical example of average English work of the early fifteenth century. The colouring is the best part of the book, the rather ugly and heavy types of the faces and the distinct ungainliness of the figures being accentuated in a monochrome reproduction.'[9] Neither Elfrida Saunders nor Joan Evans showed any awareness of the manuscript, and Margaret Rickert, who mis-numbers it B.2.7, dismisses it in half a sentence as possibly containing work by Johannes.[10] Derek Turner alluded to the book in a footnote in his article on the Bedford Psalter-Hours, assigning it to the Johannes atelier.[11] The most perceptive comments to date are to be found in Jonathan Alexander's 1972 article on William Abell, where he points out stylistic links with Abell, and also notes the Trinity artist's compositional indebtedness to Herman Scheerre, a point also made by Gereth Spriggs.[12] In an essay on 'Painting and Manuscript Illumination for Royal Patrons in the Later Middle Ages', published in 1983, Alexander further observed that Trinity B.11.7 was illuminated by the same artist as that of the Hours of Catherine de Valois, and suggested that it, too, might also have been a royal commission.[13]

This hint of royal patronage is the nearest approach yet made to a discussion of the original ownership of Trinity B.11.7. The book's anonymity has, I am sure, contributed to its neglect by art historians. In this paper I wish to consider the evidence for its provenance, and then set it in its context. There is a coat-of-arms, rather eccentrically set at the beginning of None, but this is very clearly an early sixteenth-century insertion. The arms are those of Leigh (Gules a cross engrailed within a bordure argent) quartering Colepeper (Argent a bend engrailed gules), pointing to Queen Catherine Howard's

---

[7] Burlington Fine Arts Club, *Exhibition of Illuminated Manuscripts* (London, 1908), p. 74 (no. 151), pl. 103.

[8] E. G. Millar, *English Illuminated Manuscripts of the XIVth and XVth Centuries* (Paris & Brussels, 1928), pp. 37, 41, 89 (no. 282), pls. 92, 93.

[9] Ibid., p. 37.

[10] Rickert, *Painting*, p. 198.

[11] D. H. Turner, 'The Bedford Hours and Psalter', *Apollo*, 76 (1962), p. 270 n. 12.

[12] J. Alexander, 'William Abell "lymnour" and 15th Century English Illumination', in *Kunsthistorische Forschungen: Otto Pächt zu seinem 70. Geburtstag*, ed. by A. Rosenauer and G. Weber (Salzburg, 1972), pp. 166-72 (p. 169); G. M. Spriggs, 'The Nevill Hours and the School of Herman Scheerre', *Jnl of the Warburg and Courtauld Institutes*, 37 (1974), p. 122.

[13] J. J. G. Alexander, 'Painting and Manuscript Illumination for Royal Patrons in the Later Middle Ages', in *English Court Culture in the Later Middle Ages*, ed. by V. J. Scattergood and J.W. Sherborne (London, 1983), p. 149.

half-brother Sir John Leigh, the son of Rafe Leigh, undersheriff of London, by Joyce, daughter and heiress of Richard Colepeper. Sir John had a daughter Anne, who married Thomas Paston, which may be the means by which the book came to be owned by a member of the Suffolk family of Copinger.[14] There is also what M. R. James termed 'a certain East Anglian flavour' about the original text.[15] The calendar includes the Norwich synodal feasts,[16] and the *memoriae* at Lauds include St Edmund and, more unusually, St Etheldreda, the latter illustrated by a delightful miniature of the saint blessing a blind man and two cripples. The litany, on the other hand, points more towards the diocese of Worcester.[17] Also significant are the Dominican elements. Dominicans are prominent in the funeral scene at the beginning of Vespers of the Dead, and one of the two *memoriae* added soon afterwards at the end of the book is of St Peter Martyr. Furthermore, there is evidence that St Anne, the subject of one of three full-page miniatures (Pl. 24), was particularly venerated by the English Dominicans.[18]

The next piece of evidence to consider is the miniature on folio 31v, illustrating the standard prayer for peace at the end of Lauds (Pl. 25). On the rare occasions when this is illustrated, the subject chosen is usually either Christ in majesty or the owner in prayer.[19] Trinity B.11.7 appears to conform to the latter type. Alexander captions this miniature 'a king, Henry V (?), praying at Mass'.[20] In my opinion there is no need for the question mark. Despite the distortions caused by the artist's stylistic mannerisms, the figure of the king was undoubtedly intended as a portrait of Henry, who was described by a contemporary in the following terms:

---

[14] *The Visitations of the County of Surrey...*, ed. by W. B. Bannerman, Harleian Society, 43 (London, 1899), p. 21.

[15] James, *Trinity College*, I, 343.

[16] Felix (8 Mar.), Translation of Edmund (29 Apr.), Dominic (5 Aug.), Thomas of Hereford (2 Oct.), and Francis (4 Oct.). Cf. R. W. Pfaff, *New Liturgical Feasts in Later Medieval England* (Oxford, 1970), p. 7.

[17] The grouping 'Wulfstan, Benedict, Oswald, David' is significant. The inclusion of SS. Milburga and Winefred may point to a Shropshire connection. See Appendix II for the saints in the litany.

[18] D. Park, 'Form and Content', in C. Norton, D. Park, and P. Binski, *Dominican Painting in East Anglia: The Thornham Parva Retable and the Musée de Cluny Frontal* (Woodbridge, 1987), p. 52 n. 103.

[19] e.g. Berkeley Castle, Nevill Hours, fol. 31v, Christ in majesty (Spriggs, 'Nevill Hours', p. 106); Edinburgh University Library MS 40, fol. 46, owner at prayer (C. R. Borland, *A Descriptive Catalogue of the Western Mediaeval Manuscripts in Edinburgh University Library* (Edinburgh, 1916, p. 67)). London, British Library (hereafter B.L.) Egerton MS 2781, fol. 80v has an initial of worshippers in a church (L. F. Sandler, *Gothic Manuscripts 1285-1385*, 2 vols, A Survey of Manuscripts Illuminated in the British Isles, 5 (London, 1986), no. 115).

[20] Alexander, 'Royal Patrons', pl. 9.

His hair is smooth and brown and thick.
His nose is straight, his face becomingly long;
His countenance is fresh, inspiring both affection and respect.
....
His ears small and becoming in shape.
He has a cleft chin, and his neck is everywhere adequately thick;
At the same time one notes that his skin is completely white.
His cheeks are not puffed out, and are graced with whiteness,
Though rosy in part; but his lips are scarlet.[21]

Confirmation of the identification is provided by comparison with an early sixteenth-century painting of Henry which, it has been demonstrated, preserves a contemporary portrait type.[22] The same *'facies decora'* can be recognised among the Scheerresque portrait-initials in the Bedford Psalter-Hours.[23] However, this does not necessarily mean that Henry V was the intended recipient of Trinity B.11.7. This miniature should be seen rather as a visualisation of the litany prayer *'ut regi nostro ... pacem et veram concordiam donare digneris'*. Nevertheless, it would be reasonable to presume that the book was intended for someone closely connected with the king, and was almost certainly produced during his reign, that is between 1413 and 1422.

There are in fact two miniatures at the beginning of the *memoriae* in Lauds which seem to depict the book's owners. The first, a full-page miniature on folio 20, shows a bare-headed man in armour kneeling in prayer before the Blessed Virgin and Child (Pl. 26). Over his armour he wears a brownish-purple tabard of the same form as that shown on the 1424 brass of John Wantele at Amberley.[24] On folio 21 there is a half-page miniature of a woman kneeling in prayer before Christ crucified (Pl. 27). Her mantle has a turned-down collar, a fashion which was introduced in the 1410s.[25] On top of the wide cauls of her headdress (again, very much a feature of the late 1410s) she wears a high coronet, similar to that shown on the effigy of Beatrix, Countess of Arundel (a daughter of the King of Portugal), rather

21 The *Versus Rhythmici in laudem Regis Henrici Quinti*, cited in translation in F. Hepburn, *Portraits of the Later Plantagenets* (Woodbridge, 1986), p. 38. For the Latin text see *Memorials of Henry the Fifth, King of England*, ed. by C. A. Cole, Rolls Series (London, 1858), p. 66.

22 Hepburn, *Portraits*, pp. 27-40.

23 B.L. Add. MS 42131, fol. 74.

24 *Monumental Brasses: The Portfolio Plates of the Monumental Brass Society 1894-1984*, introduction by M. W. Norris (Woodbridge, 1988), pl. 143.

25 M. Scott, *A Visual History of Costume: The Fourteenth and Fifteenth Centuries* (London, 1986), ills. 58, 61, 62.

than the low coronet normally worn by English peeresses.[26] There are no arms to identify the couple, but fortunately the artist of Trinity B.11.7 adopted the Scheerresque habit of incorporating inscriptions in his compositions. The lady's mantle is strewn with the motto '*jammes ne changer*'. In the border of the full-page miniature of St Anne on folio 29 (Pl. 24) this motto, in the form '*Jammes ne changeray*', alternates with another, '*lessez dyre*'. The same pair of mottoes are woven into the backgrounds of the Nailing to the Cross and the Entombment.[27] Since '*Jammes ne changeray*' is associated with the lady, it is reasonable to presume that '*lessez dyre*' was used by the knight.

The clue to their identification is provided by an engraving by Wenceslaus Hollar of stained glass formerly in Ampthill church, Bedfordshire, showing Sir John Cornwall, Baron Fanhope, and his wife Elizabeth kneeling in prayer (Pl. 28).[28] The border incorporated the motto '*lessez dyre*', rendered in a slightly garbled form by Hollar. Examination of their biographies provides support for this identification. 'Grenecornewayle', so called because he was born at sea off St Michael's Mount, was the son of Sir John Cornwall, a descendant of Richard, Earl of Cornwall, and a niece of the Duke of Brittany. In 1400 he married Henry IV's sister Elizabeth, having, according to the *Annales Henrici IV*, captivated her by his prowess at a tournament at York in June that year.[29] She had previously been married to John de Holand, Earl of Huntingdon and Duke of Exeter, who had been executed at Pleshey in January 1400, following the failure of the conspiracy against the new king.[30] Sir John, who served as M.P. for Shropshire in two of Henry IV's parliaments, was appointed Constable of Sheppey Castle in 1402, and in 1409 was made a K.G. In the following reign he played a prominent role in the Agincourt campaign and the siege of Rouen. The French wars brought him profits, which he devoted to the building of a new castle at

---

[26] For the effigy of the Countess of Arundel see A. Gardner, *Alabaster Tombs of the Pre-Reformation Period in England* (Cambridge, 1940), fig. 188; for examples of low coronets see ibid., figs 171 (Duchess of Exeter), 178 (Lady Bardolf), 183 (Duchess of Suffolk), and M. W. Norris, *Brass Rubbing* (London, 1965), fig. 89 (Lady Willoughby d'Eresby).

[27] Fols. 45, 57v. The background of fol. 57v also incorporates part of the Apostles' Creed.

[28] F. Sandford, *A Genealogical History of the Kings of England, and Monarchs of Great Britain* (London, 1677), pp. 252-53. The stained glass at Ampthill survived until the early 19th century, when it was destroyed by a gale (C. G. S. [Foljambe], 4th Earl of Liverpool and C. Reade, *The House of Cornewall* (Hereford, 1908), p. 168).

[29] G. E. C[okayne], *The Complete Peerage*, ed. by V. Gibbs *et al.*, 13 vols in 14 (London, 1910-59), V, 199 n. f, 253-54; Liverpool and Reade, *House of Cornewall*, pp. 166-88.

[30] *Complete Peerage*, V, 196, 198.

Ampthill, but they also led to the death of his only son and heir, who was killed at the siege of Meaux in December 1421.[31] Princess Elizabeth died on 24 November 1425 at the age of 62 and was buried at Burford, Salop., where there is a monument to her.[32] In 1432 Sir John was belatedly created Lord Fanhope.[33] Five years later he founded a Lady Chapel in the churchyard of the London Blackfriars, where he was buried in December 1443.[34] We thus have a couple with close royal connections, which are manifested in the inclusion of Henry V and the princess's coronet worn by the wife, and a link with the Dominicans. The one troubling discrepancy is the lack of any obvious connection with the diocese of Norwich.

One possible explanation of this is that the book was begun for someone else. Apparent support for this is provided by stylistic differences within the book. Three hands can be discerned: the main artist (whom I shall refer to hereafter as the Cornwall Master), an assistant working in the same style, to whom slightly coarser work in certain initials should be assigned,[35] and the vignetteur, who also executed the corner roundels. This artist clearly belongs to an older generation, and this stylistic dichotomy prompted Alexander to state that 'the book itself is of the late 14th century, and most of the borders and the initials, and all the calendar scenes are of this date'.[36] The borders, with their monochrome lion masks and *retardataire* daisy buds and 'bubble foliage' (Pls 29-31, 34), are of a type that can be traced back to the Lytlington Missal of 1383-84.[37] It is possible that the artist is none other than the

---

31   *Complete Peerage*, V, 253-54; M. S. F. George, 'The Builder of Ampthill Castle', *Bedfordshire Magazine*, 5, no. 37 (1956), 185-89.

32   Sandford, *Genealogical History*, p. 252; *Complete Peerage*, V, 254; Gardner, *Alabaster Tombs*, fig. 249.

33   *Complete Peerage*, V, 254. He was also created, in 1442, Baron of Milbroke.

34   John Stow, *A Survey of London*, ed. by C. L. Kingsford, 2 vols (Oxford, 1908), II, 350. Leland provides a description (of sorts) of a monument: 'This Lorde Fannope lyith at the blake freres in London, as I have lernid, and his wife on the right hand of hym and a childe' (*The Itinerary of John Leland in or about the years 1535-1543*, ed. by L. T. Smith, 5 vols (London, 1907-10, repr. 1964), I, 103). Lord Fanhope's will is printed *in extenso* in Mrs H. Jenkinson and G. H. Fowler, 'Some Bedfordshire Wills at Lambeth and Lincoln', *Bedfordshire Historical Record Society*, 14 (1931), 108-12. The residue of his goods, after payment of debts, funeral expenses and legacies to 125 members of his household, was to go to his executors.

35   Fols 58v, 80 and 107v, and perhaps also the miniature on fol. 31 (Pl. 29).

36   Alexander, 'William Abell', p. 169 n. 29.

37   Daisy buds occur on e.g. fols 29v, 43v and 44. More clearly 15th-century in date are the acanthus whorls on fol. 45. For the border decoration in Westminster Abbey MS 37 see L. E. Dennison, 'The Stylistic Sources, Dating and Development of the Bohun Workshop, ca. 1340-1400' (Ph.D. thesis, University of London, 1988), pls 561, 564, 568; Sandler, *Gothic Manuscripts*, ills. 393, 402.

illuminator of the Coronation *Ordo* now in Pamplona.[38] It is instructive to compare the swaying figure of Libra (Pl. 30) with the kings in the border panels on folio 3 of Archivo General 197.[39] The *Ordo* has been dated to the mid to late 1390s. However, recent work by Lynda Dennison and Sylvia Wright has highlighted the continuation of the 'Lytlington' stylistic tradition into the first two decades of the fifteenth century, alongside International Gothic artists such as Siferwas, Johannes and Scheerre.[40] There is nothing about the fashions shown in the calendar roundels which is incompatible with a date in the 1410s, especially if one allows for the conventional nature of the subject-matter.[41] Furthermore, the integration between borders and initials is such as to indicate that the Cornwall Master and the vignetteur were working side by side.[42]

The initial of the Annunciation (Pl. 31) may provide further dating evidence. Compositionally it is closely related to Scheerre's version of the subject in the Bedford Psalter-Hours, which post-dates 1414.[43] In both the Virgin, kneeling on a cushion, half-turns, one hand raised in surprise, the other placed on the book on the altar of her oratory, as she is greeted by the angel, who points upwards. Variations of this composition, which like Scheerre himself can be traced back to Flanders, occur in the artist's earlier works.[44] However, the similarity of detail is such as to make it likely that Trinity B.11.7 is dependent on British Library Additional MS 42131. This is

---

[38] For a facsimile of this MS see F. Idoate, *Ceremonial de la coronación, unción y exequias de los reyes de Inglaterra*, 2 vols, Navarra: Temas de cultura popular, 254-55 (Pamplona, c.1976). See also Sandler, *Gothic Manuscripts*, no 157; Dennison, 'Bohun Workshop', pp. 224-25, fig. 653.

[39] Idoate, *Ceremonial*, I, 7; Sandler, *Gothic Manuscripts*, ill. 416.

[40] Dennison, 'Bohun Workshop', p. 231; S. Wright, 'The Big Bible. Royal 1.E.IX in the British Library and Manuscript Illumination in London in the early Fifteenth Century' (Ph. D. thesis, University of London, 1986), pp. 171-72.

[41] Libra's costume can be compared with that of the statue of a herald from the Emperor Sigismund's palace at Buda, datable to the late 1410s or early 1420s (L. Zolnay and E. Marosi, *A budavári szoborlelet* (Budapest, 1989), pl. 84).

[42] This integration can be seen clearly in the relationship between initial and border on fol. 7 (Pl. 31).

[43] Turner, 'Bedford Hours and Psalter', fig. 1.

[44] e.g. B.L. Add. MS 16998, fol. 17 (A. F. Sutton and L. Visser-Fuchs, *The Hours of Richard III* (Stroud, 1990), fig. 2); B.L. Royal MS 2.A.xviii, fol. 23v (Marks and Morgan, *Golden Age*, pl. 32). On the iconography of the Annunciation in early 15th-century England see Sutton and Visser-Fuchs, *op. cit.*, pp. 9-18. Earlier Flemish examples of this composition include Melchior Broederlam's Dijon Altarpiece, and Rouen, Bibliothèque Municipale, Leber MS 137, fol. 13 (E. Panofsky, *Early Netherlandish Painting: Its Origins and Character* (Cambridge, Mass., 1953), ills. 104, 156).

not the only instance where the Cornwall Master used a Scheerresque model. Gereth Spriggs has pointed out that the Betrayal in Trinity B.11.7 repeats the design used in the Berkeley Hours.[45] A reduced version of this composition was painted by Herman Scheerre in Oxford, Bodleian Library, MS Gough liturg. 6.[46] The Cornwall Master's technique of painting flesh tones over a green ground also links him with Scheerre.[47]

Although the Cornwall Master had access at the very least to a Scheerre model-book, his stylistic affinities lie elsewhere. Where Scheerre would prefer a static, introverted figure, the Cornwall Master opts for a more dramatic presentation, setting a figure in a narrative setting. Rather than a solitary Mary Magdalene holding her ointment pot he paints a *Noli me tangere*.[48] This liking for narrative, emphasized by vigorous gestures, the strongly characterized heads which sometimes verge on caricature, the rich, bright, but not garish colours, and broad frames filled with trailing acanthus or ribbon work are all features of the artist who signs himself as 'Johannes' on folio 220 of *Li Livres du Graunt Caam*.[49] It is possible that one of Johannes' assistants in this great work is none other than the Cornwall Master at the beginning of his career.[50] The gnome-like figure types which are to be found in places in Trinity B.11.7, as on the left of the martyrdom of St Laurence on folio 25, are very much in the tradition of the Bodley Marco Polo. That Johannes and the Cornwall Master are distinct may be

[45] Spriggs, 'Nevill Hours', p. 122, pl. 27c, d.

[46] Fol. 11v. On this MS see G.M. Spriggs, 'Unnoticed Bodleian Manuscripts, illuminated by Herman Scheerre and his School', *Bodleian Library Record*, 7, no. 4 (1964), pp. 199-202.

[47] This technique is Italian in origin. For a rare instance in 14th-century English illumination under strong Italian influence see L. Dennison, '"The Fitzwarin Psalter and its Allies": a Reappraisal', in *England in the Fourteenth Century: Proceedings of the 1985 Harlaxton Symposium*, ed. by W. M. Ormrod (Woodbridge, 1986), p. 51. The green ground can be discerned in the colour plate of Scheerre's Annunciation in the Beaufort Hours in D. Gordon *et al.*, *Making and Meaning: The Wilton Diptych* (London, 1993), pl. 30. For the use of *terra verde* undermodelling in the Wilton Diptych see ibid., p. 80.

[48] Cf. Oxford, Bodleian Library (hereafter Bodl.), MS Lat. liturg. f.2, fol. 141v and Trinity B.11.7, fol. 29v.

[49] Rickert, *Painting*, p. 165, pl. 164A. Bodl. MS Bodley 264, fols. 2, 218-74 comprise an addition to the Flemish Romance of Alexander MS, which may have belonged to Thomas, duke of Gloucester (d. 1397), and it is worth considering the possibility that the Marco Polo was executed for Henry IV. However, nothing certain is known about the provenance of the MS prior to its purchase in London by Richard Woodville, Lord Rivers, in 1466 (O. Pächt and J. J. G. Alexander, *Illuminated Manuscripts in the Bodleian Library Oxford*, 3 vols (Oxford, 1966-73), III, no. 792).

[50] Stylistic links can be made with e.g. fols. 226, 235, 237, 249v.

appreciated by comparing a late work by Johannes, a miniature of the Coronation of the Virgin in the Hours of Elizabeth the Queen (Pl. 53), with the scene of Christ before Pilate in Trinity B.11.7 (Pl. 32). Johannes' figures are slighter, more elegant, with small mouths and beady eyes, whereas the Cornwall Master models his faces more heavily, and often makes his heads over-large, a feature exaggerated still more by his followers.[51] Often Johannes' compositions convey an almost claustrophobic sense of crowding, which cannot be said of the miniatures in Trinity B.11.7. The fascination with physiognomy that both artists display is in line with a general trend in English art, and can also be seen in the enigmatic frieze of heads in Westminster Chapter House,[52] in the gallery of 'portrait' initials in the Bedford Psalter-Hours,[53] and in the work of John Siferwas.[54]

Siferwas can also be invoked in connection with one of the more unusual iconographic features of Trinity B.11.7. The *memoria* of St John the Evangelist is illustrated not by the youthful chalice-bearer but by the white-bearded exile on Patmos (Pl. 33). In French books of hours of this period St John on Patmos is the usual subject for the initial Gospel lection,[55] but the beard suggests that the ultimate source of the Cornwall Master's image may have been an Apocalypse miniature.[56] The immediate origin of this treatment, however, seems to have been either Siferwas or Scheerre: the miniature for St John's day in the Sherborne Missal shows a similar rather Petrine figure seated on Patmos,[57] and Scheerre included a white-bearded St

[51] e.g. in Cambridge University Library MS Ii.6.7, Sarum Hours, early 1440s; Oxford, Keble College, MS 14, Sarum Hours, 1450s; Stonyhurst College MS 2, Cistercian Missal, early-mid 1440s.

[52] Rickert, *Painting*, p. 164, pl. 156A.

[53] Turner, 'Bedford Hours and Psalter', p. 270, figs. 2-9. For the most part these are character studies rather than specific portraits. The Hungarian types on fols. 40v and 50v may reflect the visit of the Emperor Sigismund in 1416.

[54] J. A. Herbert, *The Sherborne Missal*, Roxburghe Club (Oxford, 1920); Marks and Morgan, *Golden Age*, pp. 25-26, fig. XVI, pls 28-30.

[55] R. S. Wieck, *Time Sanctified: The Book of Hours in Medieval Art and Life* (New York, 1988), p. 55, fig. 29, pl. 16. A bearded St John on Patmos occurs on fol. 13 of New York, Pierpont Morgan Library, MS M.287, Hours of the use of Rome, N. France or Lille, *c*.1445 (J. Plummer and G. Clark, *The Last Flowering: French Painting in Manuscripts 1420-1530 from American Collections* (New York, 1982), pl. 17a).

[56] e.g. Lambeth Palace MS 209, fol. 1 (N. Morgan, *Early Gothic Manuscripts (II) 1250-1285*, A Survey of Manuscripts Illuminated in the British Isles, 4 (2) (London, 1988), ill. 133); B.L. Add. MS 42555, fol. 5 (ibid., ill. 146). On contemporary Italian examples of the bearded St John Evangelist see *Lexikon der Christlichen Ikonographie*, VII (Rome & Freiburg, 1974), col. 116.

[57] Trustees of the Will of the Ninth Duke of Northumberland (B.L. Loan MS 82), p. 40 (Herbert, *Sherborne Missal*, pl. XXVIId).

John on Patmos in B.L. Add. MS 16998, a collection of select Masses and devotions made for a member of the Chudleigh family of Devon.[58]

Three unusual subjects were occasioned by the expansion of the usual programme of illustrations of a book of hours. Having decided to provide, after the initial Annunciation at Matins, both a Passion cycle of half-page miniatures from Betrayal to Entombment, and a Nativity cycle of initials from Visitation to Massacre of the Innocents for the hours from Prime to Compline, the illuminator or his adviser was faced with the problem of finding a subject for the initial to Lauds. Adhering to the established Nativity sequence, he chose the one event which fits between the Annunciation and Visitation, the dream of Joseph, in which an angel appears declaring '*Joseph fili David noli timere accipere Mariam coniugem tuam*' (Pl. 34).[59] The subject can be found in contemporary French books of hours, for example as a subsidiary roundel in Paris, Bibliothèque Mazarine MS 469,[60] but for an English example within the context of a book of hours it is necessary to go back to the mid thirteenth-century de Brailes Hours (B.L. Add. MS 49999).[61]

Having painted a funeral scene for Vespers of the Dead, the Cornwall Master had to find another suitable subject for Matins. The image of Job, covered with ulcers, debating with his three friends (whose hats appear to take part in the argument) (Pl. 35), is clearly inspired by the text of the Matins lessons. Although it is only in late fifteenth-century France that it is found with any frequency as an illustration to the Vigils of the Dead,[62] the story of Job is also found in this position in two of the later Bohun manuscripts, the Bodleian Psalter-Hours and the Copenhagen Hours.[63] A very similar head of Job is also to be found in one of the initials in the Office of the Dead in the Bedford Psalter-Hours.[64]

The most remarkable of the three subjects is undoubtedly the initial of Susanna and the Elders, illustrating the Gradual Psalms (Pl. 36). On the rare occasions when this devotion is illustrated the usual subject is either Christ blessing, the patron at prayer or the Presentation of the Virgin, who ascends

---

58 Fol. 87. The arms of Chudleigh (Ermine three lions rampant gules) occur on fol. 8.

59 Matthew, i.20.

60 M. Meiss, *French Painting in the Time of Jean de Berry: The Boucicaut Master* (London, 1968), fig. 262.

61 C. Donovan, *The de Brailes Hours: Shaping the Book of Hours in Thirteenth-Century Oxford* (London, 1991), p. 51, fig. 22.

62 Wieck, *Time Sanctified*, p. 132.

63 Bodl. MS Auct. D.4.4, fols. 244, 248v (M. R. James and E. G. Millar, *The Bohun Manuscripts*, Roxburghe Club (Oxford, 1936), p. 32, pl. XXXVIII (a), (b)); Copenhagen, Kongelige Bibliothek, MS Thott 547.4°, fol. 43 (ibid., pp. 51-52, pl. LXI (b)).

64 Turner, 'Bedford Hours and Psalter', p. 270, fig. 6.

the fifteen degrees of the Temple.[65] The last two subjects are combined in a miniature in the Hours of Margaret, Duchess of Clarence.[66] Outside its biblical context, the history of Susanna is of considerable rarity in art between the early Christian period and the sixteenth century, since Susanna, unlike other Old Testament women, did not take on a typological role.[67] There is only one other manuscript known to me where the Gradual Psalms are in part illustrated by the story of Susanna: B.L. Add. 49999.[68] There is a curious, and possibly significant, link between the two books, separated by about 180 years, in that the patrons of both had Dominican connections.[69] Perhaps the explanation is to be found in some Dominican Psalter commentary. Certainly the tenor of psalms 119 to 123, the first beginning 'In my trouble I cried to the Lord: and he heard me. O Lord, deliver my soul from wicked lips, and a deceitful tongue', fits the circumstances of Susanna's ordeal.

Turning to a brief consideration of the other works in which the Cornwall Master had a hand, one is even more remarkable iconographically, to judge by the two surviving leaves. The first to come to light was the large detached miniature (142 x 90 mm) sold at Sotheby's on 19th June 1990 (Pl. 37). The subject was identified by Martin Kauffmann as the murder of Darius; Christopher de Hamel was closer when he noted the compositional relationship to a Betrayal of Christ.[70] The leaf in fact depicts the Old

---

[65] e.g. Vienna, Museum für angewandte Kunst, Cod. Lat. XIV, fol. 173v, woman at prayer (Morgan, *Early Gothic Manuscripts (II)*, no. 104, ill. 42; Křivoklát (Bürglitz)), Castle Library, MS I.b.23, fol. 120, Augustinian canon at prayer (ibid., no. 184); Norwich, Castle Museum, MS 158.926.4f, fol. 95; Christ blessing (Sandler, *Gothic Manuscripts*, no. 47, ill. 112); Bodl. MS Douce 231, fol. 88, man at prayer blessed by Christ (ibid., no. 87); New York, Pierpont Morgan Library, MS M.700, fol. 57, man at prayer (ibid., no. 88); B.L. Yates Thompson MS 13, fol. 139, queen and princess kneeling before Christ (ibid., no. 98); Dublin, Trinity College, MS 94, fol. 109v, Presentation of the Virgin (ibid., no. 118, ill. 313); Edinburgh University Library MS 42, fol. 90v, Presentation of the Virgin; Blackburn, Museum and Art Gallery, MS 091.21035, fol. 62v, Presentation of the Virgin.

[66] Former J. R. Abbey MS JA.7398, fol. 65v (Sotheby's, *Catalogue of the Celebrated Library of the late Major J. R. Abbey. The Eleventh and Final Portion*, 19 June 1989, lot 3018, col. pl. on p. 64).

[67] Cf. *Lexikon für Theologie und Kirche*, IX (Freiburg, 1964), cols 1195-96. A *memoria* of St Susanna is occasionally found in 15th-century books of hours, e.g. the Hours of Charles the Bold and Margaret of York formerly in the R. A. Lee Collection (J. D. Farquhar, *Creation and Imitation* (Fort Lauderdale, 1976), p. 95, fig. 73).

[68] Donovan, *de Brailes Hours*, p. 24, pl. 16a.

[69] Named Dominican friars are specified in one of the Anglo-Norman prayers added at the end of Add. 49999 (Donovan, *de Brailes Hours*, pp. 125-27).

Testament type of the Betrayal, Joab's murder of Abner.[71] Therefore the miniature most probably came from a grand book of hours in which the hours were illustrated by full-page miniatures of Old Testament types of the Passion, facing depictions of their anti-types.[72] This interpretation has been given support by the recent appearance of another leaf, depicting Joseph's coat being shown to Jacob, a type of the Deposition.[73] I would place these leaves c. 1410, closer in date to the Marco Polo, which also has examples of the ribbon-patterned frame.[74]

Slightly later in date than Trinity B.11.7 is the Cornwall Master's contribution to B.L. Lansdowne MS 451, a Pontifical evidently made for the use of a bishop of London.[75] The costumes of the laymen on folio 198 point to the 1420s.[76] Later still is the book of hours of the use of Paris which he illuminated for Catherine de Valois, now B.L. Add. MS 65100.[77] Not only is the text of this book based entirely on a French model, but the artist has based his compositions on an exemplar evidently from the circle of the Boucicaut Master. The badly rubbed Coronation of the Virgin shows angels supporting a canopy on poles, as in Mazarine 469,[78] and the portraits of the Evangelists in the two books bear close comparison.[79] It may be not irrelevant to note that Mazarine 469 was in England at some point in the fifteenth century.[80] This direct French influence, as well as the scale of the work (Add. 65100 is 121 x 76 mm, compared with the 268 x 185 mm of

[70] Sotheby's, *Western Manuscripts and Miniatures*, 19 June 1990, lot 53, col. pl. on p. 41.

[71] *The Bible of the Poor (Biblia Pauperum): A Facsimile and Edition of the British Library Blockbook C.9 d.2*, transl. and commentary by A. C. Labriola and J. W. Smeltz (Pittsburgh, 1990), pp. 35, 77, 120, 165.

[72] Cambridge, Fitzwilliam Museum, MS 53, a Sarum Hours executed in Bruges in the early 1460s, has initials with types of the Passion illustrating the Hours of the Cross.

[73] *Les Enluminures*, cat. 1 (1992), no. 40 (pp. 97-99). I am most grateful to Dr Christopher de Hamel for this reference.

[74] Fols. 218, 228, 237.

[75] W.H. Frere, *Pontifical Services illustrated from Miniatures of the XVth and XVIth Centuries*, 2 vols, Alcuin Club Collections, 3-4 (London, 1901), I, 90-91, 105-09, II, pl. XI, figs. 33-36. The most likely patrons are John Kempe, bishop of London 1421-1425, and William Grey, bishop 1425-1431.

[76] Cf. e.g. *Portfolio Plates*, pls. 133, 134 (brasses of c. 1420 at Thornborough, Bucks., and Furneux Pelham, Herts.).

[77] Alexander, 'Royal Patrons', p. 149, pl. 8.

[78] Meiss, *Boucicaut Master*, fig. 268.

[79] B.L. Add. MS 65100, fols 14v, 18v, 21v, 24v; Paris, Bibliothèque Mazarine, MS 469, fols. 5, 7, 9, 11 (Meiss, *Boucicaut Master*, figs. 258-61).

[80] Meiss, *Boucicaut Master*, p. 113.

Trinity B.11.7), occasioned a greater delicacy of style. The Hours of Catherine de Valois probably dates from the mid to late 1420s.

The last work known to me in which the Cornwall Master participated is Brussels, Koninklijk Bibliotheek MS IV.1095, a Sarum hours executed for an as yet unidentified patron with the motto *En atendant*.[81] A date in the late 1430s is indicated by the fashions depicted.[82] In this book the Cornwall Master, whose mature style is well illustrated by the miniature of St Anne (Pl. 38), collaborated with another artist, probably the assistant hand in Trinity B.11.7. It is interesting to compare the head of the priest elevating the Host, a work of the second artist, with those of the clergy in the procession of relics in Trinity B.11.7 (Pls. 39, 29).

The metropolitan style of which the Cornwall Master was perhaps the most distinguished practitioner proved remarkably enduring. In the hands of William Abell it continued, and developed, well into the third quarter of the century. In his article on Abell, Jonathan Alexander has noted how that artist uses the facial types and landscape conventions of Trinity B.11.7, and has speculated about a workshop link.[83] Where Abell most obviously differs is in his adoption of a hard-edged, angular drapery style, which betrays the alien influence of the Fastolf Master.[84] A hardening of drapery style is apparent also in the fine burial scene on folio 66v of Edinburgh University Library MS 308, of the 1450s, by an artist who, unlike Abell, developed the Cornwall Master's interest in characterization.[85]

At present it would be possible to write two accounts of London illumination in the fifteenth century, one based on documentary evidence and the other on the artefacts, which would mirror each other but rarely coincide. Christianson's *Directory of London Stationers and Book Artisans* gives a good picture of the commercial book trade,[86] although it underplays the

[81]   *Vijf jaar aanwinsten 1974-1978*, exhibition catalogue, Koninklijke Bibliotheek, Brussels (Brussels, 1979), no. 28; *Vlaamse Miniaturen voor Van Eyck (ca. 1380-ca. 1420*, exhibition catalogue, Romaanse Poort, Leuven (Leuven, 1993), no. 59, afb. 62. The calendar includes the obit of William West, son and heir of Thomas West, lord La Warr (11 July), and the feast of St Eanswythe of Folkestone (2 July) has also been added.

[82]   Cf. Scott, *Visual History*, ills. 76, 78.

[83]   Alexander, 'William Abell', pl. 169.

[84]   *Pace* Alexander, 'William Abell', p. 170. On the work of the Fastolf Master see J. J. G. Alexander, 'A Lost Leaf from a Bodleian Book of Hours', *Bodleian Library Record*, 8, pt. 5 (1971), 248-51.

[85]   N. R. Ker, *Medieval Manuscripts in British Libraries*, II, *Abbotsford-Keele* (Oxford, 1977), pp. 600-01. He is the more talented of the two miniaturists working in this book.

[86]   C. P. Christianson, *A Directory of London Stationers and Book Artisans 1300-1500* (New York, 1990). See also idem, *Memorials of the Book Trade in Medieval London: The Archives of Old London Bridge* (Cambridge, 1987).

still significant involvement of regular clergy in book production. In London, in addition to Siferwas, we have the Augustinian John Cok[87] and the Carthusian John Homersley[88] (both scribes), and the Austin Friar Thomas Westley, the illuminator of Caius 433/432.[89] For some named artists, such as Herman Scheerre, the documentary evidence is both exiguous and ambiguous.[90] Johannes could be any of at least seven limners bearing that name in the first quarter of the fifteenth century.[91] As for the Cornwall Master, there is no certain clue as to his identity. A possible contender is one Thomas Fysshe, first recorded in Paternoster Row between 1404 and 1410, Warden of the Limners' and Text-writers' Guild in 1423, who died in 1450, bequeathing the terms of apprenticeship of two of his apprentices to William Abell, whom he made the supervisor of his will.[92] This is speculation; however, the Cornwall Master's employment by royal and semi-royal patrons leads me to hope that a diligent searcher in the Public Record Office may be able to give him his name. But anonymity should not lead us to ignore the vitality and skill of the main artist of Trinity B.11.7, or the

[87] Alexander, 'William Abell', p. 167, pl. 3; A. I. Doyle, 'Book Production by the Monastic Orders in England (c.1375-1530): Assessing the Evidence', in *Medieval Book Production: Assessing the Evidence*, ed. by L. L. Brownrigg (Los Altos Hills, Ca., 1990), pp. 1-19 (p. 13).

[88] Sir W. St. J. Hope, *The History of the London Charterhouse from its Foundation until the Suppression of the Monastery* (London, 1925), pp. 60-62.

[89] On fol. 1 of this MS, the *Liber soliloquiorum beati Augustini*, which belonged to London Charterhouse, is an initial of St Augustine signed 'Westle'. Cf. Rickert, *Painting*, p. 248, n. 86. Thomas Westley fl. 1423-1438 (F. Roth, *The English Austin Friars 1249-1538*, 2 vols. Cassiacum, 6-7 (New York, 1961-66), II, nos. 728, 789).

[90] On Scheerre see M. Rickert, 'Herman the Illuminator', *Burlington Magazine*, 66 (1935), 39-40, figs. opp. 40; C. Kuhn, 'Herman Scheerre and English Illumination in the Early Fifteenth Century', *Art Bulletin*, 22 (1940), 138-56; Rickert, *Painting*, pp. 166-73; G. M. Spriggs, 'Herman Scheerre and Cologne Painting about 1400 - Some Recent Attributions', in *Vor Stefan Lochner ... Ergebnisse der Ausstellung* (Cologne, 1977), pp. 118-21; Christianson, *Directory*, pp. 157-58. Christianson's interpretation of the name Skereueyn as an 'aural interpretation' of Scheerre is unconvincing. It seems more like a variant of the occupational surname Scrivener. The only reasonably certain documentary references are two London wills of 1407 which mention a 'Herman lymnour'. On Scheerre's Flemish roots see Kuhn, op. cit.; E. Dhanens, 'De plastische kunsten tot 1800', in *Gent: Apologie van een rebelse stad*, ed. by J. Decavele (Antwerp, 1989), p. 206; and M. Smeyers *et al.*, *Naer Natueren ghelike: Vlaamse Miniaturen voor Van Eyck* (Leuven, 1993), p. 57.

[91] John Anys, fl. 1404-08 (Christianson, *Directory*, p. 61); John Asshe, fl. 1417-23 (ibid., p. 61); John Broune, fl. 1395-1430 (ibid., pp. 74-75); John Hun, fl. 1404 (ibid., p. 124); John Northwode, d. 1424 (ibid., p. 141); John Poynaunt, d. 1412 (ibid., pp. 143-44); and John White, fl. 1389-1421 (ibid., p. 174).

[92] Christianson, *Directory*, pp. 109-10.

importance of his contribution to English art of the first half of the fifteenth century.

APPENDIX I
Description of Trinity B.11.7

fols. ii + 123. 268 x 185 mm. Justification 182 x 104 mm. 20 lines to a page. Ruled in brownish black.

Text

fols 1-6v	Calendar, graded, in gold, blue, red and black.
fols. 7-57v	Hours of the Virgin (use of Sarum). Hours of the Cross intercalated. *Memoriae* in Lauds of the Holy Ghost, Holy Cross, Holy Trinity, St Michael, St John the Baptist, St John the Evangelist, SS Peter and Paul, St Andrew, St Stephen, St Laurence, St Edmund, St George, St Christopher, [St Thomas of Canterbury] (*memoria* erased *c.*1539), St Nicholas, St Anne, St Mary Magdalene, St Catherine, St Margaret, St Etheldreda, All Saints, Relics, and Peace. The *memoriae* of St Etheldreda and All Saints are misbound in Prime.
fol. 58	Salve regina.
fols. 58v-66	Penitential Psalms.
fols. 66v-72	Gradual Psalms.
fols. 72v-79v	Litany.
fols. 80-107	Office of the Dead.
fols. 107v-119	Commendation of Souls.
fols. 119v-120	Added *memoriae* of St Peter Martyr (*O petre martir inclite*) and St Leonard (*Salve pater pietatis*).

Iconography

fol. 1	Men at fireside; Aquarius (roundels).
fol. 1v	Man digging; Pisces (roundels).
fol. 2	Men pruning vines; Aries (roundels).
fol. 2v	Men planting tree; Taurus (roundels).
fol. 3	Maiden holding wreaths; Gemini (roundels).
fol. 3v	Man weeding; Cancer (roundels).
fol. 4	Man mowing; Leo (roundels).
fol. 4v	Man reaping; Virgo (roundels).
fol. 5	Man threshing; Libra (roundels) (Pl. 30).
fol. 5v	Man sowing; Scorpio (roundels).

fol. 6	Man killing pig; Sagittarius (roundels).
fol. 6v	King feasting; Capricorn (roundels).
fol. 7	Annunciation (initial) (Pl. 31).
fol. 13	The angel appearing to Joseph (initial) (Pl. 34).
fol. 20	Sir John Cornwall kneeling before the Blessed Virgin and Child (full-page miniature) (Pl. 26).
fol. 20v	Pentecost (½-page miniature).
fol. 21	Princess Elizabeth kneeling before Christ crucified (½-page miniature) (Pl. 27).
fol. 21v	*Gnadenstuhl* Trinity (½-page miniature).
fol. 22	St Michael trampling on devil (½-page miniature).
fol. 22v	Baptism of Christ (½-page miniature).
fol. 23	St John on Patmos (½-page miniature) (Pl. 33).
fol. 23v	SS. Peter and Paul (½-page miniature).
fol. 24	Crucifixion of St Andrew (½-page miniature).
fol. 24v	Stoning of St Stephen (½-page miniature).
fol. 25	Martyrdom of St Laurence (½-page miniature).
fol. 25v	St Edmund enthroned (½-page miniature).
fol. 26	St George slaying the dragon (½-page miniature).
fol. 27	St Christopher (full-page miniature).
fol. 27v	IHS monogram (16th-century insertion) (½-page miniature).
fol. 28	St Nicholas and three children in tub (½-page miniature).
fol. 29	St Anne teaching the Virgin to read (full-page miniature) (Pl. 24).
fol. 29v	Christ appearing to St Mary Magdalene after the Resurrection (½-page miniature).
fol. 30	St Catherine between two wheels broken by angels (½-page miniature).
fol. 30v	St Margaret emerging from dragon (½-page miniature).
fol. 31	Procession of relics (½-page miniature) (Pl. 29).
fol. 31v	Henry V at Mass (½-page miniature) (Pl. 25).
fol. 32v	Betrayal (½-page miniature); Visitation (initial).
fol. 36	St Etheldreda and three cripples (½-page miniature).
fol. 36v	God enthroned between eight saints (½-page miniature).
fol. 38	Christ before Pilate (½-page miniature) (Pl. 32); Nativity (initial).
fol. 41v	Carrying of Cross (½-page miniature); Annunciation to Shepherds (initial).
fol. 45	Nailing to Cross (½-page miniature); Adoration of Magi (initial).
fol. 48v	Crucifixion (½-page miniature); Flight into Egypt (initial).

185

fol. 53v   Deposition (½-page miniature); Massacre of Innocents (initial).

fol. 57v   Entombment (½-page miniature).

fol. 58v   Last Judgement (initial).

fol. 66v   Susanna and the Elders (initial) (Pl. 36).

fol. 80   Requiem (initial).

fol. 85v   Job on the dunghill (initial) (Pl. 35).

fol. 107v   God holding three souls in cloth (initial).

APPENDIX II
The Saints in the Litany of Trinity B.11.7

Peter, Paul, Andrew, John, James, Thomas, Philip, James, Matthew, Bartholomew, Simon, Jude, Matthias, Barnabas, Mark, Luke. Innocents.

Stephen, Linus, Cletus, Clement, Alexander, Laurence, Vincent, Thomas, Marcellus, Quintin, Maurice and companions, Denis and companions, Eustace and companions, Nichasius and companions, Hippolytus and companions, John, Paul, Leodegar, Blaise, Mark, Gervase, Protase, Julian, Adrian, Fabian, Sebastian, Edmund, Christopher, Alban, Oswald, Cornelius, Cyprian, Kenelm, Alphege, Apollinaris, Symphorian, Lambert, Valentine, George, Vitalis, Peter, Edward, Saturninus, Valerian, Crispin, Crispinian, Quintin.

Silvester, Hilary, Martin, Gregory, Julian, Ambrose, Augustine, Jerome, Nicholas, Dominic, Francis, Dunstan, Wulfstan, Benedict, Oswald, David, Hugh, Cuthbert, Germanus, Maurus, Giles, Anthony, Leonard, Botulph, Bernard, Richard.

Anne, Mary Magdalene, Mary the Egyptian, Felicity, Perpetua, Agatha, Agnes, Cecilia, Lucy, Scholastica, Catherine, Margaret, Radegund, Florentia, Columba, 'Sytha', Fides, Spes, Karitas, Juliana, Helen, Sabina, Mildred, Martha, Milburga, Sexburga, Euphemia, Frideswide, Etheldreda, Winefred.

The Royal Library in England before the Reign of Edward IV
JENNY STRATFORD

It is now just over a hundred years since Omont edited the earliest known inventory of the English royal library, the brief list of a hundred and forty-three books seen at Richmond Palace by an anonymous French visitor in 1535.[1] Thirty years later, Warner and Gilson's great catalogue of the royal collection paved the way for all later work on the manuscripts of the Old Royal library. In his introduction Gilson wrote, 'the Old Royal Collection is of respectable though not extreme antiquity. Its real founder was King Edward IV.'[2] As the first king to leave us a coherent collection of books, the large and expensive illuminated histories and chronicles in French, made for him and imported from Flanders, Edward has obvious claims to be considered as the 'founder' of the royal collection as we now know it. Edward's manuscripts, including those which used to be attributed to Henry VII, have been the subject of much recent work.[3] This paper has a different emphasis. What can we say about the royal library before the reign of Edward IV, both as a collection, and about the places where it was kept? Do the tentative conclusions we can reach help us to know more about the readership of books and about the balance between imported and English books? This paper will look mainly at documents rather than at surviving books; great care is needed in interpreting this fragmentary evidence.

There is a notorious contrast between the surviving English and French documentary sources. Firstly, there are no formal inventories in England before the Tudor period,[4] that is no source comparable with the French and

[1] H. Omont, 'Les manuscrits français des rois d'Angleterre au château de Richmond', *Études romanes dédiées à Gaston Paris* (Paris, 1891), pp. 1-13.

[2] G. F. Warner and J. P. Gilson, *British Museum Catalogue of Western Manuscripts in the Old Royal and King's Collections*, 4 vols (London, 1921); I, xi.

[3] J. Backhouse, 'Founders of the Royal Library: Edward IV and Henry VII as Collectors of Illuminated Manuscripts', in *England in the Fifteenth Century: Proceedings of the 1986 Harlaxton Symposium*, ed. by D. Williams (Woodbridge, 1987), pp. 23-41, with bibliography; S. McKendrick, *'La Grande Histoire Cesar* and the manuscripts of Edward IV', in *English Manuscript Studies 1100-1700*, 2, ed. by P. Beal and J. Griffiths (Oxford, 1990), pp. 109-38. I thank Scot McKendrick and Janet Backhouse for their generous help. See also the proceedings of the 1993 Harlaxton symposium [in preparation], and *A History of the Book in Britain 1400-1557*, ed. by L. Hellinga and J. B. Trapp [in preparation].

[4] For the Tudor inventories, see A. J. Collins, *Jewels and Plate of Queen Elizabeth I: The Inventory of 1574* (London, 1955), pp. 231-56.

Burgundian inventories which allow us to know so much about the books, jewels, plate, textiles and other movables of the Valois kings and princes. The French inventories include the 1380 general inventory of the goods of Charles V, which also describes books dispersed among all the royal residences.[5] Separate inventories of the Louvre Library were made in 1373, 1380, 1411, 1413 and 1424, when the books were bought by John, duke of Bedford, as regent of France; after 1429 they were brought via Rouen to the duke's wardrobe in London.[6] The Louvre inventories made in France, not in England, are explicit enough to identify books which have survived. Over a hundred are known today. A similar contrast could be drawn with the inventories of the Visconti, the Medici and the Aragonese kings of Naples.[7] Secondly, in spite of the much greater loss overall of medieval records in France than in England, we know much more about the personal expenditure of the French kings in the fourteenth and fifteenth centuries than we do about that of English kings. This is largely because in England by the second half of the fourteenth century the chamber, the department which dealt with the personal expenditure of the crown, was accountable only to the king, and was exempted from accounting at the exchequer.[8] Some evidence about books can be found in other types of crown record, notably those of the wardrobe and the treasury, but on the whole this evidence does not concern the personal books (except some service books), in use in the chamber by the king himself.

In a paper published in 1983, Jonathan Alexander undertook an invaluable survey of the surviving illuminated manuscripts which can be

5   J. Labarte, *Inventaire du mobilier de Charles V, roi de France*, Collection de documents inédits sur l'histoire de France (Paris, 1879). Many of the published Valois inventories are listed in *Les fastes du Gothique: Le siècle de Charles V*, Exhibition catalogue (Paris, 1981), pp. 436-37.

6   L. Delisle, *Le Cabinet des Manuscrits de la Bibliothèque impériale [nationale]*, 3 vols (Paris, 1868-81), I, 20-56, III, 114-70, 328-36; L. Delisle, *Recherches sur la librairie de Charles V*, 2 vols (Paris, 1907), passim, both with bibliography; J. Stratford, 'The Manuscripts of John, Duke of Bedford: Library and Chapel', in *England in the Fifteenth Century: Proceedings of the 1986 Harlaxton Symposium*, ed. by D. Williams (Woodbridge, 1987), pp. 339-41.

7   Delisle, *Cabinet des MSS*, I, passim; E. Pellegrin, *La bibliothèque des Visconti et des Sforza ducs de Milan, au XVe siècle* (Paris, 1955); *La Biblioteca Medicea Laurenziana, Cenni Storici* (Florence, 1981); E. B. Fryde, 'The Library of Lorenzo de' Medici', in *Humanism and Renaissance Historiography* (London, 1983), pp. 159-227.

8   T. F. Tout, *Chapters in the Administrative History of Medieval England*, 6 vols (Manchester, 1920-33), IV (1928), 227-348; C. J. Given-Wilson, *The Royal Household and the King's Affinity: Service, Politics and Finance in England, 1360-1413* (New Haven and London, 1986), pp. 85-92. See also R. F. Green, *Poets and Princepleasers: Literature and the English Court in the Late Middle Ages* (Toronto, 1980), esp. pp. 4-8.

connected with royal patrons from Edward III to Henry VII, and of some of the documents which concern them.[9] Subsequently, one of the manuscripts, the Hours of Catherine of Valois, has been acquired by the British Library,[10] and a few new pieces of documentary information (not necessarily all concerning illuminated books) have come to light. The account of John de Flete, keeper of the privy wardrobe in the Tower from 1324 to 1341, is a survivor so exceptional that it must be mentioned, although it considerably predates the Lancastrian period. It belongs to the last years of unconcealed chamber accounting, and is precious evidence of what may have been in existence (although undocumented in the public records) at a later date.[11] The receipt section of Flete's account shows that stored in the Tower (but not necessarily all at one time), were at least 160 *libri diversi* and many other books. The issue of fourteen 'romances' and a French psalter in 1324 to William de Langley, clerk of Edward II's household, suggests that these books may have been read in the king's household. The books for which Flete accounted included canon and civil law and a bestiary, some sixty-seven liturgical books, a Bible, fifty-one unbound quires and fifty-nine books and pieces of 'romances'. Some titles in Latin and French are recorded but almost nothing about their contents. Many, if not all, the books had come to Edward III from his father, Edward II.[12] Juliet Vale, in *Edward III and Chivalry*, plausibly concluded that 'there was in effect a royal library within the privy wardrobe in the Tower'. The circumstances in which at least some of these books came to be in the Tower may bear further investigation. Many were sent within a few months of Edward III's accession to the leaders of the

9   J. J. G. Alexander, 'Painting and Manuscript Illumination for Royal Patrons in the Later Middle Ages', in *English Court Culture in the Later Middle Ages*, ed. by V. J. Scattergood and J. W. Sherborne (London, 1983), pp. 141-62. A few details now require revision. See also S. H. Cavanaugh, *A Study of Books Privately Owned in England, 1300-1450*, 2 vols (Ph.D. thesis, University of Pennsylvania, 1980).

10   B(ritish) L(ibrary), Add. MS 65100. Christie's sale-catalogue, 2 Dec. 1987, lot 34.

11   BL, Add. MS 60584, Account of John de Flete, clerk, keeper of the wardrobe in the Tower of London; J. Vale, *Edward III and Chivalry: Chivalric Society and its Context, 1270-1350* (Woodbridge, 1982), pp. 49-50, and appendix 9. I am very grateful to Dr Juliet Vale and to Dr Jennifer Ward for their help.

12   For the books issued to Langley, BL, Add. MS 60584, fol. 24v; Vale, *Edward III and Chivalry*, p. 49. The total number of books is over 340. The *summa* of the receipt of books gives: 'De libris diversis, clx'. This is in addition to a list of 67 liturgical books (13 breviaries, 12 graduals, 2 ordinals, 3 primers, a legendary, 2 manuals, 7 psalters, 8 graduals and tropers, 6 antiphoners, etc.), a Bible, 'De quaternis diversis, lj', and 'De libris et peciis de romancie, lix', and a few other specified items (BL, Add. MS 60584, fols 10v-12v). Books specified in other sections of the receipt include 11 books of canon and civil law received from John [Stratford], bishop of Winchester, 27 November 1326 (fol. 8v). The expenses begin fol. 13v.

dominant court party, Isabella, the Queen Mother, and her lover, Mortimer, but others went to the widows and executors of great magnates who had been implicated in the political troubles of Edward II's reign. Significantly, the three books 'De surgere', and the missal and four books of 'romances' delivered to Elizabeth de Burgh, lady of Clare (whose third husband, Roger Damory, was executed in 1322), the four 'romances' and six or seven liturgical books sent to her sister, Margaret, countess of Cornwall (widow of Piers Gaveston, murdered in 1312, and wife of Hugh Audley, who was implicated in the 1322 rebellion), and the three 'romances' and a bestiary sent to the executors of Thomas, earl of Lancaster (executed in 1322), were issued from the Tower with other movables such as chapel vestments of cloth of gold, secular textiles, clothes and a horse trapper.[13] The descriptions of these 'job lots' of liturgical and secular goods, issued under indenture, suggest that they could be confiscated property from chambers and chapels restored to the heirs of the original owners or represent compensation for such confiscations. Further editing and detailed study of this roll (now cut up and rebound as an exceptionally inconvenient tall manuscript) is needed.[14] Whether or not some of the books Edward II acquired can be shown to have come through forfeiture, and whether or not those issued early in Edward III's reign were alienated permanently or just lent out, the existence of a royal collection of books stored in the Tower at the beginning of the reign of Edward III is firmly established. Some of the books in the French royal collections in the fourteenth century, such as the Belleville Breviary (and the lost Belleville Missal), came into the king's possession through confiscations, and other books were alienated when they were lent out by the king.[15]

The known documents for the reign of Richard II have been investigated by Professor Richard Firth Green and others. Little evidence for the existence of a royal library in Richard's reign has so far come to light.[16] But it is worth recalling the history of one of the books securely connected with Richard, the *Epistre au roi Richart*, the letter to King Richard II of Philippe de Mézières, a presentation manuscript written and illuminated in Paris for

---

[13] BL, Add. MS 60584, fols 13v-15v, *liberaciones*; fol. 27v.

[14] I hope to undertake this during 1994.

[15] For the alienations, Delisle, *Recherches*, *passim*; for the Belleville missal, Labarte, *Inventaire de Charles V*, p. 339, no. 3300; for the breviary (Paris, Bibliothèque Nationale, MSS lat. 10483-10484), ibid., p. 338, no. 3294; Delisle, *Recherches*, I, 182-85; *Les fastes du Gothique*, no. 240, with bibliography. Both were in the king's study at Vincennes in 1380.

[16] R. F. Green, 'King Richard II's Books Revisited', *The Library*, 5th ser., 31 (1976), 235-39; V. J. Scattergood, 'Two Medieval Book-Lists', *The Library*, 5th ser., 23 (1968), 236-39; Cavanaugh, *Books Privately Owned in England*, II, 725-33; V. J. Scattergood, 'Literary Culture at the Court of Richard II', in *English Court Culture*, ed. by Scattergood and Sherborne, pp. 29-43.

Richard and sent to him by Charles VI of France at the time of the negotiations in 1395 for Richard's marriage to Isabella. This is a rare example of a manuscript which beyond question belonged to an English king before Edward IV, which was recorded among the royal books under Henry VIII at Richmond in 1535, and is still in the Royal Collection.[17]

Something is known about at least one of the places where royal books were kept in the Lancastrian period. The payments in 1401-2 for works at Eltham Palace, rebuilt for Henry IV and one of his favourite residences, describe a new study (*novum studium*), one of the rooms attached to the king's new chamber.[18] It was warmed by a brick fireplace with a chimney, and lit by seven large and expensive stained-glass windows. The windows required a total of 78 sq. ft. 4 in. of glass, ordered from the London glazier, William Burgh, at the high cost of 3s. 4d. per square foot, amounting to a total of £13. The glass was sent down to Eltham carefully packed in straw. The windows were ornamented with birds and beasts and with figures of St John the Baptist, St Thomas, St George, the Annunciation (two windows), the Trinity and St John the Evangelist, perhaps with French inscriptions.[19] The ceiling was of wood (*waynescotbord*), perhaps panelled; just possibly decorated like other parts of the new work with carved wooden bosses of archangels, angels and shields. One of two wooden screens (*spera*) may have been for the study. It was furnished with two desks: 'a great desk made of two stages to keep the king's books in, bought with two benches from Roger Joynour for the king's study, cost 20s. And another smaller desk bought from John Deken for the king's said study, cost 13s. 4d.'[20]

Aspects of these payments at Eltham (in particular the glass) have received much attention, but the purpose of the payments, to build and

17   BL, MS Royal 20 B. VI; see *Philippe de Mézières: Letter to King Richard II*, ed. by G. W. Coopland (Liverpool, 1975); J. J. N. Palmer, *England, France and Christendom* (Oxford, 1972), both with bibliography. Omont, 'Manuscrits français des rois d'Angleterre', p. 10, no. 89.

18   London, P(ublic) R(ecord) O(ffice), E101/502/23, mm. 3-4; see H. M. Colvin, *The History of the King's Works: The Middle Ages*, 2 vols (London, 1963), II, 935.

19   The entries relating to the glass and ironwork are printed in translation by L. F. Salzman, 'Medieval Glazing Accounts', *Jnl of the Brit. Soc. of Master Glass-Painters*, 3 (1929-30), pp. 26-27, no. 59. For William Burgh, who supplied glass for Westminster Hall and for Eltham, and the context, see R. Marks, *Stained Glass in England during the Middle Ages* (London, 1993), pp. 48, 94-95. The possibility of inscriptions in French is suggested by the wording: 'la salutacion saincte Marie', 'la Trinité', whereas the account is in Latin; cf. an earlier entry: 'coronez et florez cum soveignez vous de moy', where French inscriptions are certainly meant.

20   Among the *necessaria*: 'Et in uno magno deske facto de ij stagez pro libris regis intus custodiendis cum ij formulis emptis de Rogero Joynour pro studio regis, xxs. Et in uno alio deske minore empto de Johanne Deken pro dicto studio regis, xiijs. iiijd.'

furnish a luxurious study for Henry IV's books, deserves much more emphasis than it has hitherto received. There may well have been similar studies and desks for books in other English royal palaces. There are many points of comparison with the *estude* of Charles V at Vincennes; the payments made by Charles V for the newly-installed Louvre Library in 1367 and 1368 for panelling, protective wire trellis over windows and reading desks differ, however, in being for a library on three floors detached from the king's private apartments.[21]

A recently discovered record of a suit brought and dismissed in the King's Bench against the London stationer, Thomas Marleburgh, has added to our knowledge of the books Henry IV owned – although not what he did with them.[22] This document also names in the accusation a keeper of Henry IV's books, Ralph Bradfield, who seems to have been a valet of the chamber.[23] The nine books, valued at prices between £5 and £10, were in English and in Latin. The values mean that they must have been illuminated. The vernacular books included a *Polychronicon*, a Bible and a Gower.[24] Two points need to be made. First, the cooperation of a great many people is needed to uncover the scattered records about royal or other books which happen to turn up at widely separated and unpredictable chronological intervals in large and uncalendared classes of records of this kind. Secondly, biographical studies, which have not yet been undertaken, of minor crown

---

21 Labarte, *Inventaire de Charles V, estude*, pp. 317-19, nos. 3045-3066; chamber, pp. 336-41, nos. 3279-3309; A. Berty, *Topographie historique du vieux Paris, Région du Louvre et des Tuileries*, I (Paris, 1885), pp. 181-99; Delisle, *Recherches*, I, 7-9.

22 PRO, KB 27/632 Rex, m. 4, Easter Term 7 Henry V [1419], cf. C. Meale, 'Patrons, Buyers and Owners: Book Production and Social Status', in *Book Production and Publishing in Britain, 1375-1475*, ed. by J. Griffiths and D. Pearsall (Cambridge, 1989), p. 203; K. Harris, 'Patrons, Buyers and Owners: The Evidence for Ownership and the Rôle of Book Owners in Book Production and the Book Trade', in ibid., pp. 163-99. For Marleburgh, see A. I. Doyle and M. B. Parkes, 'The Production of Copies of the *Canterbury Tales* and the *Confessio Amantis* in the Early Fifteenth Century', in *Medieval Scribes, Manuscripts and Libraries: Essays presented to N. R. Ker*, ed. by M. B. Parkes and A. G. Watson (London, 1978), p. 198 and n. 91; cf. C. P. Christianson, *A Directory of London Stationers and Book Artisans, 1300-1500* (New York, 1990).

23 Ralph Bradfelde de Bradfelde, Berkshire, *gentilman*, *custos librorum* of Henry IV (PRO, KB 27/632, m. 4). He appears to have been a valet of the chamber by 1405-6 (BL, Harley MS 319, fol. 46v).

24 The case, first brought in 1413, listed the following king's books: a *Polychronicon*, worth 10 marks, a *Catholicon*, worth £10, a small Chronicles, worth £5, a Bible in Latin, worth 10 marks, a Bible in English worth £5, Gregory, *Moralia in Job*, worth 10 marks, a Gower worth £5, and two Psalters, one glossed, worth 20 marks, a total value of £58 6s. 8d.

officials such as Bradfield and the other named keepers of the books after 1400 will probably prove revealing about their status and that of the library.

The rediscovery at Eton in 1978 of a copy of Henry V's last will of 10 June 1421 and its codicils of 1422 has added valuable information about Henry's books and his intentions for them.[25] There can be little doubt that by 1421, and before he obtained the books from the Market of Meaux in 1422,[26] Henry possessed a considerable learned library. He left books to different religious houses, especially to his two new foundations, the double house of Bridgettines at Syon and the Charterhouse at Sheen. A glossed Bible in three volumes was to go to the monastic library at Syon, the works of Gregory the Great (which had once belonged to Archbishop Arundel) to Christ Church, Canterbury. Apart from these few named bequests, the library at Syon was to have 'the whole residue' of Henry's books of sermons useful for preaching, Syon and the Charterhouse to share his books for meditation. The 'common library' of the University of Oxford was to have all his legal and scholastic books.[27] The nuns of Syon were to keep all Henry's books currently in their possession, except his father's great Bible, which was to be returned to the unborn child. This Bible was of particular significance to Henry V when he was compiling his will; he named it twice.[28]

It may be a reflection on the number of Henry V's books that in a codicil he specified that neither Syon nor Sheen was to have any duplicates. In both the will and a codicil the King emphasized that his child was to have the residue of his books, requiring in a significant phrase in 1422 that they should be kept '*pro libraria sua*'. Both in 1421 and 1422 the context of the clauses suggests that Henry V was thinking of books for the household and chamber. The 1421 clause is in a section with three provisions, preceded by armour, and followed by the hangings and beds called 'le stuff' at Windsor, Westminster and the Tower, all left to the unborn child; the 1422 clause places the books and library third after goods of the household chapel, and after arrangements for the tutelage and guardianship of the child. These arrangements end with the chamberlain and steward, officers within the chamber and household.[29]

[25] P. Strong and F. Strong, 'The Last Will and Codicils of Henry V', *English Historical Rev.*, 96 (1981), 79-102.

[26] G. L. Harriss, 'Henry V's Books', in K. B. McFarlane, *Lancastrian Kings and Lollard Knights* (Oxford, 1972), pp. 233-38.

[27] Strong and Strong, 'Last Will', p. 93, clauses xix, xxij; p. 94, clause xxx; p. 100, clause [9]. For Gregory the Great, Rymer, *Foedera*, X, p. 317; for Oxford, *Epistolae Academicae Oxoniensis*, ed. by H. Anstey, 2 vols, Oxford Historical Society (Oxford, 1898), I, 151-53.

[28] Strong and Strong, 'Last Will', pp. 93-94, clauses xxiij, xxvj, xxvij.

[29] Strong and Strong, 'Last Will', pp. 96, 99-100, clauses xxxvij, [3], [9]. See also for the codicil, 'volumus quod omnes libri nostri, cuiuscumque fuerint facultatis aut

Bequests of liturgical books were also made in Henry V's will, some substantially repeated in 1421 from his first will of 1415: his father's breviary in two volumes, said to be written by John, not Richard, Frampton, was left to his uncle, Cardinal Beaufort; his breviary and missal 'written in the same hand', given by his Bohun grandmother, the countess of Hereford, were left to Thomas Langley, bishop of Durham. While these books do not belong to the library, they seem to be personal service books, such as Charles V kept in his chamber and study at Vincennes. Reserved for Queen Catherine were a missal for the altar in Henry's closet or private oratory, and the service books needed for the use of the twenty chaplains of the household chapel. In 1421, the almoner and three named chaplains each were to receive a missal and a breviary worth £10. This did not exhaust the supply of liturgical books, since the residue of books and other valuables belonging to the household chapel were allotted to Henry's son in a codicil of 1422.[30]

The Bible which had belonged to Henry IV, and which was on loan to the nuns at Syon, is twice referred to by size as the great Bible, *magna Biblia*. Should it be identified with a surviving manuscript in the British Library, Royal 1 E. ix, a giant illuminated lectern Bible, entirely suitable for the use of well-born nuns? This has not previously been proposed, but a plausible case can be made out for this suggestion. The Bible has been dated on stylistic grounds to the reign of Henry IV; it was decorated in London by Herman Scheerre and by other artists associated with the Great Cowcher Books of the Duchy of Lancaster. These artists were responsible for a number of important commissions for secular and ecclesiastical patrons in the reigns of Henry IV and Henry V. Several Bibles are listed in English, French and Latin in the Richmond list of 1535. Only one is the *magna Biblia*.[31]

A large number of Latin books, over a hundred and forty at least, were kept in the Treasury during the minority of Henry VI to 1440 or later. Most, if not all, derived from the succession of Henry V, and they seem to have

---

materie, in nostro testamento aut codicillis non legati, filio nostro remaneant pro libraria sua', Harris, 'Book Owners', p. 195.

30 Rymer, *Foedera*, IX, pp. 289-93; Strong and Strong, 'Last Will', pp. 94-95, clauses xxxiij-xxxv; p. 99, clauses [1], [3]. For Richard Frampton and payments for a two-volume breviary for Henry IV, see R. Somerville, 'The Cowcher Books of the Duchy of Lancaster', *English Historical Rev.*, 51 (1936), 599-600. A. I. Doyle, 'The Manuscripts', in *Middle English Alliterative Poetry and its Literary Background*, ed. by D. Lawton (Cambridge, 1982), pp. 93-94; cf. Christianson, *London Stationers*, pp. 106-07.

31 Strong and Strong, 'Last Will', pp. 93-94, clauses xxiij, xxvj. For Herman Scheerre, see Alexander, 'Painting and Manuscript Illumination', pp. 148-50, with bibliography; see also S. A. Wright, 'The Big Bible and Royal Manuscript Illumination in London in the Early Fifteenth Century' (unpublished Ph.D., University of London, 1986).

been kept safely by the council for Henry VI during his minority, in accordance with the provisions of Henry V's will. All those known are summarily described at different dates and in several different documents by title and by secundo folio, but without other description of contents, binding or value. These are, first, the hundred and ten books taken by Henry V after the capture of Meaux on 10 May 1422. Many must have been written in France. Seventy-seven of these books were given in perpetuity to King's Hall, Cambridge, in 1440. The second sizeable group consists of twenty-seven books which went to All Souls in 1440.[32] Three of the All Souls manuscripts and one of the King's Hall manuscripts are known to survive.[33] The All Souls group contained at least one text (in Latin) by an English fifteenth-century writer, Edmund Lacy, bishop of Hereford, 1417-20, bishop of Exeter, 1420-55; this work is otherwise unknown.[34] Lists of a few other small groups of Latin books can be found among the exchequer records. These documents indicate that between at least 1434 and 1442 learned books charged to the treasurer were kept in the receipt of the exchequer at Westminster.[35] This is evidence, moreover, that even after the dispersal of substantial numbers of books to King's Hall in 1435 and 1440 and to All Souls in 1440, other books were still left in the exchequer and were circulating among men closely associated with the royal household. Most if not all seem to have been duplicates of books sent to Oxford and Cambridge.[36] They were being given or lent out to a narrow circle, the king's

[32] For the Meaux books, Harriss, 'Henry V's Books', n. 26 above, with references; for the All Souls books, *Proceedings and Ordinances of the Privy Council of England*, ed. by N. H. Nicolas, 6 vols (London, 1834-37), V, 117-19; R. Weiss, 'Henry VI and the Library of All Souls College', *English Historical Rev.*, 57 (1942), 102-05.

[33] Harriss, 'Henry V's Books', no. 9; Weiss, 'Library of All Souls', p. 104, n.1.

[34] For Lacy, A. B. Emden, *B(iographical) R(egister of the) U(niversity of) O(xford to A.D. 1500)*, 3 vols (Oxford, 1957-59), II, 1081-83; Weiss, 'Library of All Souls', pp. 104, 105.

[35] PRO, E404/56/320, 18 May 1440, warrant to the treasurer and chamberlains, discharging them for a book called 'Armachan sinons', in Latin, 'that was nowe late put into oure receyte at Westmoustier with oother bookes of ours to be kept'.

[36] PRO, E404/57/163, 21 Jan. 1441, four books (including the *Compendium Morale* of Roger of Waltham, and a corpus of civil law), earlier lent and now given to William Alnwick, bishop of Lincoln, formerly keeper of the privy seal; E404/58/127, 23 March 1442, four works of canon law lent to Fulk Bermingham, king's clerk by 1436 (for whom see Emden, *BRUO*, I, 176-77). A two-volume set of the 'Lectura hostiensis', the commentary on the decretals by the bishop of Ostia, had been in the keeping of the king's secretary, Thomas Beckington, the other three had been charged to the treasurer (*Innocentius*, perhaps the commentary of Innocent IV on the decretals; Durandus, *Speculum Iudiciale*;

confessor, a king's clerk, and secretaries and clerks of the signet office. This was recognisably a library in our modern sense of a lending library. Books which are known to have been lent, returned, and lent again to the same borrower are two from the Meaux group: Hegesippus, *Historia de Bello Judaico*, and *Liber de Observantiis Papae*. William Toly borrowed them in July 1434 for return in October, brought them back in January 1435, and borrowed them again in February 1435, this time for a year and a half. Toly had been a signet clerk, was secretary to Cardinal Beaufort by 1429, and king's secretary by 1443.[37] Perhaps the dispersal of a considerable proportion of Henry VI's books to Oxford and Cambridge should be seen as yet another example of his dangerous tendency towards excessive open-handedness after the end of his minority, as well as evidence of his patronage of learning.

The documents so far discovered among the exchequer records of the reign of Henry VI record a handful of other books inherited from Henry V; further research will no doubt bring a few more to light. For example, the same five books are listed repeatedly in the great wardrobe accounts, among the *remanencia* or goods in stock, from the accession of Henry VI in 1422 to at least 1445 and perhaps later. These are a Priscian, a Bede, *De Gestibus Anglie*, the *Sermones Dominicales in Evangelia*, a glossed Psalter and a Bible. These five turn out to be a residue of the books confiscated from Henry Scrope after 1415, left for reasons which are not clear in the charge of the keeper of the king's great wardrobe.[38] Payments for bindings are another potentially fruitful source, although these are likely to apply to liturgical books rather than library books. To take an example from 1444-45, the time of Henry VI's marriage, a pair of liturgical books in use in the King's closet, that is his altar for private devotions within the chamber, a primer and a breviary, were covered in fantastically expensive crimson and gold pile on pile velvet, the 'tissues' or straps and clasps lined with red satin.[39] Henry

---

Guido de Baysio, *Rosarium in Decretum*).

[37] *Kalendars and Inventories of the Exchequer*, ed. by F. Palgrave, 3 vols (London, 1836), II, 152-53; Harriss, 'Henry V's Books', nos. 28, 90. For Toly, see J. Otway-Ruthven, *The King's Secretary and the Signet Office in the Fifteenth Century* (Cambridge, 1939), pp. 14, 139, 154, 184; J. Stratford, *The Bedford Inventories: The Worldly Goods of John, Duke of Bedford, Regent of France (1389-1435)* (London, 1993), p. 425.

[38] PRO, E101/407/13, fol. 4v, 1-2 Henry VI; E 101/409/12, fols 47v, 51v, 105v, 22-23 Henry VI, and all surviving particular accounts between these dates listed in *Descriptive List of Wardrobe Books, Edward I-Edward IV*, List and Index Soc., 168 (1980); C. L. Kingsford, 'Two Forfeitures in the Year of Agincourt', *Archaeologia*, 70 (1918-20), pp. 71-100 (p. 83 for the books).

[39] PRO, E101/409/12, fol. 55; cf. e.g. the payments by Charles V to Dino Rapondi, 22 April 1378, for precious silks to bind books of the Louvre library, Delisle, *Recherches*, I, 371-72.

must have had many books of hours and breviaries but these must have been something on the scale of the Bedford Hours, given to Henry by Anne, duchess of Bedford, with her husband's consent at Christmas 1431.

In conclusion, brief reference must be made to the books of the king's uncles, John, duke of Bedford, who died in 1435, and Humphrey, duke of Gloucester, who died in 1447. A few books from the Louvre library, no doubt saved from dispersal after Bedford's death, remain in the Royal and Cotton collections. Other ex-Louvre books, with the same fifteenth-century provenance, may be identifiable in English, European, and other manuscript collections.[40] Duke Humphrey's learned books had been given to King's College, Cambridge, by 1452, diverted from Oxford. On the other hand, a few of Duke Humphrey's books, the illuminated French books, seem to have been kept by Henry.[41] A few books made for Henry himself are known, for example the presentation copy of Lydgate's Life of St Edmund and St Fremund, which is now among the Harley manuscripts. It does not seem to have been at Richmond in 1535, but to have been moved to Westminster by 1542.[42]

Given the dispersals which took place during the majority of Henry VI and at his own volition, it is perhaps rather Henry IV and Henry V who should be thought of as bibliophiles and founders of the royal library. They acquired their books by inheritance, by gift, by conquest and by forfeiture, as well as by purchase. There is good evidence for books made for both kings in England, as well as for luxury books imported by or for them. On the other hand, the new evidence which has come to light so far may turn out to need correction. Nothing new has yet turned up to add directly to the existing picture of what the Lancastrian kings actually read. It seems possible, however, to say with some confidence that there was a royal library in England before the reign of Edward IV.

---

[40] For Bedford's books and the Louvre library, see Stratford, 'The Manuscripts of John, Duke of Bedford', pp. 329-50; Stratford, *Bedford Inventories*, pp. 91-96 and *passim*.

[41] See A. Sammut, *Unfredo, Duca di Gloucester et gli Umanisti Italiani*, Medioevo e Umanesimo, 41 (Padua, 1980); A. C. De La Mare in *Duke Humfrey's Library and the Divinity School, 1488-1988*, Exhibition Catalogue (Oxford, 1988).

[42] BL, Harley MS 2278; J. P. Carley, 'John Leland and the Foundation of the Royal Library: The Westminster Inventory of 1542', *Bull. of the Soc. for Renaissance Stud.*, 7 (1989), p. 21. I am very grateful to James Carley for his help.

The Pulpit with the Four Doctors at St James's, Castle Acre, Norfolk
JONATHAN ALEXANDER

The village of Castle Acre is located in Norfolk, four miles north of Swaffham and some fifteen miles south-west of King's Lynn. The church and the older houses lie on a low hill to the north of the river Nar, now a narrow stream, but in the Middle Ages probably navigable to the Ouse. They are sandwiched between the twelfth-century Cluniac priory to the west and the castle to the east. Though the latter is described by Pevsner as one of the grandest motte and bailey castles in England, it seems to have played little or no part in English history.[1] It belonged to the Warennes, earls of Surrey, from the Norman Conquest to the fourteenth century. The priory was probably founded by the second earl, that is in the early twelfth century, as a cell of Lewes Priory.[2] Its history appears to have been equally uneventful, though we hear of certain disputes with the mother house at Cluny, with Lewes and with the king, suggesting that discipline lapsed at times. It had three dependent houses in Norfolk, of which that at Bromholm became much more famous owing to its relic of the True Cross.

St James's church, granted to the priory by William de Warenne the second earl, is a typically grand example of a late medieval Norfolk parish church, and though almost all its stained glass has now gone, it must have been as splendid inside as out. Dividing the chancel from the nave the lower part of the rood screen survives with paintings of the Twelve Apostles. The framing of the side aisle screens also survives together with eight of the medieval benches complete with poppy heads and bench-ends of lions and collared dogs. To the right of the chancel arch is the pulpit, reached by modern steps, but adjacent to the staircase giving access to the rood loft.

A useful index of Norfolk rood screens and pulpits by W. W. Williamson lists the Apostles on the screen from left to right as on the left (north) side: St Philip with loaves of bread, St James the Less with fuller's club, St Matthew with halberd, St Simon (?), emblem obliterated, St John the Evangelist with chalice and serpent, St James the Great with pilgrim wallet and shell; and on the right (south) side: St Peter with keys, St Andrew with a

---

[1]   N. Pevsner, *North-West and South Norfolk*, Buildings of England (Harmondsworth, 1962), pp. 111-15; *Castle Acre Castle*, HMSO for English Heritage (London, 1989).

[2]   *A History of the County of Norfolk*, Victoria County History, II (London, 1906, repr. 1975), pp. 356-58; D. Knowles, R. N. Hadcock, *Medieval Religious Houses: England and Wales* (London, 1953), p. 95; *Castle Acre Priory*, HMSO for English Heritage (London, 1990).

cross saltire, St Bartholomew with flaying knife, St Thomas with spear, St Paul with sword and lastly Christ blessing.[3] These last two identifications are unconvincing. My friend John Mitchell, to whom I am indebted for much help with this paper, suggests by comparison with other Norfolk screens that the figure with the halberd (Matthew) may be St Matthias, the figure with emblem obliterated (Simon?) may be St Matthew, the figure with the sword (Paul) may be St Simon and the last figure may be St Jude (Christ). Note that St James as patron of the church has replaced St Paul, more normally paired with St Peter on either side of the screen doors.

The panels on the pulpit, reading from the stairs, that is left to right, are St Augustine, St Gregory, St Jerome and St Ambrose (Pls 40-42). Each is labelled and holds a scroll whose inscriptions have been printed with some minor errors by Williamson and earlier by M. D. Anderson.[4] Williamson says that these pulpit panels are inserted in the pulpit from discarded parclose screens.[5] It is certainly true that the Four Doctors are represented on the central screen doors in a number of instances in Norfolk churches, for example at Salle (Pl 43). I have not been able to check all the examples listed by Williamson, but at Salle they are standing figures and thus in harmony with the flanking Apostles.[6]

Some twenty miles to the north of Castle Acre another pulpit with the Four Doctors survives in the church at Burnham Norton on the north Norfolk coast.[7] They are in the order Ambrose, Gregory, Jerome and Augustine (Pls 44-45). The pulpit also bears donor portraits of John Goldale and his wife Katherine and the date 1450. So far as I know no-one has suggested that the panels of the pulpit at Burnham Norton, which also has an Apostle screen dated 1458, are re-used. At Castle Acre the panels on which the Doctors are painted are 91.44 cm high, the same as the panels on which the Apostles are painted. They seem to me identical in style and are surely painted by the same artist. However, the combined width of the panels, four times 36.83 cm, is 147.32 cm, so they would have been too wide for the existing opening of the central screen, which measures 125.10 cm. It seems reasonable to suppose that the central screen has not been moved, because of the placement of the stairs to the rood loft.

3   W. W. Williamson, 'Saints on Norfolk Rood-screens and Pulpits', *Norfolk Archaeology*, 31 (1956), 299-346.

4   M. D. Anderson, *The Imagery of British Churches* (London, 1955), p. 214. For the texts see note 9.

5   This statement is probably derived from J. C. Cox, *Pulpits, Lecterns and Organs in English Churches* (Oxford, 1915), p. 70.

6   Williamson notes fifteen Norfolk churches with all Four Doctors represented and eight with one or two.

7   Cox, *Pulpits*, p. 70, fig. p. 23; Williamson, 'Saints', p. 306.

In consequence I do not see any reason to doubt that the pulpit is original, even though that leaves the problem of what would have been on the central doors of the central screen if *not* the Four Doctors, and I have no solution to that. The pulpit has undergone restoration, the finials above and the carved angels below being additions, though I cannot say whether nineteenth-century or more recent. About 1963 the paintings were conserved by Pauline Plummer who removed blue paint to reveal the present backgrounds of the figures and treated paint flaking with wax resin adhesive.[8]

At Burnham Norton the Doctors are seated on rather ornate thrones with lap desks and are engaged in writing activities such as sharpening their quill pens. Inscriptions above their heads identify them but they do not hold texts. At Castle Acre, however, the figures are seated on benches, probably thought of as stone, and their scrolls refer to the function of preaching.[9] At Burnham Norton their role as Doctors of the Church centres on their writing of texts rather than on the preaching of Christian truth. The Castle Acre figures are thus more suited to their placement on a pulpit than are the Burnham Norton figures.

St James's, Castle Acre, is a Perpendicular rebuilding of an earlier Decorated church of which three windows survive on the north side, and also the sedilia, and, according to Pevsner, the re-used quatrefoil piers of the nave aisles. Money was left for the tower in 1396 and in 1438 there was a bequest for an image of the patron saint to be placed in the chancel.[10] In 1413-14 Mettingham Priory sent its carpenter, Richard Buck, to see the new stalls at Castle Acre and at Lynn. Pevsner suggested a date of *c.* 1400 from the figure style of the paintings, but a later date of *c.* 1440 is more likely in my view. More convenient than the 1413-14 date, therefore, is the record of a William Castleacre 'steynour and peyntour' in 1445.[11]

Cox, in his book of 1915, which is an excellent example of the strengths of the British antiquarian tradition, is already at pains to emphasize the importance and frequency of preaching in the medieval English church.

8　As she kindly confirmed verbally.

9　I read the inscriptions as follows: Gregory: *Gloria predicantium est profectus* (?) *audientium;* Jerome: *Ne te decipiat sermonis pulchritudo;* Ambrose: *Evangelium mentes omnium rigat;* Augustine: *Impleti* (Anderson *-tus*) *spiritu sancto predicant* (Anderson *-avit*) *veritatem* (Anderson *-Trinitatem*). I have used CD Rom of the *Corpus Christianorum* (CETEDOC Library of Christian Texts) at the Warburg Institute to search for these texts. Only that of Ambrose came up as *Expositio Evangelii secundum Lucam, Corpus Christianorum. Series Latina,* 14 (Turnhout, 1957), Liber 1, linea 47: *Itaque Evangelium ... mentes omnium rigat.*

10　S. Cotton, 'Medieval Roodscreens in Norfolk – their Construction and Painting Dates', *Norfolk Archaeology,* 40 (1987-9), 44-54.

11　G. Fox, 'Medieval Paintings in Norfolk', *A History of the County of Norfolk,* Victoria County History, II (London, 1906, repr. 1975), pp. 551-52.

Considerable work has been done since then on sermon literature, of course, and G. R. Owst's books, one of which also discusses pulpits, are well-known.[12] Cox had a clear polemical purpose in refuting ignorant claims that sermon preaching was an introduction of the Reformation. Many of the texts he cites are of importance in the present context, for example the requirement of the Synod of Oxford of 1223 exhorting clergy to regular preaching, or Bishop Grosseteste's listing of sermons for parish priests in his diocese of Lincoln, or Archbishop Peckham's constitutions of 1281 requiring parish priests to expound the Articles of Faith in the vernacular four times a year. The parishioners of Colyton in Devon complained to Bishop Stapleton of Exeter (1308-26) that their vicar's sermons were too short and that he would not allow friars to 'eke out his insufficiency' as his predecessor had done! The acts of Bishop Langham in 1364 in the neighbouring diocese of Ely (Castle Acre is in the diocese of Norwich) required parish priests to preach regularly and to expound the Ten Commandments in English (*in idiomate communi*).

Cox also lists according to counties the very considerable number of pulpits in wood and in stone surviving in England. His earliest examples, excluding the monastic refectory pulpits, are of the fourteenth century. They greatly increase in the fifteenth century. He also refers to their repair as recorded in contemporary documents, which makes it clear how many have not survived. In Norfolk, besides the two examples already mentioned, the pulpit at Horsham St Faith has painted figures of the Virgin and Child, and Saints John the Baptist, Andrew, Stephen, Christopher, Benedict, Thomas of Canterbury and Faith. A fragment of the support of another wooden pulpit at Diss is recorded, though it apparently no longer survives.

A preaching pulpit should be distinguished from a pulpit used for the liturgical Gospel and Epistle readings, usually referred to as an ambo. It seems that structures primarily for the latter function are earlier in date, though it is not clear whether they were also used for preaching either originally or later. Well-known examples occur in churches in southern Italy, in the cathedral at Ravello, for example, and in Rome, at S. Maria in Aracoeli, for example, both of the twelfth century. The latter has paired ambos on the Gospel and Epistle sides, as is often the case. Other notable examples are, or were, that at Klosterneuburg with its enamel plaques by Nicholas of Verdun, and the Pisa Cathedral pulpit which was moved to Cagliari, Sardinia, when it was replaced by Giovanni Pisano's structure in the

---

[12]   G. R. Owst, *Preaching in Medieval England: An introduction to sermon manuscripts of the period c.1350-1450* (Cambridge, 1926), discusses pulpits on pp. 3, 156, 160-64, 199, 214. Interesting is his reference to a Franciscan brother punished for decorating a pulpit with pictures, p. 164. See also his *Literature and Pulpit in Medieval England* (Cambridge, 1933). For more recent bibliography see *Medieval Sermons Studies. Newsletter*, in progress.

early fourteenth century. We see representations in the south Italian Exultet Rolls of readings from such ambos for the blessing of the Paschal candle at Easter.[13] The rectangular shapes of the Cagliari ambo or pulpit and of other Tuscan examples lent themselves to decoration with panels with Gospel scenes appropriate to their function.[14]

Representations of preaching in manuscripts or in paintings often show it as taking place outdoors and on wooden structures which were presumably temporary. It is not always easy to be sure of either setting or material.[15] The congregation in such scenes, whether outdoors or in, is mostly seated on the ground.

The question of the function of the structure must have bearing on its decoration. Many ambos have a lectern formed of an eagle whose wings support a flat surface for a book to rest on. If the purpose was the reading of the Gospel then the use of the Eagle, symbol of St John, is intelligible. Free-standing lecterns with Eagles are also, of course, common. The tradition of figure scenes, as on the Cagliari pulpit, continues on Nicola and Giovanni Pisano's pulpits,[16] and later still on the twin ambos by Donatello at S. Lorenzo in Florence, for example.[17] But if preaching is the only or the primary purpose of the structure, though the Gospel scenes would not be out of place, scenes referring to the activity of preaching or teaching or stressing the authority of the preacher might be expected. In this respect the Four Doctors seem an ideal subject.[18]

[13] M. Avery, *The Exultet Rolls of South Italy, II. Plates* (Princeton, 1936), e.g. pl. 51, British Library [hereafter cited as BL], Add. MS 30337.

[14] G. H. Crichton, *Romanesque Sculpture in Italy* (London, 1954), with examples of ambos, pls 84-85, 89, and for the Cagliari pulpit, pl. 53, and San Bartolomeo in Pantano, Pistoia, pl. 69.

[15] For scenes of outdoor preaching and reading see E. Salter, 'The Troilus Frontispiece' in *Troilus and Criseyde, Geoffrey Chaucer. A Facsimile of Corpus Christi College, Cambridge, MS 61*, introductions by M. B. Parkes, E. Salter (Cambridge, 1978), ills. 32-9 (repr. in *English and International: Studies in the Literature, Art and Patronage of Medieval England*, ed. by D. Pearsall, N. Zeeman (Cambridge, 1988), pp. 267-71). Some of these examples are clearly made of wooden planks. Another representation is of Archbishop Arundel preaching in support of Henry of Bolingbroke in the early 15th-century copy of Jean Creton, *Chronicle*, illuminated in Paris, BL, Harley MS 1319, fol. 12. This seems to be outdoors, but the pulpit structure looks more as if in stone than wood.

[16] J. Pope-Hennessy, *Italian Gothic Sculpture* 2nd edn (London, 1970), pp. 170-72, 177-79, pls 1-10, 16-22.

[17] H. W. Janson, *The Sculpture of Donatello* (Princeton, 1963), pp. 209-18, pls 102-20.

[18] Apparently a full treatment of the iconography is lacking. A useful but very incomplete introduction (the only example cited from England is the Chapter House door at Rochester) is by G. Jászai, in *Lexicon der Christlichen Ikonographie*, II, ed. by E. Kirschbaum (Rome, 1970), pp. 530-38, s.v. 'Kirchenlehrer'. In

The identification of the Four Latin Doctors already occurs in the Carolingian period, but it appears that though representations of the Four Doctors individually occur quite frequently in both the Early and the Late Middle Ages, as a group they only appear in the later Middle Ages. The earliest example known to me is on an ivory book cover dated 1022-36 from Minden, where the four figures are seated, writing at lecterns.[19] Examples of the twelfth century are in the mosaics in Norman Sicily at Cefalù and in the Cappella Palatina, Palermo, where the figures are standing, and at San Clemente in Rome, where they are seated.[20] Boniface VIII in 1297 published a Constitution entitling the Four Great Doctors to equal veneration with the Four Evangelists, and this was no doubt an impetus to their representation, in company with the Evangelists at Assisi in the crossing vault of the first bay of the nave.[21] Another well-known monument where they appear is Ghiberti's first bronze doors of the Florence Baptistry.[22]

Even in the later Middle Ages single figures are more frequent, however. Ambrose occurs as patron of Milan especially in altarpieces and illuminated manuscripts from Lombardy. Augustine has an additional role as patron of the Augustinian canons and friars.[23] Much commoner than either Ambrose or Augustine, however, are two particular representations of Jerome and Gregory which are very frequent both north and south of the Alps in the fifteenth century. The first is the Mass of St Gregory.[24] The second is St Jerome with his lion, either in penitence before the Cross or as Biblical scholar in his study.[25]

---

addition to other general iconographical sources such as Réau, I have consulted the photographic files at the Warburg Institute and the Princeton Index. A general account, but, like much of the literature, concentrating on Italian Renaissance material, is X. Barbier de Montault, 'Le culte des Docteurs de l'Église à Rome', *Revue de l'art chrétien*, 9 (1891), 275-90, 498-505; 10 (1892), 104-15, 193-200, 293-307; 11 (1893), 25-33, 106-121, 204-15.

[19] A. Goldschmidt, *Die Elfenbeinskulpturen aus der Zeit der Karolingischen und Sächsischen Kaiser VII-XI Jahrhundert*, II (Berlin, 1918, repr. 1970), p. 44, no. 146, Taf. XLI.

[20] O. Demus, *The Mosaics of Norman Sicily* (London, 1949), pls 7b, 38b, c. They are opposed to the Four Greek Doctors. For San Clemente see W. Oakeshott, *The Mosaics of Rome* (London, 1967), pl. 159.

[21] A. Smart, *The Assisi Problem and the Art of Giotto* (Oxford, 1971), pp. 12, 30; J. Poeschke, *Die Kirche San Francesco in Assisi und ihre Wandmalereien* (Munich, 1985), p. 83, Taf. 135-41.

[22] R. Krautheimer, T. Krautheimer-Hess, *Lorenzo Ghiberti* (Princeton, 1970), p. 216, p. 218.

[23] J. and P. Courcelle, *Iconographie de Saint Augustin, les cycles du XIVe siècle* (Paris, 1965).

[24] G. Schiller, *Iconography of Christian Art*, II (London, 1968), pp. 226-28.

[25] B. Ridderbos, *Saint and Symbol: Images of Saint Jerome in Early Italian Art*

In the absence of a more thorough listing, I am left with the rather imprecise impression that the representation of the Four Doctors together is a late medieval iconography more frequently met with in Italy than in Northern Europe, though there are a number of German fifteenth-century woodcuts and engravings of them either standing or seated together. An early example in England may be the four seated, writing figures carved on the chapter-house doorway at Rochester Cathedral, perhaps datable to 1342 (Pl. 46).[26] However, this must remain uncertain, since the figures have none of the necessary attributes of pope, cardinal and bishop. They may have been meant as Evangelists, though in that case they lack their symbols. The Four Doctors also occur in English stained glass of the fifteenth century, including a number of examples in Norfolk, and there they are again often in company with the Four Evangelists both in the glass and on the screens.[27] The only other surviving pulpit with the Four Doctors in England appears to be that at Trull in Somerset, a fifteenth-century one carved in oak.[28]

In manuscript illumination there is no obvious context for the Doctors to be represented together, since their works were copied separately, but an example in an early fifteenth-century Augustine, *City of God*, illuminated in Paris c. 1410, shows them surrounding God in Majesty (Pl. 47).[29] Since they are writing they form a parallel to the Burnham Norton figures.

Though clearly more work needs to be done, it seems to me likely that the Four Doctors ranged as a group on the pulpit are there to signify in the first place orthodoxy of doctrine and in the second place stress that such orthodoxy emanates from the hierarchy of the Church. On the Norfolk

---

(Groningen, 1984); R. Jungblut, *Hieronymus: Darstellung und Verehrung eines Kirchenvaters* (Bamberg, 1967).

[26] A. Gardner, *A Handbook of English Medieval Sculpture* (Cambridge, 1935), pp. 219-20, figs 263-64; L. Stone, *Sculpture in Britain: The Middle Ages*, Pelican History of Art, 2nd edn (Harmondsworth, 1972), p. 258, note 14. Another contemporary English example, kindly drawn to my attention by Nicholas Rogers, is in the Psalter, Cambridge, Sidney Sussex College, MS 76. The Doctors are shown in the border of Psalm 52, thus opposing orthodoxy to the Fool who denies God in the historiated initial (L. F. Sandler, *Gothic Manuscripts 1285-1385* (London, 1986), cat. 86, p. 95, as 'c. 1325-30').

[27] C. Woodforde, *The Norwich School of Glass Painters in the Fifteenth Century* (London, 1950), pp. 175-76.

[28] Cox, *Pulpits*, p. 74, pl. p. 75. For German pulpits with the Four Doctors, of which the most famous is that by Anton Pilgram in Vienna of c. 1500, see P. Poscharsky, *Die Kanzel: Erscheinungsform in Protestantismus bis zum Ende des Barocks* (Gütersloh, 1963), pp. 40-46. I am grateful to Nigel Morgan for this reference. I have not had access to A. Lecoy de la Marche, *La chaire française* (Paris, 1886).

[29] The Hague, Royal Library, MS 72 A.22, fol. 6v (*Schatten van de Koninklijke Bibliotheek* ('s-Gravenhage, 1990), no. 33 and plate).

pulpits as on the Norfolk screens the hierarchy of pope, cardinal, bishop is stressed by their placement, dress and positioning. Gregory is placed in the centre with Jerome beside him and the two bishops either flanking, as at Castle Acre, or as a pair, as on the right, very damaged, door at Gooderstone, Norfolk, c. 1480.[30]

In a Bible made in Naples c. 1350-60 the Doctors, shown as writers, trample prostrate figures who must signify the heretics whom they confounded in their works, such as the Manichees, Arians and Pelagians.[31] In England in 1440 the implied heretics would be the Lollards, records of whose trials in Norwich at this time survive. On the Burnham pulpit the donor, John Goldale, and his wife, Katherine, are represented on the last two panels. The last panel at Castle Acre is blank. Could it, too, have shown a donor? In any case here we have, it seems, either direct lay patronage or imagery which is as it were turned out towards the people. Orthodoxy is represented as residing in the Twelve Apostles, the witnesses of Christ's life, who then preached the Word to all the world, and the Four Doctors who expounded the truth of Scripture. Significant texts of this period, *Dives and Pauper* for example, stressed the importance of listening to the sermon for the laity as equal to if not even more important than hearing Mass.[32] In closing off the choir and its altar with screens, and orienting the images on the screen and pulpit towards the congregation, a similar point is being made.

An illustration found in two copies of a preaching text written in 1457 by Jean Germain, bishop of Châlons-sur-Marne, *Le chemin de paradis*, puts over the same message visually and in its inscriptions. One of six miniatures which portray a procession, it shows the Four Doctors with their wheels of *anagogie* (Augustine), *tropologie* (Gregory), *ystoire* (Jerome) and *allegorie* (Ambrose) conducting the 'chariot of scripture' forward (Pl. 48).[33] The scene

---

30 Williamson, 'Saints', p. 306.

31 Biblioteca Apostolica Vaticana, Vat. lat. 3550, fol. 1 (*Biblioteca Apostolica Vaticana: Liturgie und Andacht im Mittelalter*, (Cologne, 1992), no. 33). In the Sacristy of the Siena Duomo St Ambrose triumphs over a heretic. The painting is given to Niccolò di Naldo, 1410 (B. Berenson, *Italian Painters of the Renaissance. Central Italian and North Italian Schools*, II (London, 1968), figs 485-86).

32 See Cox, *Pulpits*, p. 14, for this and other texts, for example Richard Whitford, monk of Sion.

33 The two illustrated manuscripts were both formerly in the Phillipps library. Brussels, Bibliothèque Royale, IV. 823, copied by Jehan Board, priest of Farges in Burgundy, c.1473-4, was Phillipps 2840. See *Cinq années d'acquisitions 1969-1973*, Brussels, Bibliothèque Royale, no. 40, entry by M. Debae with further bibliography. She refers to the second illustrated copy, Philadelphia, Free Library, MS E. 210, formerly Phillipps 219, for which see *Saints, Scribes and Scholars. An exhibition of illuminated manuscripts and early printed books from the collections of the Rare Book Department of the Free Library of Philadelphia*, ed. by S. I. Parker, W. A. Frankel and M. E. Korey (Philadelphia, 1988), p. 31, ill. I thank Mr Frank

extending from verso to recto is described as showing: '*comme les trois estas* (sic) *clergie noblesse et peuple en unite de foy sont lesglise militant et sont menes sur le charriot de la sainte escripture a lesglise triumphant*'. The church with a Crucifixion in the centre is shown as if carried on a cart. Inside are, on the recto, the pope on his throne, accompanied by cardinal, bishops and clergy, and, partly concealed in the gutter of the manuscript, the emperor, accompanied by the nobility. Behind the Crucifixion on the verso are the people. Here, too, St Gregory as pope is to the front of the chariot, followed by St Jerome as cardinal, and behind are the two bishops, St Ambrose on the left and St Augustine on the right. No wonder such images were done away with at the Reformation, and it is only surprising that at Castle Acre and at Burnham Norton it seemed sufficient to neutralize them by disfiguring the faces by incised crosses over mouth and eyes.[34]

Halpern for facilitating access to this manuscript. Probably datable to *c.* 1460, it measures 275 x 198 mm, is not foliated, and is on paper with six inserted bifolia for the six miniatures which extend from verso to recto and show the chariot of Holy Scripture as if pulled by a long procession. The first miniature, not found in the Brussels copy, shows Jean Germain preaching to his congregation from a wooden pulpit and the start of the procession. The drawings, like those in the Brussels manuscript, are coloured, but its quality is not so high as the latter. Two unillustrated copies of the text are Paris, Bibliothèque Nationale, MS fr. 342 and New York, Mrs Phyllis Goodhart Gordan. For the Brussels manuscript see also N. Reynaud, 'Un peintre de la fin du quinzième siècle: Le Maître des prélats bourguignons', in *Études d'art française offerts à Charles Sterling*, ed. by A. Chatelet and N. Reynaud (Paris, 1975), pp. 152-53, pl. 10. She argues that the illustrations are not in reality designs for a tapestry, as has sometimes been supposed. Their description as such is only a fiction of the author. I am grateful to François Avril for these references.

[34] Eamon Duffy's important new study of the pre-Reformation church in England, which illustrates the Castle Acre pulpit, appeared after the completion of this article, so that I have not been able to benefit from it as I should have wished. E. Duffy, *The Stripping of the Altars: Traditional Religion in England 1400-1580* (London, 1992).

British Library Harley MS 1740 and Popular Devotion
C. W. MARX

Popular religion is bound to remain one of those challenging areas of medieval popular culture which is forever in search of definition: we know that it should be possible to recover aspects of it, but questions arise concerning the degree of lay and clerical involvement, urban and rural contexts, institutional and non-institutional control, and how it can be seen as distinct from predominantly bookish religion.[1] Within this problematic area of medieval studies can be identified also the concept of 'devotional piety' which Richard Kieckhefer has located between the liturgical and contemplative aspects of religion.[2] The liturgy is the church's public practice while contemplative piety Kieckhefer describes as 'what the individual does in those moments when she or he stands alone before God'. Whether this precise mapping of the concept of devotional piety can be sustained is open to question, but approaching popular religion in this way shifts the inquiry from problems of control to questions of practice: we can think in terms of devotional practices and responses as available to both the laity and those in orders and not as exclusive to one group or the other. Further, Richard Kieckhefer has emphasized that popular devotion is a religious activity and consequently much of what we associate with it, such as literary texts and visual arts, served as aids to devotion; they were means to an end. This is not to say that these sources do not reveal something of devotional attitudes. Literary texts are not conceived in a vacuum but assume an audience: presentations of the suffering of Christ or the compassion of Mary must inevitably be seen as indications both of what inspired the devout to acts of piety and of what was thought to inspire acts of devotion. To argue in this way is not to suggest a uniformity of response. Rosalind and Christopher

---

[1] I am grateful to Veronica O'Mara for drawing my attention to the texts in London, BL Harley MS 1740. I would also like to thank Janet Burton, Roger Ellis, Flora Lewis, and Oliver Pickering for valuable information and advice.

[2] R. Kieckhefer, 'Major Currents in Late Medieval Devotion', in *Christian Spirituality: High Middle Ages and Reformation*, ed. by J. Raitt (London, 1989), pp. 75-108 (p. 76). The literature concerned with popular religion is extensive; recent contributions include: R. and C. Brooke, *Popular Religion in the Middle Ages* (London, 1984); J. Van Engen, 'The Christian Middle Ages as a Historiographical Problem', *American Historical Review*, 91 (1986), 519-52; M. Rubin, *Corpus Christi: the Eucharist in Late Medieval Culture* (Cambridge, 1991); eadem, 'Religious Culture in Town and Country: Reflections on a Great Divide', in *Church and City 1000-1500: Essays in Honour of Christopher Brooke*, ed. by D. Abulafia, M. Franklin and M. Rubin (Cambridge, 1992), pp. 3-22; B. Dobson, 'Citizens and Chantries in Late Medieval York', ibid., pp. 311-32.

Brooke have stressed the variety of gradations among the laity and those in orders,[3] and devotional literature and art were therefore open to different types of use.

There survive in Middle English a large number of texts concerned with the Passion of Christ and the Compassion of Mary; many of the prose texts remain unedited and unpublished, which has meant that our understanding of fifteenth-century attitudes in this area is far from complete.[4] There is still something foreign about the extreme views presented in fifteenth-century accounts of the Passion: Margery Kempe's devotional responses are probably not as eccentric as is frequently suggested. London, British Library, Harley MS 1740 is a small manuscript of the fifteenth century; it contains three items written in two hands:

dimensions: 205 mm x 135 mm

collation: iv + i + iii + 26 [1-2^8, 3^6, 4^4] + iv

contents:

1. fols 5r-22r, Passio domini nostri Ihesu Christi (hand 1), unpublished.

2. fols 22r-24r, Item de passione Christi bona contemplacio (hand 1), edited as Appendix to this essay.

3. fols 24r-29v, Homo quidam fecit cenam magnam & vocauit multos (hand 2), unpublished.[5]

The third item is a later addition. This essay is concerned with the two texts which occupy most of the manuscript, the Passion narrative (1) and the meditation (2), and the question of how this compilation, that is, these two texts occurring together in this manuscript and written in the same hand, might give some insight into attitudes which helped to motivate fifteenth-century popular devotion.

The first text, the Passion narrative, holds some surprises, but, at the same time, it is a late example of a tradition of affective piety which has its roots in the eleventh and twelfth centuries in texts such as the *Orationes* of Anselm of Canterbury (1033-1109) and the *De Institutione Inclusarum* of

---

3 Brooke, *Popular Religion in the Middle Ages*, p. 9.

4 See, for example, E. Salter, 'The Manuscripts of Nicholas Love's *Myrrour of the Blessed Lyf of Jesu Christ* and Related Texts', in *Middle English Prose: Essays on Bibliographical Problems*, ed. by A. S. G. Edwards and D. Pearsall (London, 1981), pp. 115-27; M. G. Sargent, 'Minor Devotional Writings', in *Middle English Prose: a Critical Guide to Major Authors and Genres*, ed. by A. S. G. Edwards (New Brunswick, N.J., 1984), pp. 147-175. See also *The Middle English Prose Complaint of Our Lady and Gospel of Nicodemus*, ed. by C. W. Marx and J. F. Drennan, Middle English Texts, 19 (Heidelberg, 1987).

5 V. M. O'Mara, 'A Checklist of Unedited Late Middle English Sermons that Occur Singly or in Small Groups', *Leeds Studies in English*, n.s. 19 (1988), 141-66 (p. 157).

Aelred of Rievaulx (1110-1167),[6] and which includes the *Quis dabit* of the late twelfth or very early thirteenth century,[7] the pseudo-Anselm *Dialogus* of the early to mid thirteenth century,[8] and the pseudo-Bonaventure *Meditationes Vitae Christi* of the late thirteenth century.[9] The *Quis dabit* is especially important for an understanding of the theme of the Compassion of Mary, but much work remains to be done on its textual history.[10]

The Harley 1740 Passion text has several threads running through it, and one of its most prominent features is that late medieval preoccupation with the physical suffering of Christ, unconcerned, it would almost seem, with the larger issues of the redemption. There is an unremitting factuality about the account of the way Christ's body is tortured and wounded; for example:

> And þer þei dispoyled him and bounde him to a piller of marbell so straytly
> þat þe flessch bolled oute aboute þe cordis þat vnneth þe cordes miȝt be seen
> for swellynge of þe flessch. And þe blode sterlt from his handis & nayles.
> (fol. 8r)

F. P. Pickering and those who have followed him have been keen to stress that this use of precise physical detail has its typological dimension in that it can be shown to represent the fulfilment of prophecy,[11] and it is not difficult to see a passage such as this implying the typological image of the wine-press

---

[6] *Sancti Anselmi Cantuariensis Archiepiscopi Opera Omnia*, ed. by F. S. Schmitt, 6 vols (Edinburgh, 1946-61), III, 5-75; Aelred of Rievaulx, *De Institutione Inclusarum*, ed. by C. H. Talbot, in *Aelredi Rievallensis Opera Omnia*, Corpus Christianorum, Continuatio Mediaevalis, I (Turnhout, 1971), 635-82.

[7] The *Quis dabit* or *Liber de passione Christi et doloribus et planctibus matris eius* is available in three printings, all of which are inadequate: *PL* 182.1133-1142; W. Mushacke, *Altprovenzalische Marienklage des XIII Jahrhunderts* (Halle, 1890), pp. 41-50; G. Kribel, 'Studien zu Richard Rolle de Hampole, II, Lamentatio St Bernardi de compassione Mariae', *Englische Studien*, 8 (1884), 85-114. See also C. W. Marx, 'The Middle English Verse *Lamentation of Mary to Saint Bernard* and the *Quis dabit*', in *Studies in The Vernon Manuscript*, ed. by D. Pearsall (Cambridge, 1990), pp. 137-57. An edition based on one of the earliest witnesses along with an account of aspects of the history of the text appears in C. W. Marx, 'The *Quis dabit* of Oglerius de Tridino', *Journal of Medieval Latin*, 4 (1994, forthcoming).

[8] *Dialogus Beatae Marie et Anselmi de Passione Domini*, *PL* 159.271-290. See F. P. Pickering, *Literature and Art in the Middle Ages* (London, 1970), p. 237.

[9] *Meditationes Vitae Christi*, in *Opera Omnia S. Bonaventurae*, ed. by A. C. Peltier, XII (Paris, 1868), pp. 509-630. A useful translation from an Italian version is found in *Meditations on the Life of Christ*, trans. and ed. by I. Ragusa and R. B. Green (Princeton, N.J., 1961; repr. 1977).

[10] I am compiling a list of manuscripts of the *Quis dabit* in British libraries.

[11] Pickering, *Literature and Art in the Middle Ages*, pp. 223-307; J. H. Marrow, *Passion Iconography in Northern European Art of the Late Middle Ages and Early Renaissance* (Kortrijk, 1979).

(Isaiah lxiii.3).[12] Nevertheless, here the text seems to be mainly pre-occupied with the immediacy of Christ's physical suffering. Another passage illustrates this same point:

> And þen þei sette all to þe crosse togedir and lyfte it vp & set it more strongly & harder into þe morteis, and made it fast into þe stone with so grete vyolence and strength þat all þe woundes of þe nayles breste oute of blode in handys & in feete. & þen þe blode ren downe grete plenty & the ioyntes and þe synnous began to shrynke and þe veynes began to blede, and þe blode congelid and hong by þe woundes all arawe cloddid togeder as dropes of wex doth by the tapers. And so straytly he was done on þe crosse þat a man miȝte nombre all þe bones of þe bodi. (fol. 15v)

The last line, *þat a man miȝte nombre all þe bones of þe bodi*, is a common typological reference in this kind of description; it fulfils the prophecy of Psalm xxi.18 (Vulgate), *Dinumeraverunt omnia ossa mea. | Ipsi vero consideraverunt et inspexerunt me.* And the simile in the penultimate sentence, *as dropes of wex doth by the tapers*, breaks the illusion of realism. However, the effects of the tormenting of Christ are described in precise, anatomical terms. There are many more such passages, and these are not uncommon in accounts of the Passion. But what is the nature of the devotion they suggest?

The narrative is initially conceived as a vision: a monk desires to know *þe sondre paynes & anguysches þat our lorde Ihesu Criste sufferd for mankynde* (fol. 5r), and he is rewarded with a vision which is this detailed account of the Passion of Christ. In passages of the kind given above – and these dominate the text – the emphasis, quite literally, is on the body of Christ. The assumption seems to be that devotion to the 'paynes & anguysches' of Christ is devotion to the torment of the physical body. By the fourteenth and in the fifteenth century especially, accounts such as this had become commonplace, and in an important way they are different from descriptions of the torturing of Christ in, for example, the *Meditationes Vitae Christi* where the reader is actively encouraged to participate emotionally and imaginatively in the scene. An important role is assigned to the reader:

> Pay diligent attention to this and consider His stature in every part. And to make yourself more deeply compassionate and nourish yourself at the same time, turn your eyes away from His divinity for a little while and consider Him purely as a man. You will see a fine youth, most noble and most innocent and most lovable, cruelly beaten and covered with blood and wounds, gathering His garments from the ground where they were strewn and dressing Himself before them with shame, reverence, and blushes however much they jeer, as though He were the meanest of all, abandoned by God, and destitute of all help. Look at Him diligently, therefore, and be moved to pity and compassion: now He picks up one thing, now another,

---

[12] Marrow, *Passion Iconography*, pp. 83-94. See also R. Woolf, *The English Religious Lyric in the Middle Ages* (Oxford, 1968), pp. 199-202.

and dresses Himself before them. Next return to His divinity and consider the immense, eternal, incomprehensible, and imperial Majesty incarnate, humbly bowing down, bending to the ground to gather His garments together.[13]

This passage keeps both the physical and divine aspects of Christ in focus, and the reader is encouraged to participate imaginatively and spiritually in the scene. By comparison passages such as those found in Harley 1740 have a limited perspective.[14]

There is a parallel for the pre-occupation with the tormenting of the physical body as found in Harley 1740, in a well known popular practice, namely devotion to the instruments of the Passion or the *Arma Christi* (Fig. 1), where the physical torment of the body of Christ is scrutinized in precise detail.[15] But does the Harley text present Christ in terms other than physical suffering? Are the 'paynes & anguysches' only of the body?

Another thread running through the text can be described as the psychological or the spiritual. One place where this is introduced is in the Agony in the Garden. The episode is too lengthy to give in full, but the following passage illustrates something of how it is dramatized:

> & þen he lefte þem & went forther frome þem þan he did at eny tyme afore & come ni ʒh to a roche & þer he toke vp a grete crye for anguysch of þe sorowful paynes þat pressid and environed al his passible nature, & seid, 'Abba Pater; behold þe paynfull anguysshe of þi sonne. And if it be possible or in þi forknawne wysdome by other way of deliberacion þat þou aforeseest, be it so þat I be deliuerde fro þis shameful dethe, for þou knowist well my spirit is redy to fulfill it, but þe flesch is freill and not stable.' And whan he had seid so, he was in an agony þat þe anguysshe of deth peresid as a sharp swerde þe nature of þe humanite....And þen he fell to þe erth a longe tyme & not meued like a man þat for anguysshe of deth ʒelde vp þe last spiritte, ferst hauyng so grete colde þat it perichid all his body. And after þat he had soo vnspekable heete þat it semed his manhode schuld ʒelde þe goste....Þan aperid to him an angel of heuen and said to him in comfortyng of him, 'In þi diuine vertue arise þiselfe, for þou schalt breke þe bondis of Adam and deliuer þem þat be bounde þerin, & of þi pitte shalte heel all languores & reconsile all mankynde. Goo strongly and þe vertue of þi fader shal be with the.' (fol. 6r-v)

---

13 *Meditations on the Life of Christ*, pp. 330-31.
14 This problem in late medieval spirituality is discussed in E. Cousins, 'The Humanity and the Passion of Christ', in *Christian Spirituality: High Middle Ages and Reformation*, pp. 375-91. See also D. Gray, 'The Five Wounds of Our Lord', *Notes and Queries*, 208 (1963), 50-51, 82-89, 127-34, 163-68 (p. 84), and J. C. Hirsh, 'Two English Devotional Poems of the Fifteenth Century', *Notes and Queries*, 213 (1968), 4-11.
15 See below and note 20.

Although this scene is based on the biblical accounts, it is here used to develop Christ's humanity and to suggest his human reactions. There are two indications of this early on in the passage. Christ says ...*my spirit is redy to fulfill it, but þe flesch is freill and not stable.* This alludes to Matthew xxvi.41/Mark xiv.38, the words of Christ to Peter concerning his (that is Peter's) human frailty. Then follows the comment: ...*he was in an agony þat þe anguysshe of deth peresid as a sharp swerde þe nature of þe humanite.* The *swerde* refers to the prophecy of Simeon concerning Mary's grief for the suffering and death of Christ (Luke ii.35) which is at the basis of a vast literature on the sorrows of Mary.[16] What we have in both instances are examples of language traditionally associated with the human reactions of Peter and of Mary being applied to Christ. The language echoes its traditional contexts but the connotations of the original usage have been subtly transferred to Christ whose reactions are aligned with the human reactions of Peter and of Mary. Further, in the account in Luke of the Agony in the Garden an angel appears to Christ to strengthen him (Luke xxii.43), but no details of what this means are given. In the Harley text the angel reveals the divine purpose to Christ, and this reflects a shift in emphasis. In a text like the *Quis dabit* and some vernacular texts, it is Christ who articulates the divine purpose to the sorrowing Mary; he is firm and clear in his purpose whereas Mary is in a state of profound grief and needs to have explained to her the purpose of Christ's suffering and death.[17] The traditional division of the roles is strategic: Mary reflects the human reaction whereas Christ reflects the divine purpose. But here it is Christ who is shown to have human reactions and a limited human understanding; the voice of divine authority is the anonymous angel. The limited human perspective makes Christ's spiritual and psychological agonies that much more credible, and this is a recurring feature of the text, to emphasize the human aspects of Christ, almost at the expense of the divine.

The treatment of the Resurrection also develops this conception of Christ:

> And þe nyʒte of þe Sabote Day anone after mydnyʒte came þe miʒte of God þe fader to þe blissid body of Ihesu and with a glad voys said, 'Arise my glorie, arise my ioy, arise now without sorow and withoute payne, and take þi spirit lyuyng with euerlastyng ioy. And deth shal neuer hereafter haue lordschip on the.' And anone Criste arose bodely, enduyd with euerlastinge glorie and with godly miʒte of permanable mageste. (fols 20v-21r)

---

[16] Pseudo-Anselm, *Dialogus*, *PL* 159.274, 276, 277 etc., and *Quis dabit*, PL 182.1137; Mushacke, p.47.

[17] Marx, 'The Middle English Verse *Lamentation of Mary to Saint Bernard* and the *Quis dabit*'.

Here, it is God the Father who raises up Christ. This idea is firmly rooted in biblical usage but tends to become obscured in later writing.[18] However, the compiler of the Harley Passion narrative has found this usage to his purpose, to suggest the humanity of Christ.

A third instance reveals another aspect of the humanism which governs the Harley 1740 Passion narrative and which distinguishes it from earlier writing. The late twelfth- or early thirteenth-century *Quis dabit* is an account purportedly given by the Virgin Mary of her sorrows at the suffering and death of Christ. The text gives voice to a flood of human emotion and provides models for developments in the tradition of affective piety. A question raised by the *Quis dabit*, which emerges in different forms in later literature, is how to reconcile the picture of Mary's profound human grief with the traditional view that she alone maintained the faith of the Church in the Resurrection of Christ. In the *Quis dabit* and elsewhere her grief is too much like despair to make convincing the idea – which the *Quis dabit* insists upon – that she had a firm belief in the Resurrection.[19] The Harley Passion narrative dramatizes the issue in this way:

> Than sche maide an sorowful lamentacion and in her spirit þus: 'O þou depe stone, how hast þou my desirous and dere belouyd sone hid frome myne eeyn? Thou hast hid þe souereyn godly natures vnspeckable of þe fader of mercy and God of all consolacione. O þou riȝte hard stone, þou hast enclosed þe glorie of God þe fader, þe ioy of angelis, the sauacion of mankynde and þe only solace of my herte.' O what all depe wepynges and gret sighes þis soroful moder þan owte threw. And as she made þis grete dole, she herd a voys þat seid to her, 'O þou blessid virgine & moder & ladi of al gode spirites, be of gode comforte for þou shalt haue þi sone within þis .iii. dais alyve aȝen'. And be þese wordes she was somdell comforted, and sufferd her of þe women to be led to þe cite. (fol. 19r-v)

The Harley text copes with the problem largely by ignoring it; that is, it presents Mary both here and throughout as one whose understanding is

[18]   For example, Acts ii.24, 32, iii.15, 26, iv.10, v.30. The A version of *The Devils' Parliament* refers to the Harrowing of Hell and Resurrection in this way: *And thus God harowed helle | And ledde hys lombe to paradys* (ll. 345-46); the revised B version has: *Thus Ihesus Crist harewide helle | And ledde hise louers to paradiis* (ll. 385-6). See *The Devils' Parliament and The Harrowing of Hell and Destruction of Jerusalem*, ed. by C. W. Marx, Middle English Texts, 25 (Heidelberg, 1993).

[19]   See the reading of the *Quis dabit* in Marx, 'The Middle English Verse *Lamentation of Mary to Saint Bernard* and the *Quis dabit*', pp. 140-46. This argues that in the Latin text the emotionalism of Mary overpowers doctrinal concerns, and in this respect modifies Peter Dronke's argument that the Latin tradition contributed little to the way in which the grief of Mary was portrayed in, for example, the English mystery plays: Peter Dronke, 'Laments of the Maries: from the Beginnings to the Mystery Plays', in *Idee, Gestalt, Geschichte: Festschrift Klaus von See*, ed. by G. W. Weber (Odense, 1988), pp. 89-116 (pp. 114-16).

limited in human terms; as with the scene of Christ's Agony in the Garden, it is an external and divine voice which reassures Mary.

These two elements in the Harley Passion narrative, the pre-occupation with the physical suffering of Christ and the episodes which reveal the limitations in the understanding and power of Mary and Christ, suggest the focus of this text: it is concerned to emphasize the humanity of Mary and Christ. This emphasis is at the expense of meditation on doctrinal issues or spiritual themes or the divine nature of Christ in the manner of the *Meditationes Vitae Christi*. The details of the narrative are vivid, but set beside the *Meditationes Vitae Christi* the Harley Passion narrative seems less concerned with generating affective piety – certainly if this were its purpose its techniques are limited – and the episodes lack a larger doctrinal, spiritual or imaginative purpose.

This is the first and longest text in the manuscript, and it is helpful to remember that it is essentially narrative. But what of the second text in the sequence? The meditation, which is edited in the Appendix, is much briefer than the Passion narrative and uses as its basis devotion to the instruments of the Passion, or *Arma Christi*. Veneration of the *Arma Christi* found widespread expression in a variety of media in the Middle Ages.[20] Its most popular literary representation in English is a verse text written before the end of the fourteenth century, which has the modern title 'The Symbols of the Passion'; this survives in 19 manuscripts and was printed by Richard Fakes, probably around 1523.[21] There was a continuous readership for the verse text from the late fourteenth to the early sixteenth century. Of the 19 manuscripts, 10 are in the form of rolls, known to art historians as the *Arma Christi* rolls, while the rest are found in codices. In the 10 rolls and 7 of the codices the verse texts accompany drawings of the instruments of the Passion, and there is a close link between the image and the text in that each verse is a prayer to a particular instrument:

> The naylys throwe fete and handys also,
> Lorde, kepe me owt of synne and woo,

---

[20] G. Schiller, *Iconography of Christian Art*, 2 vols (London, 1971-72), II, 189-97 and passim. R. Woolf, *The English Religious Lyric*, pp. 206-9. I am grateful to Dr F. M. Lewis for allowing me to consult the chapter on the *Arma Christi* in her thesis: 'Devotional Images and their Dissemination in English Manuscripts, c.1350-1470', 2 vols (Ph.D., London, 1989), I, pp. 170-240.

[21] 'The Symbols of the Passion', in *Legends of the Holy Rood: Symbols of the Passion and Cross-Poems*, ed. by R. Morris, EETS OS 46 (1876), pp. 170-96; 2577 in C. Brown and R. H. Robbins, *The Index of Middle English Verse* (New York, 1943) and R. H. Robbins and J. L. Cutler, *Supplement* (Lexington, 1965); *A gloryous medytacyon of Ihesus Crystes passyon*, Richard Fakes [c.1523] (*STC* 14550). The *Index* and *Supplement* list 17 manuscripts; Lewis lists 19 ('Devotional Images', I, 211-12).

That I haue in myn lyffe doo,
With handys handyld or on fote goo. (ll. 97-100)

The *Arma Christi* text, and more particularly the use of the text and image, has been commented on a number of times, and there is general agreement that the purpose of these texts and drawings is a limited one: they are simple prayers and images that do not aim to encourage the devout beyond a certain practical piety, namely seeking a remedy for sin.[22]

The Harley prose text on the instruments of the Passion introduces the subject in a strikingly different way. The text is addressed to a woman (*my dere moder*, l.1, fol. 22r), and it encourages the reader to look 'inward', using language associated with contemplation:

> And therfore, day & nyght, in welth & in wo, lifte vp thyne hert to þinke on heuenly thynges and forget as moch as þou may erthly þinges. And clyme vp hiȝe vnto þe hill of holi contemplacion, þe which hill þou may fynde in thine awne hert, and þou may make þer an honest dwellynge place to þi lorde Ihesu Criste. Thouȝe þou eche day go to þe chirch, I consell the þat þou beilde a fare honest chapell amyddes þine awne hert, and þe fundament of trew feith and stedfast bileue with gode werkes accordinge to þi bileue, with þe walles of true hope. (ll. 16-25, fol. 22v)

Significantly this passage sets contemplation against corporate or public worship (*Thouȝe þou eche day go to þe chirch....*), and what this text encourages is the life of inward, private devotion. This passage is only a small portion of the opening of the text which serves to introduce a contemplative framework which locates the instruments of the Passion within a spiritual chapel:

> And þat þou may suffre sumwhat for his loue þat so moch suffred for thyne, in þe one ende of þe awter set þe piller þat our lord was bounde to and for thy loue sore bett. And when þou art tempted to walke to se eny ydell thynges or veyn thyngis, take þe oþer ende of þe corde þat our lorde was bounde with and bynde þe to þe piller and bere þi lorde compeny all redy to be partiner of his disese if þou thynkest to be partiner of his blisse. (ll. 40-45, fol. 23r)

What follows from this are references to nine of the instruments of the Passion, each one of which is seen as a remedy against a specific vice or sin. In this respect the prose text is following in the tradition of the popular verse text referred to earlier, and indeed other accounts of the instruments of the Passion. In other words, both the verse text and the Harley prose text are schematic; the main difference between the two is that whereas the verse text is a series of prayers, the Harley prose text is self-consciously instructive: it directs the reader as to how these instruments of the Passion function in the

[22] D. Gray, 'The Five Wounds of Our Lord', p. 168; R. H. Robbins, 'The "Arma Christi" Rolls', *Modern Language Review*, 34 (1939), 415-21. Robbins argues for the use of the rolls in church with a congregation; Lewis ('Devotional Images', I, 232-38) challenges this hypothesis.

spiritual life. It is therefore a spiritual and moral exercise which places responsibility on the contemplative to carry out the different stages of the exercise by locating the instruments of the Passion in the spiritual chapel.

The last of the instruments of the Passion referred to in the Harley text is the water, of Christ's tears and from his side, and this is how it is to be used:

> And whan thy soule is eny tyme defouled, wasch it anone with þis water and þus thorow grace þou maist make a well of teeris in þe middis of þine hert wherwith þou maist wasch and clense al thy synnes away. Therfore besyli pray to thy lord Ihesu þat of his mercy he grante þe his grace that þou may draw þat water frome þe depe well of þi hert anone to þi eeys, wherthorow þe awter of thi soule may be wasch and made clene. (ll. 72-78, fol. 23v)

The well of tears recalls the *Quis dabit*, the very *incipit* of which uses this image:

> O quis dabit capiti meo aquam, et oculis meis imbrem lacrimarum, ut possim flere per diem et noctem [Jeremiah ix.1], donec seruo suo Dominus Ihesus appareat consolans animam meam?[23]

> (Who will give water for my head or a shower of tears for my eyes so that I may lament day and night until the Lord Jesus may appear to his servant and console my spirit?)

In this early Latin text, however, the well of tears represents the ability to feel sorrow for the suffering of Christ: this is an aspect of affective piety and is seen as a mark of grace. In the Harley text, the well of tears is part of the process of penance and a remedy for sin. In fact the Harley text actually combines the traditional idea of the wounds of Christ as fountains or wells (which wash away sin),[24] with the idea from the *Quis dabit* of the inner well of tears signifying compassion. How the two ideas are meant to function is not clear, but this problem reflects the transitional nature of the text: that is, it is trying to make something new out of old materials. Nevertheless, with the emphasis on the practical purpose of removing sin, the larger vision of the *Quis dabit* has been lost.

The most striking feature of the Harley contemplative text is its conception, the way it develops a popular devotional practice into a contemplative exercise. The form of the exercise – the placing of the arms of Christ in the spiritual chapel – may owe a debt to the tradition of Christ the lover-knight in which the arms of Christ are set up in the lady's chapel:[25]

---

23 Turin, Biblioteca Nazionale, MS E.V.4, fol. 55r; ed. in C. W. Marx, 'The *Quis dabit* of Oglerius de Tridino', *Journal of Medieval Latin* (1994, forthcoming). See also Mushacke, p. 41.

24 Gray, 'The Five Wounds of Our Lord', pp. 129-34 and 163-66; Schiller, *Iconography of Christian Art*, II, 119, 125, 133.

25 The idea appears in the parable about love in part seven of the *Ancrene Wisse*; see

Now hast þou thy swete lord Ihesu biried in thyne awter and his precious armes al aboute thine awter with þe which armes he ouercome miȝtely both his enemys and thyne, and saued the (ll. 80-82, fols 23v-24r). Hirsh suggested that in English at least there was little in the way of development in medieval writing on the *Arma Christi*.[26] The Harley contemplation, however, transforms the concept of the *Arma Christi* into a text which is self-consciously directed to private, inward devotion. The visual imagination has been abandoned in favour of the spiritual imagination.

What is the nature of the sequence as a whole, the Passion narrative and the contemplative exercise? The two texts may be by different authors, but it is the compilation which is of interest. The presence of the text on the *Arma Christi* is the most significant link with a well-known theme from popular devotion. Can the sequence provide some insight into attitudes to aspects of popular devotion in the fifteenth century? The Passion narrative lacks a sense of a larger doctrinal or spiritual purpose, but it encourages devotion to the humanity of Mary and Christ. Whether the Passion narrative were read aloud or privately, it would serve to reinforce a strong tradition of popular devotion in the fifteenth century. The contemplative exercise, on the other hand, is more of a puzzle. It shares with the Passion narrative the theme of physical suffering, but like the *Meditationes Vitae Christi* it directs the reader towards compassion: *And þat þou may suffre sumwhat for his loue þat so moch suffred for thyne....* (ll. 40-41, fol. 23r). The reader is encouraged to participate in the suffering of Christ, but this is part of a larger spiritual purpose. Like the Passion narrative, the contemplative exercise recognizes human limitations, but the reader's spirituality is at the centre of the text. There are other ways in which the two texts complement each other: the Passion narrative could be said to provide the basis for the contemplative text. The contemplative text reinvigorates well-worn themes from popular devotion, not just the *Arma Christi*, but the veneration of the humanity of Christ which is reflected in the Passion narrative. It can be seen as a reaction to the limitations of late medieval humanism.

But for whom were these themes reinvigorated? In one sense the meditation is a demanding spiritual exercise, quite different from the prayers encouraged by the visual images and texts in the *Arma Christi* rolls. The compilation – and it is important to stress this concern with the compilation – reflects the demands of an audience which is at once in touch with the

Medieval English Prose for Women, ed. by B. Millett and J. Wogan-Browne (Oxford, 1990), pp. 116-17. I am grateful to Dr Flora Lewis for suggesting this connection; see Lewis, 'Devotional Images', I, 171-78, and R. Woolf, 'The Theme of Christ the Lover-Knight in Medieval English Literature', *Review of English Studies*, n.s. 13 (1962), 1-16.

26 Hirsh, 'Two English Devotional Poems of the Fifteenth Century', p. 10.

widespread devotion to the humanity of Mary and Christ and at the same time accustomed to following elaborate spiritual discipline. As such, it calls into question a too rigid application of the distinction offered by Kieckhefer between devotional piety and the contemplative aspects of religion. The address to the female figure at the beginning of the meditation along with the different elements which make up the compilation, and the fact that the manuscript is in English, not Latin or French, may indicate that the compilation was designed for a female religious community. This hypothesis suggests that the compilation comes in a long tradition of writing for devout women who had not been given the opportunity for education in Latin.[27] If this is the case, then what we think of as popular devotion may be indifferent to boundaries between institutions and the laity.

---

[27] See *Medieval English Prose for Women*. An example of a 15th-century compilation in English for a nunnery is found in Washington, Library of Congress MS Faye-Bond 4 (formerly, pre-Ac 4), which includes translations from French of the Rule of St Benedict and *The Gospel of Nicodemus*; see B. Hill, 'Some Problems in Washington, Library of Congress MS Faye-Bond 4', in *In Other Words: Transcultural Studies...Presented to H. H. Meier*, ed. by J. Lachlan Mackenzie and R. Todd (Dordrecht, 1989) pp. 35-44.

Figure 1: Pietà with *Arma Christi*, woodcut from Thomas à Kempis, *Imytacio[n] of Cryst* (London, Wynkyn de Worde, 1515-18?) (*STC* 23956)

APPENDIX

I am grateful to the British Library for permission to reproduce MS Harley 1740, ff.22r/col. 2 - 24r/col. 1. Capitalization, punctuation and paragraphing are editorial and follow modern practice. All contractions have been silently expanded. Emendations are enclosed in square brackets.

Item de passione Christi bona contemplacio

My dere moder, amonge all thyngis þat bene to thynke vpon in þis worlde, I counsell the þat þou thynke inwardly in thine awne hert how þou miȝte best plese God and loue hym. For thorow his loue þou miȝte parfitely lerne all other vertues and withoute his loue whateuer þou do, it may [fol. 22v/col.1]
5 no thinge profit the. And þerfore if þou desirest to be croned in þe blis of heuyn, it behoueth the afor all thynges to do þi besynes þat the fier of Goddis loue be kyndeld and brenne in thyn harte. But to þis loue may no man ne woman parfitely come but if he withdraw hys wyll frome þe loue and thouȝtes of vanites of þis worlde and fleschly desires, and þat he festen not
10 his loue in none erthly thinges ne creaturs to moch. For many thyngis þat we se here be vayn and ydell & shalbe brought to nowght, but Goddis loue dwellith euermore in a gode soule. And þe more þat a man loueth the creature, þe lesse he loueth the maker þerof. Also, þe more þat ȝe occupie ȝour hert forto thynke on God besily, trewly ȝe shall fynde þe more grace,
15 comfort & heuenly techynge send to the frome God. And þan both ydell loue and vayn sorow shall sone be voyded from þine herte. And therfore, day & [col.2] nyght, in welth &in wo, lifte vp thyne hert to þinke on heuenly thynges and forget as moch as þou may erthly þinges. And clyme vp hiȝe vnto þe hill of holi contemplacion, þe which hill þou may fynde in thine
20 awne hert, and þou may make þer an honest dwellynge place to þi lorde Ihesu Criste.

Thouȝe þou eche day go to þe chirch, I consell the þat þou beilde a fare honest chapell amyddes þine awne hert, and þe fundament of trew feith and stedfast bileue with gode werkes accordinge to þi bileue, with þe walles of
25 true hope. But put awey þe stones of waynhope. Also make þe rofe of the chapell of parfite charite to God and to man. And also make it so stronge þat no wynde of pride ne no wederinges of vnstabulnes may hurte þis roofe. In þis chapell make a comly awter and in þe middes of þis awter sett thy blissed lorde Ihesu hongyng on þe cros as he was crucified on Good Fryday with
30 grysely woundes [f.23r/col.1] all fresch bledynge.   And on hym loke stedfastly with þe inward siȝte of þe soule. And take hede what tokens of loue þou miȝte fynde in hym. His armes he holdis abrode alredy to take þe to hym; his heed he bowith downe redy to kysse and to be at one with the;

his side redy openyd to schew the þe hoole loue of his herte; [his] handis &
35 feet fastenyd to abide stedfastly with the and not to fle frome the. In þis siȝte
occupy þine harte awhile knelyng, sittyng or standinge, and in al þis tyme
ceesse þou not of thankyngis and worschippinge þis blessid lorde of þe grete
fordede and loue þat he hath schewid to the, pray[i]ng him with meke hert to
ȝeue the grace to contynewe in vertuous liffe.

40   And þat þou may suffre sumwhat for his loue þat so mochsuffred for
thyne, in þe one ende of þe awter set þe piller þat our lord was bounde to and
for thy loue sore bett. And when þou art tempted to walke to se eny ydell
thynges or veyn thyngis, take þe oþer ende of þe corde þat our lorde was
bounde with [col. 2] and bynde þe to þe piller and bere þi lorde compeny all
45 redy to be partiner of his disese if þou thynkest to be partiner of his blisse. In
þe other side of þe crosse hange þe two scourges and when ony temptacion of
þe flesch commyth to the, scourge þe well all aboute and make þe a reed cote
to þi lordes leuerey till þe temptacion be voyded frome the. In þe other arme
of þe crosse, hange þe holy crowne þat prikkid ful sore þe heede of our
50 blessid lord Ihesu. And if þou haue eny hedache, sett þe same crowne vpon
thyne hede and thy payn will sone slake. In þat other arme of þe crosse
honge þe reyde þat our lord was smytten with on þe heed and scorned.
Theron thynke as men scorne or slaunder the, and take it mekely. In þat oþer
ende of þe awter sett þe thre grete ragged nales þat our lord was fastenyd
55 with to þe crosse, and þerwith fasten the to þe crosse of pennance and suffre
not thy fleschly [f.23v/col. 1] affections to passe þe boundes of his loue. And
whan þou felest the loue of þi herte any tyme remove from thy lorde þorow
þe entycynge of þi ennemy, take þe longe spere þat openyd thy lordis side
and chase away the feendis from the, and ther power wil sone asslake. Hang
60 also þe cloth þat he was blyndfelde with sumwhere beside þe awter and os
ofte as it nedith, hill þerwith þine eeyn frome ydell siȝtes, thyne eerys from
ydell herkenyngis, þine nose from euyl smellynges, thy mouth fro ydell
spekyngis, so þat þat thynge which was done to him in scorne may turne the
to profitte and himto worshipe.

65   Gedder also in a fare clene vessell all þe blode þat þi lord bled for thy
loue, first in his circumcision, þe .ii.^{de} whane he swete water & blode in
deuoute prayer, thirde in his scourgynge, the .iiii.th time in his crownynge,
the vth tyme in his crucyfyinge, the sexte tyme in his naylinge, [col. 2] the
.vii.th tyme in his side openynge. Geder þis blissid blode worthely and put it
70 in .iiii. partes of þine awter. Also geder þerto the water þat thy swete lorde
Ihesu wepte with his eeyn for mannes synnes; also, þat water þat ran oute of
his side whan it was openyd with the spere. And whan thy soule is eny tyme
defouled, wasch it anone with þis water and þus thorow grace þou maist
make a well of teeris in þe middis of þine hert wherwith þou maist wasch
75 and clense al thy synnes away. Therfore besyli pray to thy lord Ihesu þat of

his mercy he grante þe his grace that þou may draw þat water frome þe depe well of þi hert anone to þi eeys, wherthorow þe awter of thi soule may be wasch a[nd] made clene.

After þis take þe sepulcre and the body of our lorde and berry hym in þe 80 myddis of thyne awter. Now hast þou thy swete lord Ihesu biried in thyne [f.24r/col.1] awter and his precious armes al aboute thine awter with þe which armes he ouercome miȝtely both his enemys and thyne, and saued the. If thou wilt thyselfe fro payn, haue þis in mynde and aray þus þi chapell, and euer thy swete lorde Ihesu wyll dwell therin. This I write to the, moder, to 85 comforte the in soule and encrese the in vertues, and þat God graunte vs grace to life so here þat we may haue euerlastynge liffe. Amen.

Ihesu rex clementissime tu corda nostra posside ut tibi laudesdebitas reddamus omni tempore. Amen.

Apparatus

11-12 *but...þe* left margin *nota omnia bene que sequuntur* MS.
34 his(2)] *om.* MS.
38 praying] prayng MS.
78 and] a MS.

222

The Coronation of the Virgin by the Trinity and Other Texts and Images of the Glorification of Mary in Fifteenth-Century England
NIGEL MORGAN

Among the popular devotional images in fifteenth-century English art is the Coronation of the Virgin by the Holy Trinity, a theme which seems to appear first in the closing years of the fourteenth century. It is best known from its famous examples of the middle years and second half of the fifteenth century in French, Flemish and German painting, both in illuminated manuscripts and panel paintings. The Villeneuve-les-Avignon painting of Enguerrand Quarton, Dieric Bouts' Vienna panel and the examples in Jean Fouquet's Hours of Étienne Chevalier are well-known mid-century works of this subject. In Fouquet's Hours of Étienne Chevalier of c.1455 the Coronation takes place in the presence of the Trinity with the Son having stepped down from His throne to crown His Mother.[1] The miniatures of the Hours of Étienne Chevalier were cut out from their text in the eighteenth century and pasted on wooden panels so that it is not always certain what was the text on the page facing the miniature in the original book. In this miniature of the Coronation of the Virgin by the Trinity the opening verse of Compline, *Converte nos Deus salutaris noster*, locates the image at the beginning of Compline of the Hours of the Virgin, a position frequently illustrated in France by the Coronation of the Virgin, but only on rare

---

[1] C. Schaefer, *The Hours of Étienne Chevalier* (London, 1972), pl. 13. For Enguerrand Quarton see D. Denny, 'The Trinity in Enguerrand Quarton's Coronation of the Virgin', *Art Bull.*, 45 (1963), 48-52 and C. Sterling, *Enguerrand Quarton: le peintre de la Pietà d'Avignon* (Paris, 1983), pp. 36-79. For the Dieric Bouts panel in Vienna, Akademie der bildenden Künste, see F. Baudoin, 'De kroning van Maria door de H. Drieëenheid in de vijftiende-eeuwse schilderkunst der Nederlanden', *Bull. des Musées Royaux de Beaux Arts*, 8 (1959), 179-230. This article is one of the few detailed discussions of the iconographic theme but is chiefly concerned with the period from c.1430 onwards. There is a short supplement: F. Baudoin, 'Nog over "De kroning van Maria door de H. Drieëenheid" in de vijftiende-eeuwse schilderkunst der Nederlanden', *Bull. des Musées Royaux de Beaux Arts*, 9 (1960), 89-91. For general discussions see 'Dreifaltigkeit', *Reallexikon zur deutschen Kunstgeschichte*, 4 (1958), cols 438-39; G. Schiller, *Ikonographie der christlichen Kunst*, IV.2 (Gütersloh, 1980), pp. 150-53, figs. 741-42, 744-50; for some Italian 14th and 15th century examples see C. J. Ffoulkes, 'Le Couronnement de la Sainte Vierge', *Revue de l'Art Chrétien*, ser. iv. 9 (1898), 42-50, 117-27; and for England G. McN. Rushforth, *Medieval Christian Imagery* (Oxford, 1936), pp. 387-91.

occasions performed by the Trinity.[2] Another image of Mary in the presence of the Trinity, also from the Hours of Étienne Chevalier, is less secure in its textual position.[3] This shows the Virgin seated in the presence of the Trinity in Heaven with the company of the saints below. This picture could have preceded either the suffrage for the Holy Trinity or the suffrage for All Saints, and the likelihood of one of these two locations will become clear by comparison with the textual locations of the image in England shortly to be discussed. In these examples by Jean Fouquet the iconographic significance is in the hierarchic placing of the Virgin Mary in the company of the three persons of the Holy Trinity within the highest circle of the Court of Heaven, higher than the angels and all the saints.

Most of the well-known examples in French and Flemish painting, and the majority of the Italian examples, are of the mid-fifteenth century or later, in which period the iconography becomes frequent all over Europe. In England it becomes popular during the first half of the century, and its origins, development and textual parallels are the subject of this paper. On the extant evidence its development was more precocious than elsewhere in Europe with the exception of North-East Italy and possibly Burgundy. In the regions of the Veneto, Marche and Emilia Romagna during the second half of the fourteenth century God the Father is occasionally included above the Coronation of the Virgin by the Son, and from c.1400 onwards the Holy Ghost is also included, thus making a Coronation of the Virgin by the Trinity.[4] Although occurrences of the theme in lost panel paintings done for the Burgundian court c.1400 have been suggested, the evidence does not seem

---

[2] See the many descriptions of French books of hours of the period c.1380-1430 in M. Meiss, *French Painting in the Time of Jean de Berry*, 5 vols. (London, 1967-72) for the almost ubiquitous use of the Coronation of the Virgin for Compline. The subject of the Coronation by the Trinity is rare in French manuscript illumination of the first half of the fifteenth century. An unusual textual location, Psalm 80, has this subject in the Psalter of Henry VI, London, British Library [hereafter BL], Cotton MS Domitian A.XVII, fol. 151.

[3] Schaefer, *Hours of Étienne Chevalier*, pl. 27.

[4] Full discussion of the North-East Italian developments is not possible in this paper but the main examples before 1450 are: Master of S. Elsino (Fermo, Pinacoteca Civica), late 14th century (P. Zampetti, *Pittura nelle Marche*, I (Florence, 1988), fig. 111); Nicolo di Pietro (Rome, Galleria Nazionale d'Arte Antica; Rovigo, Accademia dei Concordi), c.1400 (M. Lucco, *La pittura nel Veneto. Il Quattrocento*, I (Milan, 1989), figs. 15, 22); Gentile da Fabriano, Polyptych of Valle Romita (Milan, Pinacoteca di Brera), c.1408 (Lucco, op. cit., fig. 25); Lorenzo di Giacomo (Venice, Fondazione Giorgio Cini), c.1429 (Lucco, op. cit., fig. 53); Michele Giambono (Venice, Galleria dell' Accademia), c.1447-8 (Lucco, op. cit., fig. 67); Nicolo Miretto? (Padua, Sala della Ragione), c.1405 (Lucco, op. cit., fig. 107); Martino da Verona (Verona, S. Eufemia; Verona, S. Stefano), c.1410 (Lucco, op. cit., figs. 206, 209).

to be particularly strong.[5] In Flanders the theme might have begun c.1400 in view of the Flemish origins of one of the earliest artists to present this iconography in England.[6] The abundant English material has received little attention in such general accounts as exist of the iconography of the subject. Even discussion of the English examples has been almost entirely restricted to the many surviving in alabasters.[7] Doubtless it was in the alabaster altarpieces of the Life of the Virgin that the subject must have been most visible in fifteenth-century England.

In these alabasters the subject occurs in a variety of forms, and a similar variety occurs in their counterparts in illuminated manuscripts. In the alabasters, as in Fouquet's All Saints miniature, the Virgin is placed at a lower level than the Father, Son and Holy Ghost. The Father and the Son are usually placing the crown on her head, with the Holy Ghost, the giver of grace, hovering above her.[8] From the second decade of the century onward she is often crowned with the same tiara type of crown which from that time onward became popular for the Father and the Son.[9] The Son is usually

[5] G. Troescher, *Burgundische Malerei* (Berlin, 1966), pp. 55-57, argues for the subject existing in the work of Jean de Beaumetz.

[6] This is one of the artists of the Carmelite Missal shortly to be discussed. One Netherlandish or Lower Rhenish early 15th-century panel in the Kisters Collection at Kreuzlingen shows the Coronation of the Virgin by the Trinity: A. Stange, 'Vier südflandrische Marientafeln – ein Beitrag zur Genese der niederländischen Malerei', *Alte und moderne Kunst*, 11 (no. 89) (1966), 11, fig. 14; also illustrated by C. Sterling, 'Observations on Petrus Christus', *Art Bull.*, 53 (1971), 4-5, fig. 7 and *Stefan Lochner, Meister zu Köln*, ed. by F. G. Zehnder (Cologne, 1993), 259.

[7] See above all F. Cheetham, *English Medieval Alabasters* (Oxford, 1984), pp. 206-07, 211-19. For the subject in the context of surviving complete alabaster altarpieces see ibid., pp. 70-71.

[8] Cheetham, *Alabasters*, figs. 138-41.

[9] Cheetham, *Alabasters*, figs. 138, 141, 143, 144, 146. This tiara form first appears in France in the late 14th century: E. Panofsky, 'Once more "The Friedsam Annunciation and the Problem of the Ghent Altarpiece"', *Art Bull.*, 20 (1938), 437. A discussion of the use of the tiara for the Virgin in England which also includes a valuable discussion of the Coronation of the Virgin by the Trinity is J. A. Goodall, 'Heraldry and Iconography. A Study of the Arms Granted to the Drapers' Company of London', *Coat of Arms*, 4 (no. 29) (1957), 170-83. The three-fold crown may refer to the three realms over which she has power. The 1492 will of John Hobersal refers to her as 'Quene of Heven, Lady of al the world and Empress of Hell': E. Waterton, *Pietas Mariana Britannica*, pt. 2 (London, 1879), p. 320. Goodall, op. cit., p. 180 on the source of these words in a hymn attributed to St John of Bridlington. Mirk certainly knew them, for in his *Festial* he uses them in the Sermon on the Assumption: T. Erbe, *Mirk's Festial*, Early English Text Society, E.S. 96 (1905), p. 224. They also occur in a lyric on the Seven Joys: C. Brown, *Religious Lyrics of the XVth Century* (Oxford, 1939),

differentiated from the Father by His partly bare torso, showing the wound in His side, and sometimes is wearing the Crown of Thorns, which often forms the lowest of the triple crowns of the tiara.[10] The Virgin is occasionally kneeling on a cushion but is usually shown frontally with her hands held up in an orant gesture as she receives the crown.[11] In these examples the Holy Ghost is either represented as a dove, or, as the century develops, frequently in anthropomorphic guise in the same human form as the Father and the Son. Sometimes the three persons of the Trinity bless the already crowned Virgin rather than being in the act of crowning her.[12]

In stained glass the surviving examples are from c.1450 and later, but in roof bosses early fifteenth-century occurrences are in the cloisters of Norwich and Worcester Cathedrals (Pl. 49).[13] The Worcester example is unusual in showing the three persons of the Trinity standing rather than seated. Shortly before this example in the Worcester sculpture the Coronation of the Virgin by the Trinity appears in various textual contexts in liturgical manuscripts, and it is these which help to define the significance and meaning of the image. It is these examples in English illuminated manuscripts which have been neglected in discussions of this iconographic theme. In being placed beside texts they have the advantage in providing textual parallels and possible explanations of the origins of the new form. Also, above all, they

---

no. 36, p. 64. See also in James Ryman's carol of c.1492: R. L. Greene, *The Early English Carols* (Oxford, 1977), no. 224.

10 Cheetham, *Alabasters*, fig. 138; Goodall, 'Heraldry and Iconography', p. 176, pl. III.

11 Cheetham, *Alabasters*, figs. 141-43.

12 Cheetham, *Alabasters*, figs. 142-43.

13 C. J. P. Cave, *Roof Bosses in Medieval Churches* (Cambridge, 1948), pp. 43-45, 220-21, fig. 288; M. R. James, *The Sculptured Bosses in the Cloisters of Norwich Cathedral* (Norwich, 1911), p. 23, pl. XV.5. A similar boss is in the porch at Worstead (Norfolk): M. R. James, *Suffolk and Norfolk* (London, 1930), p. 153. Cave also cites an example in Christchurch Priory (Hants.) in the Salisbury Chapel. A c.1430-50 example in a roof boss is on the choir screen of York Minster: C. Davidson, *York Art* (Kalamazoo, 1978), p. 107, and a c.1450 example in the Bauchun Chapel, Norwich Cathedral: M. R. James, *The Sculptured Bosses in the Roof of the Bauchun Chapel of Our Lady of Pity in Norwich Cathedral* (Norwich, 1908), p. 5, pls. I, III. The later examples in stained glass are York, Holy Trinity Goodramgate, with the head of the Virgin a stylistically inappropriate replacement (J. Baker, *English Stained Glass* (London, 1960), pl. 64), Doddiscombsleigh (Devon) with the figure of the Virgin destroyed (F. M. Drake, 'The Painted Glass of Exeter Cathedral and Other Devon Churches', *Archaeol. Jnl*, 70 (1913), 172-73, pl. V) and the c.1500 roundel in the Leicester Town Museum (G. McN. Rushforth, 'An Account of Some Painted Glass from a House at Leicester', *Archaeol. Jnl*, 75 (1918), 58-59, pl. IV)). There may well be occurrences in pre-1450 stained glass but I have not been able to discover them.

help in defining the devotional context, purpose and meaning of this combination of Marian imagery with the profound theology of the Holy Trinity.

The earliest instance of the iconography seems to be in the famous Missal for the Carmelite friars of London (London, British Library, Add. MS 29704), one of the most richly decorated books of the English International Gothic (Pl. 50).[14] Textual evidence perhaps dates it between 1393 and 1398 but some of the illumination may be a few years later. Regrettably, when in the possession of the Hanrott family the Missal was allowed to be dismembered by their children, who cut out its illuminated initials and stuck them in a scrap book. The mutilated text seems to have been completely destroyed, and only through the careful labours of Margaret Rickert has the original text location of most of the surviving initials been determined. In her commentary on the iconography of these initials she does devote some space to a discussion of the Coronation of the Virgin by the Trinity, but not in relation to the future development and various textual positions of the subject in English fifteenth-century illuminated manuscripts as a whole.[15] The unique version of the iconography in the Carmelite Missal has no following. It shows the Virgin crowned by a Trinity of the *Gnadenstuhl* or Throne of Grace type in which the Father holds the crucifix with the Holy Ghost in between. The imagery of that form of the Trinity is linked to the text in the Epistle to the Hebrews iv. 14-16: 'Having, therefore, a great high priest that hath passed into the heavens, Jesus the Son of God ... Let us go, therefore, with confidence to the throne of grace: that we may obtain mercy, and find grace to help in time of need'.[16] The sacrifice of the Son on the cross accepted by the Father as the inexhaustible source of grace through the Holy Spirit is the clear and explicit message of the imagery of the *Gnadenstuhl* Trinity. As a didactic image for teaching the theology of redemption and

[14] M. Rickert, *The Reconstructed Carmelite Missal* (London, 1952) gives an exhaustive account of the manuscript.

[15] Rickert, op. cit., pp. 48-49.

[16] On the iconography and theology of the *Gnadenstuhl* Trinity, which originates in the 12th century, see Panofsky, 'Friedsam Annunciation', 433-42; W. Braunfels, *Die Heilige Dreifaltigkeit* (Düsseldorf, 1954), pp. XXXV-XLIII; O. von Simson, 'Über die Bedeutung von Masaccios Trinitätsfresko in S. Maria Novella', *Jahrbuch der Berliner Museen*, 8 (1966), 119-59; G. Schiller, *Iconography of Christian Art*, II (London, 1972), pp. 122-24. For 15th century examples see also H. S. Francis, 'The Holy Trinity', *Bull. of the Cleveland Museum of Art*, 48 (1961), 58-62. For the connection of the imagery with the offering of the Mass to the Holy Trinity made explicit in the Canon (*Suscipe sancta Trinitas* and *Placeat tibi sancta Trinitas*) see R. Goffen, 'Masaccio's Trinity and the Letter to the Hebrews', *Memorie Domenicane*, 11 (1980), 489-504. On the role of the Trinity in the theology of the Mass see J. Jungmann, *The Mass of the Roman Rite*, II (Westminster (Maryland), 1992), pp. 46-59, 437-39.

grace it has never been rivalled. The visual imagery makes this even more explicit than the words of fifteenth-century poems on the Trinity as source of grace:

> Lorde, that art of mightis moost,
> ffadir and sone and holy goost,
> God in trynyte,
> Thou geve me grace daye and night
> The to serve with all my might.[17]

and

> Almyghty god, fadir of hevene,
> ffor cristis love that dyde on rode,
> I praye the lorde thou here my steune,
> And fulfill my will in gode.
> Crist, thi fader for me praye,
> ffor hir love thou lighted inne,
> He geve me might or that I dye,
> Me to amende of all my synne.
> The holy gost thou graunte me grace,
> With such werkes my lif to lede.[18]

The imagery of the Holy Trinity as source of grace is an essential element in the understanding of the devotional function of the Coronation of the Virgin by the Trinity. In the initial in the Carmelite Missal the adaptation of the *Gnadenstuhl* Trinity to function in the Coronation of the Virgin presents the artist with some problems. The Father, having to perform the function Himself rather than have the crowning done by the Son as is usual, and needing a free hand to place the crown on the Virgin, has to lean the crucifix against Himself while steadying it with His other hand. The normal arrangement of the *Gnadenstuhl* Trinity is for the Father to hold the crucifix symmetrically with both hands.[19] The central figures in the Carmelite Missal initial are surrounded by saints and angels with a group of angels seated in the foreground, and the Coronation incorporating the Trinity is thus seen at the centre of the company of Heaven. The imagery is appropriate in its textual location in the Missal, for it is the main initial for the Mass of All Saints, that of the introit *Gaudeamus*: 'Let us rejoice in the Lord as we celebrate this feast day in honour of all saints over whom the angels rejoice and praise the Son of God.' This introit is almost identical to the introit *Gaudeamus* universally used for the Mass of the Assumption of the Virgin: 'Let us all rejoice in the Lord as we celebrate this feast day in honour of the Virgin Mary over whose assumption the angels rejoice and praise the son of God'.[20] As will soon become apparent it is in texts associated with the

17 Brown, *XVth Century*, no. 49.
18 Ibid., no. 50.
19 Cheetham, *Alabasters*, figs. 223-35 for examples in alabasters.
20 For both texts in the Sarum Missal see F. H. Dickinson, *Missale ad usum insignis et*

Assumption of the Virgin that her association with the Trinity is made most explicit. The fact remains that the earliest Coronation by the Trinity in English art is an image for All Saints in which the Virgin is shown in her glory as Queen of Heaven.

A few years later, *c.*1410-20, another example of the theme occurs in the Nevill Hours (Berkeley Castle) (Pl. 54).[21] This is in a form of the seated Father and Son with the Holy Ghost as a dove between them which is frequent in the alabasters, but in the Hours red clouds cut off the lower parts of the figures (Pl. 54). These clouds, out of which the Virgin is emerging, are indeed very relevant to the iconographic genesis of the theme. As is quite frequent in the early part of the century neither the Father nor the Son is crowned. The miniature's textual position is at the beginning of the Litany of the Virgin. The text on the next page specifies that the Litany of the Virgin gains an indulgence if said daily. Here a text specifically appealing to the Virgin as intercessor with repeated invocations for her help is the context of the Coronation of the Virgin by the Trinity.[22] Here the Virgin must be identified by the accompanying text in her role as intercessor, and the image consequently suggesting that she is mediator before the Trinity. This is a different context from her intercession before her Son at the final judgement, and is more akin to her role in the double intercession with her Son before the Father.[23] In her intercession before the Trinity she is before the Throne of Grace as mediator of that grace.[24]

In thirteenth-, fourteenth- and fifteenth-century England the common iconographic types of the Trinity are the *Gnadenstuhl* type and that of the Father and Son seated beside each other with the Holy Ghost in between.[25]

---

praeclarae Ecclesiae Sarum (Burntisland, 1883), cols 865, 953. For the texts in Carmelite use see *Missale secundum usum Carmelitarum* (Venice, 1504), fols 255, 272 (photostatic copy in British Library, L.R. 263.a.3).

21   G. M. Spriggs, 'The Nevill Hours and the School of Herman Scheerre', *Jnl of the Warburg and Courtauld Inst.*, 37 (1974), 129, pl. 29c.

22   For the development of the Litany of the Virgin in England see N. Morgan, 'Texts and Images of Marian Devotion in Fourteenth-Century England', in *England in the Fourteenth Century: Proceedings of the 1991 Harlaxton Symposium*, ed. by N. Rogers (Stamford, 1993), p. 41, n. 26.

23   For the double intercession see E. Panofsky, 'Imago Pietatis', *Festschrift M. J. Friedländer* (Leipzig, 1927), pp. 261-308 and 'Interzession: Mariä und Christi vor Gottvater', *Lexikon der christlichen Ikonographie*, II (1970), cols 346-52. On surviving evidence the theme was very rare in late medieval England.

24   For medieval theological texts on the Virgin as mediatrix see J. M. Bover, 'Maria, Mediatrix', *Ephemerides theologicae Lovanienses*, 6 (1929), 439-62. Also the general historical account of E. Druwé, 'La médiation de Marie', in H. du Manoir, *Maria. Études sur la Sainte Vierge*, I (Paris, 1949), pp. 419-572. For the theology of the relationship of the Virgin to the Trinity see the article 'Dreifaltigkeit', *Marienlexikon*, II (St. Ottilien, 1989), pp. 233-39.

The image with the seated Father and Son is the favoured one for Psalters, being taken directly from the opening words to Psalm 109, the first psalm of Sunday Vespers in secular use, at which point of the text it is most usually found in the historiated initial: 'The Lord said unto my Lord: Sit at my right hand until I make thy enemies thy footstool.' This iconography is also common in the fifteenth century with the enemies often depicted as the Devil or devils as in the Bury St Edmunds Psalter of c.1420 (Bury St Edmunds, Suffolk Record Office E.5/9/608.7).[26] In the Nevill Hours of c.1410-20 a *Gnadenstuhl* Trinity illustrates the suffrage of the Trinity.[27] The use of the *Gnadenstuhl* image of the Holy Trinity to illustrate this suffrage in Sarum books of hours has further relevance to the contextualization of the image of the Trinity in fifteenth-century devotion.[28]

Other text positions in manuscripts help to define further the association of the Virgin with the Trinity. A second image in the Carmelite Missal shows an unusual linking of the two (Pl. 51). It is the initial of the introit to the Votive Mass of the Holy Trinity, and like the other Trinity image in that book its iconography seems to be unique.[29] In the upper part of the initial on first impression there seems to be a normal Trinity with the Father and Son seated beside each other with the Dove of the Holy Ghost in between them. But the Father and Son are seated on a rainbow, an iconographic feature normally associated with the Last Judgement, and the Son holds up both hands symmetrically showing his wounds in the pose normally used for the Christ Judge in Last Judgement scenes. The reason for this adaptation of conventional Trinity imagery may in part derive from the first reading of the Mass of Trinity Sunday, Apocalypse iv. 1-10. This passage describes the throne of God, the rainbow and the four beasts around the throne in heaven, and indeed the beasts are there in the corners of the

[25] Both had coexisted as popular types since the late 12th century. For examples see the iconographic index to N. J. Morgan, *Early Gothic Manuscripts, I, 1190-1250, II, 1250-1285*, Survey of Manuscripts Illuminated in the British Isles (London, 1982, 1988).

[26] On this Psalter and related manuscripts see N. Rogers, 'Fitzwilliam Museum MS 3-1979: A Bury St. Edmunds Book of Hours and the Origins of the Bury Style' in *England in the Fifteenth Century: Proceedings of the 1986 Harlaxton Symposium*, ed. by D. Williams (Woodbridge, 1987), pp. 229-44, pl. 17.

[27] Spriggs, 'Nevill Hours', 106, 127, pl. 26d. For the Sarum collect see Dickinson, *Missale Sarum*, col. 451.

[28] Other examples in 15th-century Sarum books of hours before 1450 are: Cambridge, Trinity College, MS B.11.7, fol. 21v (c.1420); BL Add. MS 16998, fol. 26 (c.1410); BL Harley MS 1251, fol. 40v (c.1435); BL Harley MS 2846, fol. 23v (c.1435-40).

[29] Rickert, *Carmelite Missal*, pp. 46-47. The discussion in M. Levi D'Ancona, *The Iconography of the Immaculate Conception in the Middle Ages and Early Renaissance* (New York, 1957), p. 33, adds little to Rickert.

230

initial.[30] The vision of the throne of Heaven in the Apocalypse mentions 'one sitting on the throne', but here the throne is occupied by the Trinity. A further unusual feature, neither in the Apocalypse text nor in normal Trinity imagery, are the twelve red streams from the beak of the Dove of the Holy Spirit, normally associated with Pentecost scenes, the giving of the grace of the Holy Spirit. Below this image of the Trinity a man and woman donor kneel before the standing Virgin in the form of the Apocalyptic Woman of Apocalypse chapter 12, crowned with the stars and with the crescent moon at her feet. In the English illustrated Apocalypses of the thirteenth and fourteenth centuries the accompanying commentary text of Berengaudus to chapter 12 identifies the Woman in the Sun firstly as the Virgin Mary and secondly as symbol of the Church.[31] The inscribed scrolls in the image help to clarify its meaning. Below the Trinity is *per ipsum, et cum ipso, et in ipso*, the biblical source of which is in Romans xi. 36, the Epistle for the Votive Mass of the Trinity in both Carmelite and Sarum use.[32] Of equal importance is that these words are the great Trinitarian invocation with which the Canon of the Mass ends: 'through Him, with Him and in Him, in the unity of the Holy Spirit all glory and honour is yours, Almighty Father'. The man and woman donors beside the standing Woman in the Sun hold scrolls with the opening invocations of the Litany of the Saints to God the Father and the Blessed Virgin: *Pater de celis miserere nobis* and *Sancta Maria ora pro nobis*. Beside the Woman in the Sun are two scrolls identifying her as the Virgin Mary firstly in her role in the Incarnation, 'I have brought forth God and man', and secondly her predestination, 'The Lord chose me and predestined me.' Combining the evidence of the texts and the images this complex iconography seems to refer to the Virgin as both mediatrix and intercessor before the Holy Trinity, mediatrix of the grace of the Holy Spirit, and intercessor before the Father and with the Son at the Last Judgement. It could be argued that in depicting her as the Woman in the Sun, symbol of the Church, there is a clear reference to the Church as dispenser of sacramental grace. This could be a topical emphasis on orthodox doctrine, for at the time of the making of the Missal members of the Carmelite community in London, notably Peter Stokes, were actively defending the Church against the heresy of the Wycliffites.[33]

A further element which is relevant to devotion to the Trinity may be implied in the figures of the kneeling donors, probably man and wife. The mass of the Order of Matrimony in Sarum use was the Mass of the Holy

---

[30] *Missale secundum usum Carmelitarum*, fol. 187v.

[31] For the text see N. Morgan, *The Lambeth Apocalypse* (London, 1990), pp. 174-75.

[32] For the Sarum Votive Mass of the Trinity see Dickinson, *Missale Sarum*, cols 735*-738*. In *Missale secundum usum Carmelitarum*, fol. 300v.

[33] Rickert, *Carmelite Missal*, pp. 49-50.

Trinity, derived from the Mass of Trinity Sunday but with different readings for the Epistle and Gospel.[34] In the ceremony the Nuptial Mass of course includes the blessing of the married couple under the veil which takes place after the fraction and before the priest's communion. The sermon for the Nuptial Mass in John Mirk's *Festial* tells the congregation: 'Ye schul knowon that this ordur (of matrimony) was not furste fondon by erthely man, bot be the Holy Trenite of Heven'.[35] He then goes on to tell them about Adam and Eve and says in conclusion 'The Holy Trynite dyde alle this offyce before sayde, in tokening therof the prest begynneth the masse of the Trenite'.[36] Relevant to this use of the Mass of the Trinity as the Nuptial Mass is the parallel with the heavenly marriage of the Virgin as *Sponsa Christi* in her coronation in the presence of the Trinity.

In the first third of the fifteenth century English books of hours have the image of the Coronation of the Virgin by the Trinity beside other texts. In the Hours of Elizabeth the Queen (London, British Library, Add. MS 50001, fol. 100) it is placed at the beginning of the Seven Joys of the Virgin for the recitation of which the accompanying rubric promises an indulgence of 100 days granted by Pope Clement (probably Clement V) (Pl. 52).[37] The opening words of the text suggest this choice of subject: *Virgo templum Trinitatis*, 'O Virgin, temple of the Trinity'. The Seven Joys originated in the thirteenth century and the text is attributed to Philip de Grève (d. 1236), not Petrus Rogerus whom the rubric of the Hours of Elizabeth the Queen specifies as author.[38] Before the fifteenth century the Seven Joys are rare in England, the Five or Fifteen Joys being the more common forms.[39] Although

---

[34] For the Trinity Sunday and Nuptial Masses in the Missal see Dickinson, *Missale Sarum*, cols 451-55, 836*-845* and for the Manual see A. J. Collins, *Manuale ad percelebris Ecclesie Sarisburiensis*, Henry Bradshaw Society, 91 (1960), pp. 50-58.

[35] Erbe, *Mirk's Festial*, p. 289. For this and other Middle English sermon texts see N. J. Ryan, 'The Assumption in the Early English Pulpit', *Theological Stud.*, 11 (1950), 477-524.

[36] Erbe, *Mirk's Festial*, p. 291.

[37] For a full description of the Hours of Elizabeth the Queen see H. Yates Thompson, *A Descriptive Catalogue of the Second Series of Fifty Manuscripts in the Collection of Henry Yates Thompson* (Cambridge, 1902), no. 59, pp. 83-89. The indulgence rubric is 'Quicunque hec septem gaudia in honore beate marie virginis semel in die dixerit C dies indulgenciarum obtinebit a domino pape clemente qui prius vocabatur dominus petrus rogerii qui proprio stilo composuit.'

[38] For the authorship see A. Wilmart, *Auteurs spirituels et textes dévots du moyen âge latin* (Paris, 1932, repr. 1971), p. 329 n. 1 and F. J. E. Raby, *A History of Christian-Latin Poetry from the Beginning to the Close of the Middle Ages* (Oxford, 1953), pp. 395-401. For the text see F. J. Mone, *Hymni Latini Medii Aevi*, II (Freiburg im Breisgau, 1854), pp. 165-66 and G. G. Meersseman, *Der Hymnus Akathistos im Abendland*, II (Freiburg, 1960), pp. 195-99. See also the Seven Joys in Mirk's *Festial*: Erbe, *Mirk's Festial*, pp. 232-33.

the opening words would suggest the Coronation of the Virgin by the Trinity as a suitable illustration it is exceptional in Sarum fifteenth-century hours, the Presentation of the Virgin in the Temple being preferred. The text occurs almost exclusively in books of hours made in Bruges or Ghent for the English market.[40] An exception which has the Coronation of the Virgin, but not by the Trinity, for this text is London, British Library, Harley MS 2982, fol. 50v of c.1430. In the Hours of Elizabeth the Queen both Father and Son wear triple crowned tiaras and are robed in royal splendour of the court of Heaven with ermine capes and borders (Pl. 53).

The Bury St Edmunds book of hours (Cambridge, Fitzwilliam Museum, MS 3-1979) of c.1430-40 places the Coronation of the Virgin by the Trinity at Compline of the Hours of the Virgin (Pl. 55).[41] The Coronation of the Virgin, but not by the Trinity, at Compline is common in French fifteenth-century books of hours, and doubtless the influence on the placing in the Bury Hours comes from such sources, but substituting the preferred English iconography of the Coronation by the Trinity.

The Coronation of the Virgin is her glorification as the final event of her life, the culmination of her role in the act of redemption through the incarnation and passion of the Son of God. She is received into Heaven and made the Queen of Heaven.[42] Other iconographic forms express her glorification in fifteenth-century England, some deriving from Italian and Flemish fourteenth-century images.[43] The most popular image which comes into England in the series of Sarum hours produced in Bruges from the late fourteenth century onwards is the Virgin in Humility glorified, as it were, by setting her in the sky among angels, surrounded by golden rays of light, with stars above her head and the crescent moon at her feet.[44] This image of the

[39] See N. Morgan, 'Texts and Images of Marian Devotion in Thirteenth-Century England', in *England in the Thirteenth Century: Proceedings of the 1989 Harlaxton Symposium*, ed. by W. M. Ormrod (Stamford, 1991), p. 75, and Morgan, 'Texts and Images, Fourteenth-Century', pp. 39-40, nn. 17, 18.

[40] Examples of those pre-1450 Sarum-Flemish Hours having *Virgo templum Trinitatis* illustrated by the Presentation of the Virgin in the Temple: BL Arundel MS 341, fol. 75 (c.1440); BL Harley MS 935, fol. 59v (c.1450). There are many more examples of the second half of the century.

[41] For the manuscript see Rogers, op. cit. in n.26.

[42] For the early development of the iconography of the Coronation of the Virgin see the excellent studies: P. Verdier, *Le Couronnement de la Vierge* (Montreal, 1980); M.-L. Thérel, *Le triomphe de la Vierge-Église: à l'origine du décor du portail occidental de Notre-Dame de Senlis* (Paris, 1984).

[43] For a good discussion of some of the Sienese material see H. van Os, *Marias Demut und Verherrlichung in der sienesischen Malerei 1300-1450* (The Hague, 1969). A study of the developments in the iconography of the Virgin in glory in Italy as a whole during this period is very much needed.

[44] One of the finest early examples is in a small high quality book of hours made for

Virgin in glory is often used to illustrate the *Salve Regina* as in Ushaw College MS 10 and the Nevill Hours.[45]

The most commonly found image of the glorification of the Virgin is her Assumption. In the sense of narrative the Assumption has two episodes, the first being the lifting up of the body of the Virgin into Heaven, and the second her reception into Heaven.[46] Her reception into Heaven is almost always represented as the simultaneous occurrence of her coronation, and in the previous episode of her lifting up she should thus logically not be wearing a crown. In fifteenth-century England she is, however, frequently shown wearing a crown as she is lifted up, or a crown suspended over her head is held by angels.[47] Often above are Christ and the angels awaiting her arrival, and in some cases not Christ alone but also the Father and the Holy Spirit.[48] An early example of this is the very poorly preserved *c.*1413 painting at the end of the tomb of Henry IV in Canterbury Cathedral in which the Father and Son are blessing the tiara-crowned Virgin as she is carried up by angels.[49] In alabasters often the Trinity is holding the crown over her as she is lifted up into the realm of Heaven. An unusual variant in an unpublished *c.*1450

---

a patron in Bruges itself, Rouen, Bibliothèque Municipale MS Leber 137. It probably reflects best the Bruges prototype followed in numerous Sarum-Flemish hours. On these Sarum Hours produced in Bruges see N. J. Rogers, *Books of Hours produced in the Low Countries for the English Market in the Fifteenth Century*, M.Litt. dissertation (Cambridge, 1982), and *Vlaamse Miniaturen voor van Eyck*, Exhibition Cat., Romaanse Poort (Leuven, 1993).

[45] For Ushaw 10 see N. R. Ker, *Medieval Manuscripts in British Libraries, IV, Paisley-York* (Oxford, 1992), pp. 516-19; *Vlaamse Miniaturen voor van Eyck*, no. 5. For the Nevill Hours see Spriggs, 'Nevill Hours', 128, pl. 24d.

[46] See a Franco-Flemish drawing of *c.*1400 (Paris, Musée du Louvre) for the two episodes combined with that of her death: G. Ring, *A Century of French Painting 1400-1500* (London, 1949), p. 192, pl. 8. In her reception into Heaven she is being crowned by the Trinity. The general development of the iconography of the Assumption is discussed by E. Staedel, *Ikonographie der Himmelfahrt Mariens* (Strassburg, 1935) and G. Schiller, *Ikonographie der Christlichen Kunst*, IV.2 (Gütersloh, 1980), pp. 143-46, figs. 714-21. For the theme in alabasters see W.L. Hildburgh, 'English Alabaster Carvings as Records of the Medieval Religious Drama', *Archaeologia*, 93 (1949), 66-69. The history of the iconography of the Assumption in late medieval England remains to be written. In view of the proliferation of guilds of the Assumption and of *Salve Regina* it must have been a very popular theme among devotional images.

[47] Cheetham, *Alabasters*, fig. 132. A good example of the crown suspended over her head is in the *c.*1460 stained glass of East Harling (Norf.): Baker, *English Stained Glass*, pl. III.

[48] Cheetham, *Alabasters*, figs. 133-34.

[49] E. W. Tristram, *The Paintings of Canterbury Cathedral* (Canterbury, 1935), pp. 10-11 with pl. For the tomb see L. Stone, *Sculpture in Britain: The Middle Ages*, 2nd edn (Harmondsworth, 1972), pp. 197-98, pl. 155A.

Book of Hours in the collection of Lord Gage (Firle Place, Sussex) has only the three hands of the persons of the Trinity emerging from clouds to bless the crown above her head. The hands are differentiated: the wounded hand of the Son, a greyish hand of the Holy Spirit, and a brown-yellow hand of the Father. In the Gage Hours the textual position of the Assumption is unusual at the beginning of the Penitential Psalms. The usual subject at this point is the Last Judgement in which the Virgin pleads as the principal intercessor for humanity. Her role as intercessor in Heaven might have been the reason for portraying her entry into Heaven at this point in the text.

Although, with the exception of Henry IV's tomb, the early examples of the combined Assumption and Coronation by the Trinity are in alabasters, a late fifteenth-century wall painting in Exeter Cathedral Lady Chapel shows this iconography.[50] It has the significant feature of portraying the angels flanking the Virgin in her Assumption in the form of the Orders of Angels.[51] This shows the influence of texts describing the Assumption, above all that of the Golden Legend. The Golden Legend of Jacobus de Voragine had first become known in its Latin version in England in the late thirteenth century, but was not translated into English until c.1438.[52] Its influence as early as c.1285 is evident in the South English Legendary.[53] The Golden Legend account of the Assumption describes the Orders of Angels: 'The Blessed Virgin was assumed joyously. With joy the heavens have taken up the Blessed Virgin, the Angels rejoicing, the Archangels jubilating, the Thrones exalting, the Dominations psalming, the Principalities making harmony, the Powers playing upon the harp, the Cherubim and Seraphim

[50] G. McN. Rushforth, 'Late Medieval Paintings in Exeter Cathedral', *Devon and Cornwall Notes and Queries*, 17 (1932-3), 99-106.

[51] For the various contexts of the Orders of the Angels in English 15th-century art see Rushforth, *Medieval Christian Imagery*, pp. 204-16 and C. Woodforde, *The Norwich School of Glass-Painting in the Fifteenth Century* (Oxford, 1950), pp. 129-37.

[52] On this see P. Butler, *Legenda Aurea - Légende Dorée - Golden Legend* (Baltimore, 1899); M. Jeremy, 'The English Prose Translation of the "Legenda Aurea"', *Modern Language Notes*, 59 (1944), 181-83; A. Kurvinen, 'Caxton's "Golden Legend" and the Manuscripts of the "Gilte Legend"', *Neuphilologische Mitteilungen*, 60 (1959), 353-75; R. Hamer, *Three Lives from the Gilte Legende* (Heidelberg, 1978). The last of these has a good introduction on the English translations of the Golden Legend. The c.1330-40 French translation of Jean de Vignay was the basis of the English version and was assuredly known in England from the second half of the 14th century.

[53] On this see M. Görlach, 'The Legenda Aurea and the Early History of the South English Legendary' and K. P. Jankofsky, 'Legenda Aurea Materials in the South English Legendary: Translation, Transformation, Acculturation', both in *Legenda Aurea: Sept Siècles de Diffusion*, ed. by B. Dunn-Lardeau (Paris, 1986), pp. 301-16, 317-29.

hymning and leading her to the supernal throne of the divine majesty .....
The most ineffable Trinity Itself applauds her, and His grace redoundeth all
in her and maketh others to serve her'.[54] In the final section the Virgin is
described as channel and mediatrix of the grace of the Holy Trinity. The
inclusion of angels singing or playing musical instruments may have been
influenced by the dramatic performances of Assumption plays which
stipulate music at the point of her being lifted up.[55] The reference to the
Orders of Angels singing a hymn of praise to the Holy Trinity occurs also in
vernacular poetry in a lyric on the Coronation of the Virgin:

A melodious myrthe it was to me,
fful pure and precious by poyntes passaunte,
So shyning upward the excelcite,
With obediaunt beemys bryghtly abundaunt,
Angellys, Archangellys, froom vicis advertaunt,
Moore gloryous than evere was gleem or glas,
Thronys, Dominaciouns, thus Crist collaudaunt,
With Benedicta sit sancta Trinitas.[56]

Another Assumption text which brings in the imagery of the Trinity is
the sequence for the Mass of the Assumption in the Sarum rite: '...to
Heaven's portals you were borne. You are dear to the Father, the good
mother of Jesus, the temple of the Holy Spirit. You are the fair spouse of
God, you have borne Christ the King, you are the Lady of Heaven and
Earth'.[57] John Mirk's two early fifteenth-century sermons for the vigil and
feast of the Assumption stress that she is joining the company of the Trinity
in Heaven before which she will intercede for her servants: 'and ys ther of on
will and one love wyth the Holy Trinyte that grauntyth hur what that ever
scho askyth, and at hur prayer rewardeth all hur servants. And thus scho

---

[54] *The Golden Legend of Jacobus de Voragine*, transl. by G. Ryan, H. Ripperberger
(New York, 1969), pp. 457, 458; F. S. Ellis, *The Golden Legend or Lives of the
Saints as Englished by William Caxton*, IV (London, 1900), pp. 245-47.

[55] See R. Woolf, *The English Mystery Plays* (London, 1972), pp. 286-91; R. Beadle,
The York Plays (London, 1982), pp. 394-95. Regrettably J. Vriend, *The Blessed
Virgin Mary in the Medieval Drama of England* (Purmerend, 1928), p. 133, states
that he has not been able to extend his study to a consideration of the Assumption
and Coronation of the Virgin. As far as I can ascertain only a 16th-century
addition to the York plays has her crowned by the Trinity: Beadle, *York Plays*,
pp. 404-05; C. Davidson, *From Creation to Doom* (New York, 1984), pp. 175-76.

[56] R. Woolf, *The English Religious Lyric in the Middle Ages* (Oxford, 1968), p. 300.
For the whole poem see Brown, *XVth Century*, no. 39. Woolf, op. cit., pp.
298-302 discusses Assumption/Coronation lyrics which are characterized by
highly ornate phrases to evoke the splendour and joy of the events.

[57] Dickinson, *Missale Sarum*, cols 868-69: '...in qua es assumpta ad coeli claustra. Tu
es enim Patri cara, tu es Iesu mater bona, tu Sancti Spiritus es templa facta. Tu es
pulchra Dei sponsa, tu regem Christum enixa, domina es in coelo et in terra.'

sittythe yn Heven next to the Trinite wyth body gloryfyet'. He ends the sermon with a poem on the Seven Joys of the Virgin in Heaven:[58]

> Be glad and blythe Lady fre,
> Sytting by the Trinite
> In blood and flesh yfer[59]
> Full of joy and full of grace
> God hathe made ther thi place
> As to hys modyr dere.

The *Myroure of Oure Ladye* from Syon has similar texts.[60] The meditation recommended for Saturdays contains this passage: 'On Saterday ye may se the holy lyfe of Oure Lady, namely from the tyme of her Sonne's passyon unto her assumpcyon, and how she was taken up in to heven bothe soule and body, and sette most nyghe the Blessed Trinyte above all creatures. And so the joye that the same Blessed Trinyte had of the same glorious Lady, endelesly ere she was made, as ye rede on Sunday, was fulfylled in her effectually indede, in her assumpcyon, as ye rede on Saterday'.[61] In the commentary on the Matins hymn for the Sunday Office of the Virgin, *O Trinitatis Gloria*: 'she ys spouse of the father of heven ... she ys mother of the sonne .... and so she ys called the fathers spouse and the sonnes mother'.[62] In the section on Compline in the meditation on the antiphon *O jocundissimam*: 'O moste joyful joye. God the Father halseth Hys Spouse, the Sonne Hys Mother, the Holy Gost His sacrary'.[63] This text is significant in its reference to the Virgin as Spouse of the Father, not as is normal the Spouse of the Son. The mystical and theological imagery of the *Sponsa-Sponsus* is replaced by the human image of a re-united family.

In the religious lyrics the theme of the Virgin in Heaven in the presence of the Trinity occurs frequently. In a poem of John Audelay she is described as next to the Trinity:

> Moder and maid gentil and fre
> Precious, perrles, princes of pes,
> Thi boure is next the Trinite.[64]

---

[58] Erbe, *Mirk's Festial*, pp. 224, 233.

[59] Yfer – together.

[60] Ryan, 'Assumption', pp. 516-21; J. H. Blunt, *The Myroure of Oure Ladye*, Early English Text Society, E.S. 19 (1873), pp. 5, 91-94, 141-42, 275.

[61] Blunt, *Myroure*, p. 5. The reference to the Sunday reading is the meditation on the Chapter for Terce: *Ab initio et ante saecula creata sum, et usque ad futurum saeculum non desinam.* The translation in the *Myroure* is: 'Endelesly before all tymes I was made and I schal never fayle.'

[62] Blunt, *Myroure*, pp. 91-94.

[63] Blunt, *Myroure*, p. 275. halseth – embraces; sacrary – temple.

[64] E. K. Whiting, *The Poems of John Audelay*, Early English Text Society, O.S. 184 (1931), p. 204. James Ryman's carols of *c.*1492 refer to her as 'chast bowre of the

In a poem on the Five Joys in the sections on the Assumption and Coronation:

> In solempne wyse assumpted wyth a songe
> Of cherubyn, thy forthe joy to atteyne,
> was thi body and thy sowle aungellys amonge,
> unto thy son browte up yn febus wayne,
> wher persons three yn On god sytte certeyne.
> Of whose presens ryght ioyful mayste thou be,
> ffor as scrypture in holy bokys sayn,
> Thow conceyuydyst clene that holy trinite.
> Ande they alle three of on affeccion
> have chosy the cheffe, the quene for to be
> Of hevyn and erthe, wos coronacione
> wes thy fyffte ioy wyth grete solempnyte.[65]

The Madonna of Mercy sheltering figures beneath her cloak is the image best showing her protection for her devotees. In the years around 1400 in the wall-paintings of Corby (Lincs.) she shelters souls as they await the particular judgement.[66] In the 1446 foundation charters of Henry VI's colleges of Eton and King's, Cambridge, there is an image combining the form of the Madonna of Mercy with the Assumption and Coronation of the Virgin by the Trinity. The Virgin is carried up by angels with the Trinity above blessing the crown on her head, and three angels holding wide her protecting cloak. She looks down at the king with the lords spiritual and temporal kneeling below for whom she is intercessor, protector and mediator of the divine grace of the Trinity.[67] In the charter of the Drapers' Company of 1439 the Virgin crowned by the Trinity has her cloak widespread with naked souls sheltering under it.[68] The theme of the Virgin's protecting mantle is found in Lydgate's poem *Ave Jesse Virgula*: 'Thy merciful mantel lete cloth al in the shade'.[69]

Trinitee' and 'triclyne of the Trinitie': Greene, *Early English Carols*, nos 199, 205, 224.

[65] Brown, *XVth Century*, no. 31, p. 56.

[66] For Corby and related English images of the Virgin of Mercy see Morgan, 'Texts and Images, Fourteenth-Century', pp. 49-51.

[67] J. J. G. Alexander, 'William Abell "lymnour" and 15th Century English Illumination', in *Kunsthistorische Forschungen Otto Pächt zu seinem 70. Geburtstag*, ed. by A. Rosenauer, G. Weber (Salzburg, 1972), pp. 166-72. The seal of Eton depicted the Assumption: Waterton, *Pietas Mariana*, pt. 1, p. 29.

[68] Goodall, 'Heraldry and Iconography', pl. III; J. Bromley, *The Armorial Bearings of the Guilds of London* (London, 1960), pl. 18. Goodall, op. cit., p. 179, cites another Coronation of the Virgin by the Trinity in a late 15th century Fraternity Book of the Fraternity of the Assumption of the Skinners' Company of London. For a colour illustration see J. J. Lambert, *Records of the Skinners of London* (London, 1933), opp. p. 108.

A relevant iconographic parallel to the Assumption of Mary with the Trinity awaiting her in Heaven is the subject popular in England from c.1400 onwards of the souls released from purgatory taken by angels up to the Holy Trinity.[70] A good example is the illustration of the Commendation of the Soul in the Hours of the Duchess of Clarence (Private Collection) (Pl. 56).[71] The bodily Assumption of the Virgin received by the Trinity seems to be the model for this image of the souls taken up to Heaven.

Undoubtedly the legends and liturgical texts of the Assumption were a prime source for the Coronation of the Virgin by the Trinity, but another image in art must have contributed to her association with the Trinity. This is the wooden or ivory figure of the seated Virgin and Child in which the body opens up in the manner of a triptych to reveal inside her body the Holy Trinity.[72] Such images are known in German and French as *Schreinmadonnen* or *Vierges Ouvrantes* but no English word exists for them. They certainly occurred in late medieval England but are known only from descriptions. Our Lady of Boulton in Durham Cathedral was an image of this type and is so described in the *Rites of Durham*: 'Our Lady of Boulton was made to open from her breastes downward .... that every man might see pictured within the Father, the Sone and the Holy Ghost most curiously and finely gilded'.[73] This image is a direct translation into visual form of the text calling the Virgin the Temple of the Trinity. As Lydgate writes in his *Ave Jesse Virgula*: 'Haile chaste lady of virginite! of the Holigost haile, richest habitacle, Aforne provided by the holy Trynite, to be his triewe chosen tabernacle'.[74]

---

[69] Woolf, *English Religious Lyric*, p. 283 with the wrong assertion that the Virgin of Mercy is not depicted in English art.

[70] On the theme see P. Sheingorn, 'The Bosom of Abraham Trinity: A Late Medieval All Saints Image', in *England in the Fifteenth Century: Proceedings of the 1986 Harlaxton Symposium*, ed. by D. Williams (Woodbridge, 1987), pp. 273-98. She argues for a possible association of this image with that of All Saints. See Cheetham, *Alabasters*, figs. 226-29 for examples of this form of the Trinity.

[71] For good colour plates and description see the sale catalogue *Medieval Manuscripts*, Catalogue 12, Sam Fogg, Rare Books, lot 14 with a plate of the souls taken to the Trinity on p. 59. In the Hours of Elizabeth the Queen (BL Add. MS 50001, fol. 67v) the souls are carried up to God the Father alone.

[72] The most important studies of the subject are A. A. Schmid, 'Die Schreinmadonna von Cheyres', *Festgabe für Wolfgang Stammler* (Freiburg, 1958), pp. 130-62; C. Baumer, 'Die Schreinmadonna', *Marian Library Stud.*, 9 (1977), 239-72; R. Kroos, '"Gotes Tabernakel": Zu Funktion und Interpretation von Schreinmadonnen', *Zeitschrift für schweizerische Archäologie und Kunstgeschichte*, 43 (1986), 58-64.

[73] *Rites of Durham*, Surtees Society, 107 (1902), p. 30; Waterton, *Pietas Mariana*, pt. 2, p. 29.

[74] H. N. MacCracken, *The Minor Poems of John Lydgate*, Early English Text Society, E.S. 107 (1911), p. 299.

The association of the Virgin with the Trinity is occasionally made in scenes of the Annunciation illustrating the words of the angel 'The Holy Ghost shall come upon thee, and the power of the most High shall overshadow thee'.[75] An alabaster in the Victoria and Albert Museum (formerly Cologne, Kunstgewerbemuseum) shows the Annunciation with a stem from the lily pot rising up to become part of the Crucifix which is held by the Father above in the form of the *Gnadenstuhl* Trinity.[76]

In the fifteenth century the mystery of the Trinity had been transformed in visual imagery into a humanised anthropomorphic Trinity which would eventually come to be attacked by the reformers of the subsequent century.[77] As a parallel to the emphasis on the intimate familial relationships of the earthly Holy Family which had been developing as a devotional theme since the fourteenth century, even the Trinity in the fifteenth century is conceived as a family in Heaven.[78] In her Assumption the Virgin comes to the glorious reunion of the heavenly family. She whose womb had become the temple of the Holy Spirit and from whom had been born the Son takes her place in Heaven as daughter, mother and spouse of the Father and the Son.[79] In such human terms the image presents family relationships, and the Reformation abhorrence of the human representation of the Trinity was a strong reaction against such simplification of the mysteries of the Trinity and the Incarnation.

The court of Heaven with Mary as its queen becomes depicted in terms of secular ritual with the long-established textual authority of the liturgy interpreted in literal imagery. The alleluia verse for the daily Mass of the

---

[75] Luke i. 35.

[76] W. L. Hildburgh, 'An Alabaster Table of the Annunciation with the Crucifix: a Study in English Iconography', *Archaeologia*, 74 (1925), 203-32. The N-Town play associates the Annunciation with a manifestation of the Trinity: 'here the holy gost descendit with iii bemys to our lady. the sone of the godhed nest with iii bemys. to the holy gost. the fadyr godly with iii bemys to the sone. And so entre all three to here bosom.' On this see Vriend, *Blessed Virgin Mary*, p. 72, and G. McM. Gibson, *The Theatre of Devotion: East Anglian Drama and Society in the Late Middle Ages* (Chicago, 1989), p. 144.

[77] M. Aston, *England's Iconoclasts* (Oxford, 1988), pp. 53, 75, 76, 78, 100, for Reformation opposition to images of the Trinity.

[78] The development of the cult of the Holy Family in art and devotion in 15th-century England has yet to be written. For a recent well-documented study of the cult in Flanders and Germany see T. Brandenbarg, *Heilig familieleven. Verspreiding en waardering van de historie van Sint Anna* (Nijmegen, 1990).

[79] For the *mater et filia* topos see Morgan, 'Texts and Images, Thirteenth-Century', p. 86 n. 53. In addition to the bibliography cited there see A. Breeze, 'The Virgin Mary, Daughter of her Son', *Études Celtiques*, 27 (1990), 267-83. I am very grateful to Dr Breeze for sending me this and his other publications on Marian texts in Irish and Welsh literature.

Virgin from the Purification to Advent in the Sarum rite is explicit in referring to such imagery: 'Hail Virgin Mother of God, temple of the Holy Ghost, you alone are worthy to be called Queen and Mistress of Heaven'.[80]

The Queen of Heaven has to be in a position to intercede for mankind at the court over which the anthropomorphic Holy Trinity presides. She has to be elevated into the presence of the Trinity to be able to perform that intercession, and like her Son to be made 'so much better than the angels'.[81] The late medieval obsession with images of the glorification of Mary is a logical consequence of this hierarchic view of Heaven. The woman who is the model of humility has to be presented in imagery which places her close to the Holy Trinity. As a c.1400 Middle English poem *Quia amore langueo* reasons with such charming simplicity:[82]

> Why was I crouned and made a quene
> Why was I called of mercy the welle
> Why shuld an erthly woman bene
> So hygh in heven above aungelle?
> For thee mankynde, the truthe I telle
> Thou aske me helpe and I shall do
> That I was ordeyned, kepe thee from helle.

The intercession of Mary is not seen primarily at the Last Judgement as in earlier thirteenth- and fourteenth-century images and texts. As the poem says it is 'to kepe thee from helle' when 'thou aske me helpe'. Another poem on her Seven Joys in Heaven expresses her joy in this act of mediation: 'Be glad moder of ihu dere, That spedist alle way thi prayere, By-fore the Trinite'.[83] She is the advocate before the Trinity for that divine grace to assist her servants of which she is mediatrix. In being 'crouned and made a quene' her relation to that source of grace is visualized.[84] Both as an image of devotion and a simple and direct presentation of the theological doctrines of the Trinity and divine grace, the Coronation of the Virgin by the Trinity, in view of its popularity, seems to have fulfilled an important role in the religious life of fifteenth-century England.

---

[80] Dickinson, *Missale Sarum*, col. 780*.

[81] Hebrews i. 4.

[82] C. Brown, *Religious Lyrics of the XIVth Century* (Oxford, 1924), no. 132, p. 236; H. S. Bennett, *Quia amore langueo* (London, 1937), pp. 10, 17, for textual variants.

[83] Brown, *XVth Century*, no. 34, p. 59.

[84] James Ryman refers to her as queen and mother of grace: Greene, *Early English Carols*, nos 205, 223. Another 15th-century carol calls her 'well of grace celestiall', ibid., no. 200.1.

Margins and Marginality:
English Devotion in the Later Middle Ages
COLIN RICHMOND

> But let us open the volume... What are these scrawls in the fly-leaves? What
> incorrigible pupil of a writing-master has been here? What crayon sketcher
> of wild animals and falling air-castles? Ah, no! – these are all part and parcel
> of the precious book which go to make up the sum of its treasure to me.
>
> Herman Melville, *Redburn* (London, 1929), p. 183.

My first direct acquaintance with single-leaf woodcuts was with those in the
Willshire Collection at the Guildhall Library, London. The third woodcut I
set eyes on that memorable afternoon was a St Dorothy. To the woodcut
someone had added a floral border with a hunting scene; he or she had also
written on it 'Ora Pro Nobis' and what I believe to have been two names
(now obliterated). This individualization or personalization of an image on
sale in bulk intrigued me from that moment on.[1]

One of the most spectacular examples of such personalization is British
Library, Egerton MS 1821. This is a Rosary Book which belonged in 1540 to
John Harris of Hackington near Canterbury. Into the book are pasted a
number of woodcuts. Three of these are English. They are pasted onto leaves
of vellum tinted scarlet and painted all over with a diaper pattern of drops of
blood. One is a Man of Sorrows; another is of the Cross, the Five Wounds,
and the Sacred Heart; the third is of the Man of Sorrows standing with the
Cross: a Carthusian kneels before Him and an inscription reads 'The greatest
comfort in al temptacyon/Is the remembraunce of crystes passyon.' Are
these John Harris's aids to devotion?[2]

---

[1] The call number of the St Dorothy is WS I.14(A). It is figure 59 in A. B. Hind,
An Introduction to a History of Woodcut, 2 vols (New York, 1963), I, 136. Other
examples of personalized woodcuts are to be found in the British Library; three
of them are reproduced in *Woodcuts and Metal Cuts of the Fifteenth Century Chiefly
of the German School*, ed. by C. Dodgson (London, 1914), pls III, XI, XXX. Also
in the British Library's collection is a Christ as the Man of Sorrows as he
appeared to St Bridget (A 37, South Germany, 1490s); on the woodcut is written
in German: 'In the same form our Lord and Saviour has appeared in recent years
to a sister of our Holy Order.' I would like to thank Dr Roger Jones for his help
with this particular woodcut.

[2] For the manuscript see F. A. Gasquet, *An English Rosary Book of the Fifteenth
Century* (London, 1894), and C. Dodgson, 'English Devotional Woodcuts of the
Late Fifteenth Century, with Special Reference to those in the Bodleian Library',
Walpole Society, 17 (1928-9), 97-98. A devotional aid of a somewhat different kind
was added to the Bolton Book of Hours (York Minster Library, MS Additional 2)
in the second half of the fifteenth century: a form of confession in English which

Almost as spectacular (and arguably more attractive) is the Bromholm card pasted into the Lewknor Book of Hours in Lambeth Palace Library.[3] Below the exquisitely painted image of the Bromholm crucifix in a space perhaps intended for just such a purpose is written, in what M. R. James has pontifically termed 'a bad hand', 'thys ys the holy cros that ys so good. be me mary Everard'.[4] Mary's hand appears elsewhere in the book: on folio 2v, for example, she has put 'thys boke is mysterys Everards'; while on the otherwise blank folio 193v she has entered 'In my cafas [coffers] xij payr and a Shet [sheet]'. Such a mixture, muddle we might think, of the sacred and profane was also intriguing. It is also endearing: so familiarly did an English woman of the later Middle Ages treat her prayer book that she entered a note of her linen in it. The image of Mary Everard counting her sheets prayer-book in hand is already one which is illuminating.

A second acquaintance was with what I regarded (in those distant days) as an incomprehensible instance of piety. This experience was also pictorial. In the Bodleian Library I had out (for no reason other than curiosity) Gough Liturgical MS 7, a Flemish Book of Private Prayers, which had belonged to George, earl of Shrewsbury, around 1500. George is discovered kneeling before a crowned Virgin Mary on folio 12v. There are some interesting (and 'whingeing') English prayers in the book, including one for those who have the governance of people, and a prayer added in a later hand on folio 131v; to added prayers I will shortly come, as they are after all the gist of this short paper.[5] However, it was the rubric beneath a miniature of the Mass of St

---

runs to eleven pages. Was that an unusually devout thing to have done (or to have had done on one's behalf)? Was it done on behalf of Agnes Lond or Thomas Sauceby of York, whose obits of 1471-2 are to be found in the calendar?

[3] F. Wormald, 'The Rood of Bromholm', in *Collected Writings*, ed. by J. J. G. Alexander, T. J. Brown, and J. Gibbs, 2 vols (London, 1988), II, 124-26.

[4] M. R. James, *A Descriptive Catalogue of the MSS in the Library of Lambeth Palace, The Mediaeval MSS* (London, 1932), p. 749.

[5] O. Pächt and J. J. G. Alexander, *Illuminated Manuscripts in the Bodleian Library, Oxford*, 3 vols (Oxford, 1966-73), I, no. 390. For the 'whingeing' nature of late medieval private prayers, see below. Here is an example from George's private prayer-book, fol. 81v: 'Most dere lorde and savyour swte jesu I beseche thy moost curteys goodnes and benyngne favour to be to me moost wretched creature favourable lorde protectour keper and defender and in all necessytees and nedes be to my shelde and protectyon ayenst al myne enmyes bodely and goostly. Mercyfull jesu I have none other truste hope ne secour but in the allonely my dere lorde swete jhesu the whyche of thy infynyte goodnes madeest me of nought lyke unto thy moost excellent ymage. And whan I was lost by my fyrst fader adams synne wyth thy precyous blood dere lorde thou redemest me and sythen ever dayly moost gracyously with thy gyftes of grace moste lovuingly thou fedest me graunte me therefore my moost dere lord and sauyour to drede the and love the above all thynge in thys present lyf and after in joye and blysse wythout

243

Gregory on folio 59v which drew my attention and trapped my imagination. It read: 'To all them that before this image of pyte devoutly say five pater nosters five aves and a credo pytously beholdyng these armes of christs passion are graunted 32755 years of pardon.' Precisely how, I asked myself, was this particular image used, if it was used at all? Did George devoutly perform before it? If he did, how often did he? Did his confessor show it him during confession? If he did, at what point? Did either, or both, of them add up the years?

It is personalized devotions of these kinds which I have been tracking down in the margins (and on the blank leaves) of manuscripts over recent years. Here I shall present my findings and make a few speculative observations on what I have found.

First, three further examples of non-devout marginalia to remind us that men and women, and (as we shall immediately see) children, did, like Mary Everard, write down mundane matters in the margins – even in the margins of, and spaces left by, the sacred. A fifteenth-century copy-book which belonged to children of the Betts family of Wortham in Suffolk has entries like 'Yt was the vij daye of July that Wyllam Prylles ded Polle [pull] my Haar.' However, is this precisely recollected indignity fifteenth century? The first signature in the book is of Richard Betts of c.1490, the last is of Edmund Betts of c.1680.[6]

Secondly, in the de Grey Book of Hours, which belonged to Elizabeth Catesby, who married as her second husband Sir John Grey, fourth son of Thomas, marquis of Dorset, and who died in the early years of the sixteenth century, beneath a miniature of the Agony in the Garden has been written 'Madame I pray you remember her that ys yours and eyver sal be.' Do two varieties of love feature on one folio?[7]

---

ende swte jhesu. Amen.' There is a good deal more in this cringing vein in George's book. Could the mode be a particularly upper class one: the English nobility behaving towards their Lord as they wished others to behave towards them? Such a posture of abasement fits the nobility's generally 'craven mood' in the fifteenth century, first indicated by K. B. McFarlane ('The Wars of the Roses', in *England in the Fifteenth Century* (London, 1981), p. 261). More attention might be paid to this conjunction of politics and religion; more certainly might be said. What might be said would have to include the Lollards, who loathed all that bowing and scraping.

6   K. F. Doughty, *The Betts of Wortham in Suffolk, 1480-1905* (London, 1912), pp. 16-17. I do not know the current whereabouts of the Betts MS.

7   Aberystwyth, National Library of Wales, MS 15537C, fol. 37v. This impeccable volume of 228 folios has four (and only four) annotations, in four different hands, of four different dates, spanning some fifty to a hundred years. One of these is the obit of Elizabeth Grey, another (the earliest) is in Latin, a third (the latest) says 'o remember not the sinnes and offences'. So disciplined an abuse makes one ponder the book's use.

Thirdly, there are on the verso of the final folio of a British Library copy of *The Art to Live Well* (published at Paris in 1503) such notes as 'Item payd for at mill' and 'Item payd for harying [harrowing] 15d'. These are in a fairly crude hand, but, whether it is the book-owner's or his bailiff's, they make one gape at a book of that nature being used for such a purpose. Or perhaps not; it may be only those with a modern sensibility (and modern aesthetics) who find it disquieting that day-to-day matters should be entered in a volume of timeless verities.[8]

Obits (the point at which the eternal intersected the diurnal) were a favourite method of personalizing psalters and books of hours. I will be content with two examples. British Library, Harleian MS 1688, a psalter, is particularly exciting in the number and amplitude of its obits.[9] Besides having an account of wheat, maslin, sheep, lambs, cattle, and horses of April 1484 on its first folio, in the calendar there are many obits of the Derham family of Crimplesham, Norfolk, and their important relations (and probable patrons), like Gilbert Holcroft, a Baron of the Exchequer, who died in 1457, and Baldwin de Vere of Great Addington, Northants, who died in 1424 and who (the entry records) had been Keeper of Guernsey and Jersey and Constable of the Tower of London during the reign of Henry V, when the King of Scots and many illustrious French noblemen were prisoners in his charge. Pride in one's connections and pride in one's descent are perfectly caught here – an incongruity which the Derhams (we may safely assume) did not notice.

Many of the births in the Derham Book of Hours are recorded precisely. Thomas Derham, 'my son, God make him a good man', was born on a Tuesday at night between 8 and 9, which day was called St Hilary's day, 13 January 1488; 'Frawnses, my son, God make him his servaunt', was born on a Friday at night between 6 and 7, that day was called St Alban, the first martyr of England, 22 June 1492. The birthdays of girls were similarly noted: Thomasin Derham, for instance, was born between 5 and 6 in the morning of 17 May 1529. This precision was necessary for the construction of

---

8 BL, C.21.d.20. I am grateful to Dr Margaret Kekewich for telling me of this volume. There is a thoroughly mundane addition in a fifteenth-century hand to Ford Abbey's twelfth-century copy of Augustine's Commentary on the Psalms in the Newberry Library: I have used P. Saenger, *Catalogue of the Pre-1500 Western Manuscript Books at the Newberry Library, Chicago* (Chicago, 1989), no. 13 (p. 28). The addition is on the last page (fol. 161): 'Edward Shepherde promysyd to pay xv.s furtnyght after seynt James day nex [sic] ensuing. Item a bargayn mayd for v pense a wek on seynt Mary Maudelyns eve with Elizabeth Whawen. Of this Sheperde is recuyed vi.s viii.d parte of this xv.s above wretyn. On sent Johanne a baptist day Rychard Gye have recuyd iii score of rede shevys.'

9 C. Wordsworth and H. Littlehales, *The Old Service Books of the English Church* (London, 1904), p. 58, was where I first encountered the manuscript.

horoscopes; these, in turn, were essential for medical prognoses. Similar examples are to be found in our second manuscript, British Library, Harleian MS 2887.[10] Here there was the birth of twins: George and John Gower were born 'at a berthe' on 10 July 1470 between 10 and 11 'of the clok'. The precision in the case of Agnes Gower extended to place: Agnes was born at 4 in the afternoon of 25 August 1467 in the parish of St Michael in 'Crokedlayn', Thames Street, [London]. Soon after the arrival of the Gower boys the book came into the possession of the Butlers, earls of Ormond and Wiltshire. They duly set down on the second folio the obits of their forebears and of their former royal patrons, Henry VI, Margaret of Anjou, and Edward, Prince of Wales. There is a poignancy in the precision with which Henry VI's death was recorded: between 21 and 22 May [1471].

Prayers to Henry VI are to be found in the Gower-Butler Book of Hours; they are in Latin. There are also prayers in English in the text; others in English have been added on the last page. It is with prayers, usually in English, which have been added to books of hours – medieval prayer books or primers – that the remainder of the paper is concerned. Whether these prayers emit the 'dense smog of self-centredness, malice and sanctified whingeing', which Professor John Bossy has recently detected,[11] we will have to decide after examining some of them.

Our first examples come from a book of hours which belonged to the Fincham family of Norfolk, one of whose number entered a curse at folio 133: 'This boke ys oon the curse of Crist ys a nothir/He that stelith thoon shall have the othir.'[12] It was effective, for it appears to be Finchams who add, about 1500, the following prayers. At folio 134 is 'A devout prayer for all maner tribulacions':

> Yf a man or woman theis masses underwritten do syng for hymself or for any otheir of his frendes in what nede or tribulacion or syknes that they be ine they shall be delyvered be the grace of god withoute dowt withine x dayes and in the same maner for to delyver the soule of thy frend out of payn for this is proved. Do syng a masse on the Sunday in the worship of the Trinite and lyght iij candell and feed iij pouer men or yef iij almes. The Monday a masse in the worship of Seynt Michell and of all Aungell and light ix candell and feed ix pouer men or yef ix allmes. The Twesday a masse of Seynt John Evangelist and lyght iiij candell and feed iiij pouer men or yef iiij almes. The Wennesday a masse in the worship of Seynt Petre and of all Apostell and lyght xij candell and feed xij pore men or yef xij almes. The Thursday a masse of the holy gost and lyght vij candell et feed vij pouer men or yef vij allmes. The Fryday a masse of the holy cros and lyght v candell

10 Ibid., p. 59.
11 J. Bossy, 'Christian Life in the Later Middle Ages: Prayers', *Transactions of the R. Historical Soc.*, 6th Ser., 1 (1991), p. 148.
12 Victoria and Albert Museum, Reid MS 44.

and feed v pouer men or yef v allmes. The Seterday a masse of our lady and lyght oon candell and feed oon pouer man or yef oon allmes. And all the said dayes thow most offer at ever[y] of the vij masses sume offeryng. And witt [know] it well for soth that this prayer shalbe hard withine short tyme. And say than this ympne [hymn] Veni Creator...

As John Fincham, Ela his wife, and Ela their daughter have their obits entered in January and February 1541 – perhaps they died of plague – presumably one of them before then had written that programme of salvation by works. It epitomizes what by 1541 was rapidly becoming the old religion, as does the prayer added on folio 18v which invokes Henry VI:

Feythfull in Cryst enoyntyd Kyng
Restoryng bodely helthe to me
In disese paynfull languis[h]yng
Shew gostly helthe thro thi peté
Disposyng my sowle dewout to be
Everlastyng helthe to hawe in blys
Now gude Kyng Harre thou purches this

The second book is John Islip abbot of Westminster's book of devotions. This is a tiny pocket-book of four by two and a half inches.[13] To it, after it had left Islip's possession (he died in 1532), have been added various prayers of a date similar to those in the Fincham Book of Hours: 1539 and 1545 are scribbled on one page. By that time the prayers added by three women were certainly old hat. Are they self-centred or whingeing?

Katherine Poole (or Pole) added the *Stella maria maris*. Katherine Fortescue added a prayer to ward off the plague and the following prayer:

The peace of our Lord Jesus Christ. The vertue of his Holy passion. The singe [sign] of The holy crosse. the Entireness of the homilitie [humility] of the Blessed Virgin Mary. The Blessing of all the Saints. The Keeping of the angela [angels] And the suffrages of all the Chosen of god. Be with me And between me and all my Enemies now In the Houre of my Death. Amen.

Elizabeth Warneford was responsible for a prayer 'To St Roche against the Pestilence':

O how magnificent is thy nome Blessed St Roche which by thy intercession knowest how to heal the languishing multitude and how to show thy selfe propitius to all those who make commemoration of thy glorious name. come and protect us from the pestelence and procure us a well tempered ayre [air]. pray for us Blessed St Roche that wee be made worthy there of.

Elizabeth also wrote the prayers to St Apollonia. One went like this:

13 The John Rylands Library of the University of Manchester, Western Manuscripts 165.

> O Apolonia noble virgin of Christ pray for us to oure Lord to free us from
> what so evar may be hurtfull unto us that wee may not Justly for the guilt of
> our Sinnes be vexed with the tooth ache or hed ach.

The other went thus:

> Omnipotent and everlasting God hope and Crowne of all those who
> faithfully serve thee who hast crowned in heaven the blessed and glorious
> virgin martir Apolonia for having indured the dashing out of her teeth for
> the faithful confession of thy holy name grant wee beseech thee to all those
> who with piety celebrate her memory [that they] may inioy [enjoy]
> perpetuall peace and be deliveredd from all perills in body and soule through
> Christ our Lord. Amen. Our Father. Haile Mary.

On the final folios Elizabeth composed a prayer to St Winifred which is four
pages long. As it includes petitions for the conversion to the Catholic religion
of schismatics, heretics, and infidels, for deliverance from the deceits of the
Devil, and that 'we may chearfully and constantly suffer crosses for the love
of Crist', possibly (probably?) these women were Post-Reformation nuns.
Even so: they prayed 'That ye soules in purgatory and all afflicted persons
may obtain heaven by consolation' and 'That God of his abundant grace will
vouchsafe to blesse all our benefactors and those that labore to save souls'. Is
this whingeing? Is this being self-centred?

The prayer John Lynn added to British Library, Additional MS 27948, a
book of hours with the 2 November 1461 obit of Joan, lady Willoughby, wife
of Richard, lord Welles and Willoughby,[14] does not seem a 'me-prayer'
either. John, who writes on folio 2, 'This ys John Lynn boke that was gyuen
by my lady Mordant that dethe ys ho sole God haue marce and I pray God to
haue marcy on and all Crysten soles', added an indulgence prayer on folio
63v, opposite a miniature of the Trinity. The heading states that to deliver a
Christian soul out of purgatory the prayer must be said every day for a year;
then the soul shall be delivered within that year: 'and yf any day fayle you
must begyne agayn'.

Even more unambiguous is the message in the Wycliffite New Testament
given by Anne Pury, the widow of Sir William Danvers of Thatcham,
Berkshire, Chief Justice of King's Bench (d. 1504), to Syon Abbey in 1517:

> Dame Anne Danvers widowe sumtyme wyffe to Sir William Danvers
> knyght hoose soule god assoyle hathe gevyn this present Booke unto mastre
> confessor and his Bretherne encloosed In Syon entendyng therby not oonly
> the honour laude and preyse to almyghty god but also that she the moore
> tenderly may be commytted unto the mercy of our lord god by the holy
> demerytes of mastre confessor and his Bretherne aforseid whiche she hertly

---

14 For a description of this MS see *Vlaamse Miniaturen voor Van Eyck
(ca.1380-ca.1420). Catalogus*, ed. by M. Smeyers (Leuven, 1993), no. 23 (pp. 67-71).

desyrethe and specyally to Remembre the lyves and the soulys of suche persons hoose names heerafter be wryten.

After herself and 'hir childerne alyve', follow the names of the souls to be prayed for: her father, his two wives, her husband, three of her children, two men servants, and Margaret Longford.[15]

Finally in this sequence, there is in the British Library a copy of a book of hours of Sarum use, printed at Paris in 1535.[16] The book has been adapted for use in England, or for English nuns or monks on the continent after the Dissolution. Alongside a woodcut of the Crucifixion on folio 67 an indulgence prayer in Latin has been inked in over an erased prayer. On folio 138 beside a woodcut of St Roche and St Raphael the replacement is an instruction in English: 'Whosoever saith this prayer following in the worship of God and St Rocke shall not dye of the pestilence by the grace of God.' There are similar English (and occasionally Latin) explanations added over erasures on other folios. One would characterize both instructions and prayers as 'me-centred'; if the 'personalizing' is by a Counter-Reformation hand, what might this tell us?

My conclusion opens with Bodleian Library, MS Gough Liturgical 19. This is another pocket prayer-book; it is the same size as Abbot Islip's (four by two and a half inches) and is of the third quarter of the fifteenth century.[17] Stuck in at the front of this tiny book is an even tinier (two by two inches) woodcut of John the Baptist. It was probably inserted by John Iwardby of Farley Chamberlayne, Hants, whose coat of arms is on folio 15v and who has written on the last folio 'Pray for me John Iwardbe'. There are numerous English prayers in this volume, which, while not being 'added' prayers, seem to summarize English lay spirituality (or one type of it) of the period.

At folio 16, for example, there is a comprehensive family prayer:

> Pray for John Iwardby and Sainche his wif eldest doughter of Nicholas Carru of Bedington in Surrey and oone of his heirres and for their children frendes and welwillers and for the soule of Katerine late wif of the said John doughter of Edwarde Nevil lord Burgeyne [Bergavenny] and for the soulis of John and Edward sones of the said John and Katerine and for the soulis of the faders moders aliaunces and frendes of all them above rehersid and for all cristen [souls].

This prayer is more or less a repetition of one in Latin on folios 70v-71 save that there Edward is the only son of John and Katherine whose soul is to be

15   The John Rylands Library of the University of Manchester, English Manuscripts 81, fol. 153v. For William and Anne Danvers, see J. C. Wedgwood, *History of Parliament 1439-1509, Biographies* (London, 1936), pp. 257-58.
16   BL, C.12.e.15.
17   Pächt and Alexander, *Illuminated Manuscripts in the Bodleian Library, Oxford*, III, no. 1100.

prayed for – John is presumably still living at that point – and the last phrase runs: 'et pro animabus filiorum uterque eorum parentum fratrum sororum serviencium amicorum benefactorum ipsorum et omnium fidelium defunctorum'.

Secondly, at folio 23v, beneath an image of an enthroned Virgin and Child, there is a so-called talismanic prayer:

> Oure blessid lady delyvered of her own hand this next praier to a bisshop and grauntid heim that saith v tymes this prayer that day he shall not confounde nor of his enemy [be] deceyved nor woman in childeburgh shal perisshe nor in fortune him shal befalle nor without confession shal deye.

Thirdly, on folio 29 there is what one might call a magic-of-numbers prayer: 'For this praier next to say in chircherthe [churchyard] as often tymes is grauntid [times] xl daies of pardon as corsis [corpses] there ben buryed'. There are also prayers to Henry VI (folio 32v), Master John Shorne (folio 33), 'St Wilgeforte aliter vocata Uncombre' (folio 41v), St Zita (folio 36), Saints Sebastian and Roch (folios 27v and 28v), and a prayer below an image of the Five Wounds (folio 22).

The John Iwardby of the prayer-book was not, alas, John Iwardby of Missenden, Bucks, who had been an official at the Exchequer for more than fifty years and who died in 1470, but that John's son by his second wife. John Iwardby of Farley Chamberlayne died in 1525. As well as adding to the prayer-book he annotated the family cartulary.[18] I have not, however, mentioned the elder John Iwardby's half century at the Exchequer without motive. A Flemish book of hours in the Bodleian is MS Rawlinson Liturgical e.8; at the top of folio 39v is the only graffito in the book: 'as God Woll John Throkmertone'. I believe that this is the John Throckmorton of William Pantin's 'Instructions for a Devout and Literate Layman'.[19] John Throckmorton was also at the Exchequer in the first half of the fifteenth century, first as Chamberlain, then as Under-Treasurer. He and the elder John Iwardby must have known each other well if not intimately. That, however, is not the connection I am seeking to establish. What is intriguing is to connect the John Throckmorton of prayer-book and rigorous, even humiliating, 'Instructions' and the actual John Throckmorton. Or not to connect, for there seems (superficially at least, to the modern mind at any rate) to be little connection, indeed a disjunction.

---

[18] *Fitznells Cartulary, A Calendar of Bodleian Library MS. Rawlinson B 430*, ed. by C. A. F. Meekings and P. Shearman, Surrey Record Society, 26 (1968), pp. cx-cxi. See also A. H. Cooke, *The Early History of Mapledurham* (Oxford, 1925), pp. 47-54, 126-31.

[19] Pächt and Alexander, *Illuminated Manuscripts in the Bodleian Library, Oxford*, III, no. 1313. William Pantin's invaluable paper is in *Essays Presented to R. W. Hunt*, ed. by J. J. G . Alexander and M. T. Gibson (Oxford, 1976), pp. 398-422.

Not only was John a busy civil servant; he was also knight of the shire for Worcestershire, sheriff of the county, and a J.P. and of the *quorum* there for thirty years. He was a councillor of Richard Beauchamp, earl of Warwick, and had served in the earl's retinue in France in 1417-18. He had other patrons – at least four of them lords – and as a lawyer had many clients. In his will of 1445 he says 'I have ben all dayes of my life in my countree Asterer [i.e. 'a stirrer'] in the world as the world asketh.' He is the perfect example of an English gentleman of the later Middle Ages. He is perfect in other respects also. He was an unscrupulous landlord, an unscrupulous tenant, and an unscrupulous custodian of the Bishopric of Worcester during a vacancy. It appears that he was willing to cheat all and anyone. How did he reconcile such contradictions? Was it because of them that his confessor drew up for his use so punishing a daily regimen, so searching a programme of self-examination, so inwardly humbling a set of 'Instructions'? They had no effect. What a contrast with another English gentleman, bureaucrat, and lawyer: Thomas More. Religion did make a difference to the way Thomas went about not only his 'country's service in the world', but also the management of his household and family. No wonder Thomas More recognized the moment when the world finally asked too much; for John Throckmorton's kind it could (and in the 1530s did) demand anything of them. What I am suggesting is that for all but a handful of the English male elite devotion was marginal; in or on the margin was where, therefore, we should expect to find it.[20]

A final, leave-taking thought concerns Professor Bossy's remarkable paper on 'Prayers'. What kept the lid on the smoggy whingeing of the 'me' prayers of the 'me' prayer-books we have been glancing at was what I will call the 'non-me' nature of the Mass, particularly (as Professor Bossy stresses) the elevation of the host during the Mass. Additionally, we have seen here a number of 'non-me' prayers. This 'pluralism in prayer' was what was good

---

[20] I have mentioned John Throckmorton before: 'Hand and Mouth: Information Gathering and Use in England in the Later Middle Ages', *Journal of Historical Sociology*, 1 (1988), pp. 244-45. For the unscrupulous John Throckmorton, see C. Dyer, 'A Redistribution of Incomes in Fifteenth-Century England', *Past and Present*, 39 (1968), pp. 22-23, 27; C. Dyer, *Lords and Peasants in a Changing Society: the Estates of the Bishop of Worcester 680-1540* (Cambridge, 1980), pp. 186, 275-76; E. B. Fryde, 'Peasant Rebellion and Peasant Discontents', chap. 8 of *The Agrarian History of England and Wales*, III, ed. by E. Miller (Cambridge, 1991), pp. 794-96; C. Carpenter, *Locality and Polity. A study of Warwickshire Landed Society, 1401-1499* (Cambridge, 1992), pp. 125, 223, 232, 239. I have quoted Dr Carpenter's reading of the will, which replaces earlier, erroneous readings (*ibid.*, p. 223). Professor Dyer has written (in a letter to me) that John Throckmorton 'presumably had double standards re rents, but that is perhaps typical'.

about late medieval religion in general.[21] If the 'non-me' dimension was reduced (as at the Reformation I would contend that it was), and the 'me' aspect was enhanced, then what dire consequences for English religion, the English people, and England might (and I would contend did) follow?

---

[21] Bossy, 'Prayers', pp. 146-48.

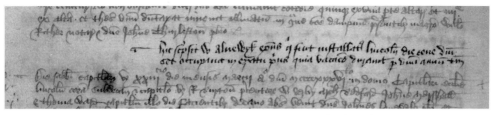

1. (Hayes) Bishop Alnwick's hand-written entry in the Chapter Acts recording his installation at Lincoln, 1437.

2. (Hayes) Norwich Cathedral, west front.

3. (Hayes) Norwich Cathedral, left spandrel above western entrance.

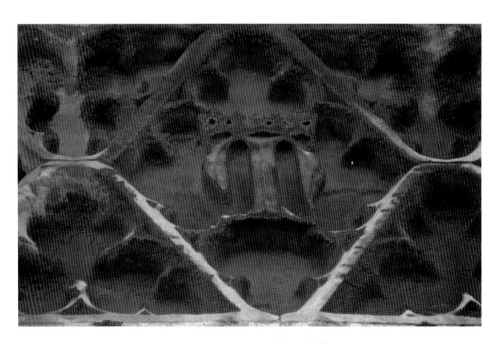

5. (Hayes) Norwich, crowned 'M' above bishop's gateway.

4. (Hayes) Norwich Cathedral, right spandrel above western entrance.

6. (Hayes) Norwich, central boss of bishop's gateway.

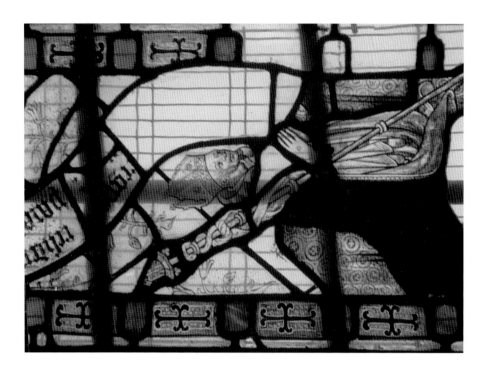

7. (Hayes) St Mary's church, Buckden,
angel corbel holding Bishop Alnwick's arms.

8. (Hayes) Bishop's palace, Lyddington,
portrait of Bishop Alnwick?

9. (Hayes) Bishop's palace, Lincoln, Buck's view of north side (1726).

10. (Hayes) William Alnwick's great seal as bishop of Norwich.

11. (Hayes) William Alnwick's signet seal as bishop of Norwich.

12. (Hayes) William Alnwick's seal as bishop of Lincoln.

13. (Hayes) Lincoln, arms of William Alnwick and
John Breton on vicars choral tithe barn.

14. (McKendrick) *Romuléon*, London, British Library,
Royal MS 19 E.v, fol. 32.

Cy commence le sixieme liure
particulier de ce traitie Romme
romuleon Contenant les faiz
de la seconde bataille puniqe
ou daufrique Depuis le tepe
que scipion laffrican fut fait
consul rommain Jusques a la
bataille ou guerze de macedone
Et contient en soy Cinquante
chapitres particuliers come
Il sensieut.

Coment apres la Reconurrace
de Capue publius cornelius
scipion de leage de xxiiij ans
fut par graint faueur de tous
decrete consul en sejur Romain
Et lui furent bailliez dix mil
pietons oultre loft ancien qui
estoit en espaigne q le consul
y auoit mene.

leer hec populi
hispanie zeet
entrementes les
peuples despaigne
qui se seroient rebellez auant
la bataille se retournerent deuers
les rommams come dist Titus
liuius en son second liure de la
seconde bataille puniqe He
nulz autres ne se rebelloient
de nouuel aux rommams Et
puis que Capue fut reconurxe
a Romme Le senat et le peuple
rommam auoient plus graint
soms de ytalie ilz nauoient
despaigne Et traittoient de
amplyer les osts et de penuoier
vnq empereur mais ilz ne
sauoient pas bien coment len
le y enuoieroit pour ce q deux
souuerains empereurs auoient

15. (McKendrick) *Romuléon*, London, British Library,
Royal MS 19 E.v, fol. 196.

des emperuns Cesars Depuis lempereur Adrien
Jusques a Constantin le grant/emperur fils de saite
Elayne fille du roy Cobel roy dangleterre Et contiet
en soy trentehuit cappitres. Lesquelz dix liures.
par le commandement et ordonnance de treshault.
tresexcellent. et trespuissant prince/et mon tres
redoubte et souueraim seigneur. Phelippe par la grace
de dieu. Duc de bourgoingne. de lothryk. de brabant.
et de lembourg Conte de flandres. dartois. et de
bourgoingne. palatin de haynnau. de hollande. de
zeellande. et de Namur. Marquis du saint empire.
Seigneur de frise. de salms. et de malines. A este
translate de latin en francois Et depuis grosse en
la fourme qui sensieut par dauid aubert Lan de
grace mil CCCC Souuante et quatre.

16. (McKendrick) *Romuléon*, Florence, Biblioteca
Medicea Laurenziana, MS Med. Pal. 156, fol. 294v.

17. (McKendrick) *Romuléon*, Florence, Biblioteca
Medicea Laurenziana, MS Med. Pal. 156, fol. 1.

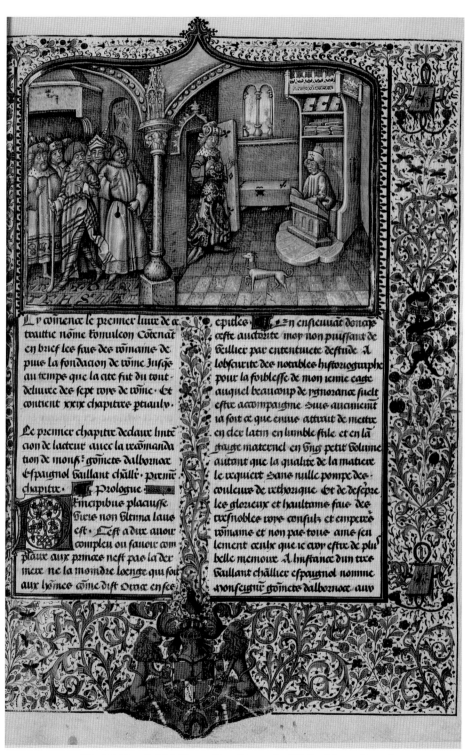

Lp commena le premier liure de ce
trauttie nôme Romuleon Cotenät
en brief les faiz des rōmainß de
puis la fondacion de rōme Jusqs
au temps que la cite fut du tout
deliuree des sept rops de rōme · Et
contient xxix chapitres ptiaulp ·

Le premier chapitre declair linte̅
cion de lacteur auec la recomanda
tion de monsₛ gōmetz dalbornoz
espaugnol vaillant chā̈ll' · premi̅
chapitre · ❡ Prologue
Incipibus placuisse
Viris non vltima laus
est · Cest a dire auoir
compleu ou fauoir com
plaure aup princes nest pas la der
niere ne la moindre loenge qui soit
aup hōmes cōme dist Orace en ses

epitles ❡ En ensieuuät donaÿs
ceste aucterite moy non puissant de
veillier par ententiuete deffide. A
lobscurite des notables historiographe
pour la foiblesse de mon ienne eage
auquel beaucoup de rgnorance fuelt
estre accompaigne. Sans aucune̅t
ia soit ce que ennie attrait de mettre
en cler latin en humble stile et en la̅
gaige maternel en ung petit volume
autant que la qualite de la matiere
le requiert sans nulle pompe des
couleurs de rethorique Et de descpre
les glorieup et haultains faiz des
tresnobles rors consulz et emperee̅
rōmainß et non pas tous ainß seu
lement ceulp que ie cuoy estre de plus
belle memoure A linstance dun tres
vaillant chā̈ll' espaugnol nomme
monseignꝰ gōmetz dalbornoz auy

19. (McKendrick) *Romuléon*, Brussels,
Bibliothèque Royale, MSS 10173-4, fol. 110.

20. (McKendrick) *Romuléon*, Florence, Biblioteca
Medicea Laurenziana, MS Med. Pal. 156, fol. 306v.

21. (McKendrick) *Romuléon*, Florence, Biblioteca
Medicea Laurenziana, MS Med. Pal. 156, fol. 37.

Ly commencent les Rubrices
ou sommaires des chapitres
du noeufieme liure de ce pre
sent traittie nõme romuleon
Contenant les fais de Iulius
Cesar augufte Et des autres
dix cesaures qui sensieuuent
successiuement lun apres
lautre · Et contient en son
Trente chapitres partiauliers

Et premierement·
Comment Gayus octauius
fils de actite fille de Iulie suer
de Iulius cesar Reuint a rome
a appolone ou il auoit estudie
Duquel la sebile tribune
Lors moustra laur estant pur
et cler · Aiant Hng cercle em
pres le soleil · Ouquel estoit
vne Hierge et son enfant Gile
tenoit quil aoura · Le chaput
premier ·

Uno ab Hui
condita ꝛc.
Lan de la fon
dation de rom
me Sept cē
et dix · Amsi come dist orose
en son sixieme liure Quant
gayus Iulius cesar fut occis
come dessus est dit Les ba
tailles ciuiles furent repareꝰ
Puis que gayus octauius
filz de gayus octauius Et de
actice fille de Iulie suer de Iule
Cesar Qui auoit prms heri
tage et le nom par le tefta
ment de Iulius cesar et qui
depuis fut appelle augufte
Reuint a rome de appolone ou
Il auoit este enuoie põ caufe
de eftudier · H ordonna sa ieu
nesse a batailles ciuiles · Et
comme dist Titus suetomus
en son deuxieme liure En son

23. (McKendrick) *Romuléon*, Turin, Biblioteca
Nazionale Universitaria, MS L.I.4, fol. 118.

24. (Rogers) Cambridge, Trinity College, MS B.11.7, fol. 29.

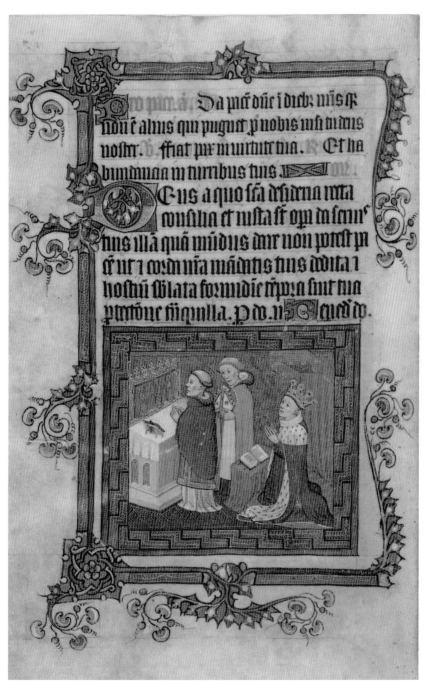

25. (Rogers) Cambridge, Trinity College, MS B.11.7, fol. 31v.

26. (Rogers) Cambridge, Trinity College, MS B.11.7, fol. 20.

27. (Rogers) Cambridge, Trinity College, MS B.11.7, fol. 21, detail.

28. (Rogers) Hollar engraving of glass formerly in Ampthill Church, Beds.

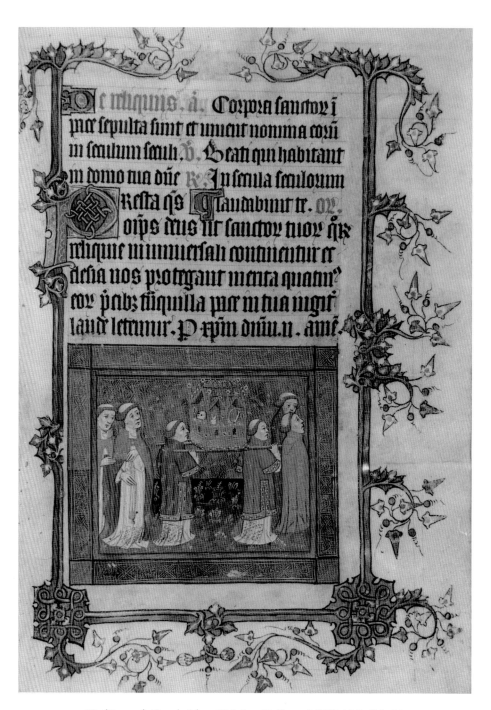

29. (Rogers) Cambridge, Trinity College, MS B.11.7, fol. 31.

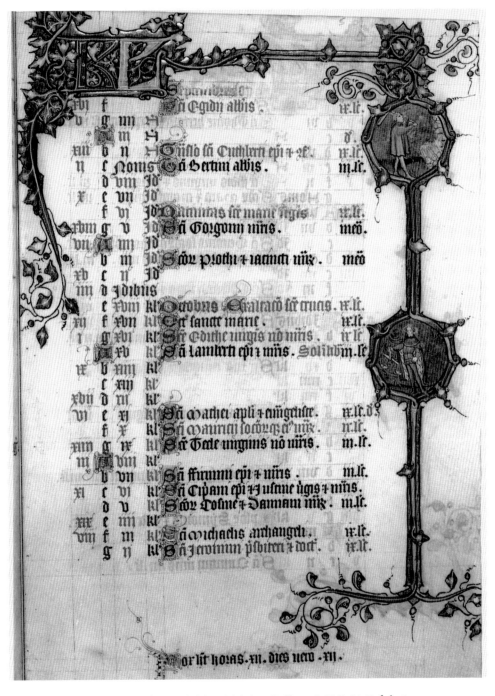

September calendar

rbi	f		Sti Egidii abbis .		ir.lc.
v	g	iii	N		
	a	ii	N		d.
riii	b	ii	N	Trnslo sti Cuthbti epi ⁊ 2c .	ir.lc.
ii	c	Nonis	Sti Bertini abbis .		iii.lc.
	d	viii	Id		
r	e	vii	Id		
	f	vi	Id	Natiuitas sce marie virgis	ir.lc.
rbiii	g	v	Id	Sti Gorgonii mris .	med.
vii	a	iiii	Id		
	b	iii	Id	Scor prothi ⁊ iacincti mrs .	med.
rb	c	ii	Id		
iii	d	Idibus			
	e	rbiii	kl	Iacobus ⁊ Raltacd sci cruas .	ir.lc.
ri	f	rbii	kl	Oct sancte marie .	ir.lc.
i	g	rbi	kl	Sce Edithe uirgis nn nñs .	ir.lc
	a	rb	kl	Sti lamberti epi ⁊ mñs . Solidem . lc	
ir	b	iiii	kl		
	c	riii	kl		
rbii	d	rii	kl		
vi	e	ri	kl	Sti Mathei apli ⁊ eūgeliste .	ir.lc.d.
	f	r	kl	Sti Mauricii soctorqz cñ mñs .	ir.lc.
iiii	g	ir	kl	Sce Tecle uirginis nn nñs .	iii.lc.
iii	a	viii	kl		
	b	vii	kl	Sti ffirmini epi ⁊ mñs .	iii.lc.
ri	c	vi	kl	Sti Cipani epi ⁊ Iustine uirgis ⁊ mñs .	
	d	v	kl	Scor Cosme ⁊ Damiani mrz .	iii.lc.
r	e	iiii	kl		
vii	f	iii	kl	Sti Michaelis archangeli .	ir.lc.
	g	ii	kl	Sti Ieronimi psbiteri ⁊ doct .	ir.lc.

Sol lit horas . rii . dies ner . rii .

31. (Rogers) Cambridge, Trinity College, MS B.11.7, fol. 7.

32. (Rogers) Cambridge, Trinity College, MS B.11.7, fol. 38, detail.

33. (Rogers) Cambridge, Trinity College, MS B.11.7, fol. 23, detail.

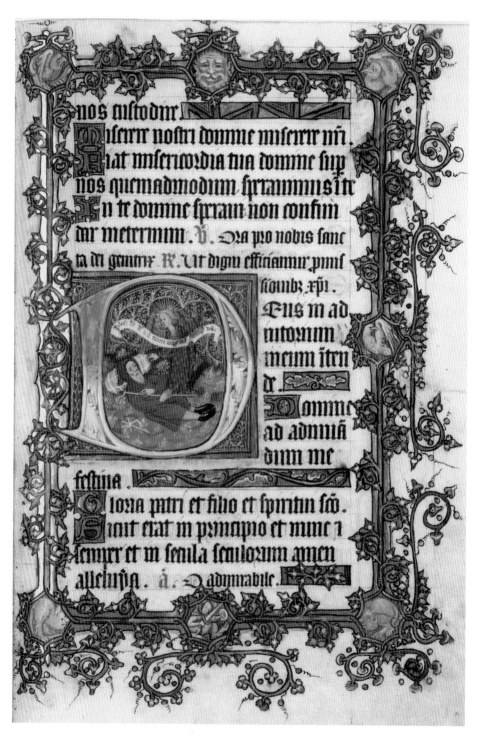

34. (Rogers) Cambridge, Trinity College, MS B.11.7, fol. 13.

35. (Rogers) Cambridge, Trinity College,
MS B.11.7, fol. 85v, detail.

36. (Rogers) Cambridge, Trinity College,
MS B.11.7, fol. 66v, detail.

37. (Rogers) Sotheby's, 19 June 1990, lot 53.

39. (Rogers) Brussels, Koninklijke
Bibliotheek, MS IV.1095, fol. 38v.

38. (Rogers) Brussels, Koninklijke
Bibliotheek, MS IV.1095, fol. 14v.

40. (Alexander) Castle Acre. Pulpit. St Ambrose.

42. (Alexander) Castle Acre. Pulpit.
SS. Jerome and Ambrose.

41. (Alexander) Castle Acre. Pulpit.
SS. Augustine and Gregory.

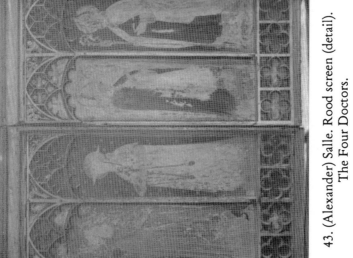

43. (Alexander) Salle. Rood screen (detail).
The Four Doctors.

44. (Alexander) Burnham Norton. Pulpit.
SS. Ambrose and Gregory.

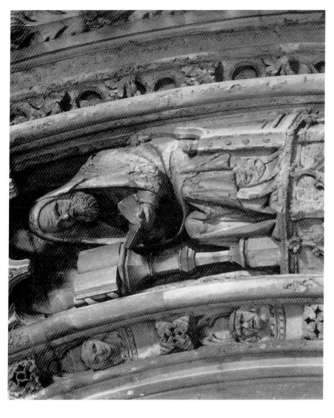

46. (Alexander) Rochester Cathedral. Chapter-house doorway (detail). Writing figure.

45. (Alexander) Burnham Norton. Pulpit. SS. Jerome and Augustine; John Goldale.

47. (Alexander) Augustine, *Civitas Dei*, The Hague, Royal Library,
MS 72 A.22, fol. 6v. Majesty with the Four Doctors.

48. (Alexander) Jean Germain, *Le chemin de paradis*, Philadelphia, Free Library, MS E. 210, fols 40v-41, 'The Chariot of Holy Scripture'.

49. (Morgan) Roof boss, Worcester Cathedral, S. walk of cloister.

50. (Morgan) Missal, London, British Library, Add. MS 29704, fol. 152v.

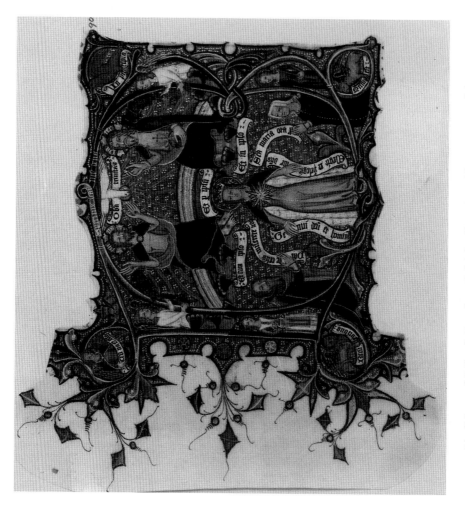

51. (Morgan) Missal, London, British Library, Add. MS 29704, fol. 193v.

52. (Morgan) Hours, London, British Library, Add. MS 50001, fol. 100.

53. (Morgan) Hours, London, British Library,
Add. MS 50001, fol. 100, detail.

54. (Morgan) Hours, Berkeley Castle, Coll.
Lord Berkeley, fol. 78v, detail.

55. (Morgan) Hours, Cambridge, Fitzwilliam Museum,
MS 3-1979, fol. 64, detail.

56. (Morgan) Hours of the Duchess of Clarence,
private collection, fol. 106, detail.